BEYOND THE ENVELOPE

Twenty-one Pioneering Architectural Projects from the Early Twenty-first Century
Twenty-one Interviews with their Architects

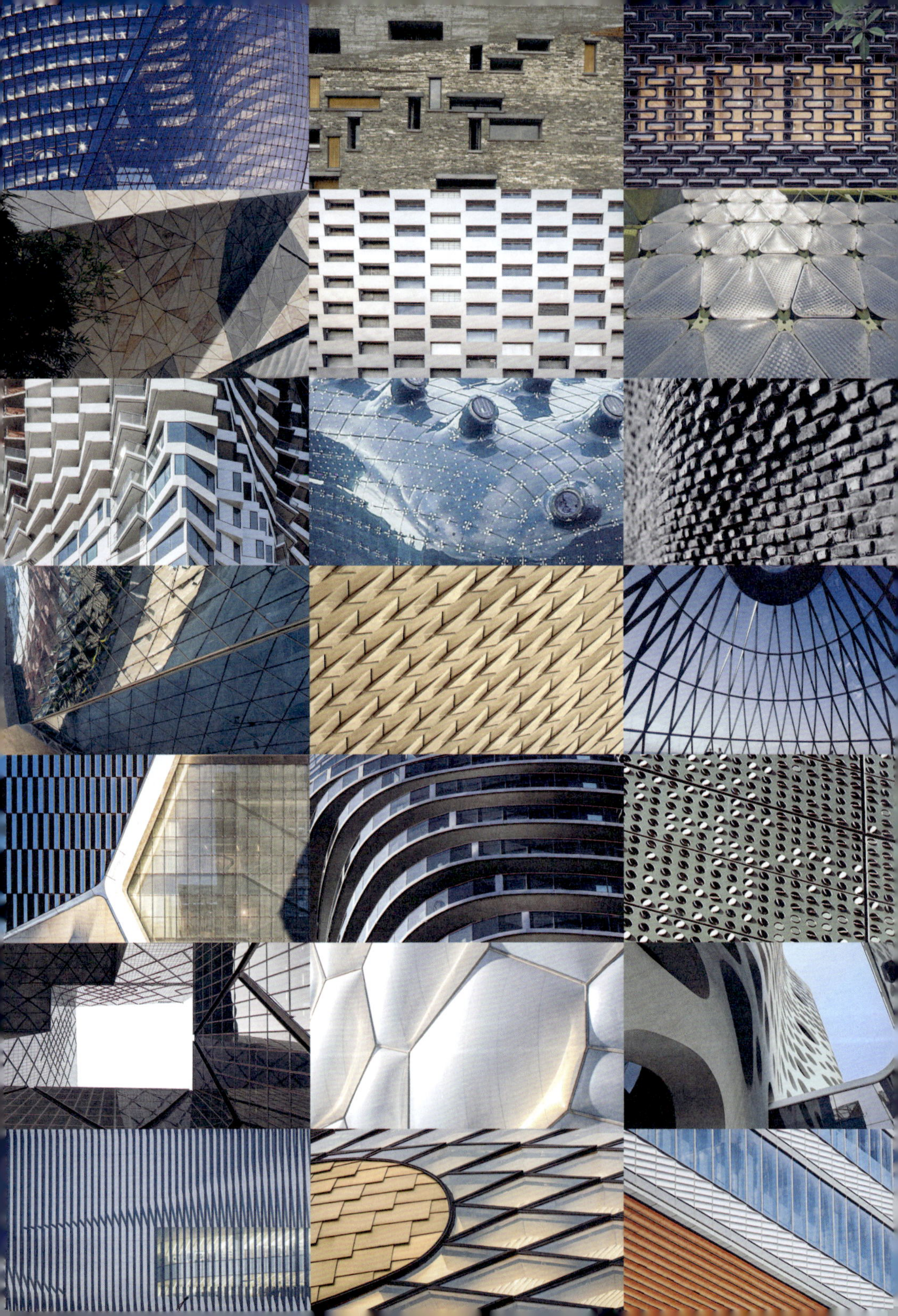

BEYOND THE ENVELOPE

Twenty-one Pioneering Architectural Projects from the Early Twenty-first Century
Twenty-one Interviews with their Architects

INTRODUCTION BY TOM VEREBES
PRINCIPAL PHOTOGRAPHY BY IWAN BAAN, HUFTON & CROW,
JASON O'REAR, RAIMUND KOCH AND SCHRAN IMAGES
DIAGRAMS BY MASTER OF ARCHITECTURE STUDENTS, SOAD-NYIT
CONCEIVED & EDITED BY TOM VEREBES

OSCAR RIERA OJEDA
PUBLISHERS

NEW YORK INSTITUTE
OF TECHNOLOGY
School of Architecture
& Design

CONTENTS

ACKNOWLEDGEMENTS

Tom Verebes

As this book's author and editor, I would like to underscore how this book is the outcome of many people's efforts: Twenty-one architects, their team, consultants, clients, fabricators and contractors. These architects' projects were researched by thirty-four final year Master of Architecture students in the School of Architecture and Design at New York Institute of Technology (SoAD-NYIT). This book stands as a testament to the collaborative spirit and intellectual rigor that defined our journey in my graduate seminar, Beyond the Envelope: Pioneering Architectural Technology, in the Master of Architecture seminar in the SoAD-NYIT in 2021, 2022, and 2023. Born in the context of the Covid-19 pandemic lockdown and remote teaching and learning in the SoAD-NYIT, the Beyond the Envelope seminar was offered on Zoom during my first academic year of service as a professor teaching at NYIT, in 2020-2021. Firstly, I would like to express sincere gratitude to Dean Maria Perbellini, for her unwavering support and encouragement to launch the Beyond the Envelope seminar, and to bring this publication to fruition. More broadly, I thank both Dean Perbellini and President Hank Foley for hiring me in 2018 as a Professor with Presidential Tenure, and Associate Dean for Academic Affairs in the SoAD-NYIT. The format of the seminar, first suggested by Professor David Diamond, Director of the Master of Architecture program at SoAD-NYIT, created the opportunity for my students to have direct contact with the architects of a series of outstanding contemporary architectural projects, through researching, preparing and conducting interviews with said architects. I am grateful for David's leadership and support throughout this journey. During three academic cycles, I worked with thirty-four talented and dedicated graduate students. The diagrams published in this book are ultimately these students' work, albeit post-produced and reframed for the context of a publication. To my students, whose diverse perspectives and relentless pursuit of excellence created an academic environment of intellectual stimulation, thank you for the countless hours of discussions, debates, and collaborative efforts in class.

Tharoonaskar Baskaran, now a graduate of the Master of Science in Architecture, Computational Technologies (MS.ACT) program at SoAD-NYIT, worked diligently as my Research Assistant during the 2022-2023 academic year to undertake the task of post producing the diagrams from 2021 and 2022.

Nidhi Nanjappa and Aneesa Warrich, current students in the Master of Science in Architecture, Urban Design program (MS.AUD), worked as Research Assistants on exhibition content in the form of a showreel for a future exhibition of the interviews, student diagrams, and professional photos.

I extend my heartfelt gratitude to the esteemed critics who joined structured final presentations of my students' coursework – the production of their own books on the twenty-one projects, including diagrams, photos and the transcribed interviews. These critics included: Jason Carlow (American University of Sharjah), Elif Erdine (AA), David Gerber (USC), Daniel Gillen (IIT), Alvin Huang (USC), Jason Johnson (University of Calgary), and Franca Trubiano (University of Pennsylvania). Together with SoAD-NYIT faculty members, David Diamond, Inanc Eray, Hyun-Tae Jung, Pablo Lorenzo-Eiroa, Nader Vossoughian,and Zhang Mengni, and I am grateful for the insights, feedback, and encouragement received from this stellar group of academic peers and colleagues.

A sincere appreciation goes to the architects who graciously shared their time, reflections, and perspectives in their presentations and interviews in my seminar and the SoAD-NYIT community in our public lectures and events series, and the published interviews included in this book. The willingness of the interviewees to open up about their creative processes, challenges, and discoveries, has added depth to my students' learning, and has greatly enriched the narrative of this compilation. This publication could never have happened without these twenty-one architectural practices' dedication to producing innovative and forward-thinking architecture, which will continue to inspire future generations of architects. A big thank you to all the administrative staff in their offices who helped with scheduling and organization, and links to the photographers published in this book. I would also like to express gratitude to the photographers, in particular Iwan Baan, Hufton & Crow, Jason O'Rear, Raimund Koch, and Schran Images, who have all so artfully captured the exceptional qualities of these twenty-one pioneering buildings through their incisive and beautiful photographs.

This research endeavor was supported by a competitive internal grant in 2021 at New York Institute of Technology – an Institutional Support of Research and Creativity (ISRC) Grant, from the Office of Special Projects and Research (OSPAR) led by Provost Jerry Balentine, and administered by Eileen Gazzola and Stella Leandrou. I sincerely thank Dean Maria Perbellini for the support of the SoAD Dean's Office, for both this grant application, and also for supporting this book with additional funds from the SoAD Dean's budget.

I am also deeply grateful to eight contributors to this book who responded generously to my appeals to crowdfund this project through Gofundme, enabling us to proceed to showcase this diverse range of perspectives and groundbreaking projects. Thank you to these architectural practices, and their principal/director/partner, for their generous sponsorship of this book, listed alphabetically: Archi-Tectonics (Winka Dubeldam); BIG (Kai-Uwe Bergmann); Coop Himmelblau (Wolf D. Prix); Diller Scofidio + Renfro (Liz Diller); Lab Architecture Studio (Donald L. Bates); Laboratory of Visionary Architecture LAVA (Chris Bosse), Morphosis Architects (Ung Joo Scott Lee), and Zaha Hadid Architects (Patrik Schumacher). I am truly grateful for their generous support and more broadly for their enthusiasm and dedication to the advancement of architectural knowledge and culture.

In 2022 and 2023, the public presentations and interviews by the architects featured in this book formed part of the SoAD-NYIT public lectures and events series. Thank you to Dean Perbellini for her interest and support for integrating the Beyond the Envelope interviews within the SoAD-NYIT public lectures and events in 2022 and 2023. I am grateful to the SoAD Lectures and Events Committee, especially Athina Papadopoulou, Marcella Del Signore, Alessandro Melis, and Susan Sternberg, for their invaluable support and dedication, and for their passion and commitment to fostering a sense of community through these events.

I express my gratitude to Professor Richard Hsu for facilitating an introduction to Wang Shu and Lu Wenyu, and Professor Zhang Mengni for facilitating communication, and his invaluable translation of the interview questions and responses to the interview with Wang SHu and Lu Wenyu.

I would like to thank editor Oscar Riera Ojeda, Carrie Tang, and book designer Florencia Damilano, and the entire editing and production team at Oscar Riera Ojeda Publishers. This is the second book we have made together, and you are all the best team an author can imagine to work with.

Lastly, a big shout-out to my wife, Nicole, who supports, and/or continues to tolerate, the time I dedicate to writing, publishing, and to my career in general.

This book is not just a compilation of project analyses and photographs, and interviews with their architects – it is a reflection of a global community of practice bound by a shared passion for researching and making architecture which transgresses conventional boundaries, for which we are all profoundly grateful.

Tom Verebes, PhD

Professor, School of Architecture and Design,
New York Institute of Technology
Director, OCEAN CN

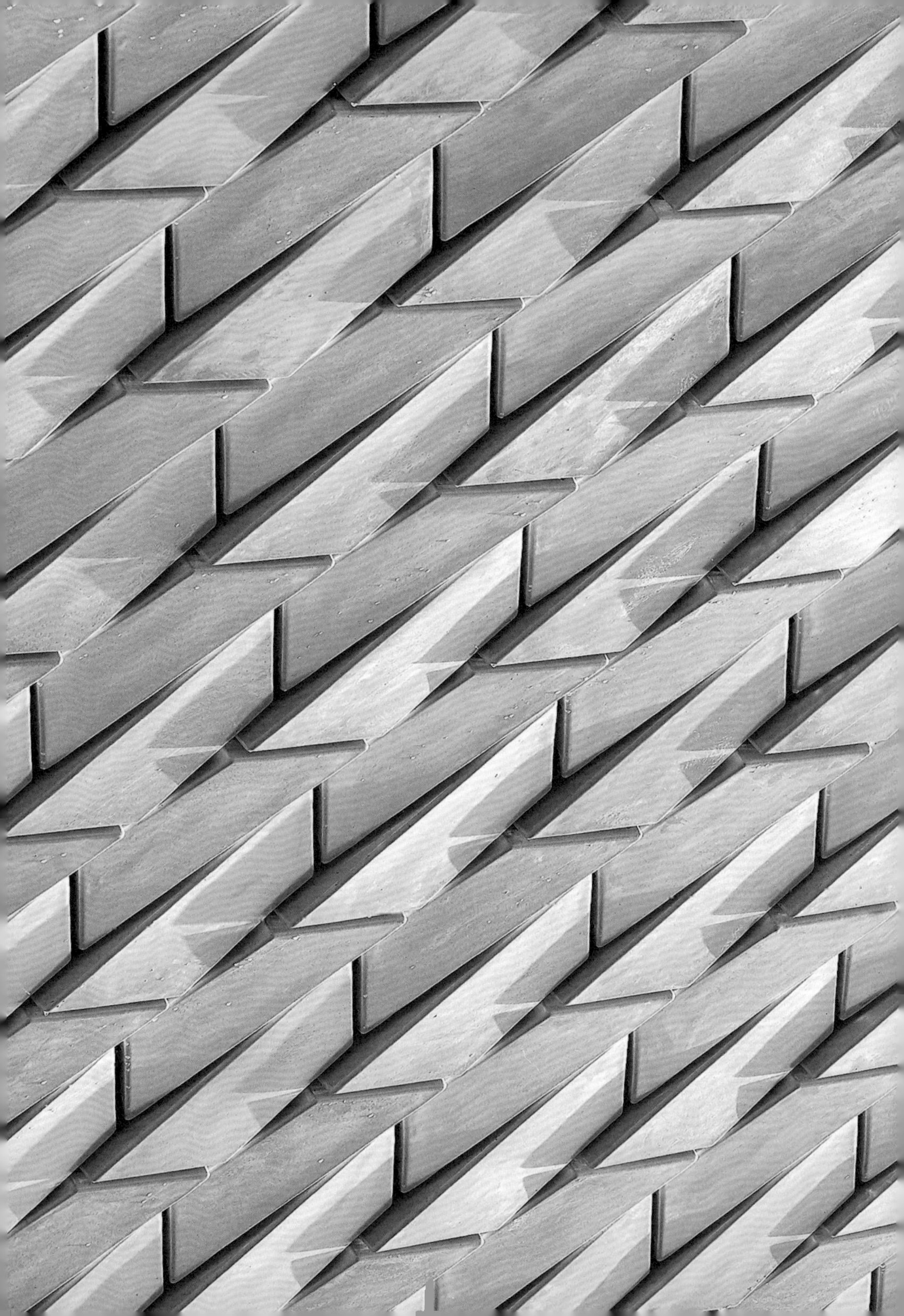

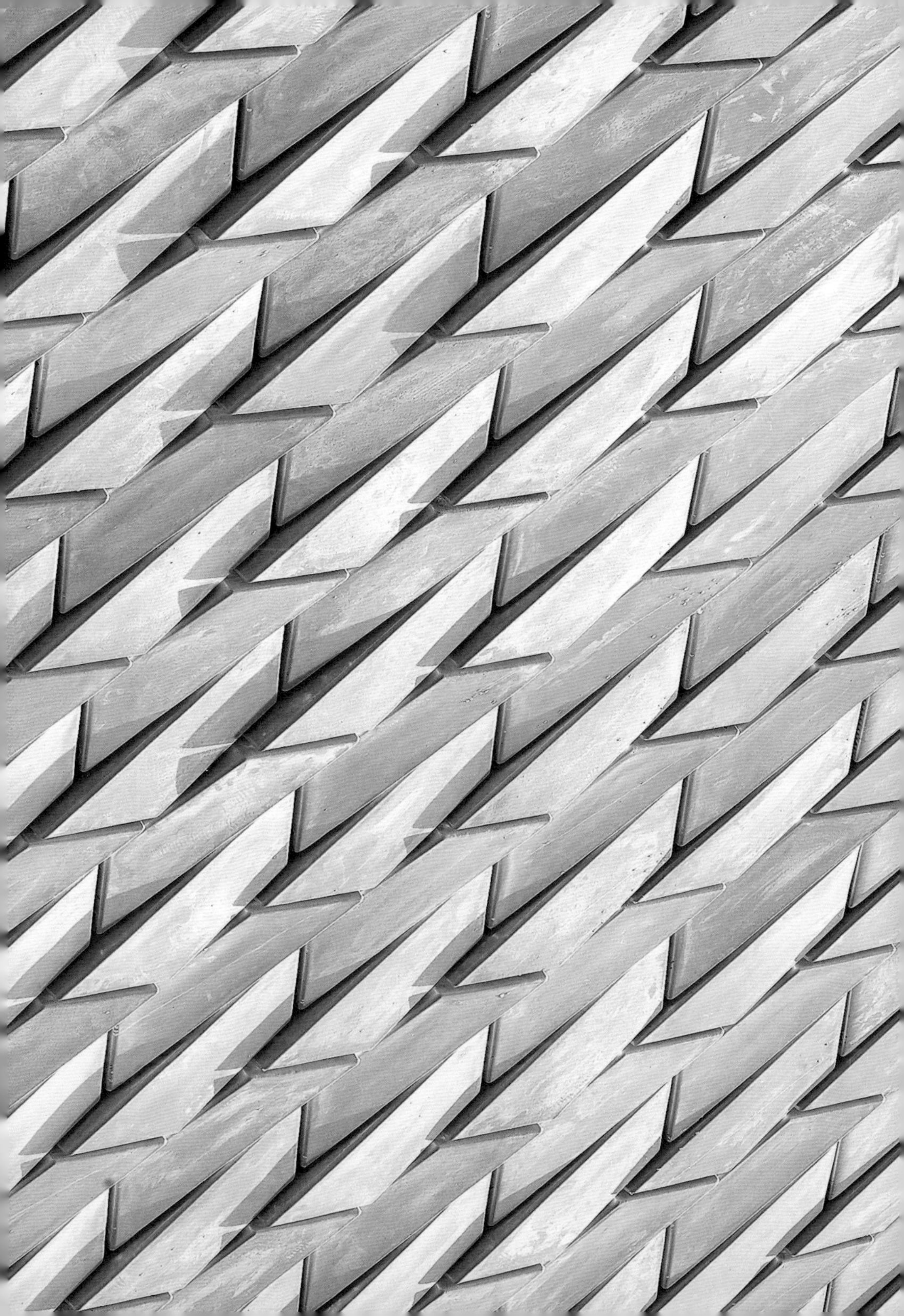

INTRODUCTION

Beyond the Envelope: Project-based Research and the Discourses of Building

Tom Verebes

"Technology is the answer. What was the question?"
Cedric Price, 1966

"The essence of what has been done to temper the environment has been – at every stage – the displacement of habit by experiment, and of accepted custom by informed innovation."
Reyner Banham, 1969

"The tactile and the tectonic jointly have the capacity to transcend the mere appearance of the technical in much the same way as the place-form has the potential to withstand the onslaught of global modernization."
Kenneth Frampton, 1980

"I really believe in the idea of the future."
Zaha Hadid, 1995

This book captures the state of architecture in the early twenty-first century, as experienced through a series of built architectural projects, representing the leading edge of architectural practice. Investigating twenty-one projects with a lens of the architectural envelope – analyzing and evaluating their forms, materials, production processes, and their performative effects and affects – *Beyond the Envelope* offers insights which no picture book of beautiful buildings can convey. Born out of the context of remoteness during the Covid-19 pandemic, this book compiles a rich database of first-hand accounts of the design, production, construction and life of one single building by each architect, with transcribed interviews with the architect of each project.

All twenty-one projects are presented under six themes: Form, Matter, Identity, Environment, Experience, and Interaction, communicated with both professional photos, as well as with diagrammatic analyses of these projects by students in the author's graduate seminar in the Master of Architecture program in the School of Architecture and Design at New York Institute of Technology (SoAD-NYIT), Beyond the Envelope: Pioneering Technology in Architectural Practice. Addressing concurrently several NAAB Program Criteria and NAAB Student Criteria, this seminar intersected technology, design, theory, and professional practice. This graduate seminar touched on several of NAAB's program and student criteria for engagement in technology, design, research and innovation, culture, and professional practice, specifically including PC 1 – Career Paths; PC 5 – Research + Innovation; PC 7 – Learning + Teaching Culture; and, SC 2 – Professional Practice. Ultimately, the student experience in this seminar was unique and unprecedented – providing opportunities for direct contact to twenty-one architects, through the series of interviews built into the class sessions, and shared publicly in the SoAD-NYIT public lectures and events program in 2022 and 2023. My students' analysis focused on design, building systems and construction, materiality, and the experience and interactivity with the realms of effects and affects. These broad aspirations of the comprehensive scope of the seminar were brought forward to this book. More than a survey monograph, the significance and contribution of this book is in its forensic investigation of the varied forms of architectural thought and production across these exemplary projects, analyzing and evaluating their commonalities and distinctions.

INNOVATION AT THE FRONTIERS OF ARCHITECTURE

Shunning mere novelty, the architects of these twenty-one examples of transformative architecture in the twenty-first century have striven for substantive innovations through incremental, compounding knowledge – and even the pursuit of The New. Through the compilation of these pioneering projects, this book explores a variety of contemporary modes of practice working at the frontiers of architectural technology. Design research in this context of experimental built architecture, as distinguished from experimental "paper architecture", engages with project-based, practice-based, and applied research. In this light, the discourse of architectural theory emerges from the field of architectural plurality and the range of different tendencies in the landscape of architectural practice in the early twentieth century.

Throughout history, building envelopes have expressed the political, social, cultural, economic, and technological constraints and opportunities of the context of the work. The agency of envelopes is understood to be delivered through a building envelope's form, matter, identity, responses to their climatic environment and context, and how we experience and interact with buildings. At once, the analysis of these twenty-one exceptional buildings focuses on their material and constructional conditions and processes, as well as the relationship of an architectural skin to the dynamic attributes of its context in time, and its impact on the human experience.

The fast-moving technological setting of the twenty-first century begs the question, that when an architectural envelope speaks about its contemporaneity and its place in

history, what does it say? How does an envelope communicate historical associations versus breaks with history? Foregrounded by the eras of Modernism, in which values of clarity, presumptions of honesty, and simplicity, then having transitioned through the various "isms" of Postmodernity towards more complex, "difficult wholes". More than conflating to mere "façade-ism", the architectural envelope serves as a mode of cultural expression, even when its external face is simply cosmetic. The semiotic function of the façade far exceeds scenography in its capacity for cultural, social and political communication. In this light, the semiological role of architecture to embody meaning beyond the fulfillment of necessities persists even when architecture's compositional rules and conventions have shifted from the trajectory of earlier guiding paradigms. Freed long ago from the burden of serving as load bearing structures, as well as from the repetitious reduction and proliferation of the curtain wall, the façade has become the site for architectural expression and a map of its technical culture.

In casual architectural parlance, architects tend to describe the building envelope as a skin – a biological membrane which holds together the insides of organic bodies and protects them from external harm – gaining significance in light of organic forms and their sensate behaviors. An architectural skin is a boundary as well as a threshold between exteriority and interiority. Great profundity is to be found in this key surface condition of architecture, in which the tension of the depth of an interior is contrasted with the exterior. A building envelope is at once a diagram of its interior activity and a projected response to its context. Embracing complexity, in which wholes are greater than the sum of their parts, the envelope has several functions. It serves as a surface for communication of values; as a screen to orient light and views; as a threshold from exterior to interior; and the envelope as a thermal climatic protector. Contemporary visual expression is characterized by organizational interests in variation, differentiation, and non-standard geometries. One of the common threads which runs across all twenty-one projects in this survey is their shared faith in complexity, driven by the accelerated technological capacity to generate, model, simulate, analyze and evaluate higher order complex forms and behaviors.

Traditionally a form of story-telling and communicating narratives about culture, ornament is also a registration of the residue of an industrial process. The contemporary expression of ornamentation lies in the articulation of intricacy, shunning standardization for the customization of components and parts, and their constructed assemblies. Expression is also the outcome of the performative affordances of building skins, and their material and environmental behaviors. As such, this compilation showcases innovations in computation, materials, and construction. These twenty-one stellar envelopes are also exemplary of the realm of effects and affects – what a building does and how it impacts human experience. The narratives of the analysis, and the interviews with the architects tell stories of the journeys in pushing forward computational design, simulation, fabrication, pre-manufacturing, on-site construction, and file to factory production processes. As projects completed in the first twenty-three years of the twenty-first century, the earliest of these projects were designed during the first digital revolution of the 1990s. All twenty-one projects are the offspring of the digital era, as well as charting new pathways towards the post-digital era in architecture. Regardless of these distinctions of pre- and post- digital, technological development has accelerated, causing great disruptions and transitions in reframing architectural culture with a new set of values.

The primacy of environmental responsibility in architecture, within the context of climate change, the increasing global population, and the limits of natural resources, all serve as important parameters for designing architectural envelopes in the twenty-first century. Buildings sealed from their exterior environments presume their autonomy from the so-called natural environmental context. When conceived and executed as an environmental buffer, an architectural skin challenges the notion of a hermetically closed building in favor of passive systems enabling more porosity as a thermal barrier, ventilator, and daylight filter. Better performing skins, achieved through energy modeling and climatic simulations of the behaviors of air, light, and heat, address performance criteria beyond efficiencies. Considered as active and interactive in these terms, architecture can be understood as part of nature, rather than distinct from it, opening the potential of a postnatural ontology of strange concoctions of the natural and the artificial. In this light, the leading edge of practice is rethinking façades and their systems by breaking familiar codes and conventions.

Beyond the Envelope explores these important areas of research and innovation in contemporary architectural practice. This is an investigation of architectural technologies and their application by leading architects working at the frontiers of design, production and construction technologies. This book explores twenty-one exceptional contemporary buildings, examining how they express architectural culture, and their role in charting the near future of architecture.

THE OPENNESS OF AN INTERVIEW

Different from a picture book of great architecture, in which photographs and the architect's drawings tell their controlled and closed narrative, this book compiles analyses of twenty-one buildings and interviews with their architects. For SoAD-NYIT students, it was an exceptionally unique experience to have direct interaction with the twenty-one architectural practices, and their principal architect or partner of the project. Twenty-one interviewees have shared their expertise and experience in a discursive arena, including some of today's most innovative practitioners, and professional and disciplinary leaders. Different from a presentation or lecture, an interview is characterized by relative informality and casualness in comparison to a prepared set of statements. An interview opens up the possibility of spontaneity, directness, and the sharing of issues usually not accessible to the public. The context of an interview supports discussions of nuances, personal experiences, interesting anecdotes and reflections on the challenges the architect can face in designing and making a great piece of architecture. Interviews offer a glimpse behind the scenes of how buildings are conceived and executed by their architects.

6 THEMES / 21 PROJECTS

Beyond the Envelope is structured into six thematic chapters: Form, Matter, Identity, Environment, Experience, and Interaction, through which twenty-one exemplary building envelopes are cross sectioned. In this book, each project is classified primarily under one of the six topics, but is also addressed through all the other five topics. The performance of architectural skins, understood as cultural, technical, experiential, thermal, etc., have been analyzed and evaluated in six classifications. Analytical 3D models and diagrams and professional photographs comprise the media with which to explicate each theme as related to the case study project. The emphasis of the compilation of analytical explorations is on the communication of the technologies – design, production, assembly and construction, and building envelope systems, as well as on concepts and discourses, and the effects and affects catalyzed by the twenty-one projects.

FORM

In this first chapter, Form, the realms of formal logic, spatial articulation, and geometric expression on the site of an architectural skin are explored. Investigating the intricacies, presence, and impact of architectural form, this chapter highlights examples of the geometry and topological conditions that shape the visual and spatial attributes of envelopes.

CCTV Headquarters, Beijing, 2012;
Office for Metropolitan Architecture OMA

Perhaps one of the most talked about buildings of the 21st century, the CCTV Headquarters in Beijing was proposed as an alternative to the exhausted typology of the skyscraper. In the words of Rem Koolhaas, perhaps the most preeminent theorist of the 20th century skyscraper, CCTV "promised to kill the skyscraper", and the repetitive banality of towers which race simply to achieve ever greater height. Reinventing the organizational model of a tower, CCTV was conceived as a loop with a 75-metre cantilever. The building offers a three-dimensional experience, visible from most of Beijing and always appearing as a different figure, CCTV is iconic by the immediate recognizability of its contour. CCTV has been a landmark of the city since its completion in 2012. OMA's instrumentality of diagrammatic generative processes establish project strategies as organizational models which encapsulate and communicate their spatial intentions. OMA's diagrams embody and embed criticality and commentary. The CCTV project broke many rules and expectations – cultural, formal, contextual, technological, statutory and regulatory. Due to the unfamiliarity of its form and presence, this is an architecture which demonstrates how architectural form can be read and received as a provocation, and how form can ultimately serve as a political tool for architecture. CCTV reminds us of the power of architecture to create meaning as a landmark, but also having the power to arouse strong opinions, and ultimately, to impact upon culture and society. Ultimately, great architecture makes us reflect and think.

Absolute Towers, Toronto, 2012, MAD Architects

Nicknamed "The Marilyn Monroe Towers" due to the way the contours of the shapely bodies of the fraternal twin towers create a unique, iconic image that has captured the public imagination, the towers are characterized by their highly identifiable figuration as they peer above the relatively flat suburban landscape of Mississauga, to the north of Toronto. Critical of the historical paradigms and formal logic of tall towers, the Absolute Towers innovate upon some prevailing legacies of the typologies of the skyscraper. Seeking to critique the replication of architectural sameness and monotonous and repetitious spatial organization, this project shuns the extrusion of a reductive plan figure. Instead, the rotation of the elliptical configuration of the floor plate is resolved in a simple structural solution, and an envelope which negotiates the curvature. These towers appear at once as monolithic and transitional, resolving the mathematics of formal differentiation with clever structural engineering and the dynamic behaviors of day lighting and views. The Absolute Towers are designed at the intersection of positions on ancient Chinese philosophy as related to nature, with contemporary global agendas on sustainability. This project expresses concern for environmental balance, in which the experience of so-called nature is set in harmony with the compounding density and complexity of our urban environments. The project consolidates a biomimetic understanding of natural processes and functionalities.

Museum of Contemporary Art and Planning Exhibition MOCAPE, Shenzhen, 2016; Coop Himmelblau

The MOCAPE project illuminates longstanding interests evident in Coop Himmelblau's work, as sites for architectural experimentation. Firstly, the institutional diagram of the MOCAPE project is formed and enabled by the assemblage of incongruous forms, bringing together the Museum of Contemporary Art (MOCA), and the Planning Exhibition (PE). The result is the involution of exterior space towards a vast interior urban space, the Plaza, framed by the Museum of Contemporary Art on one side and the Planning Exhibition on the other. The Plaza is at once a residual, yet a catalytic, democratizing space. The interior urbanism of this void is charged with the empowerment and liberation of its visitors. Coop Himmelblau attenuates the entry to the MOCAPE as a diagonal ascension of the threshold towards the raised ground of the Plaza. Elevating the ground datum and stretching the spatial sequence of movement into and up to the two museums, serve to destabilize the authority of the ground and the regulatory regime of the plan. Another experimental territory is the paradigm – or metaphor – of the cloud, which has been a persistent pursuit in Coop Himmelblau's work. Clouds are in fact formless and amorphous. In the MOCAPE project, a cloud is built in highly reflective three-dimensionally curved polished steel, containing the circulation and programmatic nexus of the building, and creating a central visual focus. The impact of the form and reflective materiality of the cloud is evident in the spatial effects of uncertainty and ambiguity staged by its presence. Considered holistically, the raised ground and the assemblage of freeform elements of enclosure of the Plaza deliver sensations of levitation and flotation of material forms and our bodies – the consummate magic trick performed by Coop Himmelblau's architecture.

One Vanderbilt, New York, 2017; KPF Architects

As the second tallest building in New York, One Vanderbilt advances and innovates the transitory typology of the skyscraper, in the city in which it was born, achieving the intellectual deepening, or rather perhaps an intellectual extension, of what is now called, the Supertall. The subtlety and sophistication of this project lies in its multiple affiliations, culturally, theoretically, and historically. At once, One Vanderbilt is sensitive to its historical context, in both its materiality and its massing. As a commercial tower, it speaks the language of transparency of mid-20th century corporate modernism, yet this supertall tower is also shaped by advanced computational approaches to generating, simulating, and evaluating architectural form understood within its context. Aside from negotiating historicity and modernity, One Vanderbilt reinvents the relationship of an urban building to its host city. The building communicates a contemporary expression and aesthetic language of a complex and coherent form, shaped procedurally from site specificities. The discrete object, made up of four component massing forms, conceived as the outcome of contextual associations, KPF carved a twenty-first century version of Hugh Ferris' expressive charcoal drawings of the 1916 Zoning Law of setbacks in New York City. One Vanderbilt shuns the autonomy of a Manhattan skyscraper. Despite consuming the entirety of its smaller subdivided urban block, this building is thoughtfully integrated and networked into the infrastructural context of Grand Central Terminal, through connections made within a complex multi-layered section.

MATTER

In Matter, the profound interplay of materiality and massing in architectural envelopes is explored. This examination spans considerations of volumetric contours of an architectural mass, material systems, structures and skins, fabrication, assembly, and construction processes, explicating the qualities of material effects such as solidity, porosity, translucency, and transparency.

Ningbo Historic Museum, Ningbo, China, 2008: Amateur Architecture Studio

The Ningbo Historic Museum critiques the normative modes of production of architecture, supporting an alternative in China – the re-establishment of a uniquely Chinese architectural culture, in which local history, customs and identity are paramount. The recuperation of collective memory and a revival of local, rural traditions is made possible by the meticulous reuse of recycled bricks and tiles for the massive façades of the Ningbo Historic Museum. Ultimately, a new relationship is formed by Amateur Architecture Studio between the architect and craftspeople on site, using unique working drawing techniques and 1:1 on-site prototypes to communicate how the recycled materials are to be reused. This project makes connections between material, cultural and environmental sustainability, as a project of resistance against a global universal architecture. This is a quest to establish and define an architectural culture with Chinese characteristics that critiques the urban, political, and economic context in China, and the pervasive model of production in architecture in China. Seen as a cultural shift from urbanization and the new towards the recuperation of collective memory and a revival of local, rural traditions, dedicated to the search for an architecture of authenticity which embeds the everyday experiences of real people, the search for the placeness of a locale is understood as paramount in the work of Amateur Architecture Studio. They have created an excavated mass of immense solidity and introversion. The museum communicates relationships with natural and environmental paradigms, as related to the concept of the mountain, valleys, caves and other landscape or geographic features, creating natural connections and profound cultural narratives. The effect of this approach on matter is a material heaviness contrasted by the groundlessness of the experience of moving from exterior to the interior of the museum.

O-14 Tower, Dubai, UAE, 2011: Reiser + Umemoto Architecture RUR

The 0-14 Tower challenges various canons and conventions of architectural envelopes, making a bold aesthetic statement about mass and heaviness through solid materiality and its perforation. Inverting the form and logic of canonic tendencies through material inversions, 0-14 is a an essay on the tower and podium type. One of the most unique projects included in this book with respect to its massing and materiality, 0-14 expresses Reiser + Umemoto's interest in occlusion, opacity and the inversion of lightness. This building is concurrently qualified paradoxically by the solidity and the porosity of its massive concrete exoskeleton, made from the distribution of five sizes of holes. The form, materiality and constructional logic of the perforated exoskeleton envelope has a landscape sensibility creating an undulating façade with an absence of corners. Beyond the first heavy layer of the building's concrete mass, a curtain wall allows for the maximization of daylight. These contrasting layers of materiality, specific to the hot climate of Dubai, prevent undesirable direct sun penetration and thermal gain. The context of rapidly urbanizing Dubai, along with its extremely hot climate, informs the project, by learning from Dubai's vernacular architectural principles for passive ventilation. The gap between the exoskeleton and the window wall creates a chimney effect for ventilation to cool the building. Conceived as a radical alternative to mainstream skyscraper design and the generic and globalized real estate context of Dubai, the 0-14 Tower deploys the complimentary and contradictory material qualities of matter: monolithic, porous, and transparent.

Chi She Pond Society, Shanghai, 2016; Archi-Union

Archi-Union's Chi She Pond Society pioneers new directions in architectural intelligence and robotic fabrication. This project emphasizes the integration of technological innovation and architectural culture, building environments, and ethics, seeking human-machine collaboration in a post-humanist era. Chi She represents the outcomes of workflows and a model of production in the specific Chinese context, fusing the application of high technology and low tech materials. As an adaptive re-use of an existing building, using recycled bricks to create a new façade with the deployment of on-site robotics – positioning a robotic arm to place bricks precisely for an overall effect – this small building encapsulates recent advancements in the architect's office to harness ubiquitous computational design and manufacturing processes, with on-site robotic construction and manual labor. The effects of the brick façade deviate from the conventions of flatness of a load bearing brick wall, towards the expression of a building envelope as a rugged three-dimensional granular topography – or, in the words of Philip Yuan, to create gradients of the smooth. The Chi She project combines both Fab Union's early adopting expertise in robotic fabrication, as a surgical intervention in the adaptive reuse of an existing building. This project also argues for sustainability with the reuse and recycling of brick for a new envelope, made on site with a robotic arm.

IDENTITY

Exploring the realms of modularity, components, and mass customization, the in-depth analysis of architectural presence and character in this chapter encompasses the complexities of part-to-whole relationships in organizational structures, subdivision, differentiated systems, and variations of types and standards, offering a nuanced understanding of how architectural identity can be shaped by pattern.

Federation Square, Melbourne, Australia, 2002; Lab Architecture Studio

Federation Square is a complex of diverse cultural, civic and commercial programs and institutions, linking the cartesian grid of the Central Business District (CBD) of Melbourne with the neglected riverside of the Yarra River – all spanning working railway tracks. The aspirations of the competition organizers called for an iconic architecture, and the "Bilbao Effect", in which the city could be transformed by a single piece of architecture. Lab's design scheme focused alternatively on the impact of Federation Square through experience and engagement with the intricacy of its spaces. The identity of the civic space of the cluster of buildings, laneways, and plazas is delivered through the subversion of the legibility of building massing figures and public routing, which create permeable figure to field relationships through the intricacies if its plan. The Atrium of Federation Square, which serves as a public thoroughfare interiorizing urban space, renders more complex the relationships of figure and field, mass and routing. This project strongly rejects spatial reductivism, minimalism, and even the conventions of modernism, positing instead complexity expressed in urban patterns, and architectural or surface organization. Its spatial order balances coherence and difference as provocations as much as guiding principles. This is a project which invests in offset and shifted geometries, both in plan, as well as in the subtle figurative opportunities in the elevations of buildings. Concerned with pattern over geometry in the fractal façades, different material systems of sandstone, zinc, and glass are distributed in a Conway Pinwheel Grid applied to the external envelopes, grouping self-similar triangles in larger triangular geometries.

MAAT Museum of Architecture, Art, and Technology, Lisbon, 2016, AL-A

More precisely described as a topography in the city than a building, the radicality of the MAAT lies in how it endorses contemporaneity while echoing the specificity of its context. The site of the MAAT is informed at once by the device of the space of flows as both a civic destination, and also by its infrastructural role for people to move through and traverse the city, impacting upon its host urbanism. The ground mass of the MAAT creates extensions of public urban surfaces, integrating what Le Corbusier called the fifth façade – a public, usable roof surface making a new civic space for Lisbon, which connects to the urban ground of the city. Citizens walk over, under, and through the museum complex from the urban ground and waterfront, to the elevated civic space on the roof – conceived more as an urban space than as an object. Demonstrating architecture's evocative power, the MAAT brings communities together in the dialogue between public spaces, materiality and constructive ingenuity. The project stages dynamic material effects with the rippling reflective texture of three types of three-dimensional ceramic tiles, establishing a deep association to Lisbon's historical use of ceramic tiles on exterior façades.The complex surface of its façade responds to the ambient conditions of different seasons, times of year, at different times of day, and to varied weather conditions. Embedding the movement of the sun path over a day, a large overhanging canopy at the waterfront has been designed to create a shaded civic space in hot summer months.

Tai Kwun Cultural Centre, Hong Kong, 2018; Herzog De Meuron

The Tai Kwun Cultural Centre is set within the historic context of the site – the disused former Police Headquarters of Hong Kong. The project transforms and reinvigorates a variety of open public spaces, as the adaptive reuse of several historic buildings and two new gallery pavilions, which are the focus of this study. Straddling the legacy of mass production methods and the customization of an entirely one-off envelope, the envelopes of the two galleries are informed by the industrial context of the project. The architectural skins of the galleries levitate above the open ground floors. The four faces of both envelopes create a texture to the façades, which behave as screens through granular material and visual effects created with arrays of four types of cast aluminum bricks. Although repeated, the arrayed aluminum bricks produce a differentiated granularity of the planes of the envelopes. The façade system deploys a principle of interlocking modules to span long dimensions without any frames or subframes, creating textured surfaces. The modules are produced using aluminum die-casting, an industrial process usually applied when casting engine parts. The modules are differentiated in four aperture sizes, each with different qualities and quantities of porosity, and have a more varied appearance than the four module types. The corners of the façade screens have open edges, rather than turning the corner with a closed mitered joint as two planes meeting at a corner. The porosity of the façade is driven by internal programmatic criteria, also absorbing the disruption of technical apparatus on the façade. The screens emit light at nighttime expressing the activation of the interior spaces. Through this screening, the building responds to different environmental conditions as the wider façade reduces solar gain by baffling direct sunlight. The sectional diagrams of each of the two new floating structures of the gallery buildings enable the public to walk underneath one of the buildings, which is programmed with music, theater performance, film screenings, lectures and discussions, and other impromptu events.

Mira, San Francisco, 2021; Studio Gang

The thematic chapter, Identity, investigates the character of an envelope as projecting a distinct identity. Mira stands as a beacon for recent innovations in material production in an era of accelerated industrial change. Amidst this transitioning technological context, the legacy of Fordism, evident in architecture's continued dependency upon the processes of standardized mass production, persists as an industrial paradigm. Modernist housing championed repetitious systems-based architecture. Well into the twenty-first century, housing remains one of the most standardized sectors in architecture, often constrained by cost limitations, codes and conventions, especially for mass housing. In this light, the Mira advances the paradigm shift to flexible manufacturing through the customization of façade systems. The window modules made out of a single, bent piece of aluminum rather than a mechanically assembled version offer a new prototype of a reinvented San Francisco bay window. In turn, the modules are mapped onto a differentiated set of apartment layouts, and distinct floor plans, shunning the uniformity of housing offerings in favor of the provision of a variety of demographic and lifestyle preferences, and differentiated spaces and views. Perhaps the most exemplary project in this compilation of the mass customization of a modular set of component parts, pre-manufactured aluminum and glass modules are repeated every eleven floors, or four times from bottom to top. The most striking impact of the Mira is brought about by the visual and urban effects of its dynamically vibrating façades, as seen and experienced from the ground and at any distance. In this project, Studio Gang states its values for an architecture of ruggedness over planarity; geometric articulation over blankness; and, differentiation over repetition. The architecture of Mira presents its public face in high resolution granularity, made possible by the dynamic visual effects of the transformational geometries of its architectural skin.

ENVIRONMENT

Environment delves into the complex intersections of climate and energy in an architectural skin. From energy usage and thermal performance to HVAC systems, ventilation, daylight, and the simulation of sustainable and resilient systems, this chapter explores a comprehensive analysis of the life-like behaviors of buildings and their association with their environment.

St. Mary's Axe / Swiss Re Tower, London, 2004; Foster + Partners

A "gherkin" is the word for a pickle in British English. Due to the building's general shape – that of a pickle – this nick-name, and its associated building figure has been embedded into the popular imagination through its imprint onto the skyline of the City of London. In this light, St. Mary's Axe is an architectural icon, manifested by its instant recognizability. Although known, and loved widely for its smoothly rounded form and its striking urban presence, made possible by its continuous curvilinear diagrid skin, the Gherkin's contribution is perhaps more pronounced with respect to the development of ecological thinking, and its unique diagram of passive cooling and ventilation. Internally, its scheme of six spiraling atria creates natural airflows which reduce energy use for cooling through natural ventilation. The first project in the thematic chapter Environment, the Gherkin has set a new benchmark for passive cooling, ventilation, and energy reduction, within the ecological and technological imperatives of this era of climate change. At nighttime, the building purges heat with openable windows in order to let the whole building cool down. Testament to the value of what a building does, rather than purely its appearance, the architectural performance of the Gherkin can be measured through its explicitly declared environmental responsibilities and contingencies. This project demonstrates how technological innovation can establish new cultural and disciplinary norms, as pioneering propositions become embedded into mainstream practice, such as environmental simulations using Computational Fluid Dynamics (CFD). What was radical about the Gherkin in the context of the turn of the century in 1997 when the project was started now seems to be a responsible mode of architectural practice. As a benchmark in high end office design, St. Mary's Axe is a great example of how architecture can take on symbolic value – culturally, civically and ecologically.

Bloomberg Center at Cornell Tech, New York, 2017; Morphosis Architects

The Bloomberg Center conceived of Roosevelt Island as a destination, the academic institution as the program, and a net-zero facility as the performance goal of this academic building on a new campus for a partnership of Cornell University in Ithaca, New York, and the Technion in Haifa, Israel. The Bloomberg Center is a beacon of environmental performance and climate resilience. Aspiring to net-zero in energy terms, with a range of climatic, HVAC and energy systems, this is an exemplary project. Deploying a photovoltaic landscape of solar energy collectors on the roof, a rainwater-collection system, together with eighty geothermal wells hundreds of meters below the ground, the impacts of climate change were considered in the design. Hurricane Sandy made landfall in New York during the design of the building. Working with Arup, Morphosis futureproofed the building and the site by moving the mechanical and electrical services up to roof to ensure their resilience. Morphosis's design approach to systems and their (re-) combinations implements environmental systems as desig elements, along with a rain screen wall system which is the outermost layer of the façade composed of aluminum panels framing 40% glazing in the envelope. Each panel has circular discs cut out from the metal panels which are unfolded on the façade, and tilted in different directions. The building skin's varied responses to daylight on the exterior maximize insulation performance, and minimize thermal bridging. The paint finish on the panels catalyzes some nuanced visual affects manifested in the envelope appearing as green, brown, bronze, or gold, at different times in different daylight conditions.

Copenhill Powerplant, Copenhagen, Denmark, 2019; Bjarke Ingels Group BIG

Through the vision and determination of its architect, BIG, the power of the architect as an agent capable of instigating change is demonstrated by this project. The broad aims of the Copenhill Powerplant are the transformation of a waste society into a non-waste society, through the conversion of 440,000 tons of waste into clean energy annually, delivering electricity and district heating to 150,000 homes. Intersecting public, social, and recreational infrastructure with clean energy infrastructure serves to rewrite the history of the relationships of dirty industry to the city. Intersecting clean infrastructure with public activities, Copenhill subverts the notion of segregated zoning of industry and residential areas, reintegrating industrial zones and living spaces. This project simultaneously creates a biodiverse landscape with capacities to absorb heat, remove air particulates, and manage stormwater runoff. Rethinking the relationships between industry and the public, and infrastructure and the city, this project has a ski slope and a hiking trail on its spiraling sloped roof, from the top of the building to its lower level, and rock climbing up one face of the elevation, made up of large scale "Alu-bricks" interspersed with large glazed panels affording glimpses to the interior of the energy plant. The climate crisis has led BIG towards radical approaches to greening industry and infrastructure. BIG's ambition to create world changing architecture applied the agency of a programmatic strategy to create strange, post-natural combinations of so-called natural elements and the artificiality of architecture. Their concept of hedonistic sustainability implies the shunning of a Puritan approach to reducing resources, and striving for the public enjoyment of clean infrastructure. The environmental, social, and urban sustainability of this building enables new experiences for the public to come closer to industry, ultimately educating its users.

Asian Games Theater Sports Hybrid Building, Hangzhou, China, 2023; Archi-Tectonics

The design for the Asian Games 2023 park and facilities challenges the polarity of the natural and human-made artifice, which has for centuries informed the distinction between the "wild" and the cultured. Unexpected side effects and relationships occur as a result of blurring the distinctions between the natural and the synthetic, in architectural and urbanistic mutations, or other stranger hybrids. Working on equal terms with the landscape architects for this project, !melk, Archi-Tectonics addressed the problem of obsolescence, dysfunctionality, and decay of architecture over time, and strategies with which to futureproof an architectural or urban design scheme. This project comprises a vast masterplan with the integration of seven buildings for the Asian Games in 2023. Embedding the Sponge City concept and techniques, the wetlands function as an "urban sponge" which acts as an absorptive lung to collect, filter and re-use storm-water runoff. Built during the time of the Covid-19 pandemic, Building Information Modeling (BIM) was used for optimization, and also to facilitate remote communication between the design team, the contractor, fabricators, and contractors. The Asian Games project is integrated into the city, with the aim for it to remain an active urban landscape territory with thriving buildings and facilities which will accommodate a range of future uses, needs and desires. By making the buildings sustainable hybrids, their lifespan and their potential agency to transform the neighborhood, is increased. The transformability of a building for multiple uses at different times potentially informs a more holistic approach to planning and design to deal with variability, flexibility, futureproofing, and the changing context, needs, and demands, of the built environment.

EXPERIENCE

Experience probes the nuanced interplay of visuality, cognition, and the immersive experience of architectural envelopes. This exploration encompasses the programming of visual content, the effects of light, color, reflection, porosity, and interactive elements, uncovering how these properties contribute to the creation of effects – atmospheres, moods and the emotive impact of a building skin within built environments.

National Aquatics Center – The Watercube, Beijing, 2008, PTW Architects

Olympic Games are often conceived as symbols of their host city and country, and how they serve to represent the city and the nation state. A building synonymous with the 2008 Beijing Olympics since its completion, the National Aquatics Center, or as it has become known, the Watercube, is wrapped in a membrane of bubbles which expresses mathematics, forms, and performances found in nature. Derived from the structure of water and the aesthetics of foam and effervescence, as a basis for communicating its programming and content. The Watercube associates the structure of water with the square, a symbolic geometry of the shape of the house in Chinese tradition and mythology. The building's envelope raises several questions about biomimetics and architecture, conceiving efficiency, intelligence and beauty in terms of the functioning of a structure and its environmental behavior. In this sense, the Watercube asks how architecture can learn from nature in the areas of structure, material and building skin. Behind the totally randomized appearance of the thick envelope hides a strict geometry that can be found in natural systems such as crystals, cells and molecular structures. By applying this material and technology, the transparency and apparent randomness is transposed into the inner and outer skins of ETFE cushions. The unique lightweight construction of the ETFE double skin is insulating, maximizes natural light and reduces the need for artificial lighting. It captures solar energy to heat the internal spaces; and harvests, recycles, and filters rainwater. The client and the architect were well aware of the risk of Olympic facilities falling into disuse after the two-week event of the Olympics. Used, and much loved by the public, as an aquatic centre since 2008, the Watercube was temporarily transformed as the Ice Cube for the Beijing 2022 Winter Olympics, thus further preventing the building becoming a "white elephant".

Galleria Centercity, Cheonan, South Korea, 2010; UNStudio

In this scheme for a shopping mall, UNStudio designed the external envelope as a low resolution media screen. The fusion of materiality and light media affect the subject, or the user, or the public, with respect to their activity, programming and didactic content. This building speaks to the impermanence of its image, as a result of illusions of time, scale, light, and people. Both perception and physical qualities are blurred in the experience of media augmenting the building's presence. This project represented a shift in UNStudio's work from diagrammatic towards more experiential visual effects. The Galleria Centercity is one of several projects by UNStudio which invest in the application of colored and polychromatic materials ifor the façades. The distinctive virtue of these projects, including the Galleria Centercity, is how the envelopes create variable atmospheres which are experienced differently at different times. The façade of the Gelleria Centercity impacts the perception of passers-by creating a dialog between two territories – the façade and the interior. Aside from the media which projects at nighttime, there is also a cinematographic effect during daytime: the building skin is static but feels dynamic as the position of the subject changes in relation to the façade. An important environmental consideration was for the façade to serve as thermal protection against the blazing summer heat in South Korea. The façade is made up of synthetic vertical elements, which cumulatively create a low resolution screen effect from the illumination of 80cm x 80cm dot LED lights.

Leeza Soho, Beijing, 2019; Zaha Hadid Architects

Leeza Soho is a single 45-floor tower with a varying elliptical floor plan featuring a spiral cut revealing the largest interior atrium ever constructed. At the risk of duplicity in its appearance, the experience of the geometric simplicity of the elliptical mass from a distance is aided by the blackness of the building. Departing from ZHA's interests in all-encompassing continuity of systems, Leeza Soho delays the surprise of the scale and impact of the atrium from the exterior to the interior. It saves the sensation of the spectacular experiences of the building for the vast interior urbanism of the project. The Atrium Effect is characterized by features as open terraces exemplified by the Bonaventure Hotel in Los Angeles in 1976 by architect John Portman. The trope of the atrium is developed by the simple external figure, and the experience of a complex, exuberant void, as an interior form of urbanism. The tower, as well as the elevational profile, are both elliptical figures.

The entire exterior surface is developed with shingle-like glazing panels which describe the three-dimensional curves of the envelope with an array of flat surfaces, shown as relief as the shingles negotiate the curvature of the building skin. Leeza Soho makes a substantial contribution towards innovating the typology of high-rise towers, challenging segmentation and serial repetition through the presence and formal expression of the interior atrium. The atrium envelope is configured by concave and convex horizontal bands at each floor level, connecting the fluid internal envelope in stark contrast to the simplicity of the external envelope. The structural expression of the atrium glass surfaces, in which instances of mathematical events mark shifts from concave to convex surfaces, are quite extreme, discreet transitions in geometry which integrate structure and surface. As one experiences views up, down, and through the transparent surface of the atrium, one grasps the atrium's crease lines and the shifts between convex and concave forms, also allowing for visual communication across floors. The atrium also serves as a climatic buffer from the extreme climate of Beijing in summer and winter.

INTERACTION

This final chapter explores the integration of smartness in architectural envelope systems through the augmentation of intelligence, emphasizing interactivity, responsiveness, and the incorporation of robotics, sensors and actuating systems. The analysis and discussion encompasses various forms of intelligence and smart/predictive systems within the context of architectural design and technology.

Kunsthaus Graz, Graz, Austria, 2003; Peter Cook and Colin Fournier

Nicknamed, "the friendly alien", this incongruous architectural jewel is set in the Baroque and medieval urban context of Graz. It is a floating, blue, shiny, smooth, three-dimensionally curvilinear bodily figure, with pointy nozzles on its roof to provide filtered daylight to its upper galleries. In the parlance of the 1990s and early 2000s, the Kunsthaus is a blob. What makes this alien blob friendly rather than adversarial, conflictive, or unsettling in its host context? It concurrently adheres to and coheres with its urban situation, yet it also subverts, transforms, and reinvents Graz. The presence of the Kunsthaus has helped to rebrand Graz, not dissimilar to the Guggenheim's famous "Bilbao Effect". From a broad perspective, the Kunsthaus contributes to, and continues the tradition of buildings which do not look like buildings of the past, the kind that jar with the present but offer glimpses of the future. The Kunsthaus negotiates past and future, tradition and innovation. The architecture of the Kunsthaus is created by the radicality of its form and colour, as well as by mediated content communicated by its programmable external envelope, saturated with visual content, and activated through embedded media technology. This project reinforces the avant-garde myth of Graz through its alien form and material, as well as with its dynamic interactive skin, fusing culture and communication media, designed in collaboration with Realities United. The art which fills the building is projected into public space, with 900 circular neon lamps that function as pixels, programmed with images, text and abstract film sequences via a central computer. Dynamic, playful, and stimulating, this truly transformative building makes people take notice, behave differently, and encourages us to reflect on our experience of the built environment.

Media-ICT, Barcelona, Spain, 2010; Cloud 9

The Media Information Communication Technology (ICT) Building in Barcelona responded to the competition's call for an architecture of information, communication, and technology. As a public building, the Media

ICT Building, together with its responsive systems, addresses the urgencies of climate change. This thematic chapter, Interaction, explores the ways in which architecture can gain sentience, and better respond to the dynamics of its environment and the criteria of its users. The building's active, adaptive and responsive systems create an interactive environment, as an incubator hosting technology thinkers, inventors, and entrepreneurs. Architectural interactivity and smartness are installed, mainly through the organization of façade systems and their responsiveness to climatic conditions. Each of the four façades are distinct. The ETFE air cushions of one of the façades are filled with nitrogen and mixed with tiny oil droplets. In the afternoon, the façade modules transform the facade from transparent to translucent, which blocks 90 percent of the sun's radiation, thus substantially reducing the building's heat gain. The material properties of ETFE have the lightness of plastics and the resistance of glass. Altogether the three layers of ETFE, each with a thickness of 2.5mm, accumulates to a total thickness of 7.5mm. As one of very few net zero buildings, this status is achieved with a range of passive systems and a pneumatic responsive façade system, together with its green roof. This project exemplifies the intersection of digital manufacturing, technologies related to energy efficiency, intelligent systems, and self-sufficiency.

<u>The Shed, New York, 2020;</u>
<u>Diller, Scofidio + Renfro</u>

The Shed has been described in the architectural and art press as an anti-institutional institution. As the newest cultural venue to arrive to New York City, this new arts and cultural institution was born out of a unique relationship between the architect and a cultural institution. The Shed is situated at the northern terminus of the High Line, as a cultural locus within the high-end mercantile context of Hudson Yards. As a beacon for culture, its architecture emanates light through its translucent lightweight ETFE envelope. Perhaps the most spectacular, and even radical, attribute of The Shed is its transformable envelope and volume, which enables the building to double in size. The telescoping envelope of The Shed performs as a responsive creative environment, in which the retractable roof, and other kinetic systems can radically transform this space, where the audience, various technologies and back-of-house functions, and artists and performers all cohabit a space tailored to the particular cultural event it houses at any given time. This project builds upon the tradition of interactive and intelligent architecture, articulating and expressing eloquently the performativity of Cedric Price's Fun Palace, and the theoretical roots of cybernetics. The legacy of Cedric Price, and the aspirations of subsequent generations of researchers, technologists, dreamers and radicals, is one of buildings conceived as infrastructure that can transform, change, learn and adapt. The Shed specifically is a large industrial shed whose mission is to augment the capacity of artists to make the building's spatial organization change in accordance with their wishes and needs. The Shed is one of those landmark architectural achievements that confirms that our job as architects, on the best of days, is to conceive and construct buildings which make possible what seems impossible.

GREAT ARCHITECTURE AS GIFTS TO THE FUTURE

Recapitulating the pioneering spirit of these twenty-one ground-breaking architectural projects, cutting-edge technologies drive the innovations of these exceptional buildings. The twenty-one projects, organized within six thematic chapters, collectively push the boundaries of what is architecturally possible to realize. On behalf of the SoAD-NYIT and my thirty-four students who are all now graduates, we express our gratitude to the interviewees and their offices, firstly for their great work, and also for their candid insights shared in the interviews, unveiling their passions and motivations, as well as their struggles and challenges, in achieving great architecture.

Beyond a picture book, this is an analytical endeavor, in which design research methods are applied to elucidate an understanding of the projects through SoAD-NYIT students' insightful observations of the leading edge of their contemporary professional landscape in architecture. The compilation of interviews, project analysis and photographs collectively chart the recent history of exceptional architectural envelopes, all of which point towards the future mainstream of architecture. The reader may wonder how this selection of exemplary buildings might shape the landscape of architectural exploration in the near future.

The visual and intellectual explorations shared in this book are meant for a global audience of students, researchers, scholars, professionals and the general public interested in experimental contemporary architecture. There remains an absence of publications focusing on the analysis of applied technology in architectural practice and its theoretical consequences – a gap this book seeks to address. Positioned at the intersection of pioneering technological research, experimental architectural practice, and transformative discourse, *Beyond the Envelope* encapsulates innovations in architectural practice, theory, and culture, in the first two decades of this century. This book stands at the precipice of the future, in which the thematic chapters and projects point towards fields of innovation at the intersection of pioneering technologies and human creativity. The reader is invited to progress beyond the pages of this book, in anticipation of a deeper understanding of the recent past, and to discover the near future implied by this compilation.

SIX THEMES BEYOND THE ENVELOPE

FORM

MATTER

CCTV HEADQUARTERS

Beijing, 2012 | Office for Metropolitan Architecture OMA

Program Offices, broadcasting, production, management, multi-purpose, administration, 9 canteens, 11 snackbars, gym, basketball field, massage space, health center, parking

Materials Glass curtain wall, structural steel, aluminum

FORM

599,548 M2	GFA
189,600 M2	Site Area
3	Floors Below Ground
52	Floors Above Ground (Tower 1)
44	Floors Above Ground (Tower 2)
35 M	Cantilever (Tower 1)
75 M	Cantilever (Tower 2)
234 M	High
70%	Open Ceramic Frit Pattern on Glass Panels
6°	Angel of Both Towers

INTERVIEW

Interviewee: David Gianotten, Managing Partner – Architect, OMA

Interviewers: Anthony Dalto, Vincenzo Orologio, final year Master of Architecture students, School of Architecture and Design, New York Institute of Technology

March 2, 2023

Tom Verebes Thank you very much, David – it has been a pleasure to receive your elaboration of the CCTV. You have presented so much background about the project that is not in any architectural publication about CCTV, a project which recapitulates the power of architectural form to provoke reactions, and how form serves as a political tool for architecture. I will shift directly to introduce, Anthony Dalto and Vincenzo Orologio, final year M.Arch students here at New York Tech, who will conduct this interview with you.

David Gianotten Thank you – it's nice to be here and part of this series.

Anthony Dalto My name is Anthony Dalto, and my partner in this interview is Vincenzo Orologio, and we would like to thank you for your fantastic presentation of the CCTV project, amongst others at OMA. We thank you also for this unique opportunity to interview you. Office of Metropolitan Architecture, OMA, was launched, as the name of the office has always implied, with an emphasis on metropolitan, urban architecture. The CCTV project aims for the reinvention of the tower typology, proposing a radical alternative. In the published words of Rem Koolhaas, perhaps the most preeminent theorist of the 20th century skyscraper, CCTV "promised to kill the skyscraper", and the repetitive banality of towers which compete simply to get taller and taller. This agenda is familiar across the history of OMA's instrumentality of diagrammatic generative processes – establishing project strategies as organizational diagrams encapsulating clear ideas and intentions. OMA's diagrams embody and embed criticality and commentary, and they have often served as provocations. You presented to us a field of study models, many in blue foam. The use of blue foam study models within the design studio environment at OMA has been one of the office's preferred 3D media with which to develop and proliferate project diagrams. Can you share with us how the LOOP emerged as an idea of a booleaned tetrahedron in early design stages, as the agent to subvert the two dimensionality of the discrete tower?

DG I was not present at OMA at the time, so I can only communicate what was told to me when I stepped in to lead the design and building process in 2009. The main idea we tested, in all kinds of models, not only in blue foam, but also in mass modeling. We had the feeling that we would disconnect the project if we went for the three-tower scheme as they had proposed in the master plan. In that scheme, you would have a broadcasting section, a production section, and a management section. We thought this would not enhance the transparency of the media or the transparency of information, because then everybody would have its own disconnected position. We thought it would be very interesting to combine these positions and therefore create an atmosphere where everybody could learn from each other, but also everybody could understand its point of view in a very complex context within the Chinese regime and the Chinese culture. Therefore, we really were only looking for massing models that combined the three main program elements. When we studied the loop of TV making, the idea of the spatial loop emerged quite quickly. We did many studies of a loop first in two dimensions, not yet breaking out and cantilevering, but more as a circle or as a square. Then, when we started looking at how we could interact with the ring road, but also with more fragile parts of the city that have smaller dimensions, we started pulling out massing models which led eventually to this way of organizing the loop. I would say that probably was in the fourth or fifth week of the competition, which we worked on for about 3 months.

AD Were there other diagrams than this particular topology of the loop which were considered in the early design stages?

DG Yes, many diagrams – and they have all been shown in exhibitions. There were many different types of ideas for the form, which is a working style of our office. We never take anything for granted. We test, and test, and test, and test, and then only when we are certain we make a commitment to a scheme. There were many different studies from a three-tower model to a one-tower model to a cube type of model, to a loop in the two dimensions as described, and then a three-dimensional loop. When that emerged we chose it quite quickly and developed it, but that led still to probably another sixty to seventy models of how this model could be done.

Vincenzo Orologio The CCTV project had broken many rules and conventions - formal, typological and contextual expectations, as well as statutory rules about controlling architectural production. The building did not comply with rigid Chinese building codes and planning guidelines at the time it was designed and constructed, but the proposal was seemingly eventually negotiated and accepted to comply with building regulations and planning conventions. As an innovative, unique and striking design, the CCTV project quickly became a symbol of Beijing. Deferring for the moment from the notion of a building as a landmark, and the politics of iconicity, the figure of CCTV continually changes the perception and reading of its form, always identifiable from a great distance as a landmark. As an icon of Beijing, what do you find to be the most significant aspect of the building in terms of the public exposure and context of CCTV?

DG I think what was really striking about CCTV is that it became a recognizable

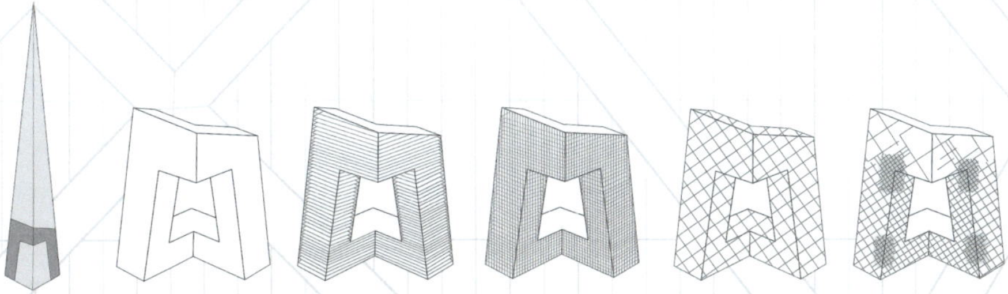

Truncated tetrahedron, booleaned; series of diagrams describing the looped figure and its suface

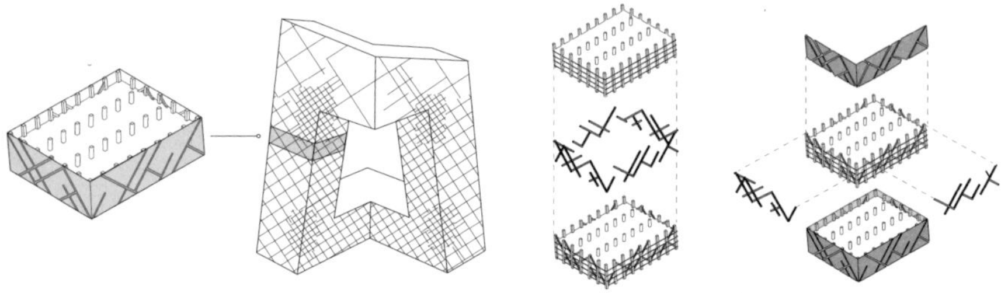

Systems diagram of structural surfaces of the structural tube

image, or an icon, quite quickly because people started to relate to it, not because it is the highest, or because it was the color red, but they started relating to the shape and understanding it. That is also why I think the nickname, "big pants", was a compliment for us because it related back to the culture of the city. I think people recognized what we were trying to do, not always liking it, but understanding that we were trying to do something very different. That helped also to make it an image or an icon. We never like to talk about icons as architects, because if you have a collection of icons, nothing is an icon anymore. We try to create buildings that are unique and that transcend the institution or the process that is happening within it. I think CCTV was a striking example of this ambition.

VO Can you share with us how you see the landmark status of CCTV. Is it recognizable based on its unusualness and its eventual recognizability and familiarity?

DG I think it is recognizable because of its curious shape and when you start looking at it and trying to understand it, you probably start understanding more of the meaning and the engagement with the surroundings and the context. And as I described it before...

"...it goes from very bombastic and iconic, to very fragile and singular, which I think is part of the myth around the building that it is never the same from whatever angle you see it, which supports the idea of being unique."

VO Also, back to breaking rules...has the building had an impact on the changing of building codes in China and planning regulations in Beijing?

DG Yes, it did, especially in the area of earthquake testing, and also, structural simulation took off in China after the CCTV for other projects.

AD Designed in collaboration with the engineer Cecil Balmond at Arup, the diagrid mapped onto the skin of CCTV acts as a "mega tube". Unnecessary and redundant elements were removed to resolve the eccentric forces of the six-degree slopes of the extrusions, seismic and wind forces, and the 75-meter cantilever of the administrative block. While working with Arup, were other options for other structural principles considered?

DG No, we did not consider other structural solutions. Simply because the tube would also relate closely to the loop and this enabled us to have spaces within the tube that were as free as possible. We wanted to translate the skin directly from the structure to show how it actually operates. Therefore, we really wanted the structure on the outside. We always worked on the idea of the tube which was folded and that is also what you see in the finished building.

AD What unique challenges led to the final architectural and engineering design? Also, at what design stage did OMA and Arup consider and develop the expression of structure as a partial diagrid exoskeleton on the façade?

AG That is a very complex question because

obviously there are, in a project of such magnitude, there are many decisions that are crucial in the end to realize it. I think one of the biggest decisions when we finally settled on the loop was to maintain that because all the forces were of course against that because it is much simpler to make standard windows. It is much simpler to make two towers, so we always had to resist referring to things that people already knew, because this was something people did not know. So, when we took the decision to go for it, we rigorously kept that original diagram of the building as the starting point of everything. That was a crucial decision because if we had given in or made a compromise to that, then the building would have been transformed back into something that people would not see as unique anymore, and that would be a compromise. Its rigor was in preserving the importance even when we had to rebuild part of the complex, and even when we had to do the interior design, which came much later. We had also done the full interior design of the building, but we kept that rigor in place and we never compromised it in any way. That is probably the most important thing for us as architects to live by.

VO In our Master of Architecture graduate seminar, Beyond the Envelope, we analyze each project across six themes. We have already discussed the themes of Form and Matter. Another theme is Identity, which entails what architecture communicates, and how the building performs contextually. CCTV stages visual effects on the skyline of Beijing. It is perceived as translucent from some angles, and opaque from other orientations. The building is quoted in publications to blend in with the notoriously polluted skies of Beijing – also designed not to look like a dirty glass façade. How was this principle of blending into the hazy skies of Beijing tested? Did OMA do renderings or color and reflection simulations?

DG We built large scale mockups. We did 1:20 scale structural models, but we also built mockups of the façade and we tested them in a situation focusing on color, not only at ground but also at height so that we could see how it would behave at an angle, how it would behave in a hazy sky, and how it would behave in a bright sky. What you see is that the building turns more to bronze and brown colors when there is sunshine, and it turns more grayish-bluish with a setting of clouds and haze. It responds to, or at least it captures some of the surrounding qualities of the air. And therefore, it sometimes disappears and sometimes it appears very dominantly. Yes, we did a lot of testing, but especially on real material at grade and at height.

VO In your view, were the desired and predicted effects accomplished in the built outcome of CCTV?

DG In general, yes, but as an architect you always see things that you would do differently if you had a second chance. That luxury though, is almost never there – only when you restore your own buildings. I think we are very satisfied with that part of the outcome.

AD We would like to now pivot to a discussion of the politics of architecture. Great architecture provokes people to think, reflect, and ultimately, has the power to make an

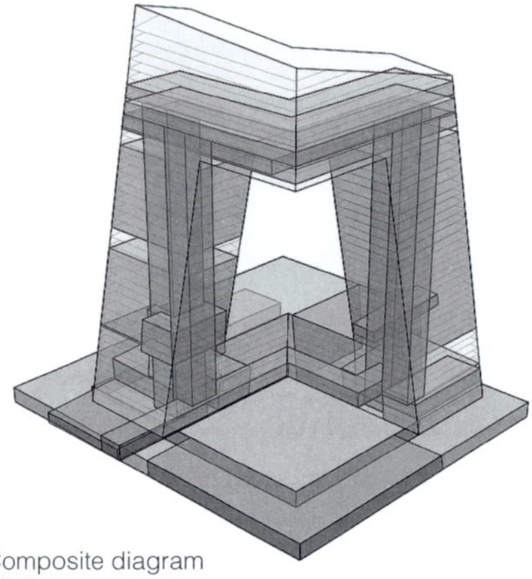

Composite diagram
of all programs

impact and, ultimately, to change society. Architecture which strives for correctness and appropriateness often fails this ambition. The status of the CCTV building as a landmark, and also as an architectural icon, substantiates its cultural value and meaning on many levels. In spite of being known by all in Beijing, and much loved, the building has grown to be deemed controversial within China. Can you share with us a historical account of the initial and eventual reception of the CCTV project; how and why the CCTV building gradually became mired in controversy by the professional communities of architects and engineers in China, the Chinese public and eventually, by the President of China, Xi Jinping?

DG When you build a project of this scale, the reception of it can have different voices. It has a voice of locality. It has a voice on level of the metropolis. It has a voice on the national level, and it has an Asian context, and it has a worldwide premise. The reception of it was in the beginning, curious and subtle, and trying to understand what we tried to achieve. OMA teaches, for example, at CAFA, one of the schools in Beijing, you still see when the students and the professor study the building, there's always the part that they really like about it, and there are also things that they see as from another era when China was upcoming and didn't yet have its own identity. Of course, the current president made statements about weird buildings and CCTV was put under that idea of weird buildings, but this was never supported by the intellectual part of the architectural community within the Chinese context or within the Asian context. It was picked up a lot in the international media because it came to the international media as "god's gift", in that they could criticize architects who would work in China and would try to achieve something in the Chinese context because China was still seen as a complex, and maybe even an aggressive context to work in. From an architecture point of view, this is at least for us, very different. We also engage with contexts that are not necessarily completely compliant with the Western idea of how a society should be. We try to learn from that and try to investigate it and see what a contextual response within that could be to bring progress, even very little progress. And for us, it was already a great idea that the largest Chinese media organization suddenly was part of the city, so everybody could view it. It was not secretly located somewhere outside the city anymore. Adding a public loop was also important although it's now closed, we hope that it opens up again. It creates this kind of engagement that was never possible there. Those are very small steps but within the perception of the Chinese culture they become larger and or aspirational in a way. That is recognized when you see the studies of the building or the writing. The building, of course, because of its shape got a response, in nicknames but also an artistic response.

"There have been many photographers, but also many artists, responding to the shape and responding to its signature skin. You could say it also became iconic not necessarily only because of the building, but also because of the interpretation of it."

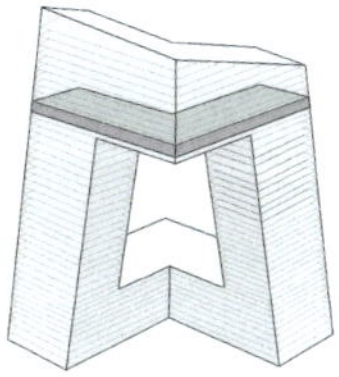

Administration

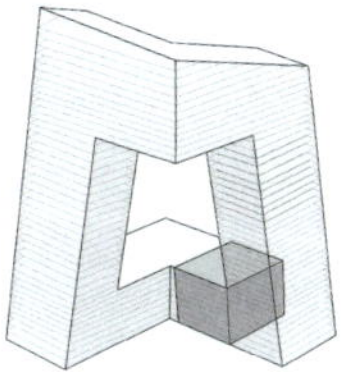

Broadcasting

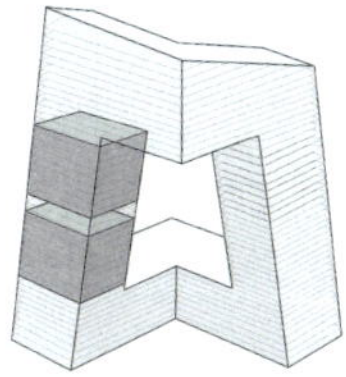

Multi-business

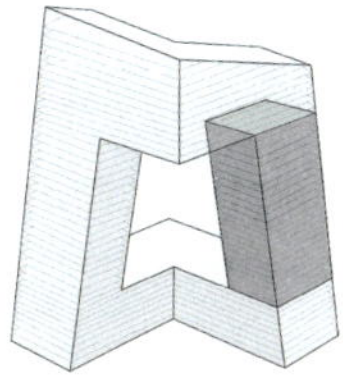

News

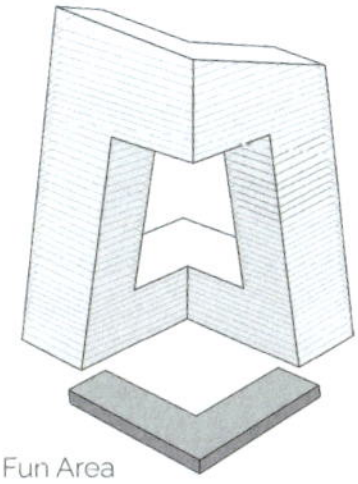

Fun Area

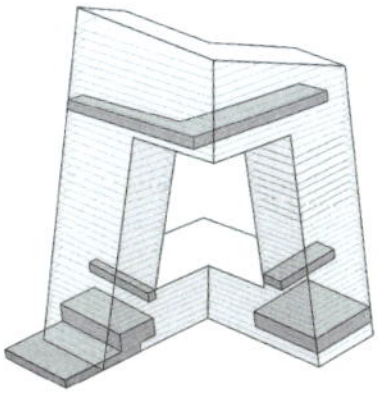

Lobbies

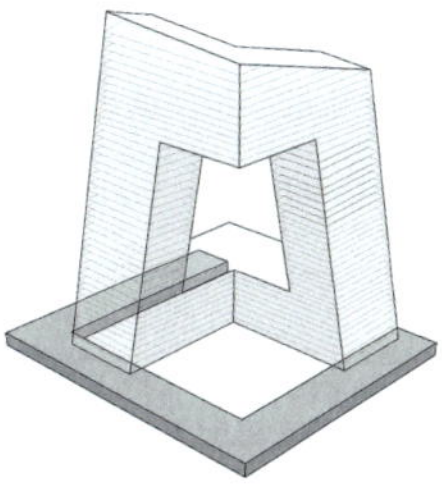

Parking

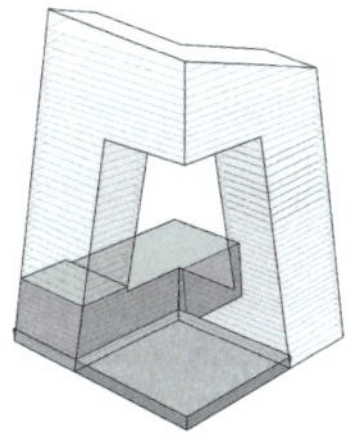

Production

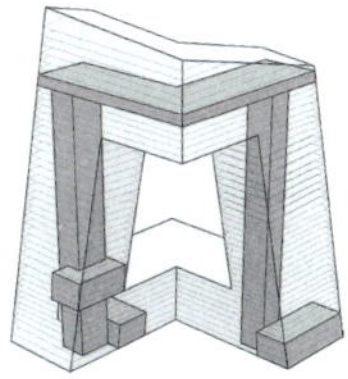

Vip Area

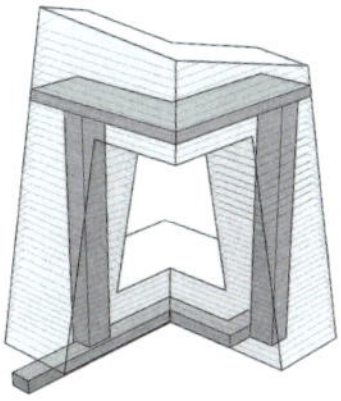

Visitors

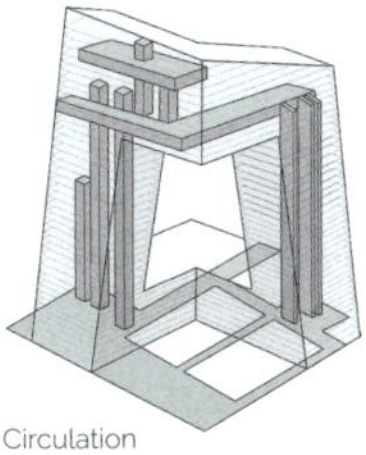

Circulation

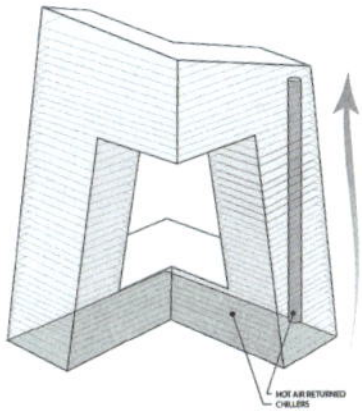

Heating Diagram

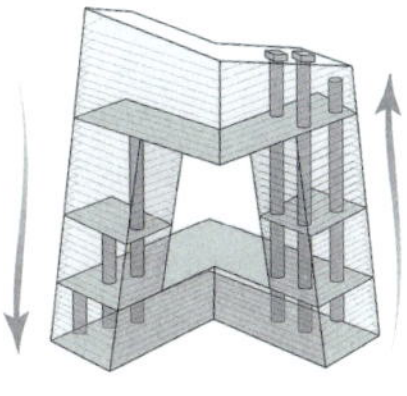

Combined Climate Diagrams

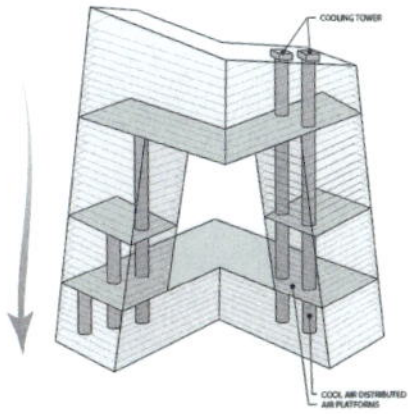

Cooling Diagram

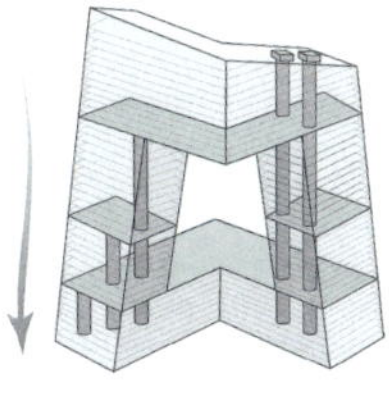

Cooling Diagram

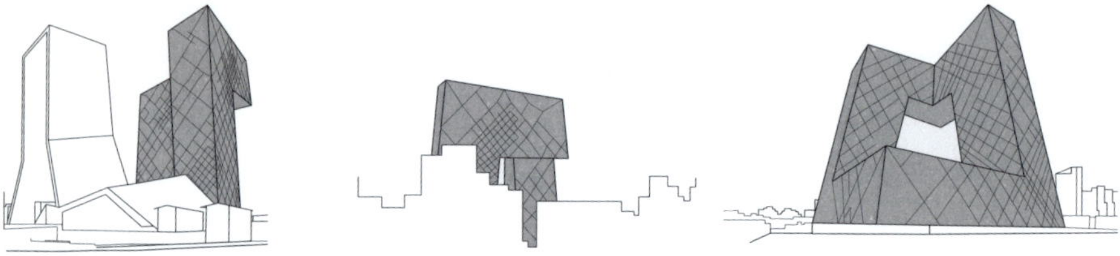

Views demonstrating the variable reading of the mass of CCTV from differnet positions.

There was an exhibition about this in Beijing, where all the art that related to CCTV was on show. It is a project of rising China. It is a project of media and maybe some people argue of dominance, but it is also a project of opening, engaging and putting things that are for society in society. It is too complex to say this is how it evolved because there's no one single voice. There are different voices around it, but we are still lecturing about it as you see today. But we are also asked a lot of questions about the ideas and what it did, and we are also not gone, we are still communicating with CCTV because the in-housing is still ongoing. But the project in our opinion is a successful project for us to do.

AD Thank you! CCTV has become a symbol of China's globalization and internationality. Do you believe a project like CCTV, designed by a western architect, can be commissioned within the cultural and political context of China today?

DG You could not do the project alone now in China from start to finish. It was possible then as foreign architect to have a significant role from start to finish. I think now it would always be in symbiosis with a local Chinese architect, but we are still working in China quite significantly in our portfolio. We keep engaging with that context because we think it's important to have that exchange. It's part of our profession. It's a part of the world that has risen quickly and is also developing heavily so that the communication and learning curve on both sides is, for us, an important reason to keep engaging with it.

AD If you were commissioned a project for the Headquarters of CCTV in 2023, more than 20 years after your initial commission, how might your decisions concerning the unusualness of the building's form be approached differently today?

DG That is impossible to answer because that would be a different process in a different context, with different leaders. That would be redoing it and probably the outcome would be very different, but it is impossible to say what we would do differently because it is a totally different context and idea. The world has changed since then.

VO Our next question concerns the relationships of the CCTV project to the larger body of work of OMA. Characterized using diagrammatic strategies, OMA has positioned architectural practice as a form of critical commentary on disciplinary spatial issues, political, economic, social and cultural conditions of the context of the work. Across countless OMA projects, interests in uncertainty, unexpectedness, and criticality, are evident. Further to your presentation, can you share with us the genealogy of the design of the CCTV project within OMA?

DG CCTV is obviously a very important project within our portfolio, not only because we were reaching out to China – a space where we hadn't worked yet, but also within developing the diagrammatic language of critique, and of striving for new models and new ideas, which are always an evolution. Porto (Casa de Musica) is an evolution of a concept for a house, and in Taipei (Taipei Performing Arts Center) we tried to push the innovation and flexibility even more, which is now pushed further again in the Factory project in Manchester. Our work is a constant evolution of ideas that continues and that are rethought and reread. In the office portfolio of OMA, CCTV has an important role to play because it shows that you can do things differently in a very logical way to create a very unique and unexpected outcome. o answer your question, the main contribution of CCTV to our portfolio is to show how we take nothing for granted and how rigorous we are. The position of it is very important. It is one of our important buildings in the portfolio and started a new thinking process about offices in other contexts as well.

AD Thank you. Are there projects which led to CCTV, diagrammatically and spatially?

DG No, it was really a process that we started from scratch and led to something afterwards. Before there was nothing.

AD CCTV was proposed 21 years ago and completed 11 years ago. We are interested in the consequences of this project on the portfolio of work at OMA in the last decade or so. Further to your presentation, can you share with us how you see the influence of the CCTV project upon the work of OMA since its design and completed construction?

DG After the completion of CCTV, we began to work in all regions of the world: the Americas, Europe, the Middle East, Africa, Asia and Australia. So, in that sense, it was important to complete the puzzle of the global. Secondly, it led to rethinking the type of the office, not the standard that developers would bring, but because it was for an institution, we could really rethink how people work together and live together while they are working. We took forward that type of thinking, which is very visible for example, in the Springer building that we delivered ten years later, but also in the Tencent headquarters building that we delivered together with BIAD in the same city. Tencent is a totally different puzzle, but there are a lot of learnings from the CCTV building in that building, which is in the same context, the Chinese context, even the same city, just one ring road further on. So, CCTV led to thinking about a topology that went far beyond the brief.

VO This interview and the study of the set of projects in the Beyond the Envelope series of presentations and interviews are set within a Master of Architecture course here at NYIT. As such, the audience of this event, and this interview, is the future of architecture. In this context, can you please share with us, from your point of view, any advice you may have for the next generation of architects?

DG I have two points of advice. Firstly, our profession is really a privilege because you are in the center pivot point of many discussions. You can have an impact on built form, but you also can have a social impact and economic impact. So be very curious to explore all the dimensions and do not do one-dimensional architecture in the sense of just putting bricks together or steel and glass together. Think beyond that about the consequences of what you do. The second thing is, architecture is sometimes taken extremely seriously, which it is, but I would really recommend you have a lot of joy and fun doing it because we are so privileged to be involved in it. It's not only about seriousness and hard work, it's also about fun and understanding what you're actually doing within a certain context. That enriches your own personality and context so also enjoy it and have fun. Maybe lastly, don't dive into the computer constantly because architecture happens in the real world. Technology is only there to support us, but it is not the tool. The tool is your brain and what you observe with that brain.

VO Thank you very much for the unique opportunity to interview you today.

DG You're welcome – this was fun! I wish you good luck in your careers.

TV Thank you very much David, for your insightful presentation and for your generosity in joining us for the interview as Managing Partner – Architect at OMA from the headquarters in Rotterdam. We look forward to years of output of new projects that OMA will nourish us with. Thank you for this opportunity for our students here at New York Tech – your participation is very much appreciated.

DG Thank you. Have a great day!

东三环北路

ABSOLUTE TOWERS

Mississauga, Toronto, 2012 | MAD Architects

Program Residential

Façade materials Prefabricated glass and aluminum

Leed Gold Certificate

FORM

95,000 M2	GFA
4090 M2	Site Area
6	Floors Below Ground
56	Floors Above Ground (Tower A)
50	Floors Above Ground (Tower B)
170 M	High (Tower A)
150 M	High (Tower B)
209	Degree Twist (Tower A)
198	Degree Twist (Tower B)
0% solid	100% Glazing

INTERVIEW

Interviewee: Yosuke Hayano, Principal Partner, MAD Architects

Interviewers: Alison Jean Iannucci, Adelina Sinanaj, final year Master of Architecture students, School of Architecture and Design, New York Institute of Technology

March 15, 2023

Tom Verebes I believe it is relevant to firstly announce the Absolute Towers project as one of the first projects built in Canada by the current generations of Chinese architects. It is a pleasure to have you with us today, Yosuke Hayano, to present this project, amongst others by MAD, and to participate in this interview.

Yosuke Hayano Thank you, Tom. It is great to be here and I am happy to contribute to NYIT.

TV I would like to now introduce Alison Iannucci and Adelina Sinanaj, our interviewers, who are final year M.Arch students at New York Tech.

Adelina Sinanaj My name is Adelina, and it is an honor to interview you. From the various publications on the Absolute Towers, and as well inferred from your presentation, this project is conceived to be situated at the intersection of traditional Chinese philosophy, spirituality, and poetics, with a highly contemporary, global, and ubiquitous concern for environmental balance. In traditional Chinese gardens, built and natural elements are integrated, as are literature, poems and music all in synthesis. Can you describe the ethos of the Absolute Towers, and more broadly the design approach at MAD, on how to achieve your ambition of environmental balance, in which the experience of so-called nature is set in harmony with the compounding density and complexity of our urban environments? Perhaps asked more simply, how does MAD aim for what your practice describes as a "balanced environment" and a "harmonious civilization"?

Yosuke Hayano Thank you. One of the main points of this project is to challenge why high-rise towers are always in the same format with typical repeated floors. We challenged this presumed efficiency in the Absolute Towers, which was critical for the client. The background of this project gave us space to challenge this, because Mississauga, where the project is located, is not so much suburbia, but also not in a very dense urban condition. Furthermore, it is a residential tower.

We asked how we can create diversity in a high-rise building, with each floor being different, which is asking how we can make a tower more like a natural setting. We can achieve this by creating particular connections and relationships. This was very challenging. We also asked how our urban gesture will appear on the skyline, and in fact, we raise similar questions in all our high-rise projects. This is why we envisioned the tower as if it had grown out of the ground.

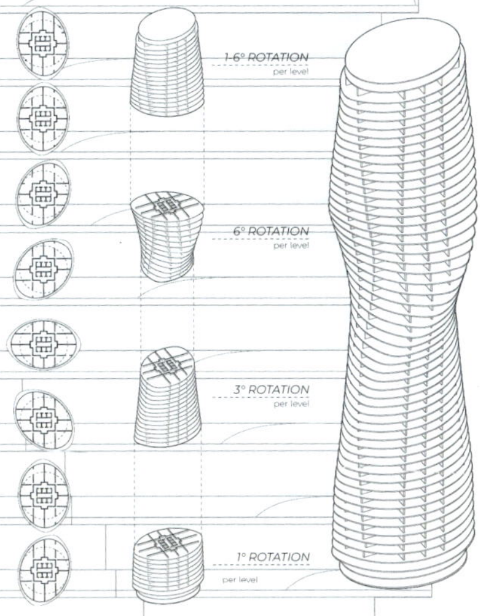

Demonstration of the degrees of rotation in plan of four segments of massing

We worked on this language of rotating floor plates to create a rounded figure, which creates a special and unique experience, but at the same time, for it to be fit for its context.

MAD never repeats work. We look for all potential possibilities for each of our projects. This site sits on the intersection of two big city roads, therefore the towers become a gateway. People will see this tower from a distance, then get closer to see more details. Our understanding of this design focused on ideas of speed, the city, and formal growth as the approach to this design. Even though the construction cost of the project is greater than an often-seen boxy building, we're happy that the market totally accepts it. Both the client and the building residents are happy about the towers. Finally, to conclude my answer to your question, we wanted this project to create value for the city, and for the towers to be elements in the urbanism of Mississauga, not as single objects. We thought about how to improve the urban condition through having the towers as part of the environment.

AS Thank you. Can you elaborate how the Absolute Towers exemplify the negotiation of the paradoxes between densification of cities and the preeminence of the environmental quality of life in cities?

YH The Absolute Towers are residential – built for those who live there in their daily lives. That is why we designed the 360 degree balconies wrapping around. Each unit has an excellent balcony, even at height. Balconies and openable windows are challenging because the wind pressure differs at higher levels. Regardless, we thought it was essential to have an outside space to see the view and to feel the natural environment. The scenes looking down are never too direct towards the ground. Sometimes you can see your neighbors above or below you. This kind of indirect encounter provides a sense of community, which is not easy to achieve in a high-rise because of management and marketing constraints. We very much appreciated our client's support to work together to make this a new type of high-rise. Many people who see this project on the internet do not have an understanding of the challenge it was to create a sense of community and emotional belonging in a high rise – this was significant for us.

AS The Absolute Towers project was designed and built in an era in which accelerated climate change is reshaping the way we think about our responsibility to the environment and our planet as a whole. Conventionally in early modernity, glass towers were unconcerned with

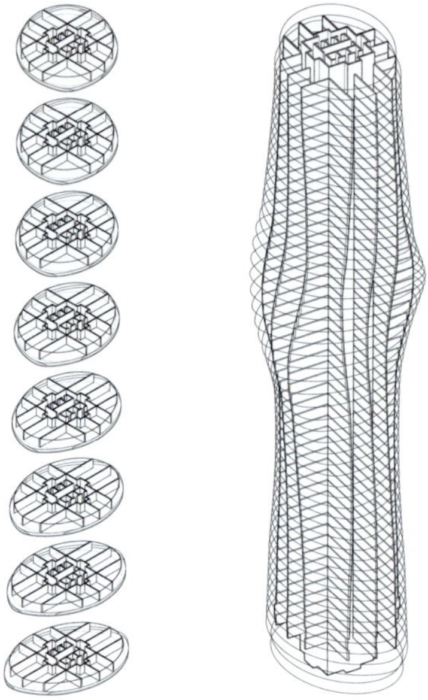

Plan rotations and their impact on the horizontal extrusion of the shear walls of the core.

environmental performance, and this legacy of the glass envelope presents a challenge for agendas of environmental sustainability. Can you share with us your position at MAD on agendas of sustainability aside from the pervasive ambition of augmenting energy efficiency and cost savings? Or in other words, can you elaborate how architecture can target more holistic intentions for ecological sustainability?

YH Our sustainable design approach is not only about numbers – it is not about what percentage of a façade should be solid, or the value of insulation. The design of the form looks very organic and carved, but each balustrade panel uses a flat panel, because of its large radius. When seen from a distance, people can tell whether this is curved glass or flat glass. This is also the same for the glazing panels on the façade. Because of the overall curved shape of the envelopes, the wind pressure on the upper levels can be dramatically reduced. We did lots of CFD (Computational Fluid Dynamics) simulations. We also tested how we can reduce the pressure on the structure, reducing some cost of structure. Of course, thermal efficiency is an important topic, but we also need more perspective to zoom out to see an architectural project as part of the environment, and how it can work as part of the natural setting.

We have to be careful not only to consider targeting with numbers, but what the numbers mean. In other words, making a building more sustainable depends on how it is used. For one, we should try hard to have a deep understanding of the criteria for how the design should respond to the sustainable design agenda in each project. Secondly, how can we provide a better urban setting, or optimize architecture's social and public value over time.

AS Perhaps related, do you believe architecture needs to resemble or mimic nature in order to be in harmony with the environment? Please can you share your thoughts on this topic.

YH We conduct quite a lot of research work that considers nature, and I think your professor (Tom Verebes) is also quite knowledgeable about this. Natural beings respond more purely to their environment, such as gravity or other forces, therefore nature has its agenda for the survival of their species. But I don't think we should directly transform the appearance of nature into architecture. Nevertheless, we need to look more into the natural system. For example, we do many studies about animal skins, for example, about how the skin responds to different humidity levels; or more generally, how species respond to their environment.

AI Our next question concerns the context of the project, and the project's relation to the cultural imagination of the public towards the identity of the architecture of the Absolute Towers. The towers are characterized by their highly identifiable figuration as they peer above the flat suburban landscape of Mississauga, to the north of Toronto. Not so different from the public branding of Frank Gehry's "Fred and Ginger" buildings in Prague, which capture the dynamics of two interacting figures, the profile of the Absolute Towers has been likened to the body figure of Marilyn Monroe, as the profile of shapely bodies.

We understand biological processes are intricate systems, but we try to understand how we can adapt that into architecture and make the overall system perform better. We had looked into how a fish moves easily in dynamic streams of water pressure, while its thermal function prevents it from freezing. In this way, it is not only about the building, the object itself, but how architecture can better serve people who use and live in it. Ultimately, we develop an understanding of natural performance and how it can be transformed into an architectural language on a more human scale, architecture scale, or urban scale.

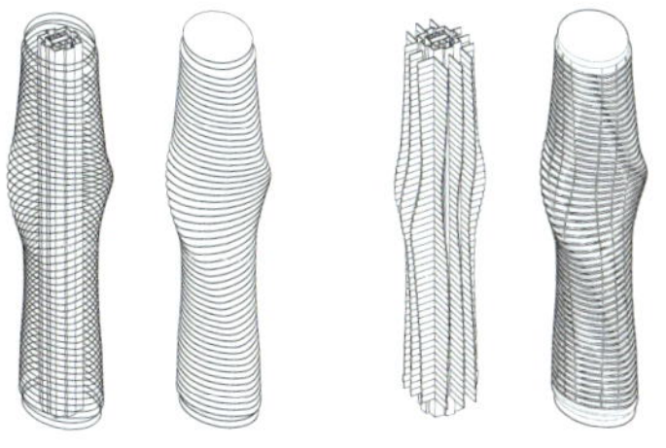

Structural and material systems

You shared with us in your presentation how the nickname, "The Marilyn Monroe Towers", had arisen from early newspaper publications of the project in the last stage of the competition. Were you pleased with the nickname?

YH Yes! We were very pleased with the way the community responded to the design. It is rare to hear the community being vocal with comments on design, and the popularity of the Absolute Towers does mean a lot to all teams during the entire process. We also received emails from local community residents thanking us for how much they enjoyed the transformation from the original design to the actual building. In a positive way, the towers have become a landmark in Mississauga. But, it is not just a landmark that people see every day, instead the background of their daily life. This is about making a personal connection to the design through architecture and urban space.

AI Can you please share with us your values regarding iconicity in architecture? Please tell us honestly, do you mind if we categorize the Absolute Towers as "iconic architecture"?
YH The term iconic is quite difficult to define. Absolutely, the towers in Toronto make an iconic cityscape for the citizens. For us, it is not so important to make an iconic building, but rather how we understand local society and people's lives, and how our architecture can bring different dimensions and settings for the future. That is why people see this design as bringing new possibilities to the urban context. In this sense, the project is iconic, but it is an urban icon, which I hope the city will accept this kind of challenge again in the future.

AS Shifting our discussion to paradigms of the skyscraper, and the ways in which the Absolute Towers innovates upon some of the prevailing

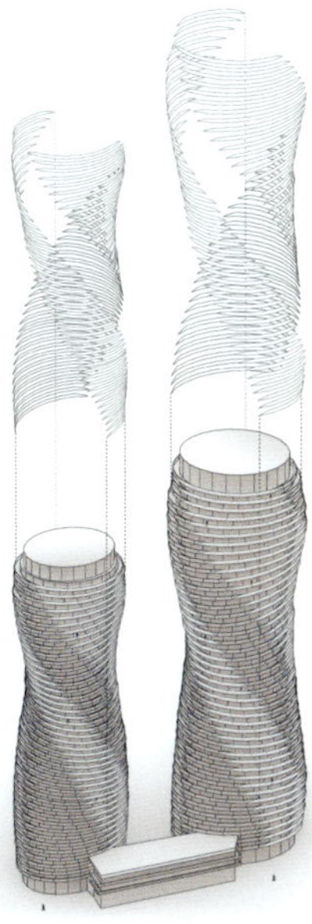

Massing and balconies

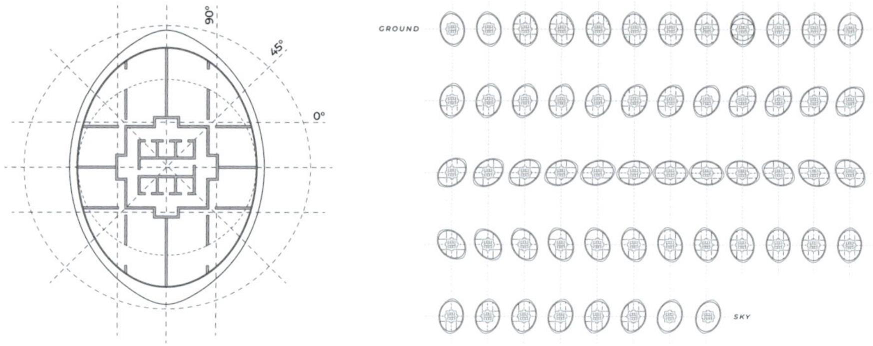

Plan of the building core rotations

legacies of the formal and material typologies of the skyscraper, we are interested in what the Absolute Towers are NOT, and what this project critiques, implicitly. Related to MAD's interests in paradigms which can be defined as naturalistic, organicist, humanistic, and ecological, we are interested in how these worldviews can be instrumentalized as alternatives to the context of towers driven by formal and typological rationalism. Given the backdrop of the history of modernism, and vertical extrusion and orthogonality as the prevailing techniques of tower design, can you share with us how you conceived the Absolute Towers as an alternative to this history and mode of practice?

YH The pure challenge of this project was to have our interpretation of a high-rise. What is the future of the high-rise for us? We had many high-rise projects after the Absolute Towers, and we always have similar challenges of how the future high-rise can be a better place for people. This vertical connection can be a new kind of urban space. How can this vertical space bring more pleasure and more dynamics to urban communities? This is a big challenge as high-rise architecture is all about square meter efficiency and functionality. In this sense, we very much appreciate our clients for granting us absolute freedom to share our vision.

AS To quote MAD Architects in publications, your practice views towers in general, as quote, "symbols of bravado, (and the) expression of wealth and prosperity". Can you comment and elaborate on this position?

YH We're more concerned about the following series of questions: How can we break through the traditional understanding of urban or architectural design, but how can we provide more dynamics from a different perspective for the people or the community. Is it a good place to trigger social happenings for the community? For example, in the urban space of the Harbin Opera House, we now see many people taking wedding photos and or dancing in groups, which we didn't expect when first designed, but this is how the community finds potential in this space and how they take it as the background of their daily life. All our projects can trigger people's imagination, pushing the society and communities a little bit forward in the future.

AS Thank you. Considering the global and urban consequences of the Absolute Towers, this project is situated, as discussed earlier, in a suburban context, yet it speaks to a fundamental critique of the replication of architectural sameness in business districts

A rotational tower can be different from a previous traditional tower, not just differentiated for the sake of being iconic. Also, this cannot be realized by one single tower. If you have a cluster of towers, how can they make a more diverse, dynamic, and differentiated urban setting? This is a key critical topic for MAD.

worldwide. Can you please comment on the specificity of form and the uniqueness of character of towers, and when multiplied, the implications for the emerging densification of cities? Asked simply and more directly, you clearly do not want box-like vertically extruded towers, but can you imagine organic building forms proliferating in every city?

YH Countless high-rise projects have repeated typical floors without asking what is the meaning behind it. We want to see what life could be like for people in this tower, what they see and experience, and how we can provide more differentiated and variable spaces for the inhabitants. We now see many organic shaped towers in suburbia – it has become the new normal. Nothing sticks out. This is why we always have to work with a much bigger agenda. What do people need? How can our design participate, and how can we help the area to be more harmonized as an urban setting and as a natural setting. We have to be very careful not to jump into form, but to see the background and the context behind it.

AI Thank you. We are interested in the technologies and performance of the Towers – the intersection of the mathematics of formal differentiation with the performance of structural engineering and the behaviors of day lighting. What was the basis of generating the rotational logic of the plan from a range of increments, from 1 degree to 3, 6, to 8 degrees?

YH Firstly, the ground level had to respond to the corner condition to become the main entrance. Then we started the rotation, clockwise and anti-clockwise. For the floors lower to the ground, or the bottom part, we tried to make very gradual changes in the rotation. Then, for floors that are taller than the surrounding high-rise buildings, at around 60m to 80m, we worked on how to start showing a quick rotational move, because this is where people can see the towers from a distance. As the form comes to the top, from a distance, you can see everything. We looked for how to end at the top, not with a movement, but moving towards the sky as elevation. So, the formal transformation, and the articulation of the rotation was very much a response to the urban context.

AI Can you describe how the rotation of the floor plan impacts the deflection and reflection of sunlight?

YH Some parts have quite a deep cantilever, which creates an excellent shading effect. We conducted a lot of tests of the effects of shading sunlight. This also occurs on the back façades as well. You are reaching this urban gesture, creating a distinct experience either from a distance or getting close up. This is one of the determining factors in the design.

AS Pivoting to the body of work of MAD Architects, can you please share with us the genealogy of projects which preceded the Absolute

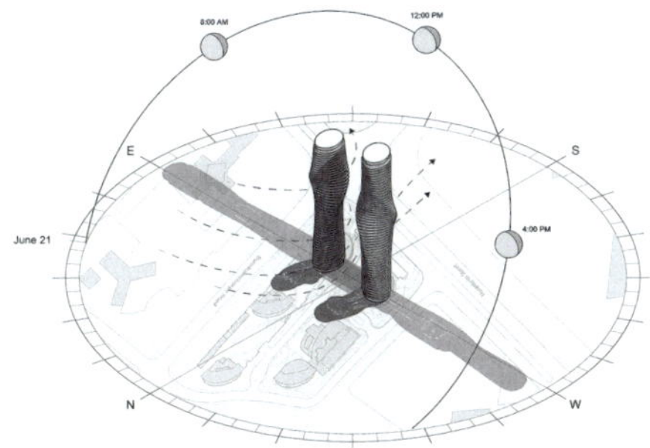

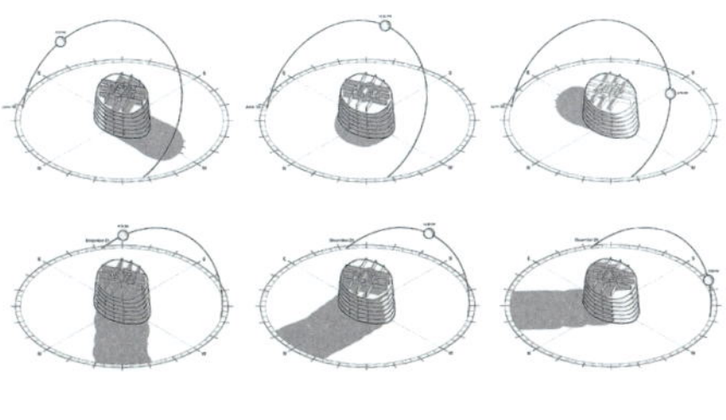

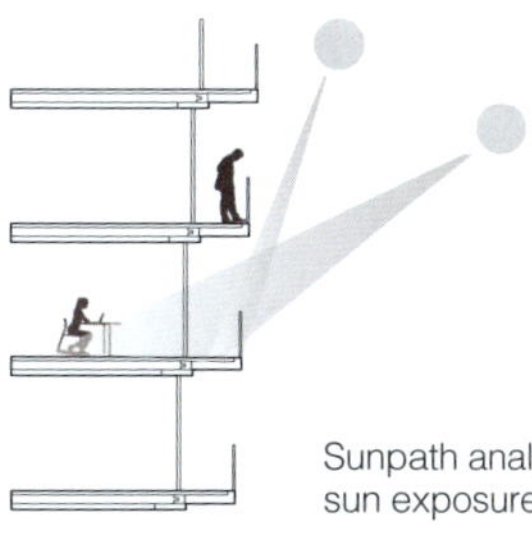

Sunpath analysis and sun exposure in section

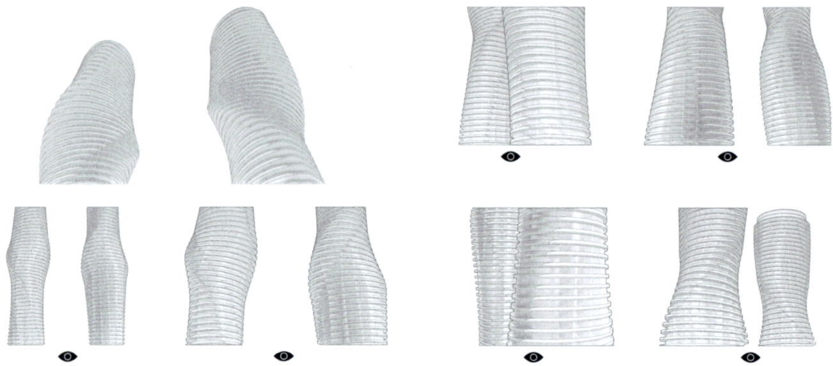

Variable experiences of the dynamic form of the envelope

Towers, and also the impact of this project on MAD's projects since its completion?

YH The two years before we won the Absolute Towers competition, we did more than 100 projects, including proposals and competition entries, but none of them were realized. After we won the Absolute Towers competition, clients started to come to us because they believe that we can realize this kind of project, as they see our organic forms built to excellent quality. They believe in our capability to turn ideas into reality by working with our expert team who could control all aspects such as cost, construction, and so on. That was quite helpful for us to develop across the challenges of various categories of architecture. While we were working on the Absolute Tower, we were also doing the Ordos Museum in China – two together – one project in Canada, one in China. For the Ordos Museum, we tried to refine the details of the façade system, but the workers who had the job to put the patterns on site, of course, do not have any architectural background, so we had to rely on fabrication and construction. That's a totally different working method to the Absolute Towers. In the end, each project has a different context, design and vision, but they share the same thing: MAD's high expectation and standard, which leads to a series of "next steps", how to communicate with clients, how we pick our collaborators, what we need to pay attention to during construction, etc.

AS MAD Architects are credited with being the first post-Open Door Policy China-based practice to build impactful and highly recognized architecture abroad. Also, as a Japanese national partnered with Ma Yansong, a Chinese national, in Beijing, can you reflect on this achievement and its global significance?

YH We worked on the Absolute Tower in Canada since 2006 while China was experiencing the architecture boom period because of the Beijing Olympics 2008. We witnessed Chinese cities' rapid transformation, and luckily we started to have more and more projects in China. We were fortunate to have these experiences in contrasting contexts of Canada and China. Our position has always been to ask how architecture can be part of urban space to bring benefits for the people and for the community. At the same time, we keep developing how we can learn from the natural environment, and how architectural space or urban space can be a natural extension of the urban context environment.

We are interested in challenging the boundary of architecture – how we can bring more elements to move between interior and exterior space; how to have a more dynamic conversation with the context. I think this attitude is more oriental. Instead of making an extreme form on the site, our architecture can become part of the context, responding to and reflecting local energy flows, or the flows of people, which is a more ephemeral approach. This is our fundamental core approach towards architecture and urban space.

We now have several projects in the US, and we continue to pursue this crucial understanding to go deeper so we can have a personal feeling about a site, the community, and the people related to a project. We focus on how our architecture is situated as part of their urban space, their city.

AS More broadly, can you comment on the importance of organic, curvilinear forms in contemporary architecture, and also, can you position MAD Architects' contribution to this disciplinary culture?

YH I would not say organic forms are a key element to define our practice, but this is our attitude towards how our architecture can hold to the requirements of a community and to functional requirements they are looking for, and how a project can be more dynamic as an urban response. For example, car design is not coming from a computer or mathematical calculations, but it is more like an emotional response. We do many sketches, and we try to find a line that fits the context from many possibilities, developing as an internal response or conversation about how to make architecture or design much more natural as an organic response to the contexts.

AI This interview and the study of the set of projects in the Beyond the Envelope series of presentations and interviews are set within a Master of Architecture course here at NYIT. As such, the audience of this event, and this interview, is the future of architecture. As our last question, in this context, please share with us, from your point of view, any advice you may have for the next generation of architects.

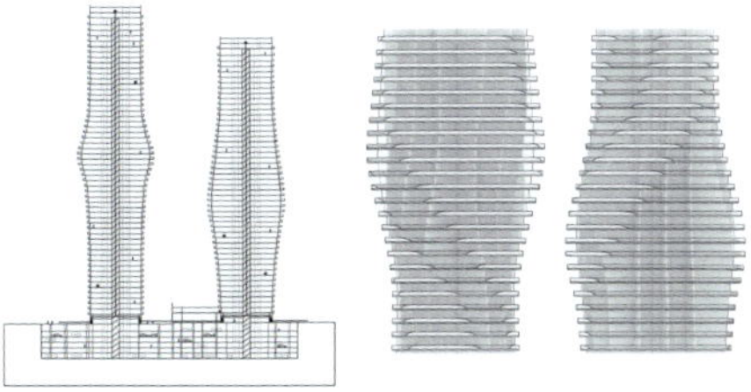

Section and detail elevations.

YH Because of Covid I believe many of you experienced a time of detachment from university life. Remote studying and working suddenly becomes normal, in which you can challenge yourself about the future of architecture and how architecture can provide a better life and better urban space for people. Challenge yourself and ask yourself what is the architecture you want to create and what kind of architect you want to be. Stick to your dream and vision. In short, be yourself. I recall now, here in front of Tom (Verebes), some twenty years ago sitting in studio at the AA working on my project. It is the same every day for me, as we ask how each project can be more meaningful for the people who will use it in the future; what kind of feelings will the users have; and how will the project benefit the city.

Dig into your emotions. What kind of moments do you feel? What touches you? What kind of spaces remain in your memory? Lastly, everything will be better after the pandemic. You will again be able to travel to many places and experience different architecture so you can define what kind of architecture you like. Then ask why you like it, and this will show you your path for the future. I hope you will enjoy architecture.

AI Thank you so much. We sincerely appreciate the chance to interview you today. Thank you for joining us.

TV This has been such a special and meaningful opportunity for us today. You have been so thorough in your presentation, and so generous with your responses in this interview. A big heart-felt thank you on behalf of everyone at New York Tech.

YH Thank you. I look forward to seeing you after the pandemic!

30,000 SQ.FT. OF AMENITIES SPACE
absolute

MUSEUM OF CONTEMPORARY ART AND PLANNING EXHIBITION MOCAPE

Shenzhen, 2016 | Coop Himmelb(l)au

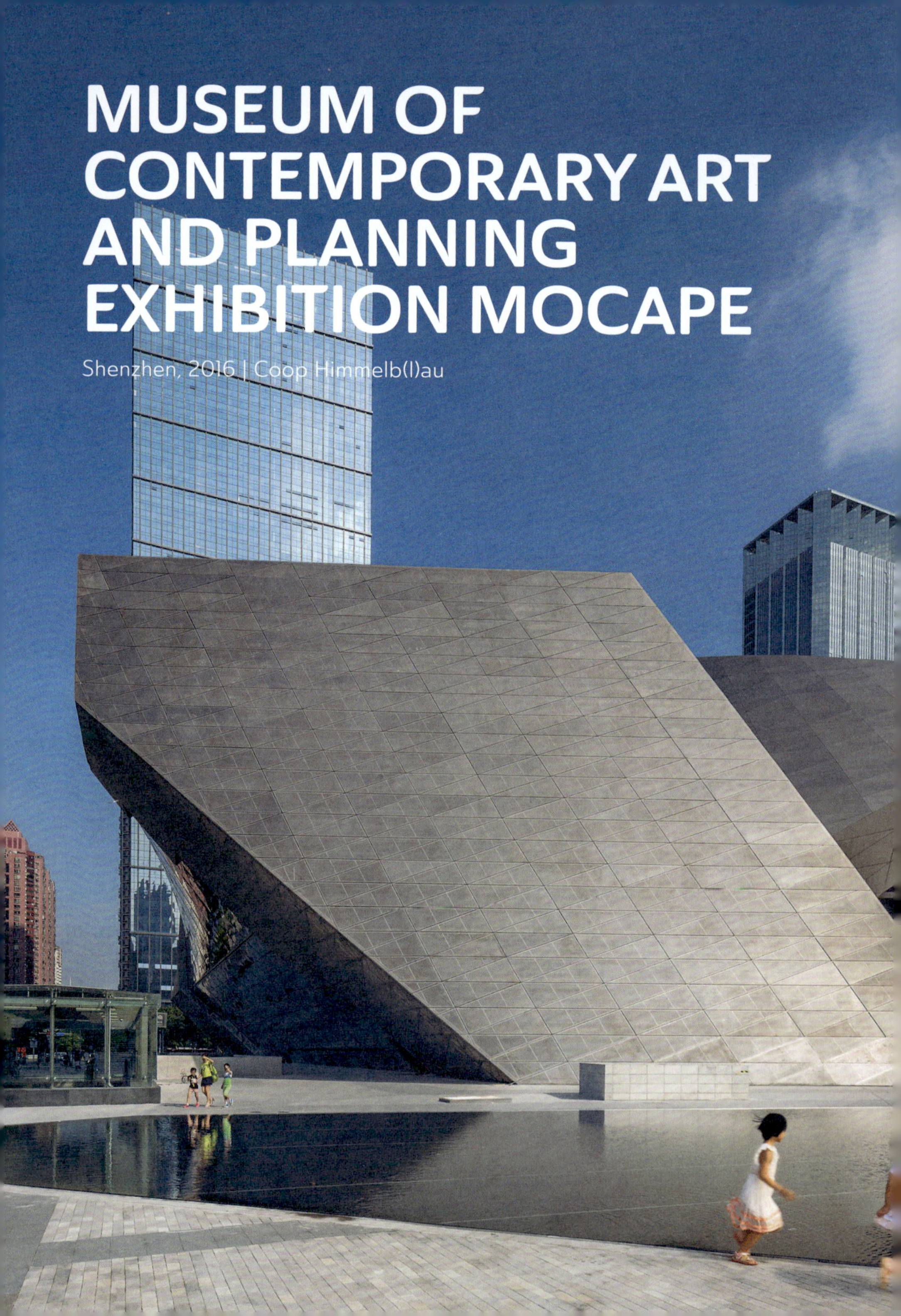

Program Contemporary Art Galleries, Planning Exhibition Galleries, Offices, Café, Interior Open Plaza, Exterior Pedestrian Plaza

Façade Materials Glass, Aluminum, Stone, Polished Steel

FORM

GFA	80,000 M2
Site Area	21.688 M2
High	40M
Floors Below Ground	0
Floors Above Ground	7
Facade Modules Total	41.567 M2
Different Types of Facade	3
Glass Facade Modules Total	18.874 M2
Aluminum Facade Modules Total	16.298 M2
Stone Facade Modules Total	6.395 M2
Glazing	45.4%
Solid	54.5%

INTERVIEW

Interviewee: Wolf D. Prix, CEO and Design Principal, Coop Himmelb(l)au

Interviewers: Michelle Enkhbaatar, Devanshi Shah, M.Arch students, School of Architecture and Design, New York Institute of Technology

March 9, 2022

Tom Verebes Thank you for your comprehensive, enlightening, and spectacular presentation, Wolf! For our students unable to experience this building due to being landlocked in our pandemic, and unfortunately, we are unable to travel to China – your presentation takes us on a spectacular tour of the design process, and the experience of the built outcome. I would like to now introduce our interviewers, Michelle Enkhbaatar and Devanshi Shah, M.Arch students here at New York Tech.

Wolf D. Prix Thank you. But have you been to the building, Tom?

TV Yes I have. This is a truly transformative and extraordinary building, bravo!

Michelle Enkhbaatar Thank you for your presentation. My name is Michelle Enkhbaatar and together with Devanshi Shah, we are grateful for this opportunity to interview you today. The impact of architecture, on both the individual and on society has been central to the work of Coop Himmelb(l)au. In which way for you is the practice of architecture a deeply political enterprise? How do you imagine the impact of the MOCAPE project upon its surroundings, which are the political and cultural center of Shenzhen?

WDP How do you think a museum interacts with the city? The building challenges the symmetry of the city planning and its surroundings and it plays with it. We twisted it around, and cut off the edges from the mass to let the dragon fly through it. This is what the building does. How does the content impact people and society? Through exhibitions of current art and of new (planning) projects. It creates a new point of interest. It creates, through the shape of the building, a new kind of environment inside and out, by design. And to be honest, we don't follow rules which other people have formed. We present new rules. No reaction, but action.

Devanshi Shah We would like to ask about your experience of working as a foreign architect in China, creating several iconic and transformative buildings. Can you share

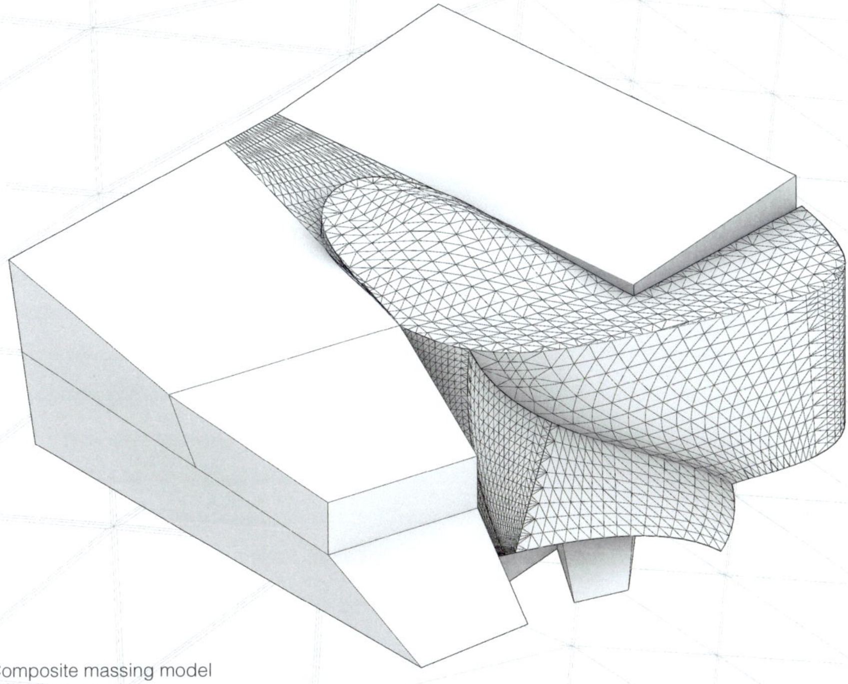

Composite massing model

with us how you have navigated the changing political context of China during the time of designing and completing this project?

WDP After we won the competition, we were looking for a local architect in China. We sent three people from our office to the office of the Chinese architects, and we worked together. The other way of working in a foreign country is to invite the architects to come into our office, and we create a team with the local architect, so that they have a better understanding of what we are designing, and we transfer our knowledge and how we work to the local architect. Moreover, we shared our methods and knowledge with the locals. We had a project which we would have loved to build in China. It was important to invite the local architects to our office. We invited a total of 6 Chinese architects and taught them how to create with the 3D modeling programs. After three months, they had learned the programs and how to make the project, they went back to China and they took the project with them.

ME As a cultural context, this project was conceived, commissioned and completed during the era of a substantial building boom, in which thousands of museums have been built in China, within the first two decades of this century. Can you summarize the contribution of the MOCAPE project to the larger societal ambition of building cultural institutions in China? In which ways is the MOCAPE project distinctive from other museums in China?

WDP Go there and you will see!

DS We hope to some day! In our M.Arch seminar, we are looking at six exemplary built projects, analyzed in relation to a set of six themes. This week we are focusing on the theme of Form, with the Museum of Contemporary Art and Planning Exhibition speaking to this topic. We are interested in what form does - its performance with regards to the social and political impact of form and spatial/material articulation, and its psychological effects on the subject. At the urban scale, the MOCA-P project simultaneously maintains and subverts

Louvres on envelope

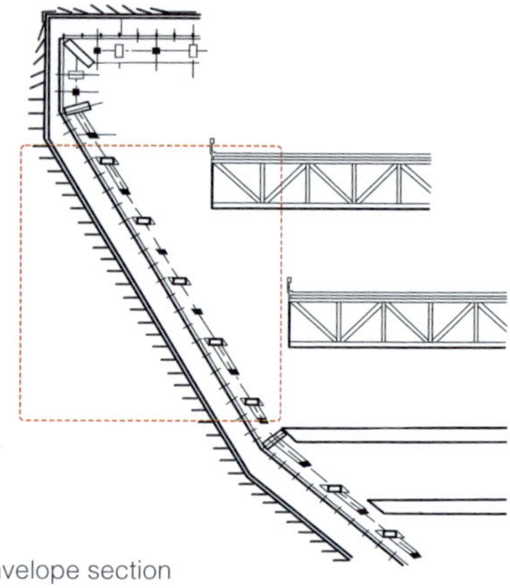

Envelope section

its relationship to the gridded orientation of the city grid of Shenzhen. Can you share with us the reasons for the distinctions in form between the twisted mass of the Planning Exhibition, and other freeform elements, and the relative neutral box of the MOCA mass, which affiliates closely to the urban grid?

WDP If you want more information about our method of designing, visit our web page. It is all public. To fully explain, I would need to give you a separate lecture which takes not only 20 minutes, but one hour. Then it would be clear that we work in a very special way of finding new ways for the development and evolution of architecture. How does a black spot appear on the red wing of a butterfly? It's not a geometrical issue, nor a matter of calculation. It is a coincidence which happens in evolution. If it's good, it stays. If not, it will vanish – this is in nature as well as in architecture. Of course, in architecture, there are other influences.

Trial and error is the main issue for an Open Society. Trial and error, and using coincidence, and even the subconscious of the designer as a driving force for creating new shapes and forms. This is our way. We don't believe there are geometrical truths in architecture. For us, this is just an excuse to have no ideas. Did I answer your question?

ME In 1969, you wrote, provocatively, "our architecture has no physical ground plan". The raising of the ground in the MOCAPE project can be understood as an action which undermines the authority of the ground. Can you elaborate on the effects of raising the ground from the surface of the city; and the attenuation, or stretching, of spatial sequences between the city and the interior urban plaza; and the diagonal movement to the MOCA, Museum of Contemporary Art spaces, and PE, Plan-

The invisible path to architecture is very strong. And the conventional way of thinking is that there is boundless possibility in this invisible thing. The aesthetic issue is discussed in the ivory tower of theory. These are things we have to break through in order to get the black spot on the red wing of ideas.

ning Exhibition spaces on long diagonal stairways and escalators?

WDP You are touching on the issues of the psychological ground plan and the physiological ground plan. You are touching on the topic of Deconstructivist methods of designing, which is a lecture that takes me one and a half hours to deliver. It is about using the subconscious as the driving force of coincidence and decision making. It will take too long to explain this deeply this late in the evening in Vienna.

DS Thank you. In your programmatic text written in 1995, *The Architecture of Clouds*, you expressed how the paradigm of the Cloud represents "an architecture of fantasy, as buoyant and variable as clouds", and you declared clouds as "symbols of rapidly changing states". You have in fact built a cloud as the central interior feature of this project. How do you imagine the individual experience of the cloud, as an object? And how did you convince your client to build a cloud?

WDP (Laughs) If you find out how I did this, please let me know! There is a programmatic idea that the story of the building must be as complex as the story of a dramatic theatre or an opera. Many, many stories coming together to change the room. Since we cannot fly, and no one wants to pay to design a flying building. Perhaps AI will help us and we will get there sooner.

If you walk around the MOCAPE, you see a lot of changing forms as you move. It is not a boring box. It is not a one trick pony. It is a serial drama. You can feel it. And for me, when a building is finished, I walk around it and if I can say "okay, I am proud of it, this is what I wanted to achieve. Never judge an unfinished building. In this case, when I entered this building when it was finished, I can say that so far, I think it is the best building I have done.

We're working on a better one right now. Maybe, we'll see.

ME We understand BIM (Building Information Modeling) was used in delivering the project from design stages to construction and fabrication documents. Can you share with us how and why BIM has been used by your office on the MOCAPE project and others in the office?
WDP The computer is a tool – a very necessary tool. Robots, computers, and AI liberate us from daily stupid work. So my dream is of AI – we're working on it and not finished yet – my dream is I am sitting on the beach under a palm, with a computer to control the AI

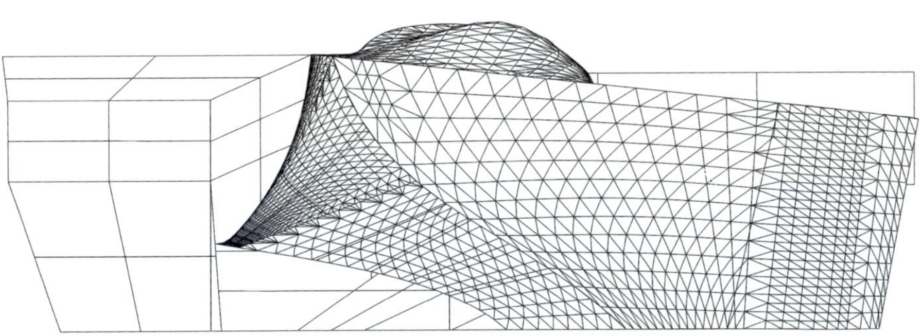

Elevation indicating multiple expressions of surface

computers in my office, which are doing the work for me. We have all the forms, shapes, all archived in a big library, where we have ground plans, and sections, and details, already uploaded. We have to train the stupid machine to use this data in a coincidental way like we are using our work.

ME Could this project be achieved without the use of BIM?

WDP No. This project could not be achieved without the use of BIM.

ME How might it have led to a different result without the use of BIM?

WDP Let me tell you. In 1987, it took our structural engineer one month to calculate the structure for a rooftop project we wanted to achieve (Falkestrasse). Now, that calculation could be done in one day. That is the advantage of this machinery.

DS In your work with Daniel Bolojan, Coop Himmelb(l)au has been interested in the development and advancement of artificial intelligence technologies, and their application in the conception, or more precisely in AI terminology, the hallucination of architecture. How has your experimentation with AI informed the more recent design methods of Coop Himmelb(l)au? And can you please share with us how you are exploring AI and Machine Learning?

WDP (Laughs) You should ask Daniel. With Daniel, we have been using all our experience to create organization, shapes, forms, and structural ideas in a library, and then we have been teaching the machine to use this information in a very special way. Namely, like we are working. Like story tellers. Until now, we have not made a project like MOCAPE, with its spaces with AI. I do not know a museum that looks like that – with its ramps and spaces. The Guggenheim is organized along a spiral ramp – it is a great museum. The idea of circulating in space without feeling the force of gravity too much. So, don't call it artificial intelligence, it is architectural intelligence.

ME Our next questions concern the relation of the MOCAPE project and your larger portfolio in Coop Himmelb(l)au. Which projects had led to the design of the MOCAPE project in Coop Himmelb(l)au's portfolio of work in the 1990s and early 2000s? And more recently, can you describe the influence and impact of the MOCAPE project on other projects in the office in the past since its design?

WDP I think it's one of the last finished buildings we have done. I am really bad about remembering the past – I am always looking forward. It came closer to the idea of how I see architecture. Nowadays it is very hard to discuss architecture, because in Europe

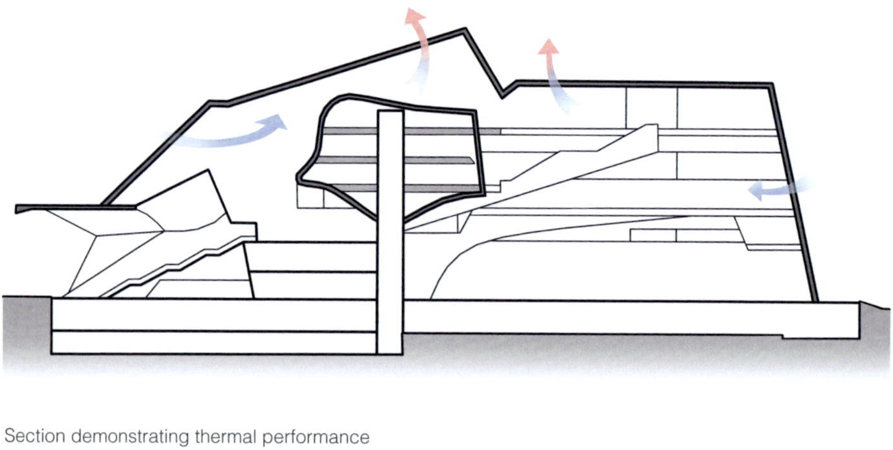

Section demonstrating thermal performance

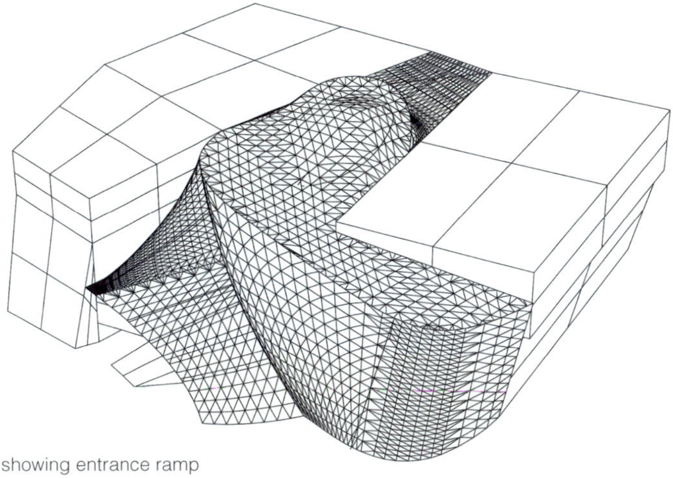

Axonometric showing entrance ramp

and I'm sure in the United States as well, they are talking about moral issues instead of architecture and they're focused on clay as building material instead of the future. We have always had an enormous amount of visitors to our public buildings.

We all have a city that we like the most. If you try to memorize what you like about that city and implement that in your project, then it could become a good solution. I don't like to give recipes, but this is my number one recipe.

DS What do you believe to be the future for architecture? What advice do you have to young architects at the early career stage?

WDP (Laughs) Don't worry, and carry on, is my advice. But don't carry on the recent discussion of architecture where a so-called "morality" is more important than a building. I had a meeting recently with young architects, who seemed not to care about buildings, but rather about the plants growing on the wall, or how the building is a sociological issue. I told them they are studying the wrong issue, because the central issue of architecture is creating space and nothing else. For all the other things you have better educated consultants. You only have to know what you want to do, and this is your main issue. Not planting vegetation on the façade, because there are a lot of companies which can do that much better. But you have to think about how the plants will affect the microclimate of the space in front of the façade, and how that space should react. So, this is your competence – creating space. Nothing else. If you go to the next step that we do not want to be responsible for the space we are creating, and because of the social impact, we can return to make clay huts. This is the wrong way to make our environments. So, the issue is not morality, it is architecture, meaning creating space, and creating the future.

DS Can you share with us your views on how the discipline and practice of architecture has changed since your early career in the 1960s to current times?

A museum is a trading spot of knowledge. When people go inside a museum, they acquire information about what is happening throughout other parts of the world. So, designing a museum, an apartment building or city plan is not really about shapes and forms, but it is always about creating spaces.

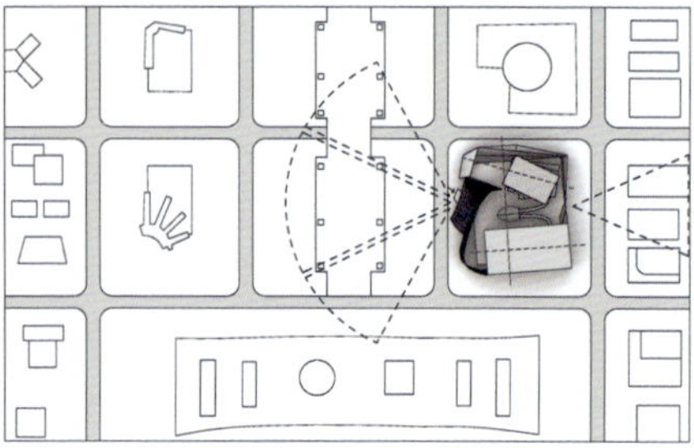

Plan describing contextual conditions

WDP I will tell you how architecture has changed. When my father was an architect the mayor came to him and said, "Mr. Architect! Please design me a landscape with swimming pools for the city, and the residents of Vienna!". Handshake, and he would start to work on it. Now we are sitting with our lawyer against six or seven other lawyers of the client in order to get the contract. This is the biggest difference. And the mediocrity of these people is that they have no respect for art and architecture. Once you embrace that, then you are prepared for the next step in your architectural career. Get ready to experience the people who are much younger than you are. I'm now 80 and 40-year-old lawyers tell me how to build. It's incredible. And this is the wrong way for architecture. We are talking too much in an ivory tower. We have to learn how to develop a concept through our ideas to improve our existing world. The politicians, as you can see, cannot do it. They have no vision economically, and in terms of society, and of the future. They only have financial interests. All our leaders worldwide are thinking to a large extent of their own interests. I have little kids, therefore I am still in this job. I have a lot of generations in my family. I am also still here working because I do not trust politics.

ME Thank you for your generosity to join us today. We are grateful for this opportunity to interview you.

TV Thank you, Wolf! This has been an exceptional experience for my students, our school, and myself. It was great to hear your insights on the MOCAPE project, as well as the state of architecture, technology and politics today.

WDP Tom, don't lose your optimism! Bye!

TV I never will! All the best!

ONE VANDERBILT

New York, 2020 | Kohn Pedersen Fox (KPF)

Program Offices, Outdoor Garden Terraces, Restaurants, Observatory, Pedestrian Plaza

Façade Materials Glass, Aluminum, Terra Cotta

FORM

162,600 M2	GFA
3,800 M2	Site Area
427 M	High
4	Floors Below Ground
73	Floors Above Ground
42,000	White Terra Cotta Spandrel Panels
2,500	Soffit Panels
8,743	Glazing Panels
1,060	Distinct Panel Shapes

INTERVIEW

Interviewee: James von Klemperer, President, Kohn Pedersen Fox (KPF)

Interviewers: Francis Kwok, Kaymar Thomas, M.Arch students, School of Architecture and Design, New York Institute of Technology

February 9, 2022

Tom Verebes I am grateful to welcome you, James von Klemperer, to New York Institute of Technology, for the first of six presentations and interviews in this series in Spring 2022. Today's project in focus is One Vanderbilt, by KPF. This project advances and innovates the transitory typology of the skyscraper, in the city in which it was born. It achieves the intellectual deepening of what is now called the Supertall. Sensitive to its historical context, and also in its relation to modernist history, this project reinvents the relationship of a tall building to the infrastructural flows on the ground and underground of the city. I would like to introduce our interviewers, Francis Kwok and Kaymar Thomas, M.Arch students here at New York Tech. Over to you, Francis.

Francis Kwok My name is Francis, and together with Kaymar, we would like to thank you for joining us today – it is an honor to interview you. One Vanderbilt is the second tallest office building in New York City, one of the more notorious, so-called, "Supertall" towers in Midtown East. One Vanderbilt has been designed through rigorous testing and evaluation methodologies which you have presented, and are by now, well published. Despite this project's many great merits, generally speaking, there have been concerns by the public and architectural community, over the phenomenon of the Supertall, of the possibility of it limiting daylighting, creating shadows, and affecting the environmental quality on the ground. Can you share with us your position on how Supertall towers can be ecologically responsible?

James Von Klemperer Thank you, and I am glad you are launching with a critical question because it is important that we are critical of our own work and we look at the road critically as architects. However, I think there is another serious note, which is that high-rises are very particular and very intrusive buildings. Where we place them, and where we decide they are appropriate and where city planners decide, is terribly important. They do not belong in many parts of many cities and so to draw contrast to make this building the hero, I can mention some of the buildings on Central Park south, the residential buildings of apartments, costing anywhere between 20 and 220 million dollars. Many of them are empty, because they are seen as investments as opposed to places to live. They cast shadows on the park. What is the public good? Here however, I make the argument that next to public transit is where you want higher density in the city. The graph of density wants to go up where most people can come in to cities without using cars, without using excess energy. So, whether in Hong Kong, or really in any city that tolerates tall buildings, and even in the city of London, it makes sense to build up where we have transit connections. Ultimately, the cities that make our economic centers need to have engines of exchange of ideas, of commerce, of education, and a high-rise building accentuates that density. Not everywhere, but this place, is a spot right at the crosshairs of the coming together

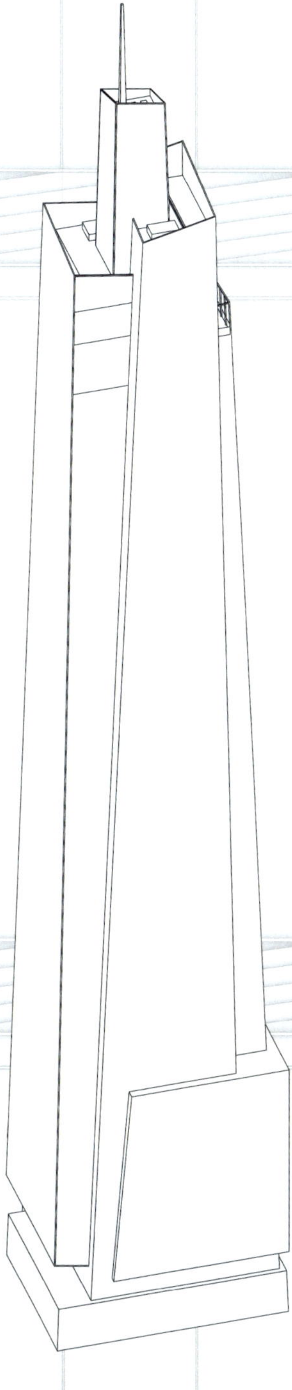

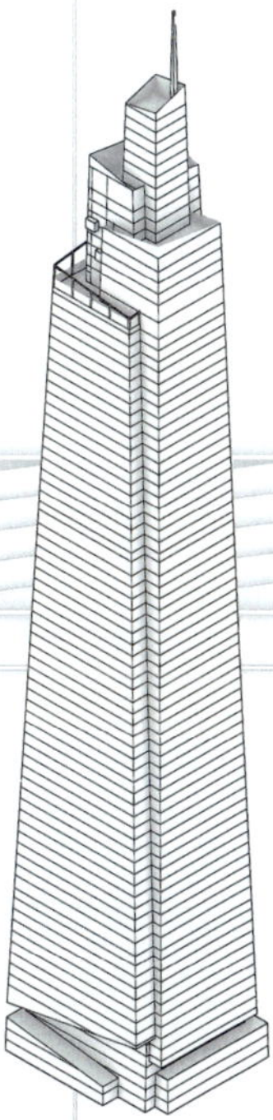

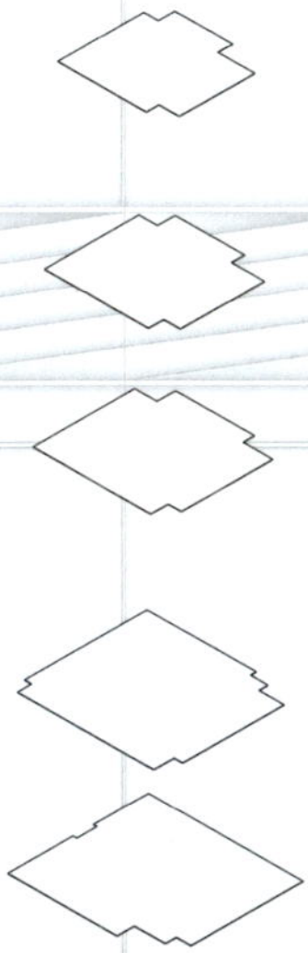

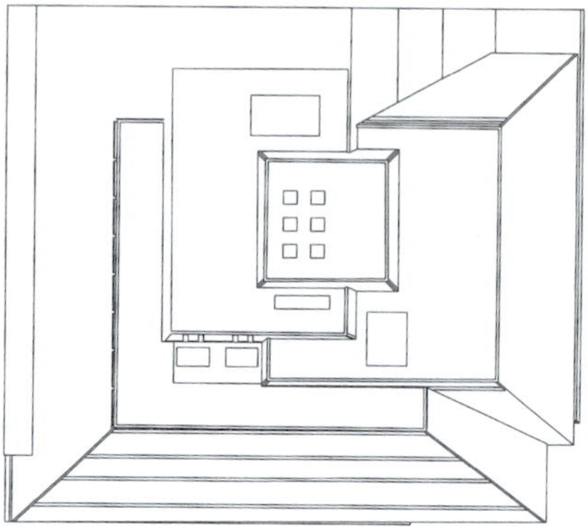

of the city's flows. If it were a body, it's the navel of New York. Environmentally, in terms of transport, energy use, etcetera, it makes good sense.

FK From another perspective, considering the impact of a tower means evaluating the relationship of a discrete tower to the immediate urban context. One Vanderbilt argues, quite successfully, for the regeneration of Midtown East. The complex section of the building is in fact an urban and infrastructural section, with its multiple network connections on ground and below ground, to the trains and subway system within and under Grand Central Station. Can you share with us how the relationship, manifested through the partnership with Grand Central, came about in which private investment into a discrete building was configured to connect with public spaces and the infrastructure of the city?

JVK I will share my observations. Many architects, planners and citizens are looking at Penn Station. Penn Station is a great example of a failure to protect our history and the ruining of the McKim Mead and White building in the 1963 demolition, but also the replacement with a very uninspired, if not soul crushing, building of the current train station from the 1960s. The reason I bring this up is to ask how are we going to improve one of the most important parts of our city? Penn Station, Manhattan's other transit hub, now has proposals from private developers, from Amtrak, from Empire State Development Corporation, and from others to increase density to be able to pay for the improvement of this area. Now whether the equation is fair or correct, I will not guess right now, as it is a complex issue. I think the density of proposals for Penn Station should be decreased and it actually was in the last stages, and may decrease again. It did take a step down in Governor Hochul's resumption of that plan, but what I am trying to get at, is to highlight our public-private collaborations in our country. Every country is different, every economy is different. In London, the British public and great architects can build High Speed 2, St. Pancras Station, and new King's Cross Station. These stations allow for direct high-speed rail connections all across Europe, which is fantastic! We need better public transit, which is good for our planet. London is the headquarters of everything; it's the capital of the country, it's one of the great centers of the world in market terms. New York is technically the capital of nothing, not even New York State, so legislatively and funding wise, we can't seem to advance the process of funding for what we should spend money on. In other parts of the world, such as Shanghai for example, there's a top high speed rail connection to all other major cities in China. Paris has a great airport connection to the city. In London you have the Paddington connection. In our culture and in our society, we don't do enough to reinforce our infrastructure, so architecture, which can help to pay for and sponsor infrastructure, is something that we should be serious about pursuing. For its small part, One Vanderbilt is a piece of that puzzle, and I hope we can learn positively from it and move ahead to Penn Station and do something extraordinary there, ultimately to make New York a better city.

FK Can you share with us the lineage of projects at KPF, in the portfolio of work before the One Vanderbilt project, which had led to its design?

JVK That is a great question. I came to New York as a student after years at Princeton

University. I went to work in Steven Holl's office, and then later, I opened my office. I never wanted to work at a large firm like KPF, but a friend of mine came to KPF and told me to come and join, and so I came to a firm that made the high-rise building its focus. Again, it was not my great interest in life, but I grew more interested. Bill Pedersen, who was one of our founding partners had the idea that you could take a very common building type, after all, putting aside the greatness of Seagram's and other buildings, many office buildings were just boxes, or just a commodity building, sliced like a loaf of white bread without anything much to offer in terms of public space or architecture. Bill took the office building type and worked on it in a way that brought it into a dialogue with its spatial context and its social context. And that became the way of working in many of our projects. Probably, about one-third of the work of our practice focuses on high rise. It's a very strong strain of studying and advancing the techniques of building while understanding design potential in broad terms as well.

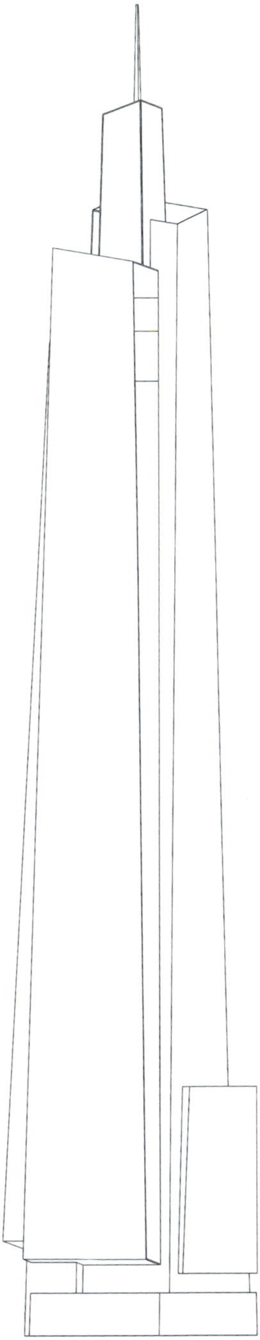

As it turns out, we have designed four of the ten tallest buildings in the world standing today which is really more than we should have as a share, but it's because we're excited by the topic. Every high-rise building is so particular and needs to almost start over again with a new set of parameters, and yet we all stand on the shoulders of those who came before.

So, understanding the steel frame, and learning from great engineers such as Les Robertson who sadly died a year ago. At the age of 32, he designed the World Trade Center as a young whippersnapper from the northwest – a brilliant thinker about forces and dynamics of high-rise buildings. We learn from this, and so in our practice there is a real integration of engineering, of

spatial design, of construction processes, of the finesse of materials, all brought together in a holistic way. We're able to move ahead in this lineage of one tall building after another, while always thinking that the tall building has a frontier ahead of it, to define new tasks. One of the issues I think now being most interestingly explored in the tall building is vertical green – of bringing public space and green space up into not just the lower parts of the building, but higher up in buildings. One Vanderbilt has a nice terrace, and 18 Robinson in Singapore, which we designed, brings up green space and park space to the midsection and top of the building. Greening the city and allowing the enjoyment of public

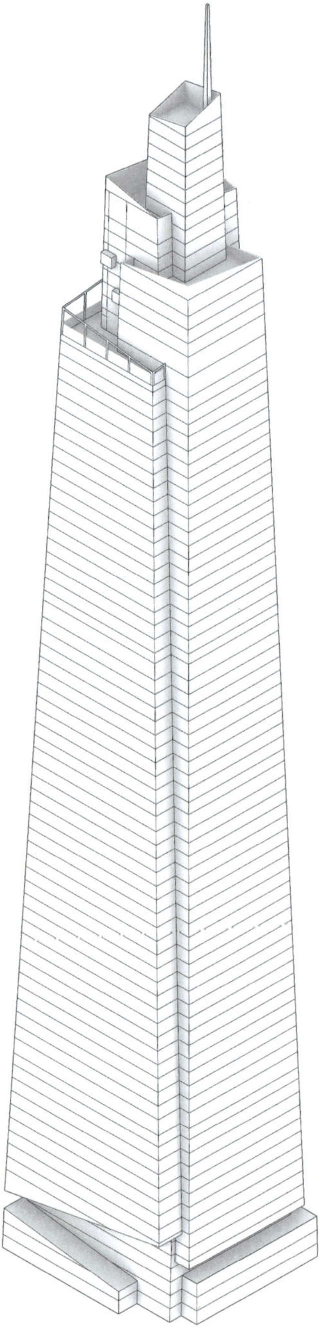

space to be had with plants in high-rises is being advanced now in many practices I see around the world.

Kaymar Thomas Our next questions concern the relation of the One Vanderbilt project to your larger portfolio at KPF. Can you please share with us any projects which had led to the design of One Vanderbilt? And more recently, can you describe the impact of the One Vanderbilt on the design of other projects at KPF since the design and completion of One Vanderbilt?

JVK The design of One Vanderbilt emerged during a competition that took place in the summer of 2012, during which we explored a variety of options. A solution similar to the winning scheme of diagonally nested volumes had been successfully realized in our Dongbu Financial tower in Seoul some 10 years prior. In each case, the reentrant carving of the building's corners helped to create a dynamic spatial effect at the base of the tower.

More recently, the One Vanderbilt project has had an effect on other projects that have since emerged from our studio. Notably, our commitment to crafting materials in meaningful ways. Our project at 520 Fifth Avenue, just around the corner, uses terra cotta glazes similar to those used in the spandrels of One Vanderbilt.

FK What advice do you have for young architects at the early launching stage of their careers?

JVK I would say, seek to make frequent connections between what you draw and what gets built. Visit construction sites, and take your sketch pad. Talk to builders, tradespeople, and factory workers, and learn about how materials come together to make buildings.

KT Thank you for your generosity to join us today, to share your presentation on One Vanderbilt, and join us for this brief interview.

JVK Thank you for this opportunity. I would

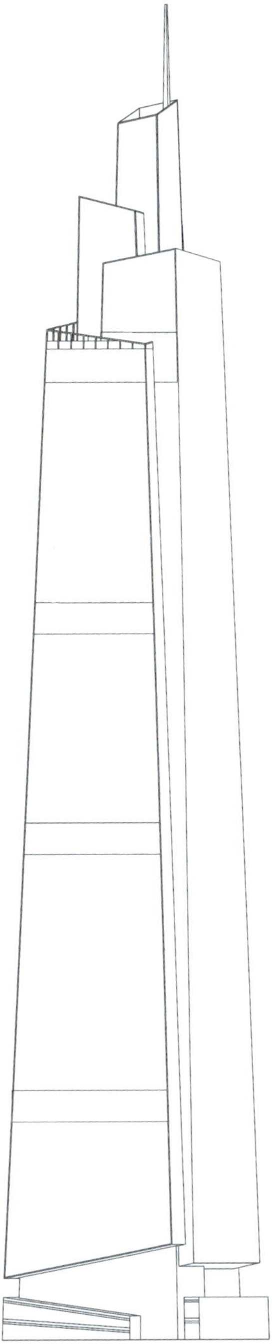

love to come back to continue to talk more with you and your students, Tom.

TV Thank you for your sharing your presentation, your insights, and your time for this brief interview. We wish you well and we look forward to seeing the further impact of KPF on the skyline of New York City, as well as many other cities worldwide. Thanks so much!

JVK Hope to see you guys on a review, or that you come to see us in the office sometime! Thank you for integrating me into your program.

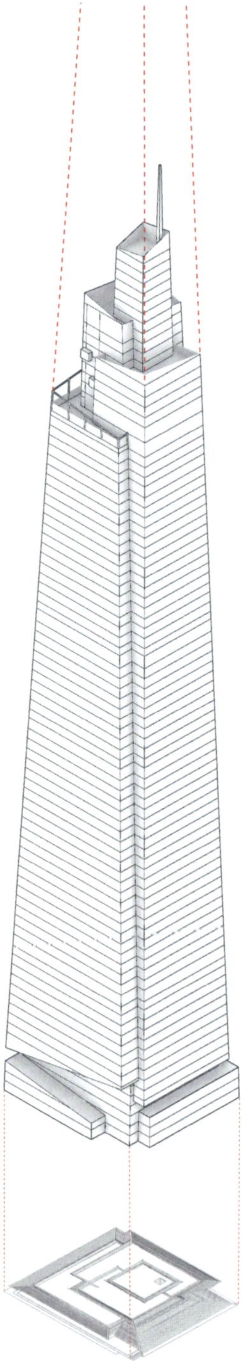

MetLife

NINGBO HISTORIC MUSEUM

Ningbo, China, 2008 | Amateur Architecture Studio

Program Exhibition Halls and Galleries, Offices, Restaurant, Café, Courtyard

Materials Cast concrete in bamboo formwork, recycled red brick, recycled blackened bricks, recycled roof tiles

MATTER

Solid	Glazing	Facade Openings in Concrete	Height	Floors Above Ground	Floors Below Ground	Volume	GFA
93%	7%	145	23.95 M2	3	0	224,640M2	30,000 M2

INTERVIEW

Interviewee: Wang Shu, Lu Wenyu, Directors, Amateur Architecture Studio

Interviewers: Anthony Acevedo, Steven Jean-Baptiste, M.Arch students, School of Architecture and Design, New York Institute of Technology

April 19, 2023

This interview with Wang Shu and Lu Wenyu was done by exchange of writte questions, translated to Chinese, and the return of written responses in Chinese and then translated to English. Many thanks to Professor Richard Hsu for facilitating contact, and to Professor Zhang Mengni for facilitating communication and translations of the interview questions and responses.

This interview with Wang Shu and Lu Wenyu is the only interview of all twenty-one included in this book which was not undertaken as a live interview. The interviewees responded in writing to our written questions, in the mother tongue of Wang Shu and Lu Wenyu, Mandarin Chinese. We would like to thank Richard Hsu for facilitating an introduction to Amateur Architecture Studio. Along with communicating with Amateur Architecture Studio, the translation for both English-Chinese and Chinese-English was generously done by Zhang Mengni, Visiting Assistant Professor in the School of Architecture and Design at New York Tech.

Anthony Acevedo, Steven Jean-Baptiste Our first question addresses the urban, political, and economic context in China, and the model of production in architecture which has driven the greatest era of urbanization ever to occur over the past four decades. Can you please share your views of the roles and responsibilities of both government and statutory authorities, of private investors, and of architects, to the public realm in China?

Wang Shu, Lu Wenyu This is a vast problem, because it involves changes in history spanning almost 70 years. However, putting aside many superficial factors, I think there are two clues. One is the change from so-called tradition to modernity. China's own culture and lifestyle, which developed gradually for thousands of years, have undergone completely disruptive changes in modern times.

The second point is that in the past 30 years or so, people have been reformatted by the construction of commercial housing, that is, from an original lifestyle based on relationships between community neighbors, formatted into a living model that is based on a fixed template for small families. During this process, I feel that there was a general lack of thinking or even no thinking among Chinese architects, where they basically just followed the popularity and changes of the commodity market, and seldom reflected or criticized the changes themselves.

In addition, if one more clue is to be added,

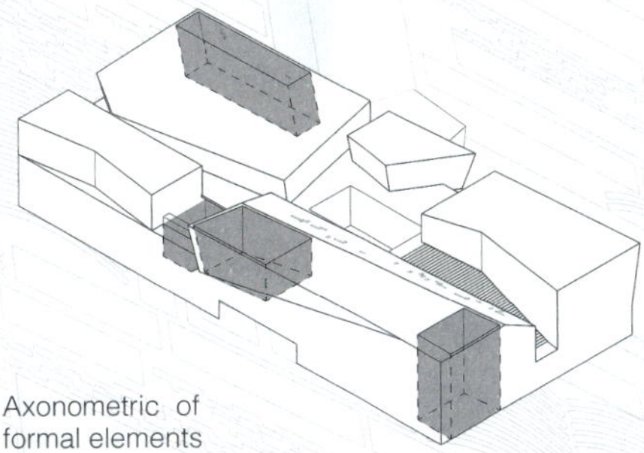

Axonometric of formal elements

it is that the entire construction and material system have changed. The traditional Chinese construction system is one based on natural materials. However, the current housing construction system has become industrialized, artificial, with synthetic materials.

Architects face such huge changes – not only changes in the housing system, but also changes in construction technology – in fact, also big cultural changes. In this kind of change, Chinese architects are basically in a state of silence and speechlessness, with little thinking and criticism. In China, it can be said that local governments and commercial organizations are in a cooperative relationship, jointly promoting the urban development of real estate focused on residential buildings. The scale and speed at which developments are happening may be rare in Chinese history, and possibly also true in world history.

AA, SJB Amateur Architecture Studio is a leading force in the search for an architecture of authenticity which embeds architectural culture, local history and customs in China. Can you share your views on the current status of the rural context, and the village as a social and architectural model in China, and in which ways has the renewed interest in the countryside impacted your worldview and your design approach in practice?

WS, LW China's villages and cities are in a relationship of pairs. The reason why our studio is so interested in the countryside and does so much work in the countryside is because we hope to maintain or seek to revive China's own architectural language and craftsman system based on natural materials, and to retain the system's place in the architecture of today. In China's cities, this system has been destroyed, and the systems that are still alive are basically in the countryside. Therefore, we take the countryside as our research focus.

AA, SJB Continuing this discussion of the recuperation of collective memory and a revival of local, rural traditions, and the establishment of an architectural culture with Chinese characteristics, we are interested in how traditional crafts are taught and learnt in China. As an architecture student some decades ago, what were you taught about your country's architectural, social and political history?

WS, LW The changes in China's cities and villages are in fact directly related to architectural education at Chinese institutions. Because Chinese architecture schools' teachings have been based on eclecticism of the Parisian school of fine arts [École des Beaux-Arts], including the so-called modern part. Also given this background, there is basically no systematic education about China's own architectural language and architectural culture, or materials and construction systems. If there are still some left [Chinese characteristics], they may only be kept in the education of architectural history, and it is completely missing in the field of architectural design education.

AA, SJB Also, as an academic leader and educator, how has the pedagogy and curricula of architecture schools in China evolved in recent decades?

WS, LW There are many changes, because each school hopes to be more creative, with more thinking. But the wave of globalization and commercialization is too powerful. Judging from the current pedagogy in China, it is still more about chasing what is popular in the world, which is essentially a form of imitation.

AA, SJB China is a vast country with many different climatic and geographic conditions.

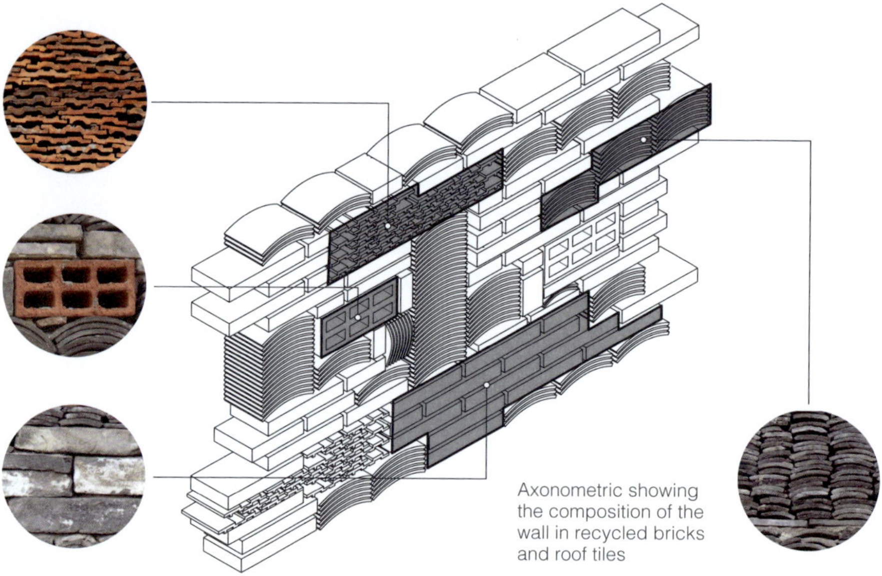

Axonometric showing the composition of the wall in recycled bricks and roof tiles

Since the 1980s, Kenneth Frampton, among others, has argued for "Critical Regionalism", critiquing the notion of a single, monolithic, and universal architecture. How has the concept of architectural regionalism in China changed during the time of the People's Republic of China?

WS, LW We are still undergoing an ongoing process of modernization. A core feature of modernization is to use a set of simplified modern language to unify the process of marketization. Such a process seriously damages the locality of various places. It is reflected in, for example, nationally unified design specifications, nationally unified construction specifications and construction regulations. All these laws and regulations represent a simplified unification, which is very damaging to tradition and regionalism. So, I have always maintained that tradition is not an abstract concept. China is a very diverse country, and each region has very strong traditions.

AA, SJB At this juncture, we would like to shift our discussion more directly towards the Ningbo Historic Museum, and the ways in which you have created an excavated mass of immense solidity and introversion. We are interested in the ways the museum creates natural and environmental connections and profound cultural narratives. How does the complex mass of the museum communicate relationships with natural or environmental paradigms, as related to the concept of the mountain, valleys, caves and other landscape or geographic features? Also, can you share how the design of this project was influenced by traditional Chinese Garden design, landscape painting, and Chinese philosophy?

WS, LW The site of the Ningbo Museum was a site that had been dismantled into flat ground. That is to say, all its historical accumulation had been demolished. But at the same time, the Ningbo Historic Museum is in itself a very large modern public building. On this basis, the thinking is to evoke the memories of the original culture, the villages that existed here, and cultural reminiscence of the original Chinese architecture to the surrounding natural environment such as mountains and rivers. It was based on this intersection that we created the design scheme. It can be seen that the plan of this building is a very simple rectangle.

Another very important distinction of the museum is related to the human experience.

From a modern point of view, a rectangular plan is the most concise form to meet program needs, and it is also the most efficient form. However, when the building develops vertically towards the sky, it gradually begins to split and change, showing some shapes similar to mountains, or small-scale forms that are similar to villages in volumes. Although it is a very abstract transition, it is a discussion between modernity and tradition.

From the way of entering this building, you will find that it is like entering a cave in a mountain range. It is different from the architectural language we are generally familiar with. From one cave to another, from the inside of the cave to the outside of the cave, from downhill to uphill, through a series of spatial shaping, people can have a more explicit, direct experience. Such spatial identities and transitions are more like the dialogue method of traditional Chinese landscape painting. It is like a memory reconstruction of a trip to natural mountains.

Any Chinese landscape painting utilizes this painting method or as a way of recording. But what is important is what people can feel directly, such as the discussion of material texture. We used a very special local technique here, which has never been used on such a large modern building before. A very important issue here is to discuss how to mix traditional and natural materials with modern reinforced concrete systems using specialized crafting techniques. The discussion on this issue should be a breakthrough.

AA, SJB The Ningbo Historic Museum used recycled bricks and tiles reclaimed from the ruins of villages demolished to make way for the new civic and cultural core of the Ningbo, in which the museum is located. Can you comment on your position regarding the connections between material, cultural and environmental sustainability? More specifically, how does the reuse of traditional materials enable the preservation of the identity of place, and the continuity of collective memory? Can you characterize this approach as a new architectural movement in China?

WS, LW The design and construction of the Ningbo Museum contains very specific practices, but also has a strong symbolic meaning. The form of practice we focused on in Ningbo solved a problem that had bothered us, that is, under the large-scale demolitions of traditional buildings in China, how can the many different kinds of rich materials be used again in modern buildings? Previously, people in Ningbo used a mixed technique for post-typhoon reconstruction, which was when people did not have time to classify and categorize materials, and within a limited scope, they used dozens of materials of different sizes for a very high level of mixed masonry construction. In addition, I think it also has a special meaning, which is about the reconstruction of diversity. Because I think one of the outstanding signs of the close connections between Chinese traditional culture and nature is its rich diversity. Reusing such a rich and diverse process in a modern and efficient construction requires wisdom. In addition, I think it is very important to consider time, including memories and so on. When all the traces of life are destroyed by the modern process and all the memories have lost their roots, such reuse is not only about the saving of materials or resources, but also has a significant cultural meaning, that is, the restoration of memories, the preservation of time, and the preservation of the experience of time. This combination is very symbolic and represents the core content of China's new architectural movement.

AA, SJB Your mode of practice requires the involvement of craftspeople to gain an understanding of your goals and to collapse the distance between the architect and builder. Can you describe the kinds of working drawings your office produced to communicate the intended textures of brick and tile?

WS, LW This question includes several

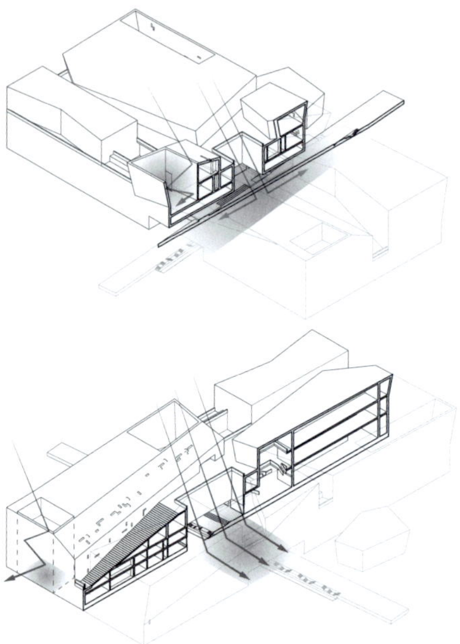

Sectional axonometrics indicating interior-exterior associations and thresholds

aspects of our working methods and interests. Firstly, we often do a lot of research, and we must become very familiar with the possible outcomes of craftsmen's techniques. On the basis of familiarity with on-site craft, we conducted small-scale experiments in the laboratory, simulating some masonry methods of craftsmen for construction. In addition, current computer technology and photographic technology are also very helpful. We can use this method to re-check the work on the computer based on our understanding of local masonry. We do not want to simply repeat tradition, but even so, there is still a very important aspect, which is our communication with craftsmen. Because during the masonry construction process, especially in modern large-scale projects, craftsmen's workload is much greater than that of traditional small buildings. Therefore, on site, for example, according to the current safety regulations, the erection of protective nets will cause the craftsmen to encounter a work environment that they have never encountered before. Their work, including the selection and delivery of materials, also happens on a larger scale, affecting the work processes.

Also, as architects, our views were blocked by the cover of protective nets, we cannot see the overall state of the masonry construction status on site. We can only see the part and judge the whole through imagination. This requires repeated exchanges with craftsmen on site. So our drawings were actually informed by these types of on-site work experiences. The drawings that the craftsmen received at the site only serve as a guidance.

The results of these experiments depend on our repeated on-site communication with craftsmen. Construction cannot simply be done with drawings, nor by the craftsmen according to traditional habits. In fact, a whole new space has emerged between the two, a process that is both controllable and not entirely controllable. Therefore, under this in-between condition of semi-control, there will often be many unexpected events and incidents happening.

So, I believe it's not quite entirely an architect's creation, nor a craftsman's creation. It transcends the individual, it is more like the accumulation of time, I even call it a

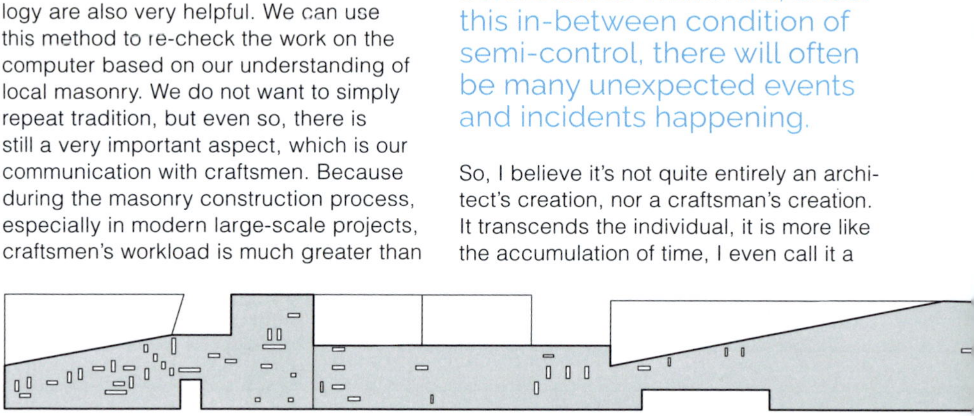

Unfolded elevation

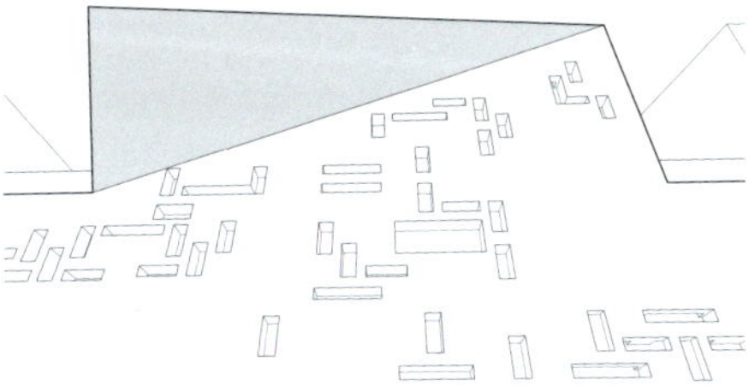

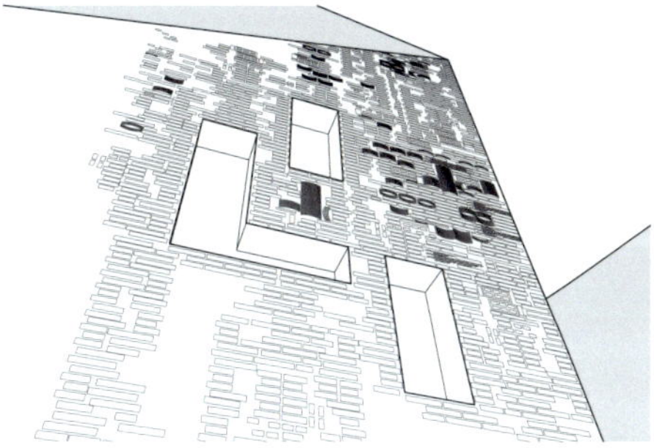

Detail views looking up.

design or craft that has gone beyond our general sense, it has become an anthropological phenomenon.

AA, SJB Please can you tell us how you use full scale 1:1 prototypes to test, evaluate and communicate your design ideas and construction processes?

WS, LW In fact, our works have never relied too much on models. Our models are basically formed in our head. Of course, now that there are computers, it can be formed through computers. But what is very important in our work is that the model formed in the computer is generated according to very clear construction steps. It is not just a concept of space, inside it has a very clear structure, with transfer and definition of materials.

AA, SJB Also, can you describe the relationship which is formed with craftsmen through the method of building 1:1 prototypes?

WS, LW This is our way of working, that is, to create a large material deposit yard at each construction site, so the materials that we want are directly visible. There must be 1:1 experiments of some of the most core mock-ups next to the site. All core techniques used in the building must be tested 1:1. In this process, architects and craftsmen will have in-depth exchanges, and based on this, masonry drawings can be done on the computer.

With the help of photography and computer technology, high-resolution material elevation drawings can be created. But even with high-resolution, it still does not convey the construction of every brick or tile. There is a space in the middle for discussion and exchange among architects, craftsmen and structural engineers.

AA, SJB There was a boom in building museums in China in the 2000's and 2010's. Literally thousands of public and private museums were built all across China. In the competition brief for the Ningbo Historic Museum, can you describe the nature of the direction, guidance, and criteria stated in the competition brief, of the relation of the museum's curation and its collection to the architecture? In simpler terms, how did the curation and collection of the museum inform the design of your architectural proposal?

WS, LW Most of the museums in China face a problem, that is, they are all brand new museums without established collections and systems of curation. Under such

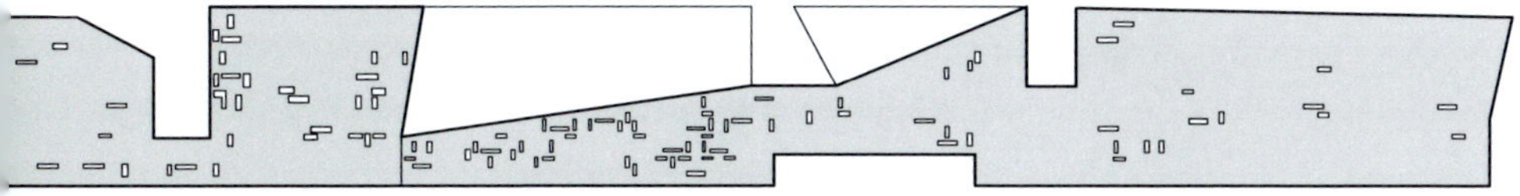

circumstances, the design of the museum is very difficult on the one hand, and on the other hand, it leaves a lot of room for architects to work. A core agenda is that you have to imagine what might happen in the future, and not be limited by people's perceptions of museums based on prior knowledge. It needs to give the building more flexibility.

AA, SJB Given the fast pace of change in China over the past decades, can we ask you about the status of history in modern China? Also, more specifically, how can you characterize the relationship of a museum of history to highlighting historical traces and forging a cultural identity for architecture?

WS, LW In fact, there has not been much museum construction for a long time. Museum building probably only became a focused topic that people cared about

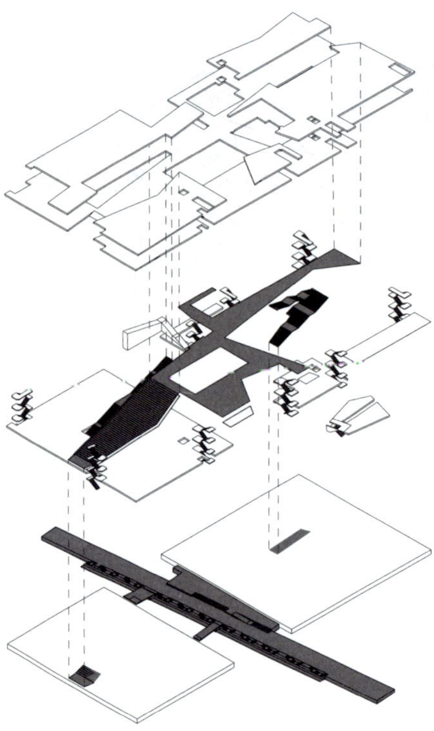

Exploded axonometric of circulation systems and surface organization

in the past 20 years. On the one hand, traditional culture is being destroyed rapidly, and society begins to realize that culture needs to be protected. On the other hand, a large number of new cities have been built, but these new cities actually have no spiritual core. At this time, museums play the role of cultural core of these new cities, confirming and recognizing cultural identities.

AA, SJB Our next question concerns the relationships of the Ningbo Historic Museum to the larger body of work of Amateur Architecture Studio's portfolio of past projects. Further to your presentation, can you share with us the genealogy of the design of the Ningbo Historic Museum within your office portfolio of preceding projects. Are there projects which led to Ningbo Historic Museum, as earlier prototypes which you developed further in the Ningbo project?

WS, LW The Ningbo Museum is actually related to two projects. One is located in the park next to the Ningbo Museum. We designed five small buildings in this city park. This project is called Wusanfang, meaning "Five Scattered Houses", which is about the basic prototypes of five kinds of buildings with traditional Chinese cultural and architectural characters. We designed five basic prototypes, and from these five prototypes two parallel large projects were derived. For example, one of the five prototypes was a small art gallery building. For the first time, we used the masonry experiment of tile walls. Another large parallel project is the Xiangshan Campus of the China Academy of Art in Hangzhou.

AA, SJB Please share with us how the Ningbo Historic Museum has influenced your practice's recent and current work?

WS, LW There has always been one very important theme in our works, both during the problem solving process of Ningbo Museum and extending to our later works, which is how to form a dialogue or co-existence system between materials and construction techniques in the modern

industrial age and traditional Chinese natural materials, such as bricks, tiles, and soil. This has become a core theme of Amateur Architecture Studio in the past two decades.

AA, SJB Can you summarize the impact upon your office of the momentous awarding of the Pritzker Prize in Architecture in 2012?

WS, LW There are two major effects of being awarded the Pritzker Prize. The first is that in our previous designs, including our exploration especially in combining modern technology with traditional craftsmanship, each time we need to overcome many difficulties to convince the client. After we won the award, this kind of persuasion seems to have become easier. Another impact is that the public has higher expectations for our works, and so the pressure we feel on ourselves is also greater.

AA, SJB From your perspective, Professor Wang Shu, as Dean of Faculty of Architecture at the China Academy of Art, and a Pritzker Prize laureate, please can you share with us any advice you may have for the next generation of architects?

WS, LW My strongest suggestion is that architects should have the ability to truly think for themselves, because what we are facing is a social reality in which traditions are broken and collapsed, and modernity itself is full of doubts. In such a reality, architects must have the ability to think independently and respond to reality, instead of turning a blind eye to what is happening and just passively drifting with the flow.

O-14 TOWER

Dubai, UAE, 2010 | Reiser + Umemoto Architecture RUR

Program Offices

Materials Cast concrete, glass and aluminum curtain wall

MATTER | 37,036 M2 GFA | 102 M High | 23 Floors Below Ground | 4 Floors Above Ground | 40 CM Thivck Concrete Exoskeleton | 1326 Openings Cast in the Exoskeleton | 5 Different Exoskeleton Openings | 100% Glazing in Curtain Wall

INTERVIEW

Interviewees: Jesse Reiser and Nanako Umemoto, Directors, RUR

Interviewers: Japheth Aleyakpo, Aditi Pancholi, Aleksandra Zatorska, M.Arch students, School of Architecture and Design, New York Institute of Technology

February 4, 2021

Tom Verebes It is such an honor to welcome you both to New York Tech, Jesse Reiser and Nanako Umemoto. As principals of your practice, we are grateful for the generosity of your time. This the very first of six public recorded sessions of presentations and interviews in this graduate research seminar in Spring 2021. What we are doing in the seminar is researching pioneering technology and its impact on contemporary architectural practice. The course explores six contemporary modes of practice through six seminal recently built projects at the frontiers of design, production and construction technologies. We are focusing on the architectural envelope and its performance as the focus of analysis in terms of their cultural, technical, experiential, thermal and other achievements, through six thematic classifications. The first theme, in which we classify the 0-12 Tower, is MATTER, focusing on issues of materiality and massing. I would like to introduce our interviewers, Japheth Aleyakpo, Aditi Pancholi, and Aleksandra Zatorska, M.Arch students in the School of Architecture and Design at New York Institute of Technology.

Japheth Aleyakpo Thank you for your inspiring presentation of the 0-14 Tower. My name is Japeth Aelyakpo. Several years after the 0-14 project was completed, and a monograph and other publications have been published, in retrospect, can you share your thoughts on the ways in which the 0-14 project addresses various architectural canons and how it speaks to this genealogy or non-genealogy, through inversion or other intellectual and strategic approaches in your work, towards cannons and disciplinary tropes?

Jesse Reiser That's a heavy first question! I see the 0-14 Tower as a project that in a way adheres to certain canonical models, such as Frank Lloyd Wright's St. Mark's Tower. Which we took as a precedent to literally invert from Wright's central trunk and tray model to our hollow exo-trunk within the slabs. Certainly, a more immediate conceptual precedent came out of a lecture that Sasaki made about his collaborations with Toyo Ito on new models for structural envelopes. In a very general way, I think our project fits into that interesting lineage between engineering concerns and factoring those into the form and aesthetics of a tower project.

We have just finished an article in *Log Magazine* which describes how blown away we were in the early nineties by Toyo Ito's Mediatheque in Sendai (Japan). While this project doesn't look like the Mediatheque, the architectural and engineering discussion between Sasaki and Ito became central to our thinking about O-14. The thing that really blew us away at the Mediatheque was the competition maquette and that we were somewhat let down by the finished building. My analysis was that this was because Ito and Sasaki were looking at the Shukhov's Russian Constructivist radio towers which had a very slender diagrid steel construction. However, because of the weight of the slabs of the Mediatheque structure and because they assumed that the structure should act in compression suddenly the diagrid shifted from being these gossamer structures in their competition model to a really massive, welded pipe diagrid. It is interesting how one thinks through precedents. Our solution to the problem of the Mediatheque would have been to keep it closer to the competition maquette by hanging the slabs from a trussed roof structure supported by bearing walls on three sides assisted by structural cores for stairs and mechanical services. Then you would get a more delicate gossamer, a mysterious structure that was as beautiful as their competition model.

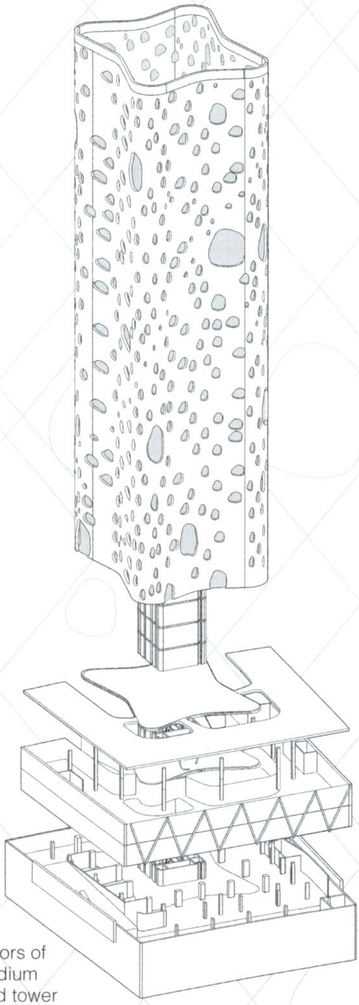

Floors of podium and tower

We see lineages as living things with logics that change and evolve with circumstance. Young architects can jump into these conversations early and not have the obligation to start from nothing, but to take up the problem where it is at present.

This approach does not strive to be entirely original but to see where the disciplinary conversation is, and where you could open something up of your own within it. That's a secret that many successful architects know very well, that their architecture comes in large part from many other designers.

JA To what extent do you believe architecture to be an autonomous discipline with its own internal discourse, and does the 0-14 tower argue for this position?

JR I think this is a tricky question because I actually believe architecture to be both internalized and linked to other disciplines. There is a certain autonomy to our discipline. Certainly, there would be a way of understanding the discipline similar to being a composer who has written symphonies or music that will never be performed. And that happens in the schools too. At certain moments, the symphony can be independently developed. There are many architectural issues that most people could care less about, the public or anyone else, which in a certain way is autonomous. Most people would be moved by the delicacy of the Mediatheque structure but would be utterly uninterested in its formal and structural genesis. At the same time, the designer is deeply enmeshed in the social, political, and material limits when you are doing buildings. So, I would say architecture partakes in both, and it has historically created its own defense-mechanisms to allow that autonomy to exist. The public, unless they are interested, would be indifferent and rightfully so to specific issues. The same could be said about a work by Mozart: not everyone would need to have special knowledge of musical composition and theory to still be able to fully enjoy it. So, the two things coexist I think, and they always have. Plus, money and power are so close to architecture that the discipline is elastic enough to deal with their inherent contradictions. Even more so I would say than the art world, architecture has always been in a fraught dance with money and power and all things bad.

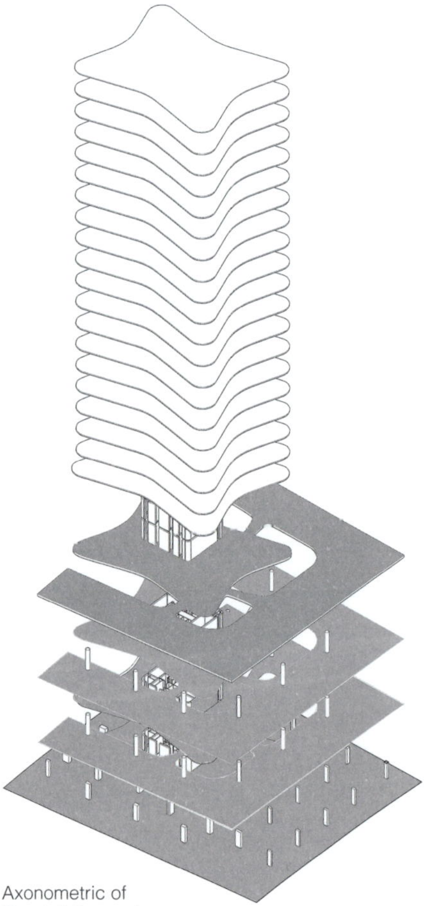

Axonometric of Exoskeleton and podium systems.

NU Really, are they all bad things?

JR Yeah, I don't know.

AZ I am Aleksandra Zatorska, and I would like to thank you for the honor to ask you some interview questions. In which ways you believe the 0-14 Tower positions itself in relation to context – its climatic context, accelerated urban development context of Dubai, and particularly its location and brief as an office tower in a Central Business District?

JR I have not been back to the building for about four years. But I guess I should back off for a second. There was a part of our pre-

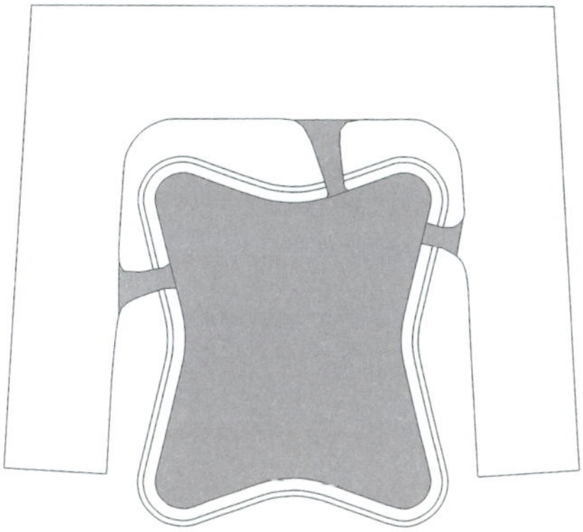

Plan of Tower connecting to podium

sentation that I did not show which was more related to the urban context and this relates to architects and what they do. The master plan was done by a big British AEC conglomerate called Halcrow who had for some time had their long fingers in the warp and weft of the urban fabric of Dubai. But for a very short time OMA assumed control of the master plan and we actually followed some of the really smart suggestions that OMA and Rem (Koolhaas) had made. As part of Halcrow's initial masterplan all new developments were to have podiums as a means of cheaply enclosing aboveground parking structures which were then decorated to provide the oversized illusion of a historical Arabic streetscape. OMA suggested that all the podiums be connected to form a new continuous public datum and so you could now have a continuous elevated garden space at the top of the podiums, keeping the ground relatively unobstructed. OMA's masterplan offered two distinct levels of programmable public space; one on the ground which, at our site, would correspond with a new waterfront esplanade, with an elevated linear park above. Ultimately this ambitious vision was only partially achieved, with our project being perhaps the true example of the diagram. This happens all the time, especially with Rem (Koolhaas). Because you know, you do what you can do. We could affect everything within the building site, but the larger utopian vision is beyond the architect's control, at best the building becomes an ideological object that points to an urbanism which may never come to pass. Of course, it never happened, but these conditions are imminent in the building. It happened to us in a similar way at Kaohsiong Port Terminal, although in that case, we created an elevated deck, that at this moment is singular, but hopefully will continue along the waterfront in successive projects.

AZ This concept of interconnected urban buildings is really fascinating prospect, and I am very curious whether this can be realized one day. Were your design decisions conscious and explicitly stated at the outset, or, alternatively subconscious and based on intuition and experience?

JR Regarding interconnected buildings, O-14 environmental performance was essentially a by-product of other decisions that we had made at the scale of building systems.

The way in which O-14 keeps its occupants and passersby cool via the stack effect, which for us emerged organically as an exaptive feature of what was initially a functional change to allow for a liminal space between window and exoskeleton for a window cleaning rig.

Then of course, once we were aware of how this arrangement could work with the gap and the stack effect, then we began to work with it deliberately. But it was not something that was there at the outset of the project.

NU The O-14 Tower is quite a short, small tower, but generally in Dubai, all new buildings are very tall. They are usually made out of curtain wall structures, so the building has to have interior columns and then the façade has a separate structural system. In the case of O-14 if we had designed a curtain wall structure, then we would have needed columns inside on the floor plates, reducing the amount, and specific quality, of the interior spaces.

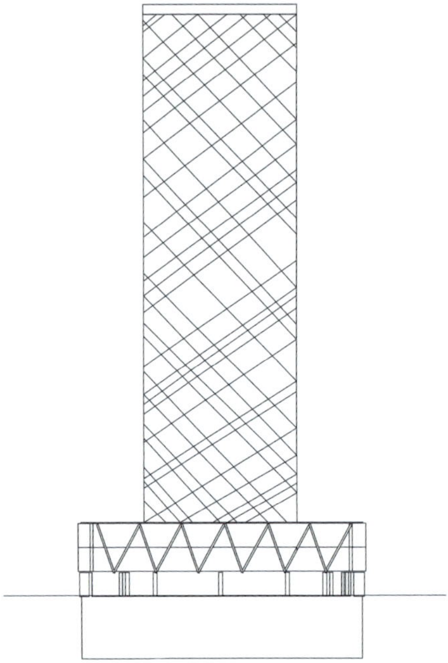

Elevation with underlying diagrid for openings

JR We were also really questioning the plethora of imported technologies and buildings in Dubai like that. Reflexively the mostly foreign architects were designing curtain wall buildings in an environment of intense heat and light. I guess indirectly through influences like Corbusier, the whole idea of a brise solei, which came before the idea of the stack effect, was something that was, we thought, more appropriate and culturally resonant with ancient building traditions in the region.

NU I don't agree with Jesse, my point is that in Dubai every building is so different. I don't know if you can argue that the 0-14 Tower had to make an urban context. Rather than following the idea of uniformity, Dubai is the other way around – every building is different.

JR We were, in a sense, working against a very conservative postmodern set of master plan guidelines. So that's why I mentioned the mandatory arcades, and the bases, and all of these sorts of rules but fortunately people who administrated the master plan were flexible enough to accept a completely different kind of building. It was a kind of battle I would say. Also, O-14 in a weird way is affiliated with the natural context of the desert more so than with the built context around it.

AZ So, can I ask you a version of the question you have just asked: what is the context of a building?

JR Right. It is not automatic at all. It is something that you should, as an architect, be questioning and inventing. It is about rhetoric too. How you argue for the many contexts necessary for your architecture.

AZ Would you agree that the process was more about form finding than form giving?

JR I would say it was both. We had formal inclinations, but were also receptive to see how it would change. How it would it modify itself.

AP In our M.Arch seminar at NYIT, we are structuring our analysis on a set of six themes. Your O-14 tower make a bold aesthetic statement about mass, heaviness, though solid materiality. This week's them, Matter, is investigated through O-14's interest in occlusion, opacity and the inversion of lightness. In terms of the methodology and procedure as the project was designed and developed, with respect to form, materiality and constructional logic of the perforated exoskeleton envelope, can you share with us how you generated, designed and evaluated the geometry of the concrete envelope, the size of grid, openings, and relation of solid and void conditions?

JR It has been a while so I would not be able to give you the exact dimensions. But we basically worked with five different opening sizes, which were more or less determined by the diagrid of structure. There was an interesting iterative process back and forth with our engineer Ysreal Seinuk, he set the parameters for a flexible diagrid shell. This gave the holes the ability to drift within certain predefined limits that combined with the five standard hole sizes would in turn modulate the particular articulation of the diagrid.

From the outset the problem was one of force transfer, the envelope initially had all of the forces track down the façade to the ring beam and ultimately into a subterranean column gird below. So, there were a series of loading streams in the façade that we were routing forces along, that was a way of guiding forces.

Once we had the parameters for the size of the holes and then established concrete strength, we had a robust working system that we could then evaluate aesthetically. There was of course the major aesthetic issue of defeating the obvious high-tech reading of the diagrid. There were interesting paths through this problem which didn't go anywhere at the time. So parametrics were used. Roland Snooks was working with us in the office, and was there initially to work through the problem of writing scripts to deal with gradients and the managing design coordination and we were continuously unhappy with the parametrically derived gradients because they looked too obviously mechanical. How the automation of the project worked very well was the way he constructed an automated drawing set and the ability to update changes – but we rejected most of the scripting, so we went manual and actually used photoshop filters as a quick way to generate patterns. We attempted a bunch of other ways for dealing with the gradients. What happened was that for each design iteration that we requested from the computational scripts prepared by Roland the number of rules would increase while the area of control would get smaller and smaller, the paradox was that rules used only once cease to be rules. It was absurd at a certain point. It was faster just to do it. Just to go manual and adjust things in a direct way. That was an interesting point and I don't know if that would still be valid today.

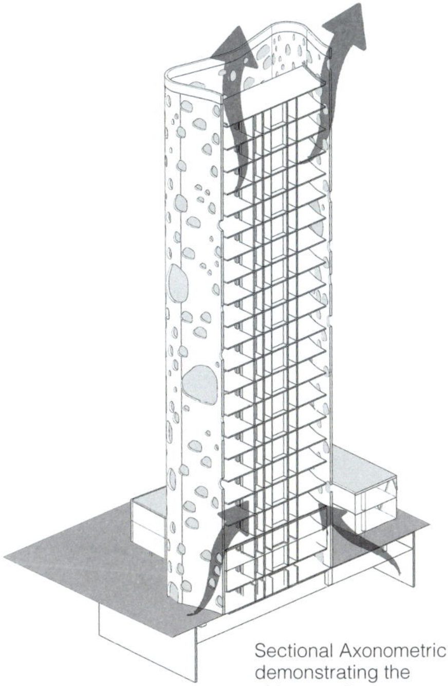

Sectional Axonometric demonstrating the chimney effect.

That was 12 years ago, but at that point that was sort of the limit of how one could deal with automation and scripting on an aesthetic level. At some point we felt we simply had to take over. Like fly-by-wire versus Chuck Yeager taking over the X1, to fly the plane by the seat of his pants.

AP I will follow with one more set of questions. How has the 0-14 project influenced your projects which have been designed since 0-14, and can you speculate on how the 0-14 has influenced design and construction by others in the discipline and profession?

JR Well, certainly one of the things that we did was that the O-14 Tower represented a certain moment in the process and when we went into another competition this time for the Shenzhen airport, we felt we had to kind of do the next iteration of O-14. Of course, it was a horizontal structure, but ultimately it is a kind of tube if only branching. So, we added even more freedom to the system. Basically, in terms

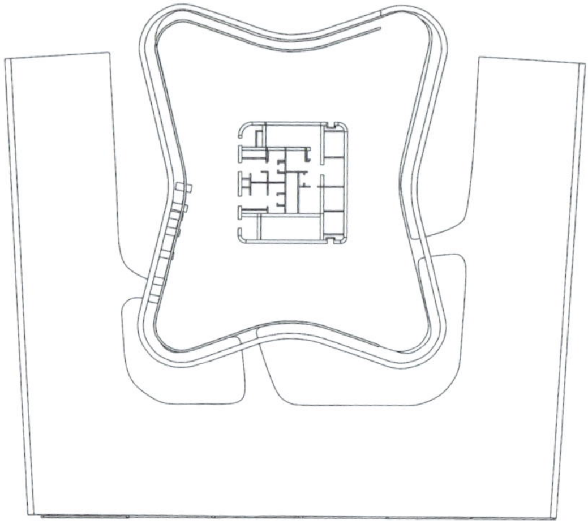

Plan at podium and tower interior

of carrying O-14 to the next project, I would say the Shenzhen airport is exactly that. The openings in O-14 are normal to the undulating surface of the shell. In Shenzhen, we added another degree of freedom to the concrete shell and began to deal with oblique projection.

NU According to movement. In our airport design, it was very important to consider the movement of light. So, we slid two surfaces diagonally, which allowed us to control the angle of sunlight reaching the space.

JR Direct light versus reflected light. We added another dimension to the idea of a tube with holes, edges, the design of a shell in long-span concrete. There was another tower that never got built as well proposed for Mexico City, which also advanced some of the ideas from O-14's design. In terms of the discipline? I don't know. It is hard to say. Certainly, Shenzhen airport was lifted pretty strongly by SOM in their airport project in India.

NU They built it!

JR Our Shenzhen airport proposal had influenced that airport way too much to our dismay. But, SOM's design was a more historicist take on the concept. I think they were definitely looking at long-span concrete and our explorations into plasticity.

JA I am going to ask a follow up question, related to this discussion. Within the portfolio of RUR's work, can you describe the trajectories of continued interests and preoccupations in methodology, and the tectonic focus of your practice, which can be located in the 0-14 tower? Regarding your longstanding interests in structural behaviors, network topologies, and computation, in which ways do you learn from your experience as designers, and where are the continuities and breaks with RUR's body of work, with respect to 0-14?

NU Our collaboration actually started in 1982. It is a long history, and in the early days, no one had a computer. The computer came quite late, and did not inform the early work.

JR I think there are a whole series of related projects within the office. We usually go from one piece of work to the next and so we don't make the argument like some offices do that every project is original or starts from scratch. In a series of longer-term projects, not just one, that we typically address when we work on a particular project. As a young office, you don't get the chance to do larger projects, so you get the work that you get. Our earliest work was landscape projects and smaller structures in gardens. So, experiments with structure happened at a very small scale, even doing fence posts, pergolas or swings. Then we started doing competitions which is something that's not so popular these days, but it was something that was very much a part of the scene as young teachers at Columbia University in the 1990s. Everybody would enter the same competition. Tom (Verebes) is well aware of the culture of competitions and also how important it was at the AA in London at the time. Those interests that we had in the small structures that we were building could then be tried out at a larger scale in a competition format. So, the Yokohama Port Terminal was a super important competition for our generation. For us it was the culmination of all of those sectional experiments we were doing with much smaller structures. So, everything is useful, I would say, even as a young practice. A project can be very simple and humble in terms of its scale and budget, but I would take it as seriously as the big projects.

JA Thank you very much. I totally agree with what you just said. Everything is useful. God is in the details, as Mies taught us. Every detail matters even in a smaller project.

JR Even a piece of furniture – for example, the great furniture of modernism, they are really miniatures or essays on what architecture should be in its most concentrated form.

JA Thank you both so much for being so gracious with your time. We really appreciate it!

TV Thank you so much, Jesse and Nanako! What a special treat it has been to have you join us at New York Tech. It has been so special to hear your reflections on the 0-14 project, and more broadly on your

work. This event is perhaps evidence one of the few benefits of the pandemic and us all communicating remotely at home, is we are able to get both of you to join us today! Thank you! Best of luck with your other current projects in Taiwan.

NU Thank you. It's really quite a pleasure to join you all today. We also really appreciate it.

JR Thank you, this was great. Best of luck!

THE POND SOCIETY
CHI SHE

Shanghai, 2016 | Archi-Union Architects

Program Galleries, Office, Social Space

Materials Recycled bricks; timber roof, tiles

Kuka Robots on Site	2
Bricks Total	31657
Floors Above Ground	2
Floors Below Ground	0
Hard Landscape	300 M2
GFA	199 M2

INTERVIEW

Interviewee: Philip F. Yuan, Professor, College of Architecture and Urban Planning; Founder, Archi-Union Architects

Interviewer: Shivani Singh, M.Arch students, School of Architecture and Design, New York Institute of Technology

February 2, 2023

Tom Verebes Thank you, Philip, for what has been a poetic and precise presentation of a series of built projects and strands of research in your office.

Philip F. Yuan Thank you, Tom. It is a pleasure to be here with you and your students at NYIT.

Shivani Singh Good evening, everyone. My name is Shivani Singh. I am a final year student in the Masters of Architecture program at NYIT. I would like to thank you for your insightful and engaging presentation. I will start a series of questions talking about the bond. The Pond Society Chi She project is an adaptive reuse of an existing building using recycled bricks to create a new façade. Although this is a small building and not a new building, we find this project to be representative of the architectural, urban, and construction context of China. Within the particular Chinese context, and of your work in general in China, what does the Chinese architectural context offer which may not be available in West? In other words, what can you achieve in China that is not possible in other parts of the world?

PFY I think this is a very good question. Last week, I gave a presentation at IAAC (Institute of Advanced Architecture of Catalonia) in Barcelona on the topic of Nonlocal Locality. For me, the non-local is about technology, in which people learn from each other globally. We had set up DigitalFUTURES as a sharing platform, with the goal of teaching people how to develop a new toolbox and also how to implement these new tools. From the sharing platform, GitHub, you can download everything and also upload robotic control systems to GitHub and share knowledge with others. This is a global culture, which is the non-local part of new technology. Locality makes its presence, for example during the COVID circumstances, we have needed to very locally address our daily lives and also our relation between each other. We need to face different local circumstances, local clients, local people, and local materials. My attitude to local practice is that we need to consider the budget and materials, whether the materials should be new or recycled. The attitude of my office

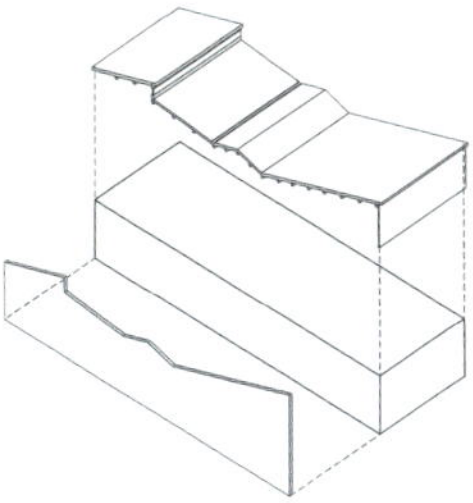

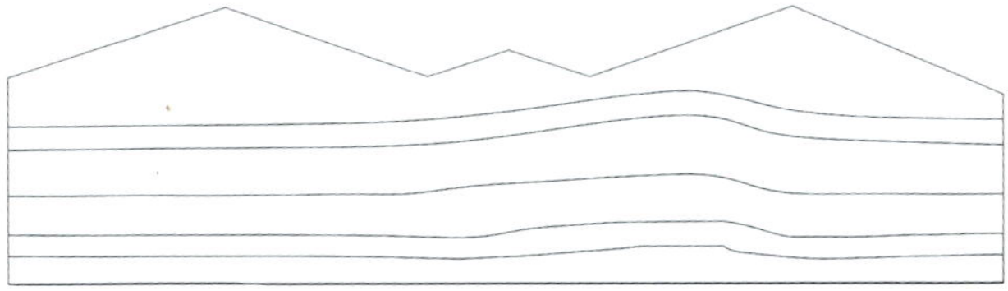

Schematic axonometric;
tool path lines on facade.

and my research team recently is about how to develop and recycle material, including traditional materiality, and also new materiality such as plastics which can create new potentials and a new materialism. There is a balance to strike between the local and non-local, so your question is a really good one. This is not about technology in the abstract – it is the designer who is shaping it through digital practice. People learn from each other, and our practice is not just about the local, we are also an international practice. I think it is super important to elaborate how I think digital technologies are driven by local scenarios towards implementation and how robotics could become a partner in the future for designers. This kind of construction process is not for contractors, it can be easily controlled by architects. If you can have six, or ten, or thirty robots on site, just imagine what you can do in the future. This may not be for the whole construction process, but robotics could be applied to a very particular materiality, or the formation and forms of the main space of a building. Robotics can easily be controlled by the designers, and this is the future of architectural education and practice. I am testing these potentials in Shanghai, Hong Kong, and other cities in mainland China, and also in some cities of South Asian countries.. In the future, I will remain open to different perspectives, and we would also like to practice worldwide.

SS This building, functioning as a gallery for exhibitions, is dedicated to cultural dissemination and cultural consumption. Set in a complex called the Pond Society Chi She Art Community, can you share with us how you see the impact of this small building upon this art community and also upon the larger urban cultural context of Shanghai?

PFY The location of Chi She – in the center of the city along the riverfront – is a very good one. The mayor of Shanghai has led an initiative to re-develop this area which was formerly an airport. There were no buildings on the site because this used to be a very large airport site. When we started the project at the development stage, most of the buildings planned for the site were using new materials to construct them, including many high rise buildings. This community is especially formed for artists. When I visited the site, we saw a lot of torn down warehouse buildings with bricks spread out everywhere. We could not use all the bricks, as some were broken. I am trying to test the possibility of not buying materials, and only using recycled materials such as recycled bricks. We introduced platform which gave us a way for design to embed the possibility of a new materiality using recycled materials. This is a special aspect of this project. Also, the budget was reduced a lot because we did not need to buy anything. The material cost saving in the budget could be transferred to the robotic fabrication process. Our client really liked this idea and gave us a lot of support. We completed this project about six or seven years ago, but it is still really meaningful to us. Thank you.

SS In broader terms, what do you see as the mission of architecture as a form of cultural practice?

PFY We believe machines are abstract machines. We are developing our software expertise and hardware in my office as we develop different solver systems for every type of robot

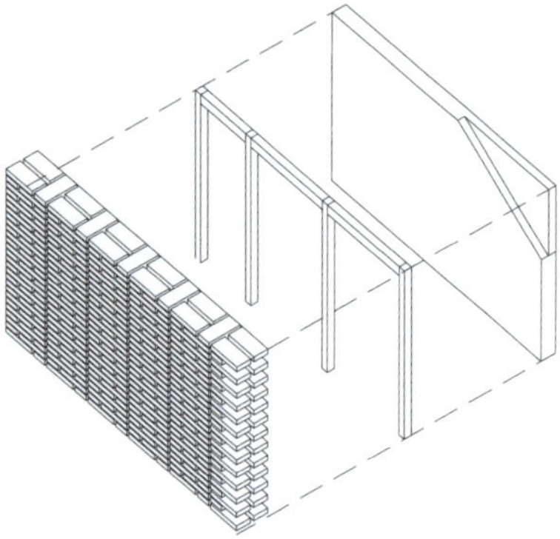

which you can download as open source from GitHub, a robotic control platform. Secondly, we are working with FU Sense, which is a positioning and motoring platform for positioning robotics accurately on site. Third, with FU Generator, we are introducing big modeling, and we have generated different form by different models. Right now, we have around 20 big models in 20 different styles driven by scripts developed by my PhD students, graduates, and post-docs. We are abstractly developing these modeling approaches with common software as a machine platform for people to share knowledge, and to stand on the other shoulders of others to develop new design outcomes in the future. Robotics is leading us to two scenarios for production, including offsite production, and large span and large material assemblages. We have the capacity to fabricate timber pieces in the lab, and in the factory, and we can also deploy mobile robotics in which we can run a group of six robots, which can engage in different real projects anywhere. We can transport our robots to different construction sites and set them up as a temporary onsite digital factory inside a tent. We set up robotics in a tent and then can very easily construct brick masonry walls on site. Each year, we construct about two to three buildings in China in this way.

So, we are sharing our gene pool with many others. I founded my fabrication company, Fab-Union, and some of my students after their graduation work with us at Fab-Union so they can engage actively to innovate our industry. I think it is super meaningful for the future of industry, because we are actively changing the working flow of design to construction, and changing the relationships between architects, fabricators, and clients. We can control, directly like designers, not only design drawings in a computer, but also we can control the complexity of construction processes as well. Thank you.

SS In a few moments, we will ask you some more detailed questions about the specific technologies used in this project, but can you elaborate on the social agenda of how Archi-Union and Fab Union deploy technology through this project? Asked another way, what is the social impact of your practice's use of technology?

PFY I am the founding partner of Archi-Union and we have around 60 architects in the office, which is like a middle scale office here in China. Most importantly, we support research into developing software processes, such as AIGC, which has been introduced to our design processes. We have also developed training models for different patents with many possibilities for their applications. Fab-Union is a robotic fabrication company and many of my former students have become leaders in Fab-Union, by working on by different crafts, including timber, 3D printing, brick, carbon fiber, and so and so forth. In practice, we need to better understand material processes, and how to create, how to construct, how to imagine, and how to fabricate within a holistic work flow. What we are doing is following our dream, which is to actually change the discipline through new work flows, and by this, we will change the way we build, and what we build. Buildings themselves are not created only by the human brain, but also through collaboration with software and hardware machinery. I believe collaborative future of the human and the machine is the basis of our human future. We are embracing this kind of new intelligence, an architectural intelligence which actually can give us a lot of new direction in the discipline of architecture. So, thank you for your excellent question.

SS Archi-Union's spatial interests seem to us to be focused on generating new modes of form-making, and the application of advanced material research. We are interested in the logic of the formalism of Archi-Union's architecture, and what serves as the inspiration of your formal interests. How do you develop your ideas for the projects in your office into forms, spaces and materials? Do you sketch? AND - At what stage is the conception of projects worked on through computation and the logic of fabrication processes, and specific materials?

PFY Thank you for this question. Over the past 15 to 20 years, our experience in practice has been about embracing digital technologies. Together with Neil Leach, we founded the DigitalFUTURES platform twelve years ago, and this global community has influenced my practice my design thinking. We do not sketch much. Computational design methodologies and robotic fabrication are in fact the main keywords of what we are doing. At the same time, we have acquired very quickly construction experience in China through our many opportunities to construct buildings. My practice is based on these two very interesting scenarios. One is about the technology development process, including AIGC, and we also try to develop different possibilities for producing new forms. We are developing a very particular style, which is about continuity, about the large, and about differential changes related to materiality. If you want to fabricate new AIGC form, you need to be able to print them, for example – you need to fabricate with some differential distance.

The robotic future is about the mechanical AIGC which can fabricate forms of materiality which the human cannot fabricate. Our office follows this idea, on the one hand to explore the possibility of new computational form, and at the same time, we focus on robotic technologies for fabrication. This is our future.

SS Within the Chinese constructional and technological context, you have presented how your work is concerned with the fusion of high technology, with computational systems feeding information to a robotic arm for on-site construction, together with low technology in the use of an ancient material, brick. In sum – sophisticated machining combined with manual labor. In the fast pace of technological change in architecture, with respect to computational tools and fabrication machinery and processes, can we ask you to share with us how you became interested in these technologies, how you developed your advanced expertise, and lastly, how do you remain at the forefront of technological experimentation?

PFY Yes, I think in the future we should redefine labors in China. The transformation is already partially here, because construction

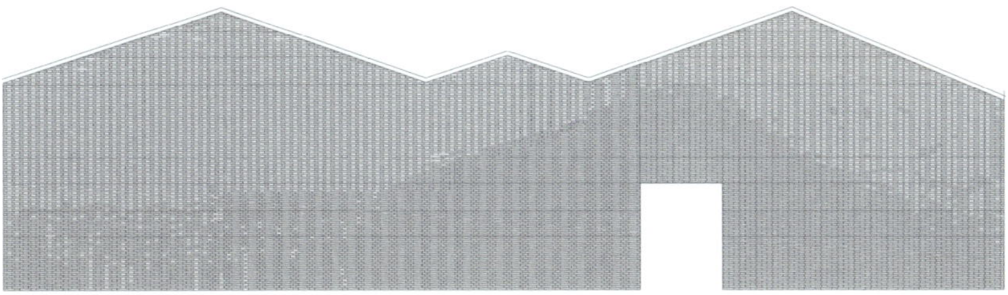

Elevation of brick wall

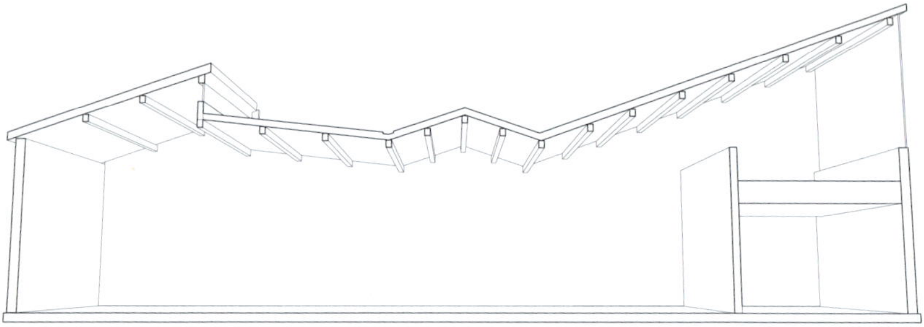

Interior perspective

workers in China have become older and older, and the young generation does not like to work in construction anymore. Perhaps the young would rather like to work in a factory controlling robotics in the prefabrication industries, which is rising in China in recent years. In the future, we should reduce human work in construction processes through collaboration between designers and robotics using prefabrication factories and on-site production. That is why our research in FU Sense is super important which can position robotics and prefabricated pieces on the site. At once reducing human labor, we should also increase the precision and accuracy and implement more efficient construction processes in the future. Our industrial paradigm is changing and this will produce new jobs in the future, and I believe architectural education should be redefined in relation to these changes. I think it is super important to not only explore new generative form, but also we should redesign our work flow, and the relationships between laborers and designers. Ultimately this is about rethinking our discipline, and these are my suggestions to respond to your question.

SS What are the biggest challenges for architecture today? And, in which ways can robotic fabrication address these challenges?

PFY I think the challenges are coming from the regulations and also from capital investment into new things. So, we also have opportunities in these challenges. In the future, renovation will become a primary agenda around the world because of the importance of sustainability. New innovation should be introduced to the discipline, and in this sense, the biggest challenge is the transfer of knowledge from research to practice. Secondly, we should also research designing social processes and social systems. This is related to Bruno Latour's ideas of how laboratory life should be transferred to social life. For this, we need a long time, as it will not happen in a one day revolution. I think we need education, not only of students, but also education of social networks. We need to contribute to this longer term process.

SS With respect to the Chi She Art Community project, we have questions about the relationship of this project to the body of work of your practice. How has the Chi She project been influenced by other previous projects which Archi-Union has done before 2016? Or in other words, which of your projects led up to your interests and the outcome of the Chi She project?

PFY Our Chi She project is already seven years old, and is an early project to us, but I think we can position it, not as a single project, but in relation to some of our other bigger projects since then. Our work is a testing process for us. We develop our tools – in Chi She, we only had one mobile robot, and recently, we have introduced working with six robots in a single project. This is like a version update in computer technology. We update a new version of software and hardware, and we update a new version of our design. Think of it as the generation of an iterative process. It is a really interesting challenge for pedagogy in education – you should think about what's new and what's next. Alongside and previous to Chi She, we have focused on what this new materialism can produce, including some of our work on 3D printing in plastics. I have also found it a very interesting to research recycled and reused material scenarios. So, this is the background of the Chi She project. Thank you.

SS How has the Chi She project influenced other Archi-Union projects since 2016?

PFY From when we started to collaborate between Archi-Union and Fab-Union, we started to produce a very special material identity, which looks local, but this actually developed a very strong material sensibility by our practice. Since then, we have further introduced computation and fabrication technologies into our practice. The year 2016 was a transformation in our studio – it was a big shift from design to human labor, towards human design assisted by robotic labor. That was a transformative moment for us!

SS Moving on to the next question, we would like to shift towards a discussion of the future consequences of your work, and specifically, the impact of your contribution on the culture and discipline of architecture worldwide. We understand your involvement in various modes of engagement, as a practicing architect, educator, and researcher. You conduct research in the context of professional practice at your office. As an academic serving as Professor of Architecture at Tongji University, you teach and conduct research, and importantly, you have launched the Digital Futures World events which have hosted over 13,000 students in architecture for free workshops and lectures, over the past three summers.

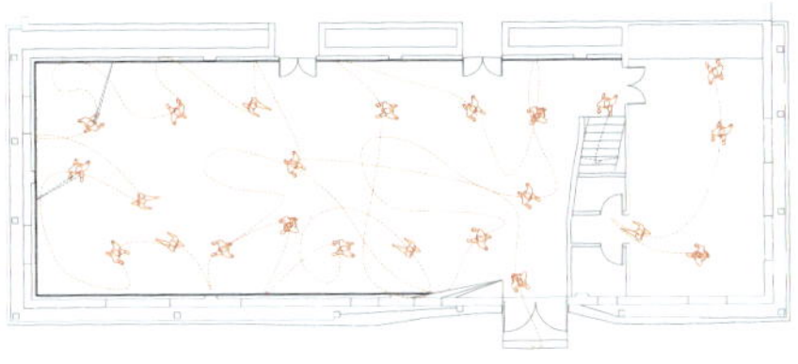

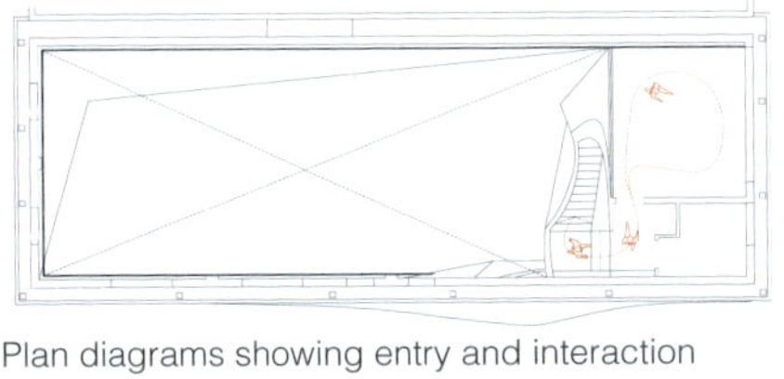

Plan diagrams showing entry and interaction

Please can you share with us how you see the impact of experimentation in architecture on practice, education and research in China, upon the world? In other words, how is the practice and study of architecture in China influencing architecture globally?

PFY This is a great question! I think China has made a great leap forward by learning so much from the world. For us in China, this has been very important. Actually, I have been influenced by your professor, Tom (Verebes), because he set up the yearly AA Visiting summer workshop (AA Visiting School Shanghai, 2007-2018), which really influenced the new generation of architects in China and worldwide. During that time, Neil Leach and I founded DigitalFUTURES. Our dream was to freely educate more people and to introduce these new computational technologies to a wider audience. In China, you can only imagine we have more than 260 universities which have architecture as a discipline, and most of the students have no opportunity to learn skills in new technology. For example, DigitalFUTURES has professors from Harvard GSD, MIT, ETH Zurich, and many other top schools, and most students in China lack the finances to travel abroad for their education. DigitalFUTURES produced a platform for short workshops, seven to nine days long, to offer students new ways of thinking, new work flows, and other themes, and to learn from professors from around the world. Actually, my team also participates in DigitalFUTURES, together with our PhD and grad students sharing our technology and expertise with the world. By linking every robot to GitHub, as I mentioned, you can download knowledge for free, and you can control more than 60 robots on this platform because it is a culture for sharing. We are learning from each other and also exchange knowledge with each other. I believe there should be friendly collaboration internationally. Also, on the platform of DigitalFUTURES, we have a lot of listeners and participants from India, Africa, and Latin America as well. This platform is bridging technology and learning, and is also creating a sharing culture in the discipline of architecture.

SS Thank you for sharing this. This interview and the study of the set of projects in the Beyond the Envelope series of presentations and interviews are set within a Master of Architecture course here at NYIT. In this context, can you please share with us in a final question, from your point of view, what advice may you have for the next generation of architects?

PFY Yes, of course. I think the best time is coming, largely because AI (artificial intelligence) is booming. What we are doing now is not only developing our expertise in robotics, but also in AIGC software development. This generation has new opportunities not only to learn new ways of thinking about the meaning of design, and the design skills embedded in the human brain, but you also need to learn how to collaborate with the computer using different software, especially to collaborate with AI. We need to control the AI toolbox. The future generation should, I believe, if you are still in university, try to find the benefits of design, because design thinking is the most important to control the entire working flow. You should collaborate with computer scientists because they know how to code, but they don't know how to design. Our design processes should embrace all new technology. That is what I believe the future generation should do. If you are asking for my advice, I think the future is coming.

AI's future is coming, and this will change our discipline. We need to embrace this new technology, and not reject it. I think we need to balance culture, balance tradition, together with the future. I think we should embrace the future at the same time, but we should look back and learn from the past.

And every day, you should learn something new. By gaining expertise in today's hardware and software you should develop the capacity to design the toolbox for design in the future.

SS Thank you so much for your time today. I have learned so much about your work and the specific context of applied technology and construction in the particular context of China.

TV Thank you so much, Philip, for your deeply enriching, engaging and enjoyable presentation. Thank you also for your generosity to join us for this interview. It is a pleasure to see you on screen and I hope we have the opportunity to see you again in person soon.

PFY Thank you for the invitation – I also hope to see you all in person soon.

FEDERATION SQUARE

Melbourne, 2002 | Lab Architecture Studio

Program National Gallery of Australia, Ian Potter Centre, Australian Centre for the Moving Image ACMI, Koorie Heritage Trust, SBS Radio and Television Offices, The Atrium, The Edge, Zinc, restaurants, cafés, Transport Hotel Bar

Materials Glass, Steel Components, Sandstone, Zinc (Including Perforated Zinc)

20% Solid The Atrium

80% Glazing The Atrium

85% Solid National Gallery Of Australia

15% Glazing National Gallery Of Australia

470,000 Kimberley Sandstone Pavers

22,000 Conway Pinwheel Triangles

24 M High

5 Floors Above Ground

1 Floors Below Ground

3.6 Hectares

45,000 M2 GFA

INTERVIEW

Interviewee: Donald L. Bates, Director, Lab Architecture Studio

Interviewers: Kashmi Shah, final year Master of Architecture student, School of Architecture and Design, New York Institute of Technology

March 8, 2023

Tom Verebes Thank you so much, Don, for your presentation – this is truly a special opportunity to be toured across the design, construction, and the life of Federation Square. I would like to introduce Kashmi Shah, final year M.Arch student at New York Tech.

Donald L. Bates It is a pleasure to be here, thank you.

Kashmi Shah My name is Kashmi Shah, and I would like to thank you for your insightful and engaging presentation. The Federation Square project elicits associations between the role of civic architecture to patterns of urban space, and the relationship between discrete institutional buildings and the city. It has been published, and you have presented, how this project recapitulates the urban order of the nineteenth century fabric of Melbourne's narrow laneways, blocks and streets. Your published sketch diagram of figure and field relationships, which you have just shown this evening in your presentation, suggests the subversion of the legibility of building figures, and also hints at narrow routes into and through the field. While in London, in the early design stages of the project, how was this diagram instrumental in the design of the massing figures and public routing of the urban pattern of Federations Square?

DLB To be honest, we did lots and lots of diagrams. Some of our research was interested in the work of Stan Allen. He had written about field orders that are not based on classical geometries, or axial planning, or centrifugal plans. Our initial diagrams took a tartan pattern and distorted it, in drawings, but also in the folding of tracing paper and then photocopying the overlapping patterns. We also looked at thin rock sections. If you take a rock and cut it very thinly and then shine ultraviolet light through it, you pick up a matrix of different minerals that are bound together. At first this looked completely chaotic, but when you study it, you realize some of the grains and some of the minerals are oriented with particular direction. Out of that, you start to see another kind of order, allowing us to question how to create order not based on pure geometries. From our point of view, what was important about it in terms of architecture was in creating a "relational" design. What we were trying to design were not specific figures that look like particular things or that were based on a kind of purity of a grid, but rather, we were trying to design organizational relationships which we could move and push. As the project changed multiple times, for instance, the largest facility on the site, the National Gallery of Victoria, was in fact not part of the original competition. Ultimately, we had to rethink the project when we won the competition. Budgets and floor areas would change and the brief would change. We did not have a strict image of a figure because it was about designing for the constant shifting of relationships.

KS At what stage in the design conception of the Fed Square project did the concept of Melbourne's urban fabric of lanes arise? Was this relationship to Melbourne's urban pattern a conscious decision, or did your diagram of figure to field relationships imply an association to Melbourne?

DLB When we did the competition, I didn't know about the laneways and Peter only knew about them a little bit. We had already been working on that sense of order on other competitions before Federation Square, so there happened to be a good meshing between them. When we got to the second stage of the competition, we had to form a joint venture with a local practice in Melbourne called Bates Smart, and they sent two people to London to work with us on the second stage entry. We started to articulate how actually this did have something to do with Melbourne's character and sensibility. For me, Melbourne is a city of experiences and it's very different to Sydney, which is a city of images. As a tourist in Sydney, you stand and take the photograph of the Opera House and the bridge and the harbor all together, and then you can say you've been to Sydney. There is not a place in Melbourne where you can stand and say, "this is Melbourne", it's something you have to participate in. Our design for Federation Square is a precinct of experiences you move through, through arcades, laneways, and zones, which make sense by being there, not by looking at it.

KS The Atrium of Federation Square, which serves as a public thoroughfare interiorizing

Patterns of shifted grids on site massing

urban space, renders more complex the relationships of figure and field, mass and routing. Was this space part of the competition brief? or, at what stage was it included as a feature in the early design stages?

DLB The Atrium was part of the competition, but it wasn't called The Atrium. They used the term, "Winter Garden", which meant it was to be an interior space you could use for events when it's cold, wet or windy outside. For a lot of the competitors, it was conceived as a commercial zone where you would have cafés, restaurants, and shopping. We saw it as this connector because before Federation Square was built over the railway, there was no connection from the CBD to the north down to the river, except at bridges. By creating Federation Square as a precinct, it made for the first time a whole block that connected the city to the river. When we were designing the atrium, we saw it as a covered street; as a way to get from the city to the river.

After winning the competition, we began to see how The Atrium could form a role as a venue – both a space you pass through, but also a space you go into. It was very important for us that The Atrium does not have a front door, that it could not be closed off, so that it had a civic quality and a civic role different from a shopping mall which is locked up at night and is privatized.

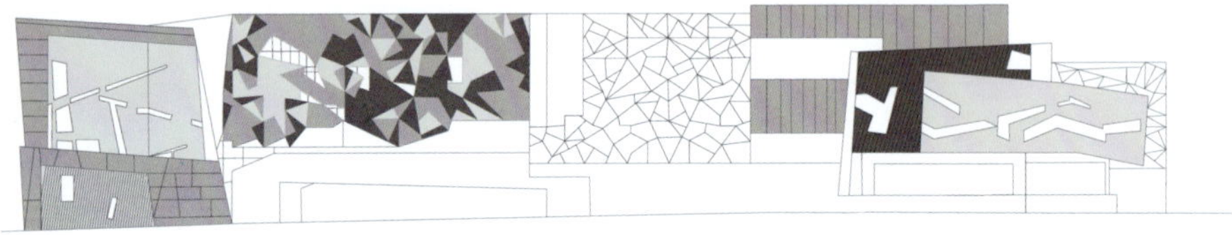

The consequence of that was we had to figure out how to heat it or cool it, and to do that economically, our consultants, the environmental services engineers, Atelier Ten, came up with something called the "Labyrinth", which is a passive cooling system. It manages the climatic environment of the Atrium, even though the structure is all glass and it's always open.

KS Civic spaces associated with comprehensive arts and cultural venues, also often referred to as cultural districts, have the potential to become symbols of their host city. Interestingly, the Fed Square project has been suggested as Melbourne's equivalent to Sydney Opera House, and you have presented the context of the 1990s "Bilbao Effect" within which the project was designed. When working on the project, did you imagine the civic and cultural space of Federation Square could attain the status of a symbol of the city?

DLB There were 177 entries for the competition for Federation Square from around the world – it was an international open competition. In the competition documents, there was an aspiration that Melbourne was looking for its "Opera House" as an architectural image. This idea that a piece of architecture could define a whole city was certainly part of the discourse that was going on during the time of Bilbao (Guggenheim Museum by Frank Gehry), but we weren't particularly interested in that. Our analysis was that it did not want to be iconic in the sense of being a single figure, but what it wanted to be was a destination of experiences, a place that people would go to, not to look at and take that one photograph, but to actually have to experience it in order to discover it. Our work was in how to let people enjoy it as a place and not feel disappointed because it's not iconic enough.

Since Federation Square finally opened, it has had ten million visitors each year for twenty years, except of course during Covid. They had hoped to attract four to five million visitors per year. Four years ago, less than 20 years since its completion, it was given heritage status. To answer your question regarding cultural districts: Melbourne Arts Precinct on the south side of the river, a bit to the west of Federation Square, also called Southbank. Brisbane and London both have arts precincts called Southbank, which lie across the river from their downtowns. In this history of these arts precincts on the south bank, it produces what we might call the Acropolis effect, where you separate out the arts domain from the rest of the city. For example, in New York with Lincoln Center as a precinct with a concert hall, a theater space, a performance space, a gallery – and if by putting it all together, you create this singular domain of culture. We didn't want

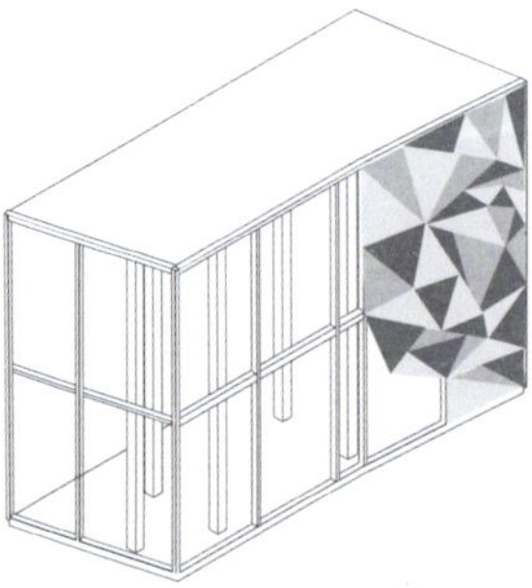

Structure and envelope panelization

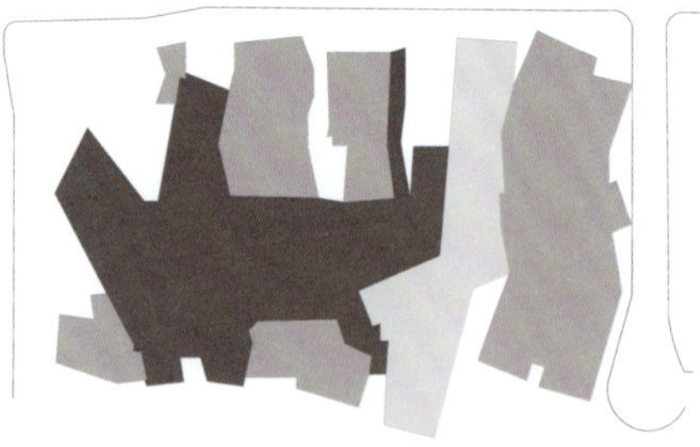

Plan diagrams of building figure, plazas, and laneways

Panel Module; Conway Pinwheel geometry; Diagram of Atrium structure

to do that. Our site is not like that. The urban permeability in the design was to say we want the arts and the culture to be part of everyday life, not a place you go to once or twice a year with your grandmother. It's a place you go through on the way to someplace else. Part of the shifting grid of Federation Square was to try to induce this sense of organization, not of singular buildings that you go into for a cultural or civic experience and then come back out again, but rather as a permeable matrix that you pass through, around and in, and it's part of everyday life.

KS Thank you. Many cultural districts, London's Southbank for example which you mentioned, grow and evolve over time, expanding with buildings and institutions added over time. Other cultural districts are built at one time, such as New York's Lincoln Centre. Fed Square was commissioned to have been completed in 2002. Interestingly one of the buildings, the Yarra Building, was recently proposed to be demolished, and an Apple shop was to be built in its place. Can you please comment on how you viewed this development of the site, which would have changed your initial design?

DLB The proposal was to replace the Yarra building with an Apple store. In the end this didn't happen because Federation Square received heritage status. There was also a lot of opposition from different sectors across Melbourne, mostly because it was Apple. They didn't want a big American technology company at Fed Square. People thought Apple would take over the image of Federation Square. Nonetheless, there is a current project that's going on right now. Melbourne is building a new metro line, an underground train line, and one of the stations is just to the north of Federation Square. One of the entry points into the station is located at Federation Square. Our building, the Western Shard, has been demolished and a new entrance point is being built, which is by the Rogers, Stirk Harbour + Partnership. Personally, I didn't like the design by Foster (and Partners) for the Apple Store but I was not against the idea of Federation Square changing. We always said when we designed Federation Square, it's important to understand the three C's: that it's a civic site; that it's a cultural site; but it's also a commercial site. To make public space work, it needs a commercial component. It needs cafés and restaurants, and places to hang out. It needs that animation when a cultural event isn't happening. We advocated strongly for a whole range of cultural and commercial facilities to be part of it, because we believe that's what makes public space. When we looked at Southbank in Melbourne, Brisbane and London, they all had beautiful venues, but they were dead 90% of the time. The opera is only on for two and a half hours a night and the rest of the time the building is completely blank. You mentioned the transitions of Southbank in London, where they've added shops, cafés, and restaurants, which have livened it up. The project for the Apple Shop to me was a part of that possibility. The Yarra building, which was originally designed without a specific tenant in mind, was not part of the original competition. It was a building component we added to Fed Square as a way to embrace the plaza from an urban design point of view. It is now being renovated to become the Koori Heritage Trust,

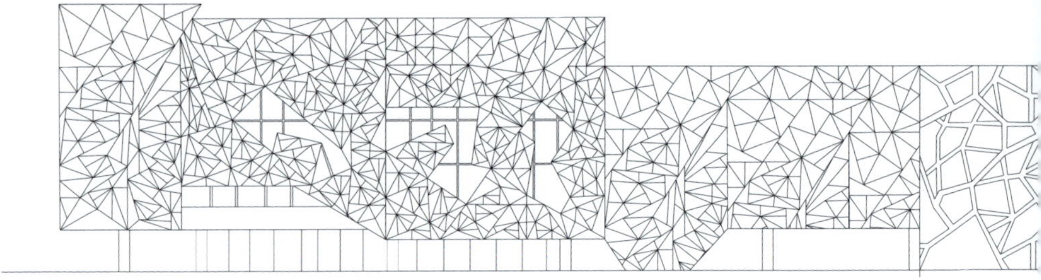

Diverse subdivision patterns on façades

for the "Koori" people, the indigenous people of Victoria, and will become another destination for people.

KS In the AD issue, "Architecture After Geometry", guest-edited by you and Peter Davidson in 1997, some months before you both started working on the Federation Square project, you argued for a shift in emphasis in architecture from geometry towards pattern. In the Federation Square project, your deep interest in the relationships between geometry, pattern, and organization, is evident in the unrelenting difference and the denial of repetition in both the urban fabric and the surface expression of the project. Further to your presentation, the Federation Square project is one of the very few buildings built with notions of Fractal geometry and self-similarity to embed multiple scales, as a basis to achieve coherence and difference. In retrospect, some 25 years after starting the project, can you situate the Federation Square within the larger shift towards complexity in architecture in the late 1990s?

DLB We were looking at all this in the issue of AD, Architecture After Geometry, which included friends and colleagues – people like Greg Lynn, Jeff Kipnis, Reiser + Umemoto, people we either went to school with, knew well, or taught next to at the AA or elsewhere. And again, Stan Allen was very influential in terms of his theoretical works, looking at how order and organization can be generated outside of classical geometries. These notions were definitely in Federation Square. Being able to work digitally meant that you could create much more complex patterns. I can't use Rhino and Grasshopper. I use simple digital tools like Illustrator and InDesign, and I use them in terms of making multiple images that can be stacked, offset, shifted, twisted, and slightly distorted here and there. The computer was in its early days in 1997, but it was part of an important process of being able to work graphically. Developing the ability to manipulate the image through computational or digital means was also an important development as well. In 1996/7, we had students who could use Microstation Triforma, which we used to design and develop all of Federation Square. It was one of the first buildings in Australia where we gave a 3D digital model to the engineers. At the time, sharing a 3D model was not yet the norm, as nobody was sure who had responsibility for the digital files if there was a mistake. Our engineers effectively redrew the drawings based on our digital model so that it came from their hand. That is actually how the atrium structure was formulated, which is a very complex structure with tolerances of four millimeters. The Atrium, both from an architectural aspiration in terms of ideas around complexity, but also the computational means to be able to make that work structurally and then actually get it fabricated and put on site, was just happening at that moment for us.

Thermal gain / cooling diagram.

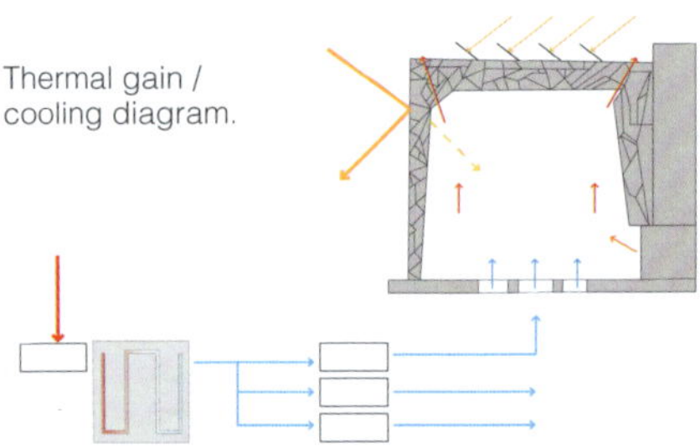

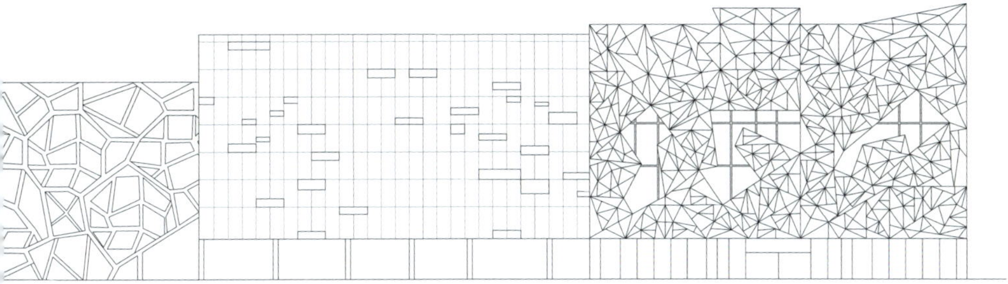

KS Thank you. Can you please share with us why Federation Square so strongly rejects spatial reductionism, minimalism, and even the conventions of modernism, positing instead complexity expressed in urban patterns, and architectural or surface organization.

DLB Partly, it's because that's what we became interested in. We did feel that it was about a different understanding of how social and cultural life is at the end of the twentieth century and into the twenty-first century. The offset geometry goes back to this desire to produce an architecture of relationships rather than iconic objects. When using Euclidean geometries, it's very easy to come up with very strongly definable and recognizable entities as objects. We felt part of the complexity of life is that we were not made up of those kinds of elements. We don't operate that way. We don't structure our life in clear, undeniably differentiated moments. It all flows and meshes together. For us, the very notion of a Federation Square is an interesting idea. Not dissimilarly to the United States, Australia used to be made up of British colonies and there was debate of whether they would form a federation or whether the colonies would each become individual nations, and they chose to federate to join together.

And in Federation, there is a question of coherence as a whole, as an entity, which allows for differences. We wanted to develop an architecture that could not just recognize the complexity of life, and certainly not try to illustrate it, but would help to facilitate its expansion as part of civic and social and cultural life.

KS My next question concerns the envelope technologies developed with the triangular Conway Pinwheel grid as the modular basis of the façade systems. How did you conceive of the three different material systems of sandstone, zinc, and glass? AND what led to the decisions for the structure, and transparency of the atrium building to be so distinct from the other sandstone and zinc buildings?

DLB We started developing the project with our structural engineers, Atelier One, and the way in which the pinwheel grid could be made operable. In part because the building was supposed to have been built within four years, so we had a sense that we would, particularly with the façades, have to develop something that was prefabricated, which could be brought to site. We didn't want a curtain wall system. The Conway Pinwheel Grid allowed us to be able to produce it as prefabricated units. We didn't spend a huge amount of time thinking about the choice of materials – we had to write something in the report for the competition, so we listed sandstone, zinc, and some glass. After we won the competition, we spent a lot of time looking for a sandstone that was variegated, that had tonalities within it, not just a beige single colored stone. When it rains, the red tonalities in the sandstone become much stronger, and the building changes. Zinc is really shiny when you first put it on the building, but over time it develops a patina, and has a different tonality of gray depending on

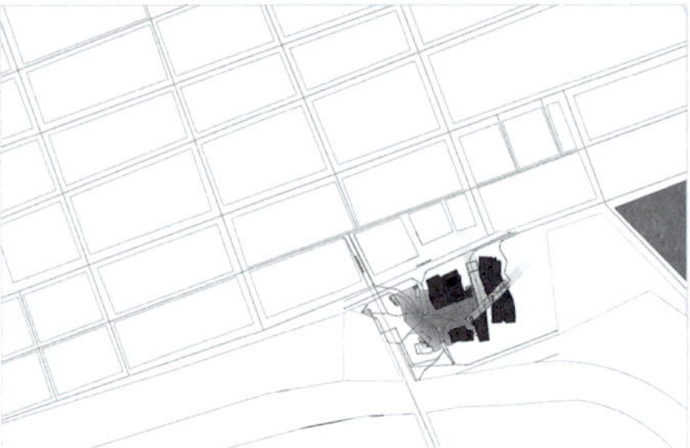

its exposure. The zinc facing towards the sun is, after 20 years, quite different from the zinc not facing the sun. Or the zinc facing to west that gets the most rain is different from the zinc that's on the east that doesn't get rained on as directly. We liked the idea that the materials show materiality – showing up by themselves. The glass is sometimes opaque glass because it's there as part of the pattern. Some of the material choices came out of those decisions about using those materials because they have very specific material qualities in their own right.

KS Can you comment on the dissonance between the twisted ribbon diagram from which the massing drives and the triangular fractal diagram from which the wrappers divide?

DLB It is interesting, because I really don't like triangles! When my students are working on designs and they come up with a triangular plan…it's terrible! Even worse is when they come up with hexagonal plans. I think every student does one hexagonal design in their life. I always tell students, "okay, you've done this, and now you don't ever have to do a hexagonal plan again". I would never plan to use a triangle in plan, but in the façade, thanks to John Conway and the aperiodic tiling grid that he developed it works. Even though it comes from a simple golden ratio triangle, it creates an incredible array of difference and variation in terms of how the triangles come together, and this is what allowed us then to have that big array of figuration on the surfaces of the buildings. The façades are the result of probably 4000 sketch drawings, because everybody in the office, for two and a half months, was drawing the façade, based on the Conway tiling pattern. You overlay the large aperiodic pinwheel grid with tracing paper and as I was showing with the colors, you connect different points. It seems very simple, but some of the emerging images, some of those figures were just not nice. We had a whole set called the Bart Simpson façades because it was all very spiky, like Bart Simpson's hair. The final façades derive from constantly going through and finding figures, figurations, that seemed to work together. The triangular grid allowed us incredible freedom, but also responsibility. It was a way of articulating those surfaces to create different effects from the east, west, north and south, from the gallery building versus the cinema building versus the office building versus the back of the Yara building. That standardized triangular grid allowed a huge array of different articulations and figuration to emerge.

KS I will shift our discussion to the way in which the project was initially received by the architectural community, and the public. In hindsight after more than 20 years, Federation Square is a civic space which is activated continuously, embedded in the urban communities of Melbourne and the cultural life of the city, and has become much loved. In advance of the Federation Square proposal, Australia, and especially Melbourne, had been the host of some experimental, unique, and even radical architecture. In retrospect, can you please share with us why there was seemingly so much controversy and so much commentary on this proposal at first?

DLB The project is right in the middle of the city, across the street from the main railway station, and on the main north-south access throughout Melbourne – it's a very prominent site. Some of the controversy was, first of all, because we weren't from Melbourne. There were a lot of Melbourne architects that were angry that this major project was given to these outsiders. Peter is Australian, but he had been living overseas for fifteen years; and I'm from Texas. Certainly, part of the architectural community made comments about our design. A lot of Melbournians and Victorians didn't know what a "Federation Square" was. Nobody had told them. There was just this

thing called Federation Square that a lot of public money was being spent on in the middle of the city. When we won the competition, Peter and I offered to launch an exhibition showing our drawings and models at the Town Hall, nearby the site. We offered to be at the exhibition for two solid days, at least 8 hours a day, to answer any question from anybody. We had lots of people telling us they hated it; it was terrible; why were they doing this? But we also had people asking, "why are you even building these buildings?" "Why don't they just make it a park? We need more grass and green trees". So, nobody really knew what Federation Square was supposed to do, not in terms of the architecture, just as a civic project. There were a lot of people that disliked the architecture, and there are still a lot of people who dislike it. They think it's too jumbled, too messed up, not coherent enough, or not ordered enough. There was a political dimension to it as well. One of the newspapers here, which is very conservative, hated it because it wasn't traditional architecture. "Could it be something everybody can understand? Why does it have to be so difficult to understand? What it's all about?" Also, this was a way people could be against the Premier of the day, and against the local politicians.

The Premier (Jeff Kennett) who commissioned the project was on the conservative side of politics. The opposition at that time, Labour (The Labour Party), is more left leaning, came out and said that Federation Square "has all the grace and charm of Godzilla", a monster. Three years later, Labour won the election and they had to finish the project, and they suddenly thought it was going to be a great project and great for the economy. There are multiple strands in terms of all of this – I could give a whole lecture just on newspaper reportage about the project, but the one that still hits me the most was a writer, again, for a very conservative newspaper. As the building was coming up, but wasn't yet completed, and he wrote this in probably July, 2001, not long after the Taliban in Afghanistan had blown up the ancient Buddhas, and two months before 9/11: "If only we could get those guys from Afghanistan to come to Melbourne, maybe they could blow up Federation Square." That sentiment hits very hard everytime I think about it.

I give a lot of credit to the Labour government who had an open day when Federation Square was still a construction site. They had shut down construction for almost a week, put up barriers, walkways, and ramps, and they let the public come onto the construction site for two days on a Saturday and a Sunday. Almost overnight, opinion changed. The buildings weren't finished, so you couldn't really figure out exactly what it was going to look like, but you got a sense of something. Public opinion changed. People understood what the point was in terms of the galleries and the multimedia spaces, and what was going to be a public outside space or a covered interior space like the Atrium. Also, it was also no longer going to be this little cake that was going to be wrapped up and handed to the public when it was finished. They actually had ownership of it, and that was an important moment also in its reception. Then, once it did open, it really became the place you go to, a destination. It is what you might call the home page for Melbourne – where you go first before you decide where else to go.

KS It has been more than 20 years since Fed Square was completed. Can you share with us your perspective of any changes in the perception of the public in Melbourne over the years towards the architecture and urban design of Federation Square?

DLB As I said, it's the place people go to, but a lot of this has nothing to do with the architecture. A management company runs Federation Square, and they put on about 2000 events every year. Melbourne is a very multicultural city and Federation Square is used for national festivals and celebrations, but it also hosts big events. Melbourne has a lot of festivals. We have a film festival, a comedy festival, a fashion festival, a food and wine festival, and it goes on and on. Some of those events take place at Federation Square. October 2022 was the 20th anniversary of the project and there was a formal celebration, and the next day we had another celebration, which was just for the people who worked on it. All together about 4000 people worked on Fed Square over 6 years, and only 100 people were from our joint office. The most gratifying thing to me is the number of people that worked on it, and who came to me during the anniversary celebrations and said, "this was the best project I ever worked on." A sense of camaraderie developed, but also the experience that we were trying to do something different – not iconic, but something that would change the way Melbourne operated – and I think it did change the way the city operates.

KS Thank you so much for sharing this. In general, do you believe it is important for an architect's decisions and interests, and the product as built spaces, to be perceived as comprehensible and legible by lay people, or the general public?

DLB Again, it is a cliche, but for me, the difference between Melbourne and Sydney is a difference between experience and image. There is a sense, as a tourist you go to cities and you want to make sure you take the photograph that was on the cover of the book about the city you've just come to visit, so that you can say you've been there. Melbourne is different. When we have visitors to Melbourne and I chaperone them around Melbourne CBD, it takes about an hour to do the tour, because to really get a sense of it, you have to go through a lot of different spaces. You have to wander through these laneways and arcades and passageways rather than looking at particular buildings. It is a city that you have to experience, so it is demanding in one sense, because you can't just be given the image and understand it. You actually have to engage in it, and for me, that's great. Certainly, we thought about this, and we wanted to create a place that won't necessarily make sense the first time - not because we're trying to hide anything - but it can only make sense by experiencing it, and that it makes sense by a visitor making it makes sense. You have to be there and be part of it for it to make sense.

KS Thank you. A deck was built above the existing railway lines, reestablishing a civic space and connection between the city and the Yarra River, making a new, inclusive civic space which is activated non-stop by the public. Did the public migrate to and activate this urban space immediately upon its opening?

DLB The building's official opening was on October 24, 2002, and it was not complete – the building on the corner overlooking the river, which is a café and restaurant, was still being constructed. On the back side of that building is where we have the big video screen, but at the time, they hadn't yet got the sound up and working. Every year, Melbourne hosts something called the Melbourne Racing Carnival, a horse racing festival. There's a big race called the Melbourne Cup which happens on the first Tuesday of every November, and it's a public holiday in

Victoria. All over Australia people put a bet down. It's a big day. We were in our office, and because we knew that they were going to show the race on the screen at Federation Square, we all left our office, a few blocks away from Federation Square. As we were walking towards Federation Square, and in the distance, we could see a line of people headed in one direction. It was in the middle of the afternoon, on a holiday, and people were not going to work, but there were trails of people on all the streets that were converging towards Federation Square. And as we arrived, the square was filling up with people who seemed to know this was the place to go, and we watched the horse race on the big screen – without sound. There was a gravitational pull to the square, and that is how it is whenever there's a public event like the World Cup or the Olympics. People know it's going to be happening there.

KS We are interested in the relationships of Federation Square to the body of work of Lab Architecture Studio, and your broader background as an educator for 15 years before proposing the Fed Square project. Were there projects, research, or teaching, which served as the springboard and led to your proposal for Federation Square? Or in other words, what was the genealogy of ideas, concepts, and techniques, which foregrounded your work on Federation Square?

DLB When Peter and I started Lab in 1994, Peter had been practicing. He had his own small office in London, mostly doing bars, cafes, and residential renovations or additions. I had mostly been teaching, at the AA, and then I launched a school in France, and then I came back to the AA as Head of Media Studies. I had worked for Daniel Libeskind on a couple of competitions (such as the Berlin Museum/Jewish Museum Berlin), and I had worked in offices in Houston and elsewhere before. So, when Peter and I started together, the only way to start doing anything was competitions. One of the first competitions we did was for the Cardiff Bay Opera House that was won by Zaha (Hadid) but then wasn't built. We did a competition in Scotland, which was an architecture and design center. We did another competition, the Wagga Wagga Civic Center, in New South Wales, Australia, and we were shortlisted as one of the last five on that. There were a lot of aspects of these projects which helped to feed into Federation Square. Federation Square was our 16th project, and the 15 projects before were all competitions, and some had aspects you could say were related or Federation Square. None of the earlier projects were a whole precinct – most other projects were singular buildings. We felt that whether we win a competition or not, it's a way of building up a body of work and a body of ideas, and that those ideas would get rethought and reconfigured and reanimated in other projects, and then that would lead to new research. We called our office "Lab" because it really came out of the notion of it being a laboratory. We didn't call it "Davidson and Bates", because it wasn't about us. It was called a "lab" as a laboratory. The school I had in France had a somewhat pretentious name called the Laboratory of Primary Studies in Architecture, shortened to LoPSiA.

When we started the practice, we called it Lab as a shortening of laboratory because we felt that that's what we wanted to do. We wanted to experiment and to test different ideas out. We didn't feel like there was just one idea. There were many ideas and different projects allowed for the articulation, development, and expansion of those ideas.

Federation Square was a part of that, but it wasn't it – there are ideas in Federation Square that came from previous projects, and there are things that we did in Federation Square that we use on other projects later as it developed.

KS How did the Federation Square project influence your thinking about architecture since its completion?

DLB When we worked on the Fed Square

competition, we had an office for Peter and myself and two students from the AA. Closer to the deadline for stage one, we had three or four more students join us. We started talking to some engineers, Atelier Ten, and Atelier One, across the street from Peter's office, and we had a landscape architect, Karres En Brands from the Netherlands. When we got shortlisted for the second stage, we had 21 people working on Fed Square in the office. Federation Square was a huge project and it was our first project, and the first building I've ever built that I've designed. We realized a project of that scale and dimension – not just with a large office - but with a lot of really good people.

Every competition, no matter what project, is the same size – 6 x A0 panels – whether you're doing a project like Federation Square, the Guggenheim Bilbao, or a competition for a new city in China, it's always presented on a fixed number of panels. You can manage that with a small number of people, but for a project that gets built, then suddenly it's not just that the size of the project demands more people, but expertise and ability, so we had to hire a lot of people. We (Peter and I) had to hire a lot of people so that they could tell us what we needed to do to tell them what to do – if that makes any sense. We had to have people that knew much more about building buildings than we did, yet we also had to control it, develop it, and lead it. We ended up staying in Melbourne because of the people who we could depend on, who could articulate and help us to develop ideas and to turn them into architectural possibilities. We didn't want to start over by returning to London. That was, for me, what we learned from the difference between working on competitions as a starting point and then moving onto another kind of scale in the development of the office.

KS Can you share with us a sense of the impact of the Federation Square project on Lab's projects afterwards?

DLB The irony is, even though I've stayed here for 26 years by now, we have never had another project in Australia. We did lots more competitions. We were shortlisted on an art gallery competition for Brisbane at the very end of Federation Square, and we were doing two competitions at the same time. We also did a competition for BMW in Leipzig, which we came in second place to Zaha Hadid, who built the project. We did other projects back in European cities, and we also did projects in cities across Asia. Peter had gone to Taiwan to present a project and passed through Hong Kong. Somebody said to him, "you should go to Beijing and give a lecture." He gave a lecture in Beijing and we got invited to do a competition for a project in Beijing with a group called SOHO China, and we won the competition. That was our second building – 170,000 m2 in two towers in Beijing. Once we did that, we started getting invited for projects in China. Peter was doing those. I went and started teaching at Cooper Union for a year and a half, and I passed through the Middle East on the way back to Europe. We received an award in Dubai for Fed Square. I met a friend who lived there, and he informed me that the Victorian Government had a business office in Dubai. I went there, they took me around and I met two dozen developers in Dubai, and then we got commissioned to do a few projects, and then we set up an office in Dubai. Then we were invited to give a lecture in Mumbai. And I went to Mumbai and then we got invited to do some projects in India. We ended up setting up an office in Delhi for a while. It is just the way it worked for us. We went to where we could get projects.

KS How has your teaching and your perspective as an academic leader been influenced by the achievements of building Federation Square?

DLB It has been influenced a lot. I still have some of the same theoretical or conceptual interests that I study, that I research, and that I look at. I am certainly not somebody who thinks that knowing what it takes to build a building means you have to change the way you think. In

terms of my interest in architecture, they remained as theoretical and as conceptual as before. I think with students, a lot has changed since I was first teaching in comparison to what it takes to teach now. Some of the fundamentals that I'm interested in remain the same.

The line is the fundamental tool of architecture because it's how we make differences. Part of the role of the architect is not about difference in terms of simply being different in the world, but that what we do differentiates the world, between inside and outside, between public and private, between social space and nonsocial space, between civic and domestic.

I think some of those things are still the same. How we produce new kinds of lines and how we understand new production techniques and technologies in our thinking about spatial relationships and spatial organization – I think that has changed.

KS Your presentation and this interview in this series, Beyond the Envelope, are set within a Master of Architecture course here at NYIT. In this context, can you please share with us, from your point of view, any advice you may have for the next generation of architects?

DLB What I have the most trouble with currently is there is so much to know. At University of Melbourne, we have a three year undergraduate degree and then a two year master of architecture degree; still only five years. My undergraduate was five years and then I did three years of a master's degree. I just feel like there are not enough teaching hours and enough learning hours to learn what one needs to learn to be a contemporary architect. It's frustrating sometimes because everything that our students are learning is absolutely fundamental and necessary. There are other things they're not getting a chance to learn and they're not expected to as part of their degree. They may come back and do a PhD, but receiving a master's degree after only five years of complete study just seems undercooked. I think it should take a minimum of six or if not seven years. I graduated in 1978 with an undergraduate degree. All that I studied then is still necessary today. Then, there's everything that we've learned since 1978 that's necessary. If anything, the school years should be increasing rather than decreasing, because there's just so much to know. I remain very thirsty for knowledge and experience and the current academic programs are just too short. I know you don't want to hear that as a student because you'd like to get out sooner rather than later. Personally, I think you should stay longer.

KS Thank you very much for the special opportunity to interview today and for your generosity to share your thoughts and reflections. Thank you.

TV Thank you so much for your generosity in your responses in this interview. It has been a treat to hear your reflections and insights.

DLB It was a pleasure. Thank you all. Goodbye.

MUSEUM OF ART, ARCHITECTURE AND TECHNOLOGY MAAT

Lisbon, 2016 | Amanda Levete Architecture AL_A

Program Galleries, education centre, shop, café

Materials Ceramic tile, moleanos limestone

IDENTITY

Solid	85%
Glazing	15%
Ceramic Tiles	15,0003D
Different Ceramic Tile Types	3
Long Elevation	190 M
High	12 M
Floors Above Ground	2
Floors Below Ground	1
GFA	8,000 M2

INTERVIEW

Interviewee: Maximiliano Arrocet, Director, AL_A

Interviewers: Nidhi Gohel, Vishesh Patel, final year Master of Architecture student, School of Architecture and Design, New York Institute of Technology

April 5, 2023

Tom Verebes Thank you, Maximiliano, for your presentation of this subtle but spectacular project – proof that impact in the urban environment can be created by a building so low it is an urban surface. I would like to introduce our interviewers, final year Master of Architecture students in the School of Architecture and Design at NYIT, Nidhi Gohel and Vishesh Patel.

Nidhi Gohel Thank you for your fantastic presentation! I am Nidhi Gohel, and it is an honour to interview you about the MAAT project. Located on the edge of the Tagus River in Lisbon's Belém district, the MAAT is the focus of EDP Foundation's masterplan for an art campus on the riverfront, creating a unique locale from which to capture views of all of Lisbon. In reconnecting the city to the waterfront, can you summarize the ways in which this project repairs gaps and disjunctions between the center of Lisbon and the waterfront? In general, was the MAAT project conceived in the larger urban context as an agent of urban regeneration?

Maximiliano Arrocet Thank you. Belém, the site of the MAAT, is not really in the centre of Lisbon. The centre of the city is considered to be the Plaza del Comercio which was once connected to the riverfront all the way through to Belém. When we started working on the MAAT project there was a clear disconnect between the city and its waterfront. Before our intervention, the riverfront only touched the city at Praça do Comércio - one of many projects that the city of Lisbon had in mind to reconnect with the river. There are a series of projects in Comércio, including the Expo. A lot of other new projects have since been completed and have actually been regenerative, moving life in the city back to the river. This helped reconnect open land and the riverfront adjacent to the MAAT museum, along with Museu Nacional dos Coches, the new museum by Mendes da Rocha. In the MAAT project, it was critical to reconnect the city and it was one of many projects the city had called the Arco del Rio, meaning the "arc of the river". It very much promoted all projects to do something similar to what we did. I could say this is a success story, and I think there are other great success stories along the river. The municipality of Lisbon and the mayor have done a great job in regenerating the city.

NG Thank you. In urban design terms, this site is informed by the flows as a civic destination, but also by its infrastructural role which allows people to move through and traverse the city. How has the city been extended by the MAAT intervention? How has the MAAT project created a community?

MA It is very difficult to capture the imagination of an entire city, and somehow the MAAT has been able to do that.

One of the many reasons that the MAAT has been a successful project is because it is a place where you can see sunrise and sunset, and somehow there is something magical about that.

This is probably rooted in how deep it is to see the sunrise and the sunset. This is a place where you can feel part of a community and I think that is one of the secrets of the success of this project. The use of shade from the sun has also been a very fundamental part of the project to create public space, because people in Lisbon really look for shade at certain times of the year.

Having an elevated platform in front of the river is unique, as it provides a vantage point that you wouldn't otherwise have. It is a mixture between the unique lighting conditions and relationships that you have with the sun, the advantage of the upper public space and the fact that we designed it as an amphitheater so people could sit. They have outdoor cinema nights in summer. This civic space is successfully activated, and I do think that having an area that is cooler and provides shade has been fundamental.

NG This is great to hear. How else does the site attract crowds? And how does the MAAT building instigate activity, and what different kinds of uses or events have been enabled by

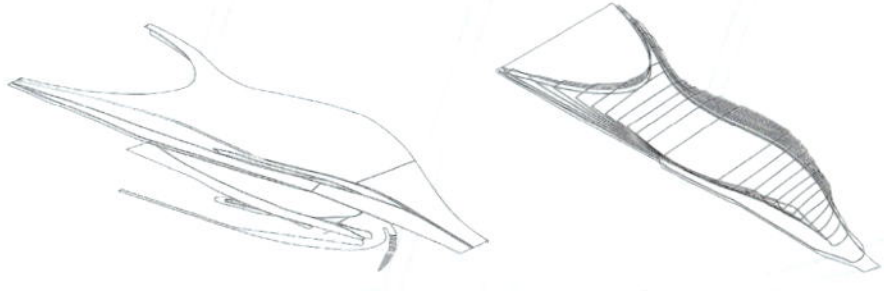

Axonometric diagrams of interior floors and exterior civic surface

the civic surfaces of the MAAT site?

MA Part of the success of this building is that it does not need to be programmed to be successful. You don't need someone to actively program activities and events at the MAAT for people to go there. People congregate there naturally because it effectively acts like a three-dimensional roundabout. If you are in Belém and you want to go to the riverfront, you have to walk across the roof, and suddenly you find yourself in the amphitheater. You find places of urban comfort, and people gather there because it is comfortable. This civic space immediately creates community. It is a hotspot for skaters and cyclists as well and they love it. Different artists have staged interventions and installations outside. There is the possibility of setting up a bar for night events. As I said, I think the fundamental success of the building is that it does not need programming to be occupied.

NG How do you see the agency of transformative new architecture to regenerate cities? And, did you expect the extent of reactivation in this part of the city?

MA No, we didn't expect this extent of activation. As an architect, you always dream that you're going to be able to regenerate a part of a city that despite time will continue to flourish. We are incredibly happy about how the people of Lisbon have adopted the MAAT

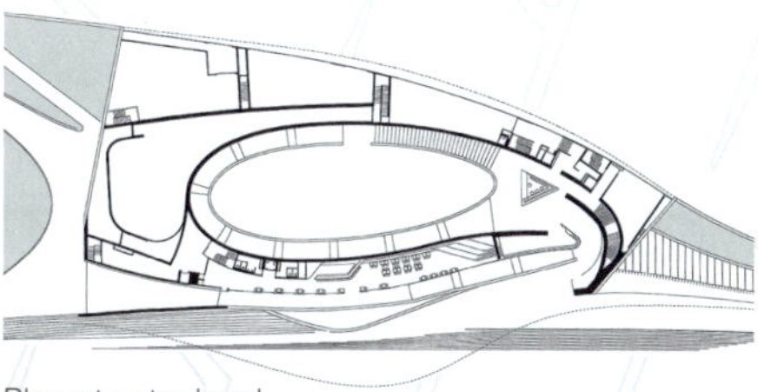

Plan at entry level

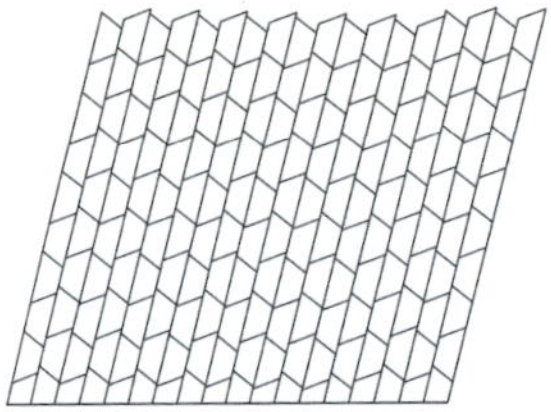

as a new cultural hub and I think that is really important. The language of this building can only be situated in Lisbon. The solar path and the curvature of the building is only possible in Lisbon, because it is unique to its location, and the materials, ceramics, are used everywhere throughout the city. It is as if all the buildings surrounding us had the same idea that all the vertical elements of architecture are clad in ceramics. So, the architecture of this particular project can only be located in Lisbon. The MAAT is definitively contemporary architecture but it is deeply rooted in its locale.

NG This masterplan includes the adaptive reuse of the Central Tejo power station as well as a new museum project in which an abstract contemporary space was created. It is rare for an architectural commission to include both a strikingly new piece of architecture and the adaptive reuse of a disused industrial building. Can you share with us how you developed the difference in architectural language and the expression between the renovation and transformation of the disused power plant (inherited from the industrial revolution) and the new building for the MAAT?

MA Firstly, to clarify, we did not take part in the refurbishment of the existing industrial building. It was a project that was happening in parallel, and obviously we worked together as a team. Our brief evolved very much from an analysis of the types of spaces that they had in the existing building which were mainly orthogonal, which is very good for a traditional kind of gallery and exhibition space. It was well lit on most occasions. Some rooms have no lighting, so they were good for multimedia exhibitions. The brief for the extension of the building actually hides a substation which most people do not know. I think it's important to understand that the brief developed alongside the existing building and the type of spaces that we generated were to complement what was already there. Also, we had interviews with different artists from which we understood there was a need for a space for artists to occupy and make their own. There is

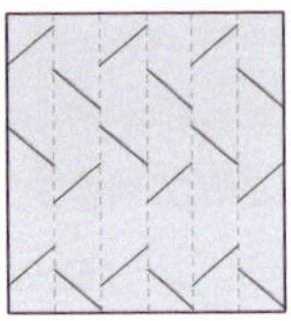

Deviated Pattern

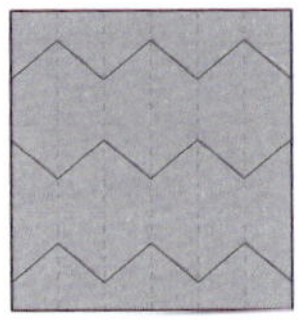

Aligned Pattern

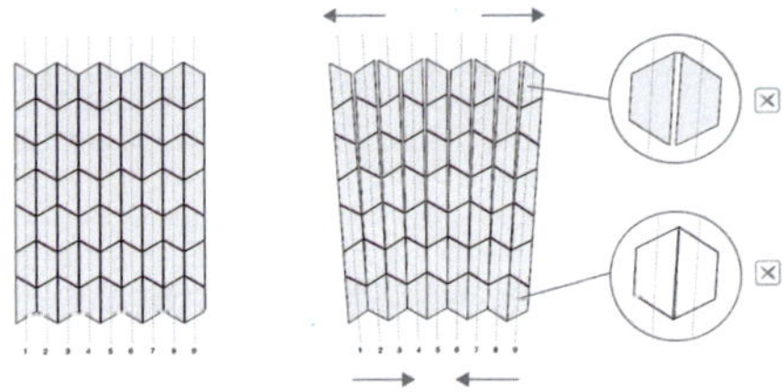

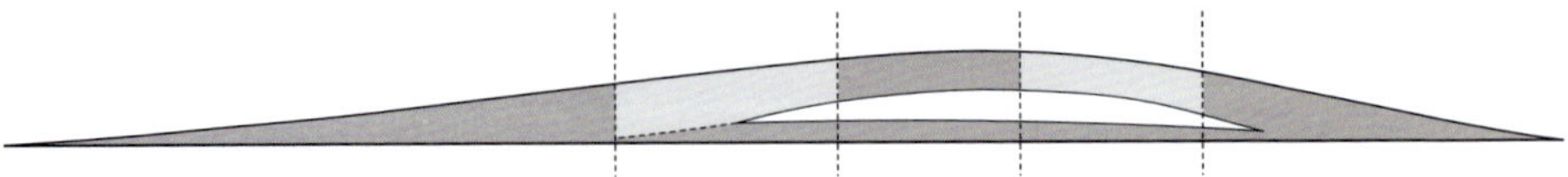

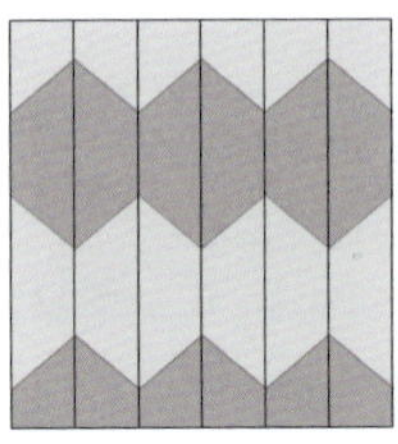

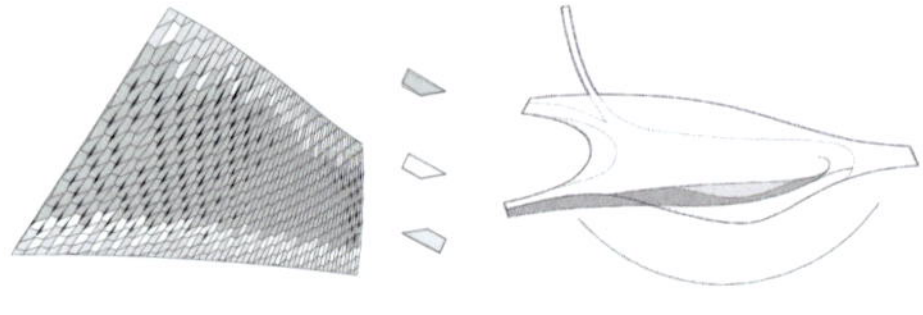

Logic of 3 patterns and their arrays

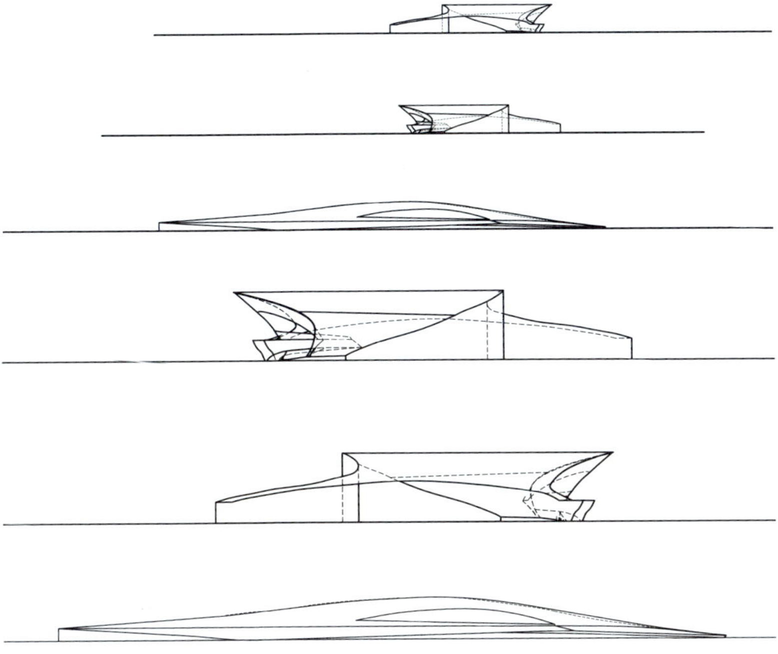

Wireframe elevations of spatial identity

a symbiosis, if you want, in the type of spaces that we had generated.

NG The MAAT explores contemporary culture through exhibitions in the disciplines of visual arts, new media, architecture, technology, and science. Museums are often conceived with the promise of benefits to their host city. Ultimately, can the impact of this architectural project upon its host city be characterized as "The Bilbao Effect", or in other words, has the MAAT had a transformative effect upon Lisbon, serving to attract large numbers of tourists and citizens?

MA I don't think the MAAT has quite created the Guggenheim effect. Lisbon already had a very healthy tourism industry and has many attractive places to visit, while Bilbao was a regional city of great industrial importance. Most people outside Spain did not really know Bilbao, so the Guggenheim Museum was transformative in a different way. The Guggenheim also has a collection of incredible art while in the MAAT, there is no permanent collection of art. The MAAT is more transformative at a public space level – redefining what public space is in a city. It definitely attracts huge numbers of visitors, but the situations are slightly different. The MAAT is also a success story, but it is a success story at a different level. The Guggenheim was very important for Bilbao as an attractor, and the MAAT is more of a way of redefining what public space is within the city.

NG Whilst the massing of the MAAT project can be read as low key and subtle due to its low profile and height, it is also an abstract, even radical building in how it endorses contemporaneity, or The New. How do you feel about calling this piece of architecture iconic?

MA Well, that is a difficult question. I do not think it is for us to define the building in that way. Generally at AL_A, there is a certain negative connotation to "iconic architecture", and when we work on our projects, we very intentionally try not to think in terms of whether it will become an "icon" or not. Unavoidably, when you create a project of this dimension, ultimately it does become a symbol. People

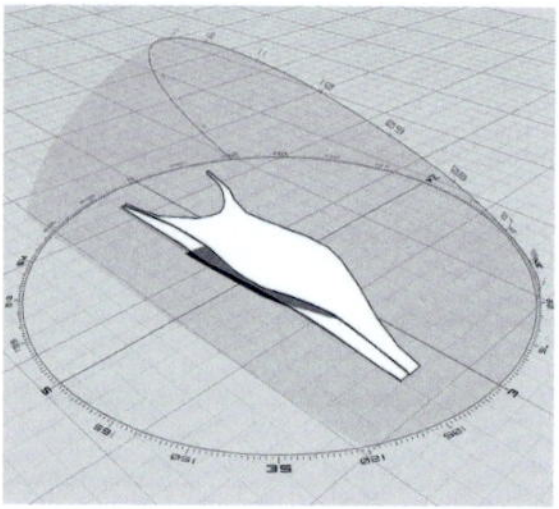

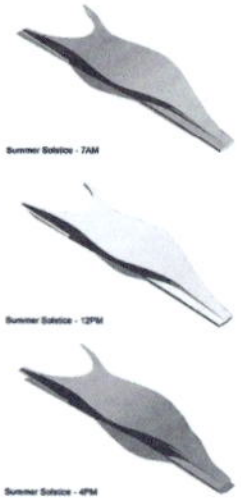

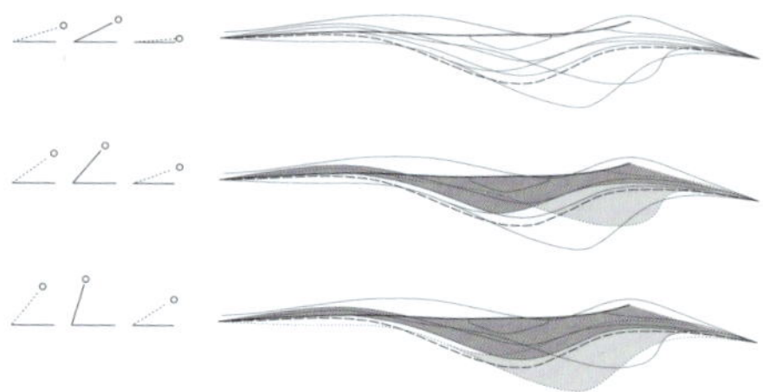

do recognize it, perhaps as an "icon", but that is not the way that we perceive architecture. I think only time will tell. It has definitely become one of the symbols of the city but we are careful not to use the term "iconic architecture".

NG Our next question concerns the spatial organization of the MAAT. The surface organization creates the urban potential, as you have published, to walk OVER, UNDER, and THROUGH the museum complex from the urban ground and waterfront, to the elevated civic space on the roof. These spatial maneuvers embed public space into the interior of the museum, sunken six meters below grade. Can you explain how the interior of the building captures the flows of an urban population?

MA The whole project is a complex network of ramps. We have ramps to go to the top of the building. We have ramps which go to different levels other than the main level. There is the level of the river walk, which is the level where we had to establish the entry of the museum, which is elevated to avoid a potential flood from the river. Once you arrive at that level, then we slowly start ramping people down, and you have an option to go in two directions, and that is where the big oval space starts. As you head towards the perimeter of the oval shape, one route is along a very long ramp that takes you to the back of the oval on the opposite side, and the other route is a generous stepped set of surfaces. Once you are in the oval, there are different connection points to different parts of the building. All these spaces are hyper connected, and this is before you know if you are on a different level, because of the experience of moving on oblique ramps. The idea was to create these interconnected spaces that could be used in different ways. In this sense, the museum can be split into different modes depending on what the artists want to do. In an organic flow of how spaces move along each other, this then leads you back to the entry point, and outside. We have always looked at the interior of the museum as part of a continuation of what is happening on the exterior. Inside and outside are actually fluidly related. We wanted to have an air curtain, and no entry doors at the entrance, but we didn't manage to convince the museum that it was a good idea. It was also incredibly expensive from an energy consumption perspective. Our ideal solution would have been not to have an entry door so that you could walk freely in and out of the museum, but practicalities did not allow for this.

NG How did you determine the final form, topography, and surface organization of the exterior civic spaces, and related to this, please tell us why the gallery level was designed to be sunken 6m meters below the ground level?

MA It all has to do with the ramps, and what we were trying to achieve. To understand the different levels of the building and the maximum level we could achieve by turning ramps. For the differently abled, this is a long route that can be taken all the way up, landing at the bridge where the ground is level. In this sense, we were limited as to how high the building could be. We also had another condition: we did not want the MAAT to be an obstacle for the visual connection to the city, so our only option was to go underground which was very complex, because obviously the site is reclaimed land, and we were underneath it. This was complicated from a construction perspective, but we really thought the building

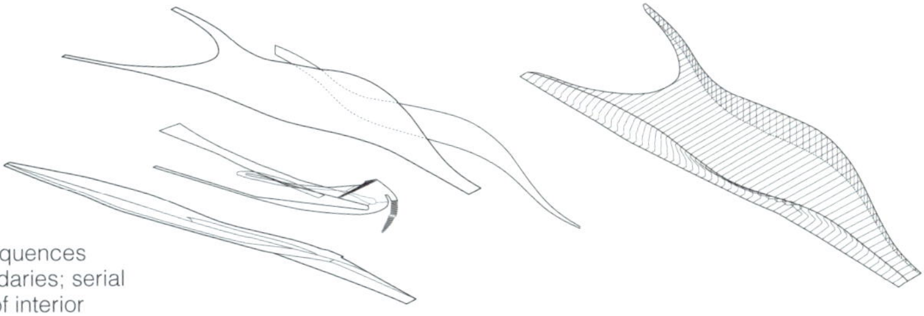

Spatial sequences and boundaries; serial sections of interior

would only be successful if we managed to maintain this external ramp at a different slope. Ultimately, the geometry of the building is generated by a very long and intense period of exploration, of flow diagrams and accessibility. And then, the fine touch to the complex pathways and geometries was the movement of time. I am quite confident to say that this was completely generated by pathways of human flow, and by the movement of time.

NG We would like to now focus on the ways in which the MAAT creates dynamic and differentiated material effects, in how we experience, perceive, and interact with the exterior surfaces. In particular, the ceramic cladding of the riverside elevation and canopy which stage different reflections of color throughout different seasons, weather conditions, and at different times of day. Please can you expand on the decision to use ceramic tiles in this project? And, has the success of these material and visual effects helped to develop wider methods to interact with daylight and ambient conditions to create material effects, ultimately which can be applied to other projects?

MA Ceramics is a wonderful material because it allows you to play with different textures, depths, and with different glazes, even if you decide to use white ceramics, and of course, there no such thing as white. We explored the material by adding different minerals to it to create different qualities. Ceramics are pretty unique. There is also a sustainability narrative of using ceramics. Using white was definitely the right decision in the project, and this project was, for us, like doing a PhD in ceramics. We have learned a lot, and not only on this project, but also in our projects in V&A in London and the Maggie's Centre in Southampton. I think we have adopted ceramics as one of our preferred materials to explore. Ceramics can create different qualities, and even different kinds of mechanical characteristics.

NG This project encourages architecture to use daylight as visual media. In our seminar, we discussed Le Corbusier's famous statement, authored one hundred years ago: "Architecture is the masterly, correct, and magnificent play of masses brought together in light. Our eyes are made to see forms in light: light and shade reveal these forms." Le Corbusier was referring to platonic solids – spheres and cubes or planar surfaces, or "pure forms" or "platonic solids", as he referred to architectural form. The geometries of the MAAT project are dynamic and complex, and not platonic, prismatic and pure forms. Can you characterize the distinction between the modernists' notions of the behavior of light qualities on planar and smooth surfaces, to the complex surfaces articulated with rippling patterns of reflections created by the ceramic tiles on these surfaces?

MA I like the quote. I do think daylight was very important for us when we were looking at the different geometries that we could use. What was critical about this façade was generating it to be used as a roof surface. The qualities of the roof purpose means that you can actually build it using a series of straight lines, if you want, and in between two straight lines. Then you can connect to straight lines that are different planes using equilateral triangles. The hexagon is subdivided into a series of equilateral triangles, and the decision to make the shape two-dimensional instead of planar gave us the opportunity to use a hexagon split in half and made three dimensional.

This is fundamental for how you perceive light, and how it plays with Platonic solids, and our perception. I do not think there is such a distinction between modern geometry and classical geometry. Geometry is a universal language, but we have new tools that allow us to explore spaces and effects with more complexity. I do not see much difference in the appreciation of light effects on geometry one hundred years ago, and how light plays with geometry as we did in the MAAT.

NG Can you tell us a bit more about the flow and movement of the sun path over a day, and how the large overhanging canopy at the waterfront has been designed to create shade and a civic space in hot summer months?

MA We worked with diagrams of projected shadows. The top line of this diagram projects the building. The pink line is the line of the oculus, the big skylight.

We worked with different projections of the shadows at different times of the year: the winter solstice; two equinoxes; the summer solstice, all project different shadows. The entire front of the project was formed using shadows – we were sculpting with shadows, which is quite a poetic way of understanding how we designed this.

We used models and ultimately, we also were assisted by early forms of virtual reality, to try to understand how we could truly sculpt using shadows.

VP We would like to shift our discussion towards the space planning of the museum. AL_A deployed the geometry of an ellipse as a space planning device. Can you characterize the qualities of spaces created, and can you explain how the flows of crowds interact with exhibition in these elliptical spaces?

MA We also had many discussions about the geometry of the space. We tried to create a new type of gallery space that did not exist in Lisbon. We traveled to Lisbon, and analysed all the existing museums in the city, including all the spaces that they had in the existing building neighboring us, the original Museum of Electricity. Most were organised with orthogonal rooms. What was interesting to us is that when you generate an ellipse, you use two focus points. A circle has a focal point at the center of the circle, and with the radius you derive the circle. With two focal points, you enter the building at a slightly higher level, and then you start to ramp down in two directions, and before you know it you are actually navigating the space around the ellipse and you experience the space at different heights. You start at a higher vantage point but by the time that you circulate around the ellipse you are at the lowest point of the museum, and that was a very interesting quality to us, because it meant that the artists could occupy that large volume and it can be seen from different vantage points. We had conversations with several artists, because we saw this as a space which could be used differently by different artists who could make it their own. The rationale behind this space involved testing many geometries, but the oval geometry was an important one. This space opened up different spatial possibilities of how a gallery space can be curated and used by artists.

VP Can you share with us the distinction of the elliptical space planning of the galleries compared with a more traditional enfilade model of organization of museums, in which a series of boxes are arranged in sequence?

MA Sure. We did not plan the elliptical space as a traditional gallery where artists could use the walls to display art. We imagined it as a spatial exploration of the elliptical space with two focal points. We imagined what would happen if an object was placed in the center and where the visual lines are drawn. The ellipse has two focus points that are deliberately relatively close to each other, and we tested this using different art objects of different sizes and different configurations. The planning of the elliptical gallery was not done traditionally – we explored and all sorts of different configurations and subdivisions of the ellipse.

VP Our next question concerns the relationship of the MAAT project to the larger body of work of AL_A. Further to your presentation, can you share with us the genealogy of the design of the MAAT project within the body of work by AL_A? Are there projects which led to this project, as earlier prototypes which you developed further?

MA We see our MAAT and our V&A projects as siblings. They were developed at the same time and although different people were working on these two projects, all the directors at AL_A work across all projects, so it is very difficult to understand how one project influences another. These are two projects in which we explored ceramics. In the case of the V&A, we used porcelain, because the V&A has a huge collection of porcelain. We also went underground for the V&A, for completely different reasons, but we also excavated. Another parallel is that the V&A could only be in London in the same way that the language we generated for the architecture of the MAAT is very much rooted in Lisbon. There are so many parallels and mutual influences, as they were developed alongside each other, which is why I call them siblings. Both the V&A extension and the MAAT were the two largest projects so far for AL_A. Both explored our approach to architecture which evolved to mark a distinction with the earlier work of Future Systems. With the V&A and the MAAT, we had developed a different way of looking at architecture, which has impacted most of the projects that we do now in the office. This is not so much an architectural language, because we rethink our architectural language every time we start a new project. These projects gave us the courage to be strong conceptually, to believe in our narratives, and to not be fearful of rethinking established typological and programmatic models of museums. A museum is similar to a public space, as we have developed both of these cases. We have been fortunate to have the opportunity to push the boundaries of designing public space.

VP The MAAT project was completed seven years ago. Can you please share with us how the MAAT project, both as a museum and an urban design project has influenced the recent and current work of AL_A? In more broad terms, what has been the impact of the MAAT project on your practice and more recent portfolio of projects?

MA The project I have been working on for the last three and a half years is a Fusion Demonstration Plant, which is quite different, and it is difficult to find parallels, other than the way we approach materiality, our understanding of sustainability, and of how people flow through spaces. The MAAT gave us the confidence to pursue an alternative way of looking at things, and it has definitely influenced the way that we think of design. What we are not doing is replicating the type of architectural language we developed for the MAAT. We never do a project that has the same architectural language as a previous project, because, as I said in the case of the MAAT, it is unique to this situation in Lisbon, and the influence of the context is at a very deep level, not a superficial level.

NG This interview and the study of the set of projects in Beyond the Envelope series of presentations and interviews are set within a Master of Architecture course here at NYIT. As such, your audience in this event, and this interview, are future architects. Given this context, can you please share with us, from your point of view, any advice you may have for the next generation of architects?

MA We face a time of real change, and this is a time to be brave. It is a time to truly explore what public space means for our cities. It is a time to challenge models that have stagnated, but it is also a time to reflect on some of architecture's more traditional values. We need to go back to the responsibilities of the architect. We can see, even in the Renaissance, or even before in Vitruvius' Ten Books of Architecture, which effectively tells the reader what the qualities of the architect should be and what he or she needs to master. It is our responsibility to go back to that polymath way of working as an architect, and this is a great challenge.

I have been playing a little bit with Chat GPT as I suspect you all have been too. There are going to be huge changes in the next 10-20 years, and the role of the architect will need to evolve. There are certain values of the classical notion of the architect that are still valid today and we should face up to the challenge to bring back of those notions. It is a challenging time to be an architect on many different levels, and it is definitely a fascinating time to be alive. You will be graduating at a very exciting time.

NG Thank you very much for your presentation and for the special opportunity to interview you today.

TV This has been a great opportunity to hear your insights on the MAAT project and your work in general at AL_A. Thank you for your in-depth presentation and for your generosity with your time to engage in our seminar and our public lectures and events series.

MA Thank you very much for having me, it was a pleasure to receive your invitation and to be here with you all today.

TAI KWUN, CENTRE FOR HERITAGE AND ART

Hong Kong, 2018 | Herzog & de Meuron

Program New buildings: Art Gallery, multi-purpose auditorium, covered outdoor gathering space, café, reception, shop Heritage buildings and spaces: Public Square, Piazza and Laneways, Visitor & Education Centre, Heritage Interpretation Spaces and Tours, Boutique Shops, Restaurants, Bars, Multi-purpose halls for events, Police Station, Offices

IDENTITY

GFA	27,000 M2
Open Courtyard Area	4,000 M2
Landscape	500 M2
Floor Below Ground	1
Floors Above Ground	4
Facade Modules Total	8,400
Different Typical Module Types	4
Glazing	10%
Solid	90%

INTERVIEW

INTERVIEW WITH: Ascan Mergenthaler, Senior Partner, Herzog & de Meuron

INTERVIEWERS: Yuti Kothari, Gyongok Tammy Noh, Sohui Noh, M.Arch students, School of Architecture and Design, New York Institute of Technology

Tom Verebes Thank you, Ascan, for your presentation of the Tai Kwun project, and for sharing your reflections and insights on the project. I would like to introduce our interviewers, final year M.Arch students at NYIT, Yuti Kothari, Tammy Noh, and Sohui Noh, who will jointly conduct this interview with you.

Gyongok Tammy Noh We would like to start this interview with several questions on the context of the project, in particular the historic context of the project, as a reuse of the former Central Police Headquarters of Hong Kong. Aside from the limited size of the Tai Kwun site, especially as it is nested within one of the densest cities in the world, Hong Kong, did you face any other challenges related to the transformation of the historical context from a formerly closed-off part of the city to become open public space?

Ascan Mergenthaler The challenge with Tai Kwun was that, on the one hand, we wanted to convey that this used to be a prison and a police station and not destroy the history of this significant site in Hong Kong. On the other hand, we wanted to open it up. As a result, the few interventions we made on the site were very precise and almost surgical. What struck us when we toured the decommissioned Central Police Station site for the very first time is that there are many different types of spaces, from tight alleys to small squares, to larger squares, plazas, yards and grounds – something we know from the European city. It felt, oddly for a prison, quite comfortable. That is what set the tone in terms of how we defined the spaces we created and our insertion of the new buildings. They pick up this language of very diverse outdoor public spaces and seamlessly continue this story and add to it. The context was less of a problem because our client, the charities group of the Hong Kong Jockey Club, was a very strong ally in this project. During the initial studies, we had many discussions, presentations, and exchanges with authorities and other stakeholders and important

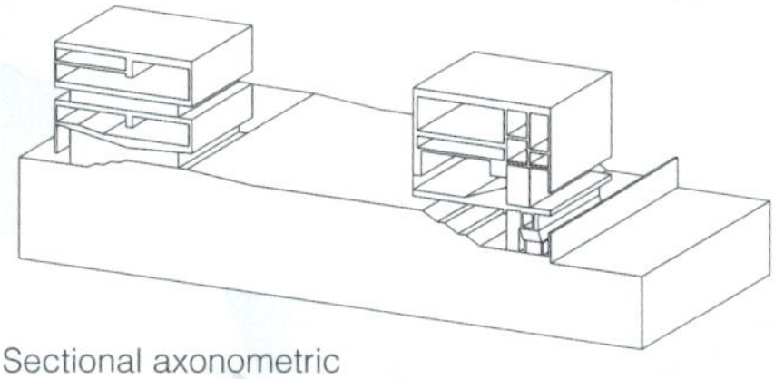

Sectional axonometric

community groups. It became clear that we would need the input of a heritage architecture consultant and, together with the client, we decided to bring Purcell on board. They were a great help in determining some of the moves we made. We prepared a very thorough storyline to explain the rationale behind keeping, altering, or demolishing buildings within the site. The original buildings are of no great architectural significance, yet they are an important part of Hong Kong's history.

GTN Our next question focuses on the materiality and context of the project, and how your design decisions and the final outcome were impacted by the proximity of "the world's factory", China. With regards to the recycled aluminum modules making up the façades of the two new buildings, in which ways did the specific industrial context of Hong Kong, and especially of Shenzhen, impact decisions made during the design and production stages, and the final outcome of the project?

AM We felt the most sustainable approach to this façade was to work with an industry which is local. We have worked on many projects in China that explored a variety of local traditional materials such as bricks, ceramics and so on. For the two new buildings of Tai Kwun, we assessed that brick or a similarly mineral material was not the right approach due to its weight and our aim to differentiate the new interventions from the existing brick and stone buildings. We looked at other local industries to create an innovative, lighter, higher functioning, and stronger façade system. This led us to the aluminum industry which is very present in Shenzhen. We approached various companies, developed our design with them and started producing a series of full-scale mock-ups. These experiments in Shenzhen were insightful but we also found that the companies could only deliver to a certain level – let's say up to a 90% of what was needed for the facade to work very well, but the last 10% was missing as it was not precise or consistent enough. So unfortunately, we could not produce the façade elements locally, despite our hope and efforts to do so. The façade modules were finally produced in Australia where we could achieve the high standards of quality required. Our only hesitation was due to the transport, which was not ideal in terms of carbon footprint and sustainability, though shipping the aluminum bricks from Australia was relatively straightforward and the distance was not so far. With our second project in Hong Kong, the M+ Museum, we had the same experience. We decided to work with ceramics for the façade and started off with local fabrication and manufacturers because ceramics are a very old tradition in Chinese and Asian culture. But ultimately they simply could not deliver the quality and precision needed for such a complex building and the ceramic components were produced in Italy. It's a complex world, full of unexpected routes.

SN Probing deeper into the design to construction workflow and processes of the modular façade, can you describe the design and production processes followed, the ways you worked in the office and with your fabricator, how design information was controlled, how decisions were made, and how you arrived at 4 types of modules?

AM In terms of computer technology, Revit was our main tool for the façade of Tai Kwun. We treated the building as a naked volume, mapping out the technical requirements of different parts of the façade which resulted in dedicated zones of varied openness. For example, in one area we needed it to be 80% open, and in other areas 40% or 20%, to accommodate windows, air intakes, or air outlets behind the façade. Based on this, we developed the four modules of bricks with different open areas, then we arranged each brick in the digital model accordingly. There was some scripting involved but basically every single brick was drawn and positioned in the 3D Revit model, and these 3D files were sent to the fabricator. The two new buildings were quite complex and required the dedication of a person in our office for a few months to coordinate and refine these elements.

SN Can you share with us how you generated the configuration and prototyped the composition of the aluminum bricks and the various openings of each component? How did you determine and manipulate the certain level of automation while still maintaining the versatility of the design?

AM We started off by building a very simple Styrofoam form in our office, immediately jumping into 1:1 scale as we wanted to understand it physically. Without losing any time building small scale models, we understood very quickly that we wanted these bricks to be about 90cm x 30cm as a reference to the important historic granite walls surrounding the entire Central Police Station Compound. We cut Styrofoam blocks of that size, then literally carved them out. We eventually built some sections of the walls in our studio and studied the size of openings, what you see through the bricks, the radius of corners, if the shape should be more squarish, and so on. All these qualities were already explored in-house before we discussed it with a manufacturer. One interesting aspect is that the bricks have a smoother side which we thought would be the visible side, facing the exterior. We modeled these in the office and made them hollow on the other side to reduce the mass. When we turned the blocks around, everyone on the team thought, "Wow that's actually much more interesting!" The back has more depth and creates a complex play of lights and shadow, especially from a distance.

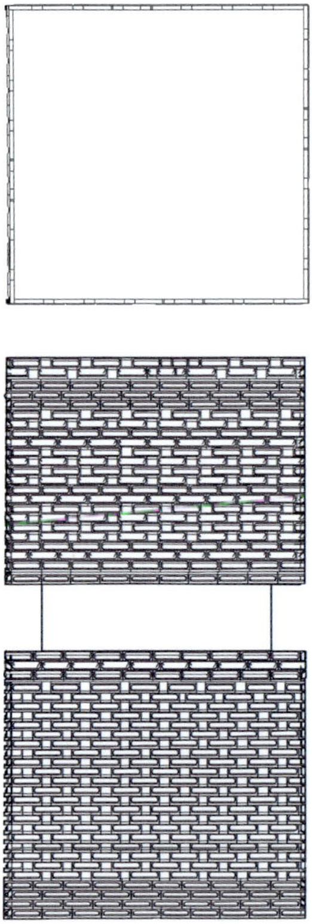

Façade modules arrayed onto the facade screen

We are always interested in how the perception of a building changes throughout the day, animated by daylight and different environmental conditions.

So, we decided to flip the brick modules inside-out. It is also compelling from the inside because then you are close to it and have the smooth and finer surface in front of your eyes which is very nice. This process of physically making the modules in-house where design parameters are tested and defined before going to the aluminum fabricator is very important, in our experience. With not only drawings but also our Styrofoam blocks, it was easier for the fabricators to grasp our ideas and intentions. We could then immediately have a back-and-forth about precise adjustments of a few millimeters, surface treatments, thicknesses, structural strength, and so forth.

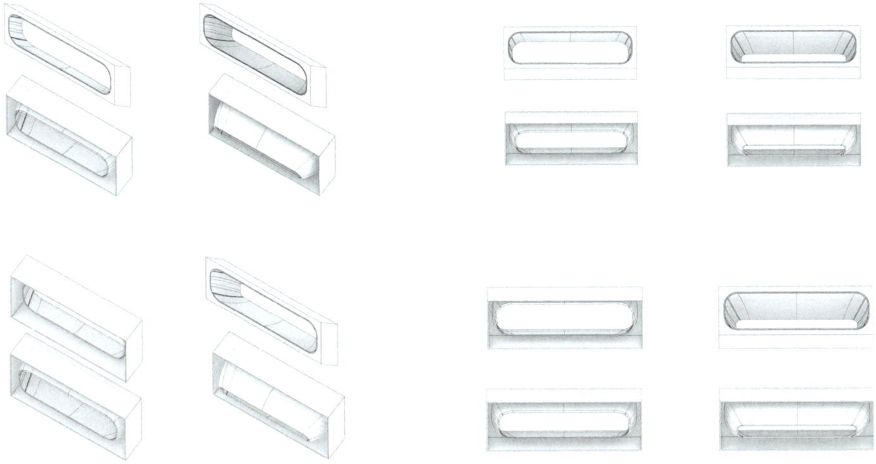

Diagrams of four facade module types

YK Thank you for your in-depth answer. I would like to shift to a discussion of the visual impact and performance of the façade. In terms of the effects and affects of porosity, patterning, and expression of the facade, how did you conceive the entire façade – with respect to daylight, artificial lighting, and views inside and out. How were the effects tested or simulated? Tell us about the prototyping process and how it assisted in the making design decisions.

AM The porosity is very important because the added buildings are the new central source of cooling for the entire site. The massive mechanical plants always need a lot of open areas in the façade – and one reason why we created these deep bricks so that from most angles you cannot see through them. With a thin metal screen which is 60% or 80% open, you would see everything. Additionally, the depth of our brick not only connotes the granite block reference, it has a much better screening effect, acting as a "brise soleil" for the windows and for the entire building. The aluminum blocks also work as a heat sink – they collect solar energy and become hot during the day while reducing the heat gain on the main building envelope, then during the night they release this stored heat. It is an effective thermal envelope to deal with the extreme heat conditions of Hong Kong. The brick's depth also had a benefit in reducing light spillage from the building to the surroundings, which was a concern expressed by the neighborhood groups in public consultations.

The louvers of the brick refract light, so there is no artificial light pollution. Instead they give a soft glow from the inside so you sense activities are taking place, which is something we really wanted and felt was important.

YK How did the extraordinary corner detail of the façade come about? What challenges did you face in developing it? In your AD article on the Tai Kwun cultural center, you discuss the corner detail as imperfect yet a strong one. Can you describe this distinction between a strong and a weak corner?

AM The most logical and cleanest way of making this corner would be a miter joint, a very simple cut to two bricks at 45 degrees each to wrap perfectly around

Daylight analysis of façade screen

the corner. We tested this in renderings and then 3D models, but it didn't feel right because this continuous vertical cut weakens the corner structurally and visually cuts apart the building into separate planes. Instead, by cutting the aluminum blocks straight and then alternating them in rotation – as in typical brick walls where a structural bond is needed at the corner – we could interlock the modules and 'knit' the facades together around the corner. The actual cut of each block reacts to the geometry of the adjacent block, which results in an interesting irregular cutting line. But it was also impossible to match the geometries of the two adjacent blocks completely, and this slight imperfection makes the corner even stronger. It adds an aspect of craftsmanship, and, like in the historic buildings where corners are often also treated in a special way, it creates a unique moment with the tools and methods of today. You could not design these special details – they just happen. Almost by accident, something becomes really striking and beautiful as a result of an inherent logic of construction.

SN Regarding the energy strategy of the Tai Kwun, given the aggregated material organization of the volume, the unit block serves to break down the façade surface, reducing reflectivity and glare especially during the daytime. Also, the façade plays an important role for rain protection. Can you describe the energy scheme for the building, including passive and mechanical cooling and ventilation? To what extent does the façade screen reduce heat gain?

AM The deep façade of aluminum reduces external solar gain by mitigating the heat transferred to the building itself. Additionally, the cavity behind this deep aluminum brise-soleil is open and ventilated so that the excess heat is removed naturally. This is new and an important contributor to the passive cooling of the building – one could say that the entire building is clad with cooling ribs. The overall mechanical system is fairly traditional and now, ten years later, one would probably try to work with a more innovative system. We looked into geothermal, wind harvesting and photovoltaic panels, but they are not so effective in Hong Kong because of the overcast skies. Today, these are systems I would have liked to explore more, yet what we have done is very different to many other projects in Hong Kong and an important step in the right direction. For example, for the interior climate control of the galleries, we are working with displacement ventilation, which is a much more energy efficient system as it is based on low velocity air coming in from below, instead of forced air from above. Energy use is reduced as it follows the natural flow of air instead of pressing the high velocity air downwards. On this basis, Tai Kwun is a very efficient building.

YK Our next question concerns the influence of your past projects and the impact of the Tai Kwun project on the larger body of projects by Herzog & de Meuron. How has the Tai Kwun project influenced the design of further projects by Herzog & de Meuron? Would you agree that the application of digital fabrication in the field of architecture has aided processes of design and construction?

AM Tai Kwun was informed by our work on many other previous projects, especially our expertise developed over many years of working with existing buildings in historic contexts. Though they are more challenging with certain issues, historic buildings can inspire the project quite a bit and trigger creative solutions and ideas. This makes it a very rewarding process. I would say about a quarter of Herzog & de Meuron projects deal with historic contexts, existing structures and adaptive re-use such as CaixaForum Madrid and the Tate Modern. In parallel to Tai Kwun, I was working on the Park Avenue Armory in New York which is very much about heritage yet at a very different scale, though some of the thinking processes and conceptual approaches are not so dissimilar. Also, in both projects, the use of digital fabrication was an important tool during the design and construction process. Our work is a constant learning curve about the care of existing structures, observing the particularities of a situation, and building upon the built. After completing Tai Kwun, we have more in our backpack for the next projects and can profit from these successes. At the end of the day, though, every project is different and new. Our previous experiences are important, and make thinking about new projects a little bit easier, but we cannot just copy-and-paste things we found from another project. Our work is constant research and development, and we never stop thinking and questioning, in order to develop very specific responses to a very specific task, context, client, program, and so on. It's a long journey and we are not at the end of it.

TV Thank you Ascan for your generosity with your time and interest today, in joining us for your presentation and interview. We are grateful for your support. I especially enjoyed the tales of planning sagas, and public consultations. I lived in HK through all those years, and of course I was a supporter of each scheme. It is great to hear your insights on the challenges to build this building. We have not discussed the relationship between higher, or advanced technology of design and coordination, and lower or existing technologies, for example of the casting processes of the façade, which is a mix between the higher and lower use of technology. This is typical of design and construction in China, and the high and low tech really comes to the fore in this project.

AM That is a very interesting topic in general. Herzog & de Meuron has always been fascinated by the intersection of digital and analogue methods, going back and forth between computer-generating and hand-making. We are in that field of different forces; we try to play with both at

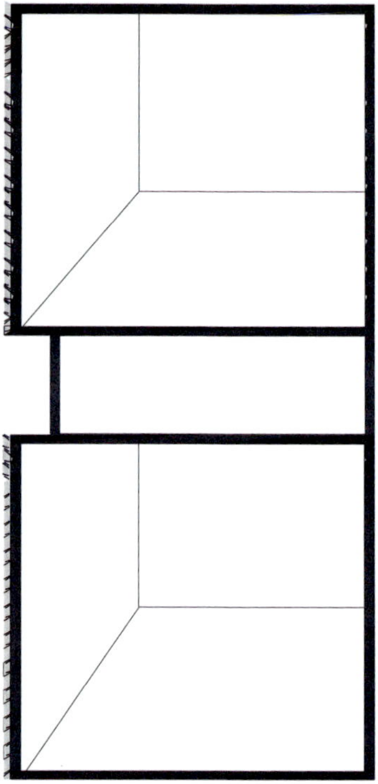

Section of interior space and façade screen

the same time and challenge ourselves. Digital design and fabrication technologies are very powerful tools, but should not overpower the sensual and spatial qualities of the built architecture. We believe it is important to complement each other, ultimately creating a better result by combining the digital and the analogue.

TV Thank you, Ascan – it has been a pleasure to have you join us today. We're grateful for your time.

硬石
THIN FOLDS OF SOFT EARTH
HERE & THERE

MIRA

San Francisco, 2020 | Studio Gang

Program Housing, retail, courtyard, rooftop deck, private dining and lounge, fitness center, children's playroom, conference room, dog washing station, valet parking

Façade materials Prefabricated glazing units and aluminum

Leed Gold Certificate

IDENTITY

40%	Residential Units Below Market Rate
392	Total Residential Units
49%	Solid
51%	Glazing
17,660 M2	Outer Skin
3 to 4	Floors of Façade Repeated
10	Facade Modules Total
122 M	High
39	Floors Above Ground
3	Floors Below Ground
929 M2	Retail at Ground Level
40,970 M2	GFA

INTERVIEW

Interviewee: Jeanne Gang, Founding Principal and Partner, Studio Gang

Interviewers: Adnan Jangbarwala, Seth Mears, M.Arch students, School of Architecture and Design, New York Institute of Technology

February 23, 2022

Tom Verebes Thank you, Jeanne, for joining us today for this interview. We appreciate your generosity for sharing so much detail of designing and constructing MIRA, in your enlightening and comprehensive presentation of this project along with other recent and current projects by Studio Gang. In the thematic structure of my seminar, this project beautifully exemplifies the theme of Identity, in which we evaluate projects invested in mass customized modularity. Housing remains one of the most standardized sectors in architecture, and MIRA stands as a beacon for recent innovations in material production in an era of accelerated industrial change. In this light, MIRA advances the paradigm shift to more flexible manufacturing modes, through the customization of façade systems to create a family of bay windows mapped onto a differentiated set of apartment layouts, and arrayed vertically in a series of distinct floor plans. I would like to introduce our interviewers, Adnan Jangbarwala and Seth Mears, M.Arch students at New York Tech, who will get started with this interview.

Adnan Jangbarwala Thank you for your wonderful and descriptive presentation. We would like now to ask you a few questions, to trigger a discussion with you regarding MIRA and more generally about Studio Gang's work. Reflecting on the historical context of San Francisco, the bay window, indigenous to San Francisco, amplifies the views out of a residence in a context with vast views. As you have stated, MIRA reinvents the San Francisco bay window. The angles of MIRA's windows not only give every unit classic views of San Francisco but also establish the historical and contextual value of this project. Does this new prototype of a reinvented bay window have the potential to become a new standard to be replicated on other, maybe high-rise, projects in San Francisco or elsewhere? Can you foresee the MIRA bay window concept leading to the emergence of a new type of differentiated bay window to influence other projects in the future in San Francisco or elsewhere globally?

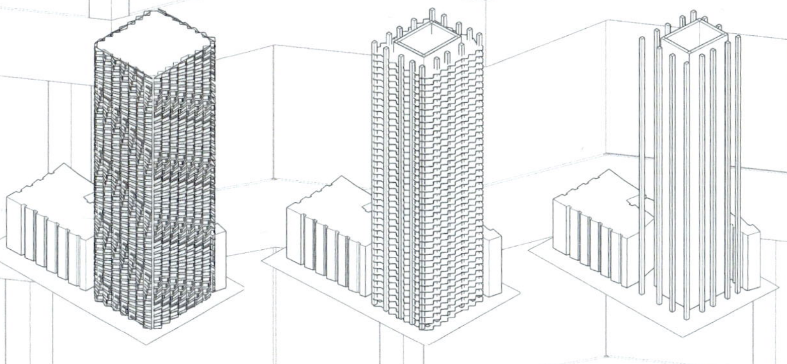

Formal logic of the tower and podium

Jeanne Gang Thanks for these questions. The point is to pave the way for others – to demonstrate what is possible. There are, of course, many buildings that have been constructed with customized façade systems. What is unique about MIRA is the nature of the spandrel units, which were made out of a single piece of aluminum. This vastly simplified waterproofing, construction logistics, and scheduling, and made the formal complexity possible – we didn't have to frame and assemble a range of sill and soffit conditions.

Importantly, our bay window concept simultaneously brings inhabitants more natural light and opens up extra space within the apartments, improving quality of life and extending what it means to live in a tower. I hope that MIRA adds to that body of knowledge and will be expanded upon going forward.

AJ Thank you for your response. I'll move on to my next question. Another way to characterize the context of this project is its industrial and technological context. Despite the enduring legacy of Fordism, architecture is actively pursuing the transition in guiding the industrial paradigm from a model of standardization and mass production towards increasingly flexible manufacturing processes with the potential for greater variation in possible products of the industrial processes or mass customization. Housing is notoriously one of the most standardized sectors in architecture, constrained by cost limitations especially on mass housing in which the ubiquity of sameness triumphs through repetitious standardization. Thank you for explaining how MIRA applies repetition to achieve the appearance of extreme specificity and uniqueness. In this sense, how much standardization was required for the customization of this project? Also, can I ask why so many of the differentiated systems of MIRA have been produced abroad by fabricators and manufacturers based far away, for example in Italy and Thailand, produced as pre-manufactured modules, delivered and installed on site? Were there no locally based fabricators with the background and credentials to achieve your intentions?

JG You have touched on a very important point. The building industry, in general, relies on a very wide global network of manufacturers and producers. I often think about this in relation to mass timber. Take Chicago, for example – it could be surrounded by sustainably produced forests that support mass timber production. At present, mass timber has to come from forests that are already established, and this is often from Europe. When it comes to specifying building components, it can be hard to win the day against companies who produce a very specific thing over and over, no matter where they're located in the world; this kind of standardization has become so efficient that it can be challenging to beat in terms of the cost, delivery, and the performance of the product or the material.

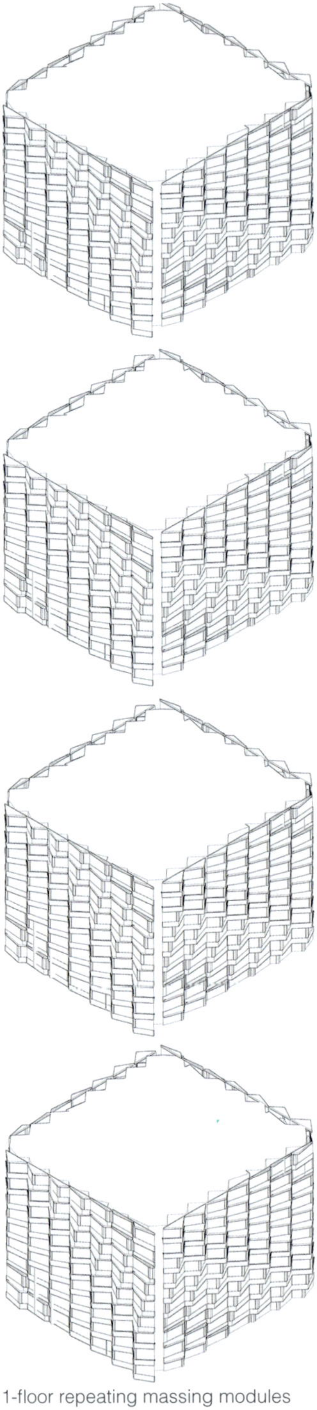

Four 11-floor repeating massing modules

To answer your question directly, there wasn't a local fabricator that could match the quality of the window wall. Italy has become dominant in manufacturing curtain wall systems and different kinds of exterior envelope systems. But this could change in the future. As the architect, your role is to first identify things that are locally made. We try to do that as much as possible. We also try to use building products that are made using recycled material. We, as architects, must work closely with clients to identify strategies that lower the embodied carbon of buildings, whether that's through locally sourced materials or adapting existing buildings and working with what's already there.

AJ Thank you for the detailed clarification. In our graduate seminar at New York tech, we are evaluating projects in relation to six themes. This week's theme is Identity, which concerns modularity, components and mass customization, with MIRA exemplifying this topic. The building reads as though it has a multitude of unique floor plans and façades. You have elaborated how you conceive the relationship between various differentiated systems in the project from bay windows, to unit types, the repetition to units aggregating in floor types, and the repetition of floors. What is the underlying logic to the custom spatial and material organization to enable the project to be cost effective yet still able to create an array of unique and differentiated experiences?

JG One of the options that we proposed for our first tower – Aqua back in 2006 – was a mass customized façade. For example, people could choose their own windows and specify colors or different details. But the problem we encountered, which I don't think is insurmountable, was the marketing of apartments and how it aligned with the design and construction schedule. Buyers would have to customize their apartments long before touring the building, as façade materials are typically purchased well in advance.

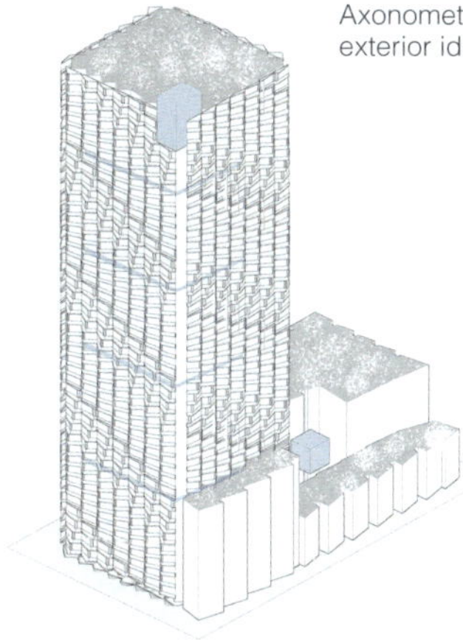

Axonometric of exterior identity

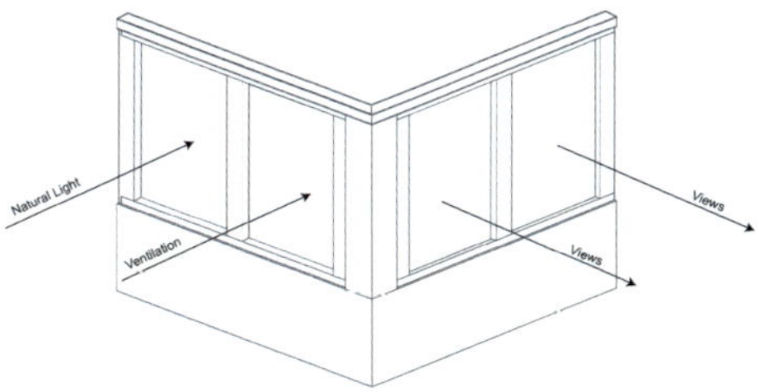

Bay window module

Customizing towers is not as easy as customizing a pair of tennis shoes! It puts the architect in the role of trying to define units with different sizes, aspects, and qualities ahead of time.

The solution that we settled on for MIRA, designed a decade later and finished in 2020, still offers inhabitants a variety of options, but it was much more feasible in terms of the project schedule and cost. Buyers are provided with the same general floor layout but they can choose between ten different façade configurations. For

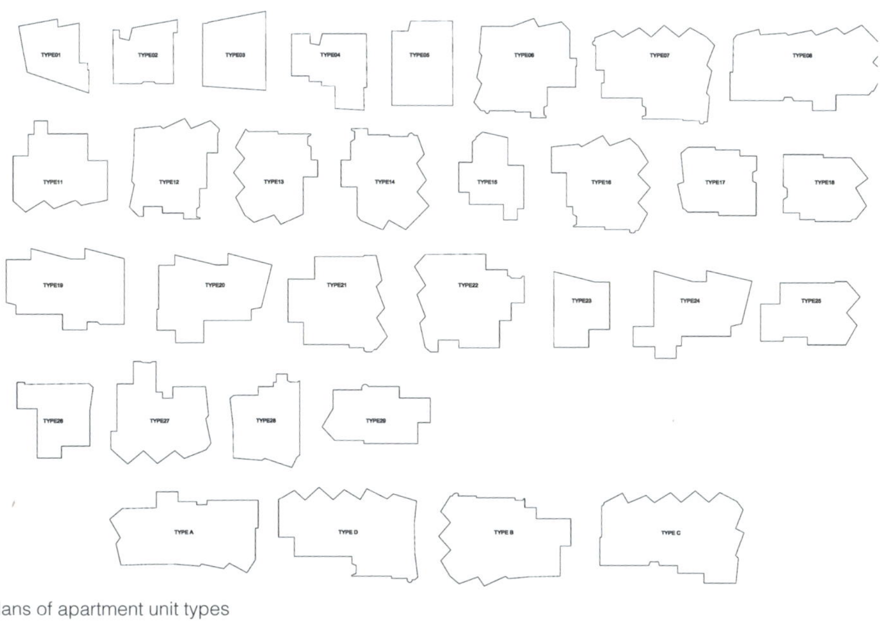

Plans of apartment unit types

Greening the podium terraces

instance, do they want additional space on the balcony, bedroom, or living room? Do they want a view of the city or the Bay? MIRA's design offers these options.

An additional factor informing the design was the seismic activity in the San Francisco area. This dictated the size and thickness of our concrete core, which had to be very simple and stiff.

AJ Thank you. I'll be giving it to Seth to continue.

Seth Mears My name is Seth Mears, and it is an honor to interview you. I would like to probe more into the technical issues of design fabrication, manufacturing, and the parametrics of façade geometries which are resolved in-house and largely pre-manufactured off-site. From your presentation, we learned about what discoveries or innovations in design and production have been learned during this project that basically led to a new set of technical rules and practices. I have some questions about the technical aspects of constructing the building. Why were the bay window modules made out of a single, bent piece of aluminum rather than assembling and mechanically fixing multiple elements together? What exactly were the construction and installation challenges based on site or related to the façade? Why was there a need to make the shape of the columns octagonal in the project? And lastly, how did the scheme arise from mounting the prefabricated façade on brackets?

JG Oh wow – lots of questions! The reason the exterior modules are made of the fewest pieces of folded metal is, firstly, to avoid seams and vulnerabilities for the folded elements of the bay. It also enabled us to reduce the number of welds to only one weld per bay. Folding is much less labor intensive than welding, and can be done with just one material. Determining how thin we could go with the metal – to reduce the amount of material used – without oil canning was an important balance to find. We collaborated closely with different manufacturers to devise different systems, knowing that sometimes they will come up with an idea, which we can take back to the design to see how it might work. The final design balanced the right gauge of metal, which could be finished for durability and easy maintenance, with the necessary stiffness. It was a back and forth process, with the aim of getting the right quality while using less material. The less material, the less carbon!

To answer your other question about challenges: MIRA was built during a very big building boom in San Francisco. There was a lot of competition to secure teams, materials, etcetera, and to get the project done quickly. Managing the project's different teams was challenging. I often think of tall buildings as having different guilds working at the same time on different floors. You have your concrete team, steel team, plumbing team, electrical team, carpentry team – and they are all deployed vertically across the building, trying to keep out of each other's way.

While the excavation and superstructure were under construction, we refined unit layouts, interior details, and the design of the amenity spaces – these were all done by Studio Gang.

Regarding your question about MIRA's columns, our solution for the building's columns was really interesting: their octagonal form allowed more light into the building and also helped marry up with the façade's different geometries.

To address your last question about how the scheme arose for the prefabricated panels mounted on brackets. The brackets are internal to the prefabricated panels, which also contain the waterproofing and insulation. It's all sandwiched together and pre-made. The panels are attached to the concrete through a mechanical connection. There's essentially one bracket on the concrete and one bracket on the panel: marry those up, tighten it up, and you're good to go! It sounds easier than it is. We tried to make the panels small enough for people to handle, but they are still big pieces of material to lock in. It was interesting to see how that came together. In general, it worked a lot better than assembling layer after layer of different materials, which would be installed by different trades. The installation was all done by one trade, reducing the number of people getting in each other's way on the site. That's a very big factor in high-rise design.

SM Great! Thank you so much. Thank you for sharing with us the precedents within your office's portfolio and other projects that inform the design of MIRA. Studio Gang engages in a great variety of projects

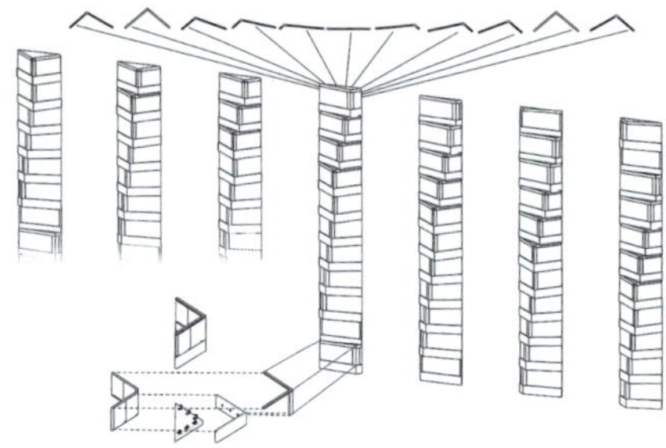

Plan and 3D vertical strips of bay windows

and your architecture engages in the broader cultural needs for society. Does the diversity of Studio Gang's projects reflect your curiosity as a designer or is it a reflection of the variety of project types, scales, programs and clients within an architectural practice? Lastly, do you see yourself as a generalist or specialist architect?

JG The diversity of our projects and design approach is unique to us. It's unique to me. At Studio Gang, we are interested in projects that can have some kind of positive impact on society. That doesn't necessarily mean designing only community centers, although that is how I first started my practice. Making an impact means asking questions of each program. Consider a program like a bank, for example. What does a bank do for society? When a new project opportunity presents itself, we always step back and ask these questions to see how a project can play a role in our cities' social ecosystem. Every building can do something. Maybe, it's offering something back to the urban realm of the street, or maybe it's changing the way that people engage with each other. In MIRA, everyone uses the same entrance, the same lobby, and the same amenity spaces, even though the residents have different economic backgrounds – forty percent of the apartments are below market rate. There's a feeling of equality when you get home. It feels welcoming for everyone. In every single project that you take on, try to look at it through these different lenses and design how it's participating in the city.

We also care about materiality and how a building is built. These are all things that I find very fascinating. I'm a designer and a creative. I like to try different things, and I respond well to new challenges. Some people like to specialize and hone a groove – and this approach can produce wonderful buildings too! The things that I'm working on honing are not exactly the same formally, but there is a cohesiveness to the work in the practice. When you see a Studio Gang project you can tell it's a Studio Gang project, even if it's made out of a different material or hosts a different program. There is a play with natural light and an expressiveness of structure. The projects share a sensibility and an experimentation, which comes from a love of discovering new things and pushing towards a bigger scale. I think you can discover new things even with a more iterative approach. It's just a different scale of discovery.

SM Thanks. Finally, we'd like to conclude our interview with questions on the future of architecture. In a rapidly evolving technological context, what technology do you feel was lacking to further facilitate the design and construction of MIRA?

JG In general, we are still working in an orthographic way as architects. It's the language not only of designers but all the people that come together to produce architecture. Visualizing a design's potential orthographically is disciplined and focused, which can sometimes be better than zooming around a 3D model even if the 3D model contains more information. An orthographic approach allows us to isolate aspects of a design and analyze them.

> But we are in a time of transition, and we will probably no longer be using orthographic ideation at some point. That is one of the field's biggest technological shifts. But it's also an imagination shift, and we're just scratching the surface of that right now.

While we still use plans, wall sections, and elevations to convey information about a building, I do see architecture and construction taking a different path in the future. It will be multifaceted with many more factors to manage. We will need to find new sophisticated ways of judging and comparing design qualities especially in the age of AI.

SM Thank you – we would like to ask you our final questions: Can you share your speculations on how architecture with respect to differentiated systems and their effects may evolve in the next decade or two? Also, what innovations in automation, robotics and custom manufacturing do you think we may see integrated in architecture?

JG What I would like to see is two-pronged. I really do like making. With the rise of robotics, there is a risk that we lose the physical "making" qualities that you can get from handmade things. I'm not talking about the design of high-rises specifically, but rather any building. How can we, together with technology, identify a way to source materials locally? Using a local source or company to produce something in a smaller batch to a quality that is acceptable moves away from the Fordism that you were talking about earlier.

I wonder if technology could help us to be more custom and more local. That could be amazing. Of course, it makes sense to do certain tasks faster and more efficiently with robotic production. But I would like to see how this evolves in terms of the distribution of making. For example, if you wanted to buy an outfit, could it be sourced from someone who is local and closer to you, rather than made somewhere far away using low wages? This would reduce the amount of carbon expended during transport, too. Perhaps technology could make recycled elements more readily available so they could be more easily deployed into our projects. There are a lot of ways projects could be even more human and responsive, and technology could be harnessed to help us achieve this. It is hard to predict the future, but I feel that reducing the distance of production and consumption is a really good use of some of our newest technologies.

SM Absolutely! Thank you so much for your time and your enlightening responses to our interview.

TV Thank you so much, Jeanne, for your generosity to join us today to present the work of Studio Gang and in particular MIRA. And this experience for our students at NYIT is especially a genuine privilege. We really appreciate it – thank you!

JG Thank you for having me. Enjoy the week. Bye everyone!

Spear

ST. MARY'S AXE

London, 2004 | Foster + Partners

Program Offices, Restaurant, Bar, Parkin

Façade materials Glass, aluminum

ENVIRONMENT

Glazing	1000%
Outer Skin	24,000 M2
Openable Facade Modules	745
Fixed Facade Modules	4,755
Facade Modules Total	5,500
High	180 M
Typical Floor Plate	1,400 M2
Floors Above Ground	41
Floors Below Ground	1
GFA	64,500 M2

INTERVIEW

Interviewee: Rob Harrison, Senior Partner, Foster + Partners

Interviewers: Dalton Lackey, Noah Seeback, M.Arch students, School of Architecture and Design, New York Institute of Technology

March 30, 2022

Tom Verebes It is a pleasure and honor to welcome you to New York Tech, Rob Harrison, to discuss your reflections on the "Gherkin". Although known, and loved widely for its instantly recognizable pickle-like figure, the Gherkin's contribution is perhaps most pronounced with respect to the development of ecological thinking and passive building systems. I have selected this project for this Beyond the Envelope series due to the value of its environmental performance, more than purely for its striking appearance. Rob, we are grateful to you for joining us today to share your presentation, and to participate in this brief interview. I would like to introduce my M.Arch students, Dalton Lackey and Noah Seeback, who will take over now as interviewers.

Noah Seeback Hello, my name is Noah Seeback, and together with Dalton Lackey, we're honored to interview you today. We would also like to thank you for your insightful and engaging presentation focusing on 30 St. Mary Axe, or as it is popularly known, The Gherkin, situated within the historic City of London. The project has rightly been praised for its achievements in creating a new benchmark for passive cooling, ventilation, and energy reduction, within the ecological and technological context of the turn of the century. We also believe the building has made a substantial contribution to the advancement of banking, finance, and other professional office building space design. Were there ever any contradictions between the ambitions of the "radical approach" and the "responsible environmental practice" of this building's design, in terms of the environmental innovations and the expectation for a landmark headquarters located in London's financial district?

Robert Harrison You raise a very good point, that is, had this been a purely commercial development, had it not been an owner/occupier, had it not been Swiss Re who were ultimately occupying the vast majority of the building, and if Foster + Partners were doing this building as a speculative development, or we were doing this as a building for a developer who had a different anchor tenant in

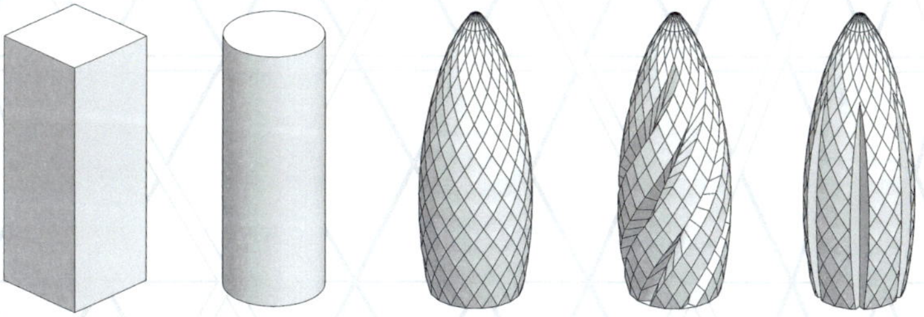

Diagrams of formal generation of the envelope

mind but was not an owner/occupier, it would have been impossible to achieve the goals that we wanted to. The spatial efficiency of this building is good but it cannot be compared to a more traditional rectilinear, more formulaic office building. It just would not stack up. We cut six triangles out of our floor plate on every single floor all the way up. You have to have a very dedicated client who is prepared to sacrifice that floor area. Since Swiss Re were located in about six different offices across London at the time. Their business, a reinsurance company, and the vast amount of their general day-to-day work is done through Lloyds of London. It involved, at the time in the early in the early 2000s, and perhaps for at least a decade after that, going to the marketplace of Lloyds and they would carry large bundles of actual paper! Their contracts were all on paper. They would go to the marketplace to do whatever they do in the reinsurance world, but it was all traded out of Lloyds. Lloyds is located 100 yards away from the Gherkin, so locationally the new site for Swiss Re was perfect for them to move to a site that was big enough to agglomerate all of their other offices together into one space. They had a very particular requirement with their brief for an environmentally progressive design, which was intended to make a statement about who they were and to get their name more broadly known.

There is no better bit of advertising than this building. It was an advantageous symbol for them so they were prepared to sacrifice many things that other developers simply would not have.

They were prepared to sacrifice some spatial efficiency within the building, because they felt that what was being achieved made for a far better working environment and it made for a better statement about them as a company and about what their ambitions were. You raise a very good point though, had this been for a different financial institution we would never have designed this building, it would not have looked anything like this form. This building is not a great example of fitting a super efficient floor plate and office design into it. It is efficient to a point and it works really well for them, but it required a very particular client so we were extremely lucky to have them.

Dalton Lackey In our seminar, we are analyzing projects in relation to a set of six themes. This week's theme is Environment, involving issues related to climate, weather, energy, sustainability and resilience, with the Gherkin exemplifying these topics. The building has been celebrated for its passive cooling strategies. In our analysis, we have wondered how the all-glass façade has performed with respect to heat loss in winter months and how passive heat gain may have helped to reduce energy consumption for heating in winter?

RH I will share some more information about the skin of the building. In the office portion of the building, at the 40 degree section of the office component, there is a very deep double skin façade which is internally ventilated. It is not unusual for us to have double skin facades, most of our projects do, but they tend to be externally ventilated. They are easier to maintain, they take up less of the overall volume of the buildings in terms of build efficiency,

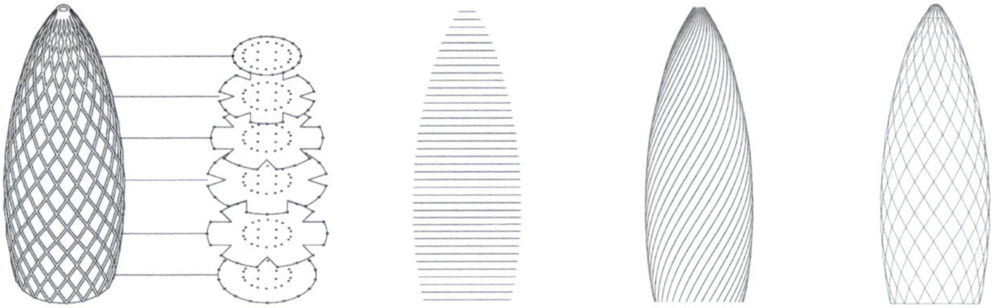

Diagrams of material and structural systems.

and they are better. But when you have a curved envelope and you are putting a floor plate across to it, the junction of the floor plate to the façade is either an obtuse angle or an acute angle. To have vertical bits like wall surfaces and glass screens to go up next to it, you end up with a triangular zone that is created. This started the thinking about why the building should be an internally ventilated system as opposed to externally ventilated.

The double skin façade allowed us to have a buffer zone between the external wall, which in summertime gets very hot and in winter time gets very cold in comparison to a 20C degree office temperature inside, for example. We had a larger zone to deal with the thermal buffer and we were able to use that zone to effectively flush office air into the space in order to temper it. So, for example, if it were zero degrees centigrade outside and it is 20C inside, the office would have a pressure differential across there of 10C. But if you can take 20C degree air out of the office and flush it through the void at the edge, you are warming, and you are tempering that space. So, you then have to provide less heating into it. It is the reverse in summertime, simplistically. If there is 30C degree air on the surface, probably more on actual surface temperature but let's say it's 30C degrees outside and 20C degrees inside. Again, you can use your internal air to help flush that space in order to reduce the comparative cooling load. What the natural ventilation does, in temperate conditions while bringing air in, is to not only help provide reasonable temperature air in the office space, the really significant difference is it is natural air and it increases air changes from maybe eight air changes an hour, which a ventilated system would give you, to up to dozens of air changes per hour. So, it just feels a much fresher environment and we have found in the tests that we have been able to do that people will accept something outside of the normal range that you would expect in an office building, which is kind of typically set here in the UK at 22C degrees, or the low 70s in Fahrenheit. Most developers will stipulate in the base building definition provided in a brief, that the air temperature needs to stay within four degrees of that so 70° up to 74° Fahrenheit or 21 to 23 degrees Centigrade. That is with a typical mechanical system with approximately eight air changes per hour, which is enough, but it may still feel a little bit stuffy. If there are instead, dozens of air changes per hour and there is fresh air coming through rather than constantly

> We used natural ventilation by opening up the light well portion at 20 degree sections. That is where the natural air comes in and then flows across the floor plate to keep the pressure differential from front to back. As it moved across the floor plate, we needed to be able to use that cooling air that comes through. It is very rare that it works in full natural ventilation but it is almost always in a mixed air mode, so you have a combination of air conditioning working with the natural ventilation coming across.

filtered air, people will accept a wider variation in temperature. So, the occupants will accept it going down to 19 degrees centigrade, which is 66° Fahrenheit, and they will accept it going up to 78° because the degree of the air flow is greater and it is fresher air that is coming in. It is very difficult to persuade a developer of that even when there is data to prove it. We try on our projects to convince our clients of this but it is still quite a difficult ask. But that is the double skin ventilation system of the façade that we had, and it really helped with that internal flushing, using the exhaust air to temper what was happening, which allowed us to reduce the air conditioning load or the heating load inside the building.

DL Thank you for your thorough response to our first question. We have also been wondering, whether the building's energy performance has been affected by climate change, and rising global temperatures since the building's completion? Have there been increments of time during months in the past 20 years, when the passive cooling strategies have not met expectations?

RH When the building is used for nighttime purging of heat, meaning when you open the windows in order to let the whole building cool down, this has been proven to be very effective. They have not used the natural ventilation system for that, rather ventilating when the office space is occupied, but the ability to cool the building down in the evening when nobody is about, that really was vindicated during the Covid-19 pandemic. With the generally increased temperatures that we are getting, whatever the temperature increase is across the 20 odd years since it was built,

Structural diagrid; glazing subdivisions for panels

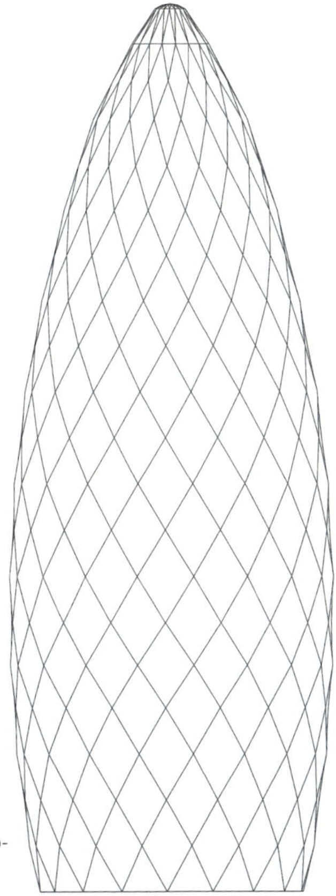

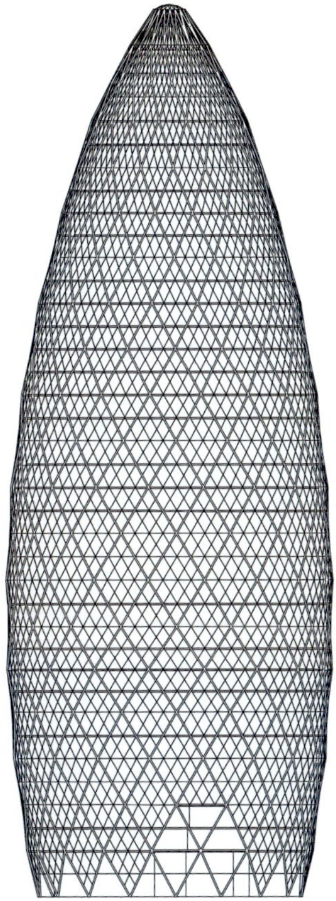

there is generally more heat in the building. The heat rejection plant is no bigger than it was and it is contained up in the top of the building as well, being pretty modest in terms of the volume that it occupies at the top of the space. It is not as though there is a lot of space where you can suddenly stick a whole load more chillers and other heat rejection equipment. It can become more efficient, but we need to make sure we do whatever we can to let the building heat and cool itself naturally, to do it itself, rather than having to rely on ever more expensive and ever more costly mechanical means to do it. With temperatures rising as they inevitably are, I really hope it gets used much more. We know that the systems in the building have not been as extensively used as they can be and would welcome them being more sophisticatedly employed. We hope that will be the case in the future. Office environments are changing quite a bit and we hope with that change will come the chance to put those measures in place in the Gherkin.

DL How were environmental simulations used to aid the decision-making process during the design of the building, and what do you recall about the initial testing and experimentation of the interior ventilation system?

RH In two diagrams I showed in my presentation, there is one that is the photo of the wind tunnel test performed in RWDI's test center

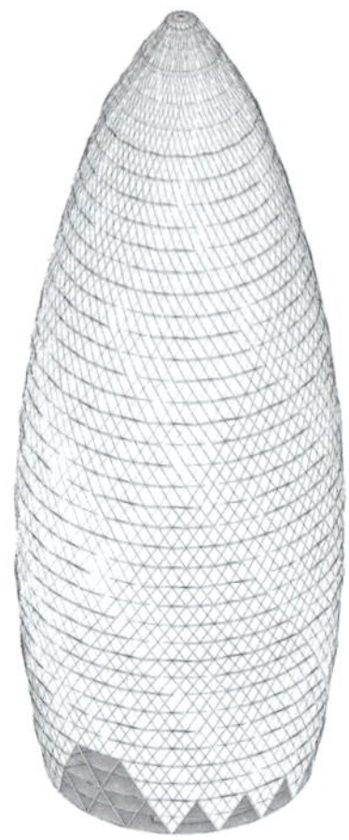

in Toronto, in which we tested a rudimentary, 1:400 scale model of the building. It had a series of little pressure sensors inside it so you could measure wind pressure and much of that was actually done for the cladding. This helped us to make sure that we knew what the specification requirement was for the glazing, but it also gave us data on what sort of wind pressures we were going to be getting there and if it was practical to open a window when we had to manage those degrees of pressure. So, it was done in the wind tunnel but then a lot of the CFD (Computational Fluid Dynamics) testing by Hilson Moran, who were our environmental and mechanical engineers, they pioneered that work with us

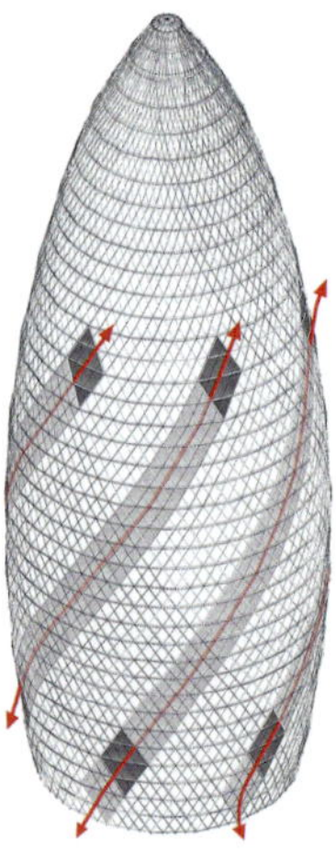

Diagram showing spiraling of the six atrium voids

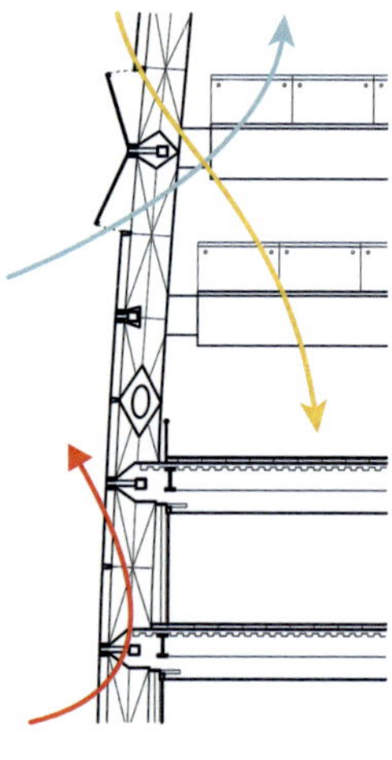

Detail section

and it was across a number of the projects that we were doing at the time but particularly so on the Gherkin. This is what led to moves such as the twisting of the atrium, which we would never have done had Hilson Moran not shown with their CFD analysis that this actually helped to push the incoming air. It helped to get the flow of air to work more effectively across the office floor plate if there was a degree of twist to it. We always hoped that would be the case, as it made for much better architectural spaces inside, but that was an aesthetic response from us. It is nice that it actually then was vindicated through the environmental performance of the building as well. So ultimately, CFD was crucial to us both internally but also to the flow of the air around the building. There is also a downdraft effect, and the simulations were able to show how much better pedestrian comfort would be because of the building having a more smooth and curvilinear surface form. So, environmental simulation was crucial to our design process. It has developed obviously an enormous amount since then, from those early days of CFD analysis, but it played a crucial role in several of the big decisions that were made in this project.

NS Significant buildings, when they capture the public's imagination, become recognized as landmarks. We have discussed how The Gherkin was driven and shaped by innovations in passive cooling and ventilation. However, various publications on The Gherkin have declared its "instant recognizability", more likely due to the distinct form and materiality of the project. In this light, our next questions address the notion of an architectural icon, a topic of debate for some time in architecture. The less desirable connotations of an architectural icon usually arise when buildings are used by their investors as branding tools to create and establish identity. Can you summarize your views on what makes this project "instantly recognizable"? And in retrospect, what do you believe to be the attributes of the project which contributed to it having become affectionately part of the public imagination?

RH It looks very distinct from most office buildings, and that is a great help. Cast your mind

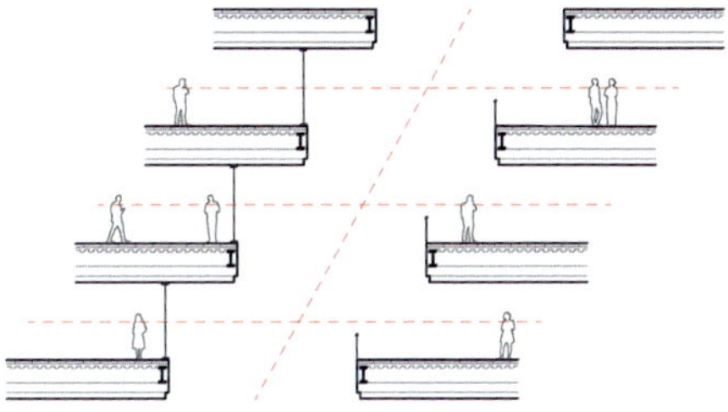

Schematic section through an atrium

back, or look back at photographs of what London was like back in the 1990s. It certainly did not have the shapes of buildings that the city certainly has now, where there are quite a lot of interestingly formed buildings. Most were rectilinear forms of good quality, from the 1960s, 1970s, early 1980s, but they were all predominantly rectilinear in form. So, our building, naturally, was very distinct from all other nearby buildings, and it is still a very distinctive form even amongst the diversity of nearby buildings that have since been built. What we wanted to ensure, and this was with the approval of English Heritage , now known as Historic England, who are the arbiters of the UK's heritage. They were very encouraging about the elegance of the building. The building is 180 meters, or 600 feet, tall, but earlier versions were more like 120 to 150 meters, or 400 to 450 feet, tall, it still had the same amount of area in it, 500,000 square feet. Volumetrically, earlier in the design stages, it was a much more condensed squashed form. One of the earlier inspiration reference points was the Fabergé Egg, so it was more like an egg shape rather than the sleeker profile with which the building was built. It was through Historic England's encouragement that the building became taller because it was felt that it was a more elegant form. It was also one of the determinants that we had, that the building could be read differently at different scales so the context around the building is different depending on what point you are viewing it at. If you are viewing the building from many miles away, and you are looking back across at the City of London, what you are really looking at is more the overall silhouette of the building but you also see the form of the primary structure. The primary structure is on a 20 degree grid and the diamonds on the façade are four stories high from the tip to the tail and they are deliberately painted white. By contrast, the hori-

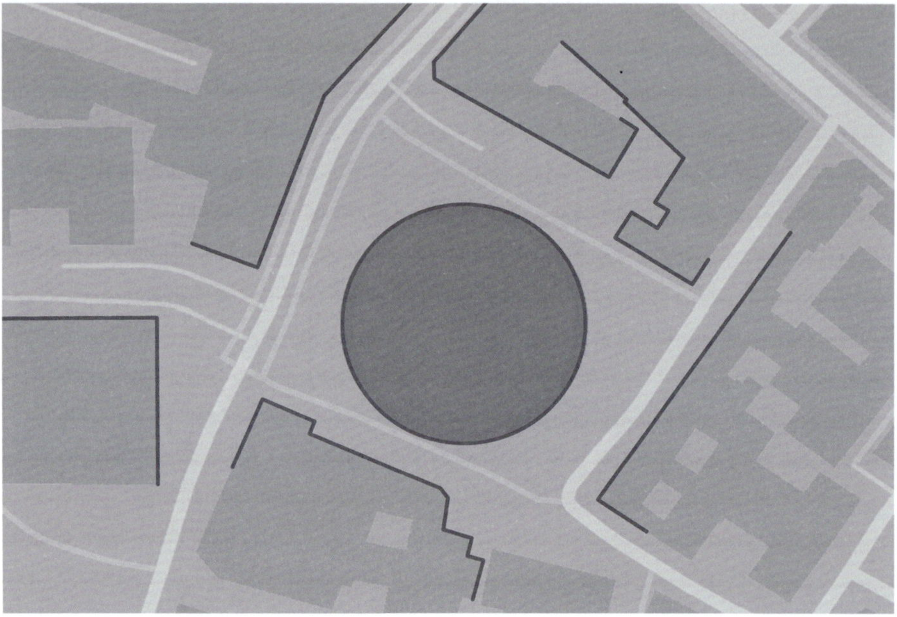

Plan figure and its urban context

zontal elements, which at a distance you do not see because they seem to disappear, as they are painted a very dark blue. What you read from a distance is the four-story high diamonds patterned around the building and you see the silhouette of the form of it from longer distance. As you get closer to it, you start to read more of the detail of the building and then that debate about when does it change scale, at what point when you get closer to it do you start to read the degree of finesse in the architecture? That was something we all debated a lot and is ultimately why the cladding grid is arranged as it is on a five degree module, and the cladding grid of diamond panels span floor to floor so that we have a triangle top to bottom. You read this at a very different scale to it when you get closer to the building and when you get right up to it all the detail is revealed.

NS Since completion, several other landmark office buildings have been completed nearby in the City of London, such as the Leadenhall Building, 20 Fenchurch Street, and several others, each also communicating unique and distinct formal expressions, yet all are vastly different from The Gherkin. In this transitory context since the completion of The Gherkin, how does the insertion of an icon alter the historic context, to welcome a multiplicity of icons, making the distinct icon a normative condition of the context?

RH I would agree that if you now look at the skyline of the City of London, it is peppered with many different shaped buildings and they create quite a contrast. If you compare the City of London against Canary Wharf, there has been quite a distinct alteration to

But addressing that notion of an icon, we were together with our client, and we wanted to create something that was very memorable on the skyline of London. The way it was finally executed with the input of a whole range of different people, including heritage lobbies, I think all contributed to a much better and more graceful form than we might originally have had.

the morphology of the City. In Canary Wharf, which is a little bit more like downtown Toronto, it has a more uniform look and form. The City prides itself on having very differently shaped buildings and the City of London, as the local authority, have been keen to push that. I will not make comment on my personal opinion of some of those buildings but that is the aesthetic desire the City of London has. They want buildings to each have a very distinct individual personality, and their view is that as an agglomeration of buildings together is what makes the City of London great. The fact that there is this distinction happening between them, they together form a cohesive clustering of buildings. But within that cluster, they all want variety, and they want to make sure that each building is very different to the others.

DL In many respects, the 30 St. Mary Axe project was ahead of its time. Environmental building technology and building codes and regulations have changed in the last 25 years. If you were to design this project now, with respect to passive environmental strategies, what would you do differently?

RH The building met the zeitgeist, and it was right for its time. If we were given the site again? We would not end up with the same building. If we had had a different client, it would be an entirely different project. It is of its time and it is of the people that took part in its creation. If we did it all over again, who knows, I think it would be fundamentally different.

DL Thank you. Urbanization, building construction, and energy use all have immense impact on the natural environment, and serve to accelerate climate change. In terms of our collective ecological responsibilities, what is the future for architecture and what needs to change?

RH One of the debates that we are having here at Foster + Partners, and I know everybody else is as well, the initial response to a commission, to our brief from a client was always: "What's the new building that we can put there? What does it look like? How does it respond to our client's requirements?" The first question we ask ourselves now on every project is: "What element of reuse is there? And particularly in urban settings, how can we reuse fabric that exists on the site?" That represents, front and center, a sea change in what has happened previously. Whenever we work particularly within an urban environment, that is the very first thing we will ask of ourselves and it is the very first thing we ask of our clients. More and more clients now have that uppermost in their mind because they know that the people they need to persuade, including the planning authorities, the local authorities, and planning committees, that is going to be one of their primary concerns as well. The more you can reuse, the more you do not need to demolish and take away, the better the overall energy performance of the entire estate and project will be. That is the shift I have seen and I can only assume that is still going to further accelerate.

TV Thank you very much Robert, we are really grateful for the time that you have taken to give your wonderful presentation and especially also to participate in a student-led interview.

RH It was a pleasure meeting you all today and thank you for your questions. They were thorough and very thoughtful, and I think they point quite pertinently to the future which lies ahead of all of us. We will continue to make sure that our involvement in our projects will as environmentally progressive as they can be, which is a phrase that our client gave us from the start of the Gherkin, and I think this still holds true a generation later.

TV Absolutely! Foster + Partners have been one of the leaders in meeting some of the environmental challenges we have faced in the past generation, and we look forward to your future projects which will advance these ideas.

Thank you, and we wish you continued success in your work at Foster + Partners.

RH Thank you! Goodbye, all!

EMMA AND GEORGINA BLOOMBERG CENTER

New York, 2017 | Morphosis Architects

Program Classrooms, instructional labs, lecture hall, huddle rooms, collaboration areas, conference rooms, café, classrooms, open work areas and shared spaces

Materials Pixelated tabs on the façade done by a robotic welding arm programmed to tilt each individual tab; glass

Net-Zero Energy
Leed Platinum (Expected)

60%	Solid
40%	Glazing
80	Geothermal Wells
337,500	Number of Pixelated Tabs
1464	Pv Panels
4000	Facade Metal Panels
4	Floors Above Ground
1	Floors Below Ground
14,865 M2	GFA

INTERVIEW

Interviewee: Ung-Joo Scott Lee, Partner, Morphosis Architects

Interviewers: Yuti Kothari, Gyongok Tammy Noh, M.Arch students, School of Architecture and Design, New York Institute of Technology

March 17, 2021

Tom Verebes Thank you so much for your fantastic, in-depth presentation on the Bloomberg Center! It is truly wonderful to hear the narrative of your experience of conceiving, designing and building the Bloomberg Center taking us through its conceptualization, its challenges, to its completion. You've generously shared so much information which is not visible from experiencing the building. Of the six buildings selected as case studies for the first run of this seminar, I know the Bloomberg Center more intimately than all others. I live in Roosevelt Island and I have spent a lot of time reading there during the pandemic, both inside and outside of the ground floor café. Of course, I knew of the building before I moved here, and like most architects, we approach buildings as we see them for the first time with a critical eye. I was blown away by the nuance of the visual effects manifested in different appearances during daylight conditions, and also, the mystery of some of the systems and forms of the building, which I really did not understand with respect to their environmental and MEP functionalities. Congratulations on realizing a great piece of architecture and contribution to contemporary discourse. I'll now introduce our interviewers, Yuti Kothari and Tammy Noh, M.Arch students in my seminar in the School of Architecture and Design at NYIT.

Yuti Kothari Hello! My name is Yuti Kothari. First of all, I would like to thank you for taking time out of your busy schedule to join us today. We are grateful for all your efforts, and we appreciate you sharing your journey and experience of the conception, design, and construction of this project, in your enlightening presentation. I will begin our interview with some contextual questions we have. The Bloomberg Center represents a unique opportunity to investigate the intersection of three territories: Firstly, the unique urban condition of Roosevelt Island, which has a legacy of architectural excellence, from Johnson and Rudolph's masterplan, Sert's buildings and Louis Kahn's Four Freedoms Park. Second, the Bloomberg Center, and Cornel Tech participates as an academic hub within the clustering of top universities in the city in New York City. Thirdly, The Bloomberg Center is a beacon of environmental performance. We would like to

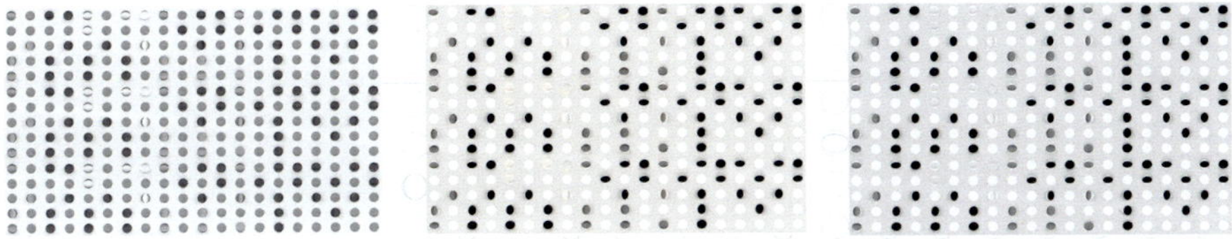

Elevations of envelope panels

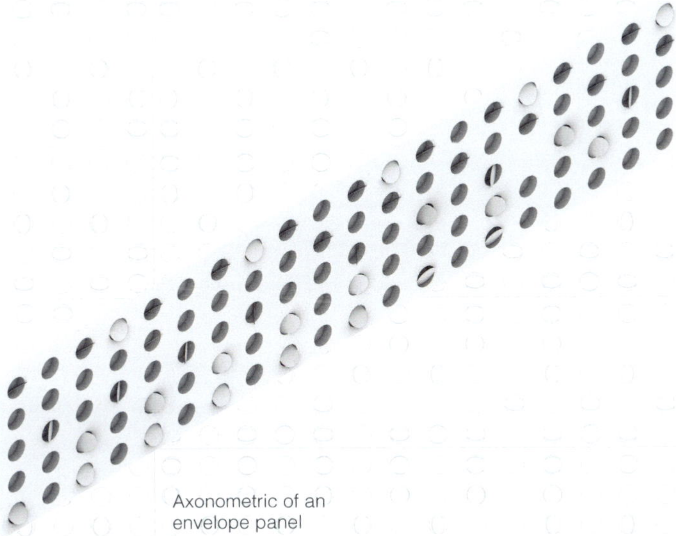

Axonometric of an envelope panel

ask some questions about this agenda of the building. While the environmental concerns of the Bloomberg Center, along with its various environmental systems, have made a bold political statement on environmental responsibility, the risks of flooding from rising sea levels and storm surges seems to be the paramount concern of the project. As the site sits on an island within the East River, can you share with us how the design scheme was impacted by the flooding of Roosevelt Island during Hurricane Sandy? What other specific impacts of climate change were considered in the design of the Bloomberg Centre?

Ung-Joo Scott Lee Thank you for the invitation – it's great to be here. I'll respond to the first item at the start of your question concerning the academic program and the unique Roosevelt Island urban context. Every project carries multiple agendas, requirements, and performance criteria. Buildings don't exist in silos and in this instance, it required deep integration of Roosevelt Island as a destination, the academic institution as the program, and a net-zero facility as the performance. The mission was to create a singular piece of architecture that not only integrated those

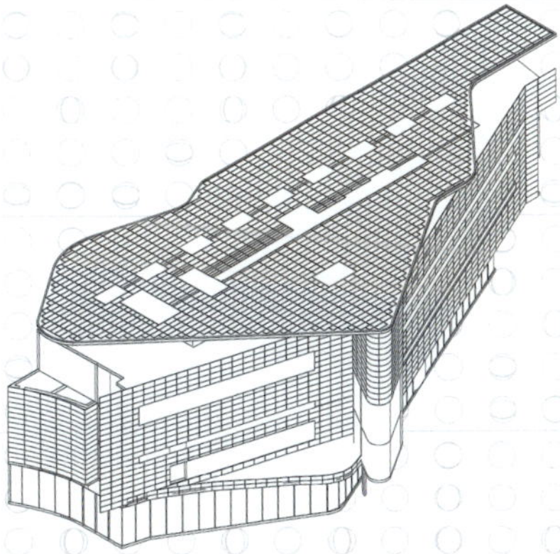

Composite form

three elements together, but augmented them and made them visible and experiential.

When Hurricane Sandy made landfall in New York, it reinforced how each of those three things correlate and affect each other. So it focused our holistic approach to the project even further. You cannot separate the project's objectives in different buckets since it's a singular piece of architecture. We were in the middle of our schematic design phase when Hurricane Sandy made landfall in New York. Every community was affected and the impact on the Roosevelt Island community was in many ways greater because it is, itself, an island.

> I have been in New York for several years and experienced several paradigm changing events: the big "black out" when the entire power grid went down, 9/11, and Hurricane Sandy. The common theme for all of these events is that it makes us think about resiliency.

Exploded axonometric of envelope and interior systems

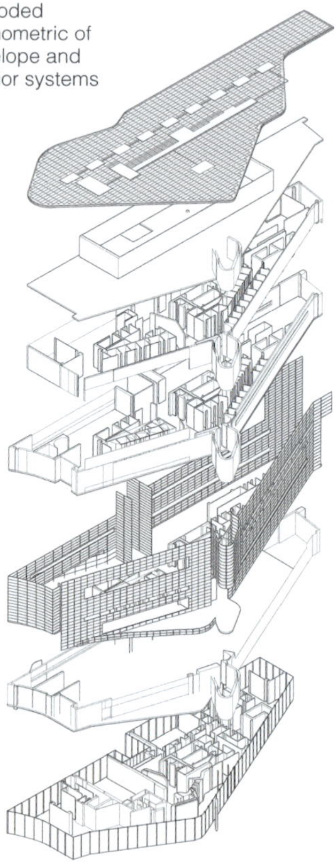

Before Hurricane Sandy, the building design included a larger basement, and a lower ground elevation. We did not have roof level mechanical spaces nor roof top equipment. At that time, most of the mechanical systems were located in the basement, closest to the incoming underground utilities. After Sandy, that was of course no longer the plan. We really needed to understand the impact of lowering anything below the ground level. We elevated everything higher than the adjacent street level by several feet, and relocated all services to the upper roof, which was not an easy change from a mechanical perspective. We were required to have some mechanical equipment remain on the lower floor, but relocating the majority of equipment allowed us to adapt to a changing environment. For example, the building uses a closed-loop geothermal well system, using ground-source water to heat and cool the building. Some of the equipment that needed to remain in the basement was connected to this geothermal well field. The equipment was then specified to be submersible, with an enclosed chassis so they are functional even if exposed to water. We also elevated every piece of machinery, panel, and incoming infrastructure conduit in the basement level to withstand two feet of water. We elevated the whole building, eliminated all lower openings so that any street level flooding would not make its way into the basement. The lower-level basement is designed as a "bathtub." We collaborated closely with ARUP, our mechanical engineers and with Cornell Tech, who were looking at the project very carefully to ensure that not only the building was resilient, but that the entire campus, including the exterior outdoor spaces, could better withstand future hurricane events.

YK In our seminar, we are looking at a series of six projects to be analyzed along a set of themes. This week's theme is "Environment", focusing on issues related to climate, energy, resilience and sustainability, with the case study of the Bloomberg Center at Cornell Tech. We believe the project to be a bold statement on sustainability as the building aims to attain net zero energy. Having the spotlight on the lily pad canopy of PVs, other green features such as geothermal wells and a rainwater-collection system for the all-electricity building, how challenging was it to achieve the net-zero building status and certification? Could you please describe the performance of the rain screen wall system which is the outermost layer of the façade composed of aluminum panels? How does this system balance exterior views and daylight, maximize insulation performance, and minimize thermal bridging in the building?

U-JSL We will be looking for post occupancy metrics to see how the building is performing. When the Bloomberg Center first opened, the facility was not fully loaded from day one. In other words, Cornell Tech is still scaling up its student, faculty and administration population so the campus is not fully occupied. The building was designed around an assumed campus population of approximately 2,000 people and Cornell Tech is not at that full capacity yet. Since the building is not fully occupied, the balance between energy consumed and energy created is not yet there but as the building achieves its full occupancy, we anticipate it will.

In terms of the building façade and sustainability, we were very conscious not to design an all-glass building with floor-to-floor curtain wall. Generally, our window-to-wall ratio for the façade rule was 40:60. What that means is that 40% of the façade is glass and the other 60% is a well-insulated, well-detailed, solid façade. Since the Bloomberg Center is not an all-glass building, we had to be very cognizant and purposeful as regards where we put the glass. We decided to put transparency in all of the public spaces, including the ground floor with its publicly accessible café, lecture spaces and classrooms. We wanted and needed transparency in the public areas to create identity, visibility, and campus activity. We also integrated glazing at the upper level work spaces, providing those spaces with natural daylight in the studio-like loft spaces. We optimized the glazing quite a bit to maximize daylight, while minimizing unwanted heat transfer and lowering electrical lighting. When you get a chance to walk through the interior, you get all the visibility looking out towards the campus and Manhattan, with really great daylighting. That's not the product of a lot of glazing, but rather of glazing in the right locations and exposures.

In the solid portions of the walls, which represent 60% of all of the exterior façade surfaces, we detailed the wall by locating the insulation outboard from the interior framing. Typically you have studs supporting the exterior façade, with insulation between the studs inside the wall cavity. The thermal bridge from the studs makes a less energy efficient wall because the framing is exposed. In the case of the Bloomberg Center, we had the stud framing the wall,

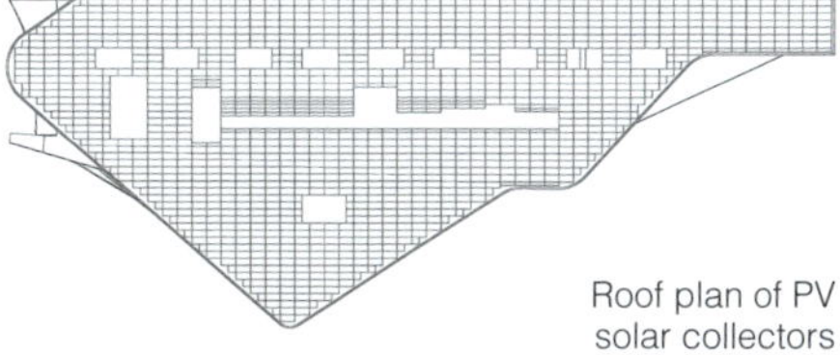

Roof plan of PV solar collectors

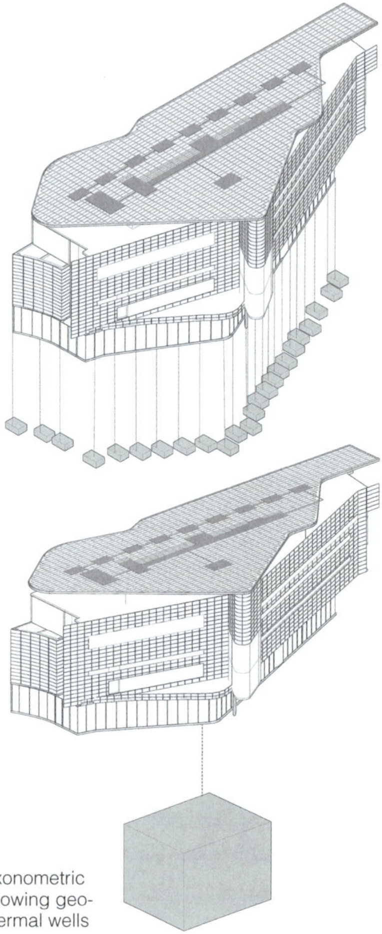

Axonometric showing geo-thermal wells

with an insulation completely outboard of that frame. Simply put, the insulation is a jacket covering the entire building avoiding the thermal bridging from the framing members. We were able to achieve the continuity of insulation around the entire perimeter which allowed us to detail the best façade from a thermal performance point of view. The disadvantage is the façade thickness. In the typical exterior wall, you have your studs, and because you have insulation between the studs, you can get the rain screen set in less than 12 inches. Because we are putting insulation outboards from the framing, our exterior wall thickness increases. What that means is there is less space inside and if you are working with a commercial investor, the increase in wall thickness decreases your net interior area, potentially affecting the overall project net area if you have many floors. A small decrease in floor size can be consequential on a tower, which was fortunately not our case.

TN Hello, I am Tammy Noh, and it is an honor to interview you. Can you please share with us the journey and process of this façade coming to life? The discs cut out from the metal panels unfold on the façade – tilted in different directions uniquely that catch sunlight in interesting ways, and the PPG paint treatment makes the building change its coloration from green to brown to bronze to gold, in different daylight conditions. Can you explain how the façade took inspiration from the waterfall in Ithaca and the Manhattan skyline to illustrate the connection between two campuses? In the design process, was it intended to have different colors on façade that vary over time during the day? Do you anticipate the façade panels becoming patinated eventually over a long period of time?

U-JSL I will start with the last part of your question. The paint coat on the façade panel is inert, so it will not patinate over its lifetime. It will remain the color and appearance of what you see today. The coat is from a manufacturer called PPG, and they are produced in very large, pre-painted coils which are then shipped to the fabricator who fabricates the panel components.

One of the images that I showed in my PowerPoint presentation speaks about the two sides of the building and what we used as their source images. For the Manhattan facing elevation, we had a photographer come in and take photos of the east side of Manhattan, exactly as seen from the campus. We then used that image to generate the patterning on the west façade, which is the building façade facing Manhattan.

For the east façade, which faces the inner campus, we used an equivalent image of the Ithaca Gorge since Cornell University is located in Ithaca. And if you know Ithaca, they are well known for many of their gorges.

If you had the photographed image next to you and you were facing the building, you would clearly identify the difference of the source image for each of these two very distinct sides. You would recognize the relationship between the façade "pixelation," and photographs in a literal way. The variability of what we call the "rocking and rolling" of each of the small façade "pixels" is based on the grayscale of the picture. If you study the façade and the photograph, you will see a clear patterning. The bright spots of the photographs register with a certain kind of patterning on the façade, that's how you can easily tell their relationship.

In terms of the iridescent color you mentioned, it's a type of coating that shifts color depending on your viewing angle and time of the day. It can look green sometimes, other times it looks bronze. We had to review this several times with Cornell and the City of New York so they could visualize and understand the color of the building – a lot of the comments we initially received was that it was too dark or how contextual the color would be around other buildings. It was very difficult to talk or even visualize what the color would be since the color shifts throughout the day, season and even weather with cloudy skies.

Sometimes it is green and sometimes it is bronze. What we ended up speaking about is that the bronze tone relates closely with the steel structure of the Queensboro Bridge. The bronze tone alluded to the infrastructure quality of the Bridge and what we liked about the bronze in our building is that this building, beyond its architecture, is an infrastructure for people to think and work.

It is infrastructure to collect energy. No different than the Queensboro bridge is an infrastructure of movement. That connection was very important to us. The green was wonderful because I do not think anyone could predict what a green building would look like at this scale. When you see the green tones from the façade, the tone connects to the campus landscape, the Roosevelt Island streetscape, and shares similar tones to the East River surrounding the building and the campus.

TN What is the relation of the Bloomberg Center to earlier projects at Morphosis Architects? Did any past projects influence the Bloomberg Center?

U-JSL Every project is different. Every client needs something that is very specific to their needs. In that sense, no project should purposely look alike since the mission is different, the site is different, the opportunities are different, and the pressure points are different. We like to think that our past projects are different from the projects we are working on currently since they deal with unique questions and problems. Some projects also operate at a more urban level, others operate at a product design level. Since each opportunity is different they require different starting points, different design strategies, and different approaches.

The shared DNA amongst them is our iterative process, often non-linear, and frequently Darwinian where the final solution is the one that survives the stress test of the project parameters. So, to answer your question directly, I do not think every project should look alike but they share a connection of a thinking process, a certain line of questioning and stress testing.

TN How has the Bloomberg Center influenced other projects by Morphosis, worked on in the office alongside this project in parallel, and those which had come on board after its completion?

U-JSL The Bloomberg Center has influenced other projects in the sense that we always strive to improve. Even for you in architecture school, I like to think that every project that you work on will be better than

the previous project because you are always advancing your line of thinking and you are honing your observation skills. You are also discovering and learning the mechanics of putting buildings together, so details always improve. Many of our peers strive to do the same, that is really important for the evolution and progression of a professional office. For example, if you want to design a stair, you cannot figure it out on one project. You do one stair, and you detail it, and you learn from it. Then in the next project you advance the detail, you learn from it and then advance it in the next project, and you keep going. When you look at buildings from many seasoned practices, you see a building and you begin to appreciate the history of a detail, and a certain level of iteration that's required to take and make a detail interesting functionally and pragmatically. In that sense, for me, this building affects the next project, which affects the next project, and so on. That requires continuity, discipline, a lot of experience, and a staff who are aware of this process. I think lineage, history, and continuity are important because if you want to keep making better work both conceptually and tectonically, you cannot break that link. You must keep it up continuously because through that continuity you advance the work.

TV Thank you so much, Scott! I have to just share one more thing before we wrap up. When coming up with a set of

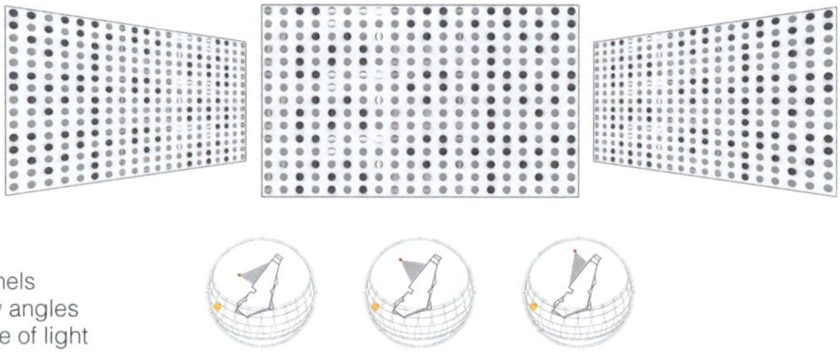

Envelope panels showing view angles and incidence of light

In that sense, we didn't imagine the Bloomberg Center as an icon. It was an incredibly important building, for a very important community, in a very special place. In our minds we are simply deploying creativity to solve challenging problems. We are just doing what we need to do to make something that is creative, something new, which can meet the budget and the schedule, in a pragmatic way. The goal was not to produce an icon.

themes which seemed relevant for my grad seminar at NYIT seminar, the theme of "Environment", comprising climate, energy, and issues of circularity, resilience and sustainability, was the most difficult of the six themes to associate with a truly fantastic case study project. I say that mainly because there aren't many seminal buildings like the Bloomberg Center, which absolutely fulfills the criteria given by your client of attaining net zero status. Often in architecture, projects that announce themselves as ecologically performative, sustainable, resilient, or green, not that these terms are interchangeable, are often buildings that either suspend, or even worse, are uninterested in aesthetics, appearance, formalism, or signature, as secondary to the main environmental aspirations of the project. In one of the publications on the Bloomberg Center, I recall reading a quote from Thom Mayne, declaring, "We don't design icons!", and I find that to be a compelling statement by a Pritzker Prize winning architect. Whilst I do not make claims about icons and the body of work of Morphosis as a practice, the Bloomberg Center seems to be iconic, if I can use this term as an adjective rather than as a noun, an icon. This is an iconic building in terms of energy and climatic performance, and would like to hear your thoughts on whether you find this classification either congratulatory or offensive.

U-JSL When we're in the middle of a design process, we never start the process saying that we are going to end up with an icon. For example, when you're passionate about cooking and you are sweating in your kitchen, your goal is to make the best dining experience for that one dish, for that one night, for that one customer. I don't think you are cooking aiming that dish to be a Michelin star, or at least that's not how I think about it. You start by sourcing the best ingredients you can find, putting them together in your way and seeing where you go. It's a little bit open ended.

Sometimes the icon is important to a client for various reasons, because they're interested in a certain kind of impact. So that's great, it's fun, and we are very fortunate that we are brought in by some clients with the specific goal to create an icon, but that is not our day one mission. We learned that from Thom Mayne himself, who immersed himself in projects, and there were no design shortcuts for him. He reminds us that these days, the world does not need more icons but rather great buildings in great public spaces that inspire people in some ways. If that is an icon, then he would be ok with it.

TV In those terms, the Bloomberg Center also underscores how buildings have an impact on us, on our emotional well-being, and also on the environment. This has been an architectural value which in last year of our pandemic, architecture has begun to embrace the association between different areas of performance, between how a building makes us feel, its impact on our own bodily health, the health of society, and the health of our planet. Thank you so much for joining us, Scott. It's been a huge treat for my students and I to have you join my seminar. You've generously given us a lot of your time, and on behalf of our school, our Dean, our M.Arch program, and especially our students, I cannot thank you enough.

U-JSL Great! Thank you! You guys hang in there - only a few more weeks of Covid, tops. Thank you, Tom, talk to you soon, and thanks for having me!

COPENHILL POWER PLANT

Copenhagen, 2019 | Bjarke Ingels Group BIG

Program Waste to Energy Plant, skiing, hiking, rock climbing, offices, après ski bar

Materials Aluminum panels, glass panels, skiing acrylic surface, hiking landscape planting

400,000 T	Non-Recyclable Waste Every Year
140,000	Households Supplied with District Heating
550,000	People Provided With Low-Carbon Electricity
45%	Glazing
2,865	Glass Façade Panels
3,724	Aluminum Façade Panels (Alu-Bricks)
11	Floors Above Ground
0	Floors Below Ground
90 M	High Rock Climbing Wall
9,000 M2	Skiing / Hiking
41,000 M2	GFA

INTERVIEW

Interviewee: Kai-Uwe Bergmann, Partner, BIG

Interviewers: Amy Goldfisher, Angie Syed, final year Master of Architecture students in the School of Architecture and Design at New York Institute of Technology

April 12, 2023

Tom Verebes Thank you, Kai-Uwe! Your in-depth presentation of the Copenhill Power Plant, among other related BIG projects was truly a thrill! Thank you for explaining to us in such great detail about the making of the project, and sharing your excitement and enthusiasm about it. Copenhill is certainly a ground-breaking project and a tremendous achievement. I'll introduce Amy Goldfisher and Angie Syed, final year M.Arch students at New York Tech, who will conduct this interview with you.

Kai-Uwe Bergmann Thank you - it is a really a pleasure to join your seminar and this live event at NYIT.

Amy Goldfisher Hi! My name is Amy Goldfisher. My partner is Angie Syed, and we'd like to thank you for your engaging and informative presentation. The story of the Copenhill Power Plant's development from the competition stage to a commission, to its eventual built outcome is one led by the vision and determination of its architect, BIG. We understand the budget for this project was partly crowd funded through Kickstarter. In your presentation, you pointed towards the power of the architect as an agency capable of instigating change. The architects in this instance acted simultaneously as an environmental activist and venture capitalist. Can you share with us how and why this alternative mode of raising capital for an architectural project was used? Was there an insufficient budget provided, and was crowdfunding used to supplement the given budget? What parts of the project were crowdfunded – and what was added to the project brief as a result of crowdfunding?

K-UB Great question! Let me clarify what was actually crowdfunded. Kickstarter was getting started as an online crowdfunding tool while we were doing this project, and we were very curious as to how to crowdfund our ideas. We crowdfunded the testing of the steam ring generator to prove that the mechanism is possible. If you think about any kind of project you are going to continuously have hidden challenges. Here in New York City we have the BIG U Resiliency Project – which is now in its tenth year. To maintain a vision through different mayoral administrations and through different funding mechanisms, through some federal funding and a lot of city funding, you have to be very resourceful and creative on where to look for funding in order to create great architecture.

AG Our next question concerns the relationships between industry and the public, and infrastructure and the city. Intersecting public, social, and recreational infrastructure with clean energy infrastructure serves to rewrite the history of the relationships of dirty industry to the city – and the legacy of the industrial revolution regarding how cities are organized which had generally zoned industrial areas and poorer economic groups in the east, where prevailing winds blow, and are more polluted. The concept of intersecting energy infrastructure with public activities aimed to mitigate NIMBY-ism, the ISM of "Not In My Backyard". Were there still people or groups who opposed the project, even with the benefits of the expanded public activities? If so, what were the reasons for their opposition? Lastly, after four years since completion, has the public embraced the Copenhill Power Plant as a public social and recreational space?

K-UB This is where I think things become quite political at times and it's interesting that architects as a whole are not very political. We don't generally pick a political affiliation or run for office. Very often, I find it's because architects are afraid that if they were political, they would alienate whoever is not in their favor. So, as an architect, you try to be open, but at the same

time you're a little bit at the mercy of what the prevailing thought is. So, to answer your question, there was a group that was still against the project. Their whole idea was that the transformation of a waste society to a non-waste society was not happening fast enough, so they wanted to go cold turkey circular, and we were saying that it's really hard to imagine a world that will be circular tomorrow and that we need to create transitional infrastructure that takes you from our current waste producing society to a less wasteful society by finding ways to turn that waste into energy.

And so a question for you and your generation of designers is how do we move the needle quickly enough to address climate change and climate catastrophe? And, how do we get there? So a project like this looks good on paper and looks great in practice, but it is not fast enough. That is what the people who were opposing it were saying; that we are spending so much money to still be trapped for another 30 or 40 years in the waste creation bubble. What we were saying is, let's put this plant out

Formal generation.

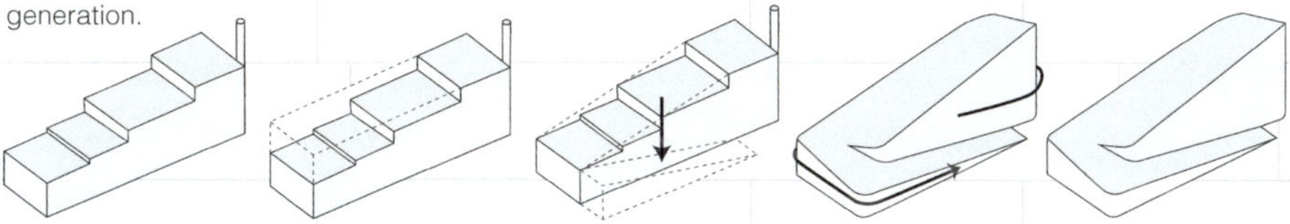

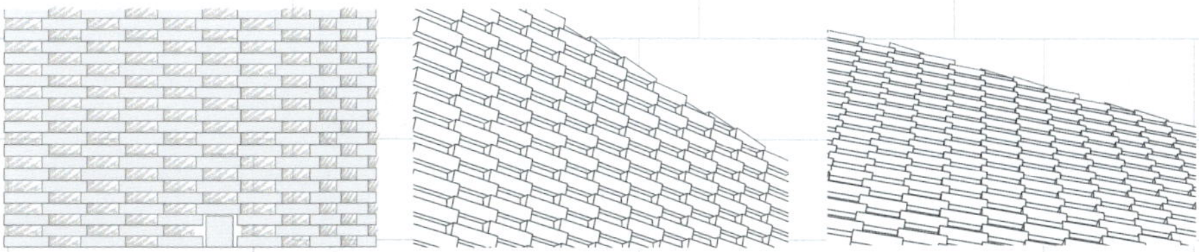

Elevation and views of "alu-bricks" and glazing on facade.

"And since there are all these athletic, sporting amenities around the project. Why not bring those onto the site? And so we came up with a breakthrough concept of taking an elevator ride up to the roof, and then being able to ski down. Having black diamond, blue and green trails, and seeing how all of these things could start to feed one another."
— Kai-Uwe Bergmann

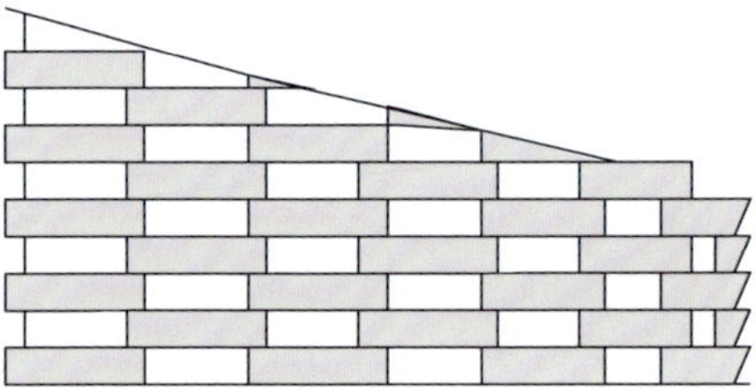

Façade block edges

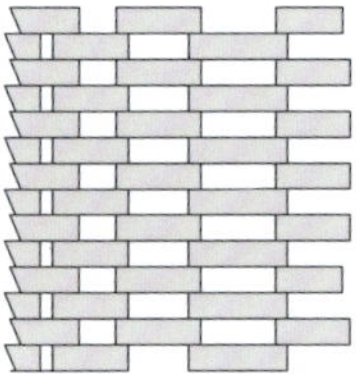

Façade block density

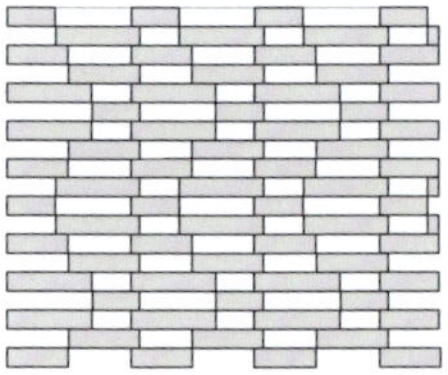

Façade block pattern

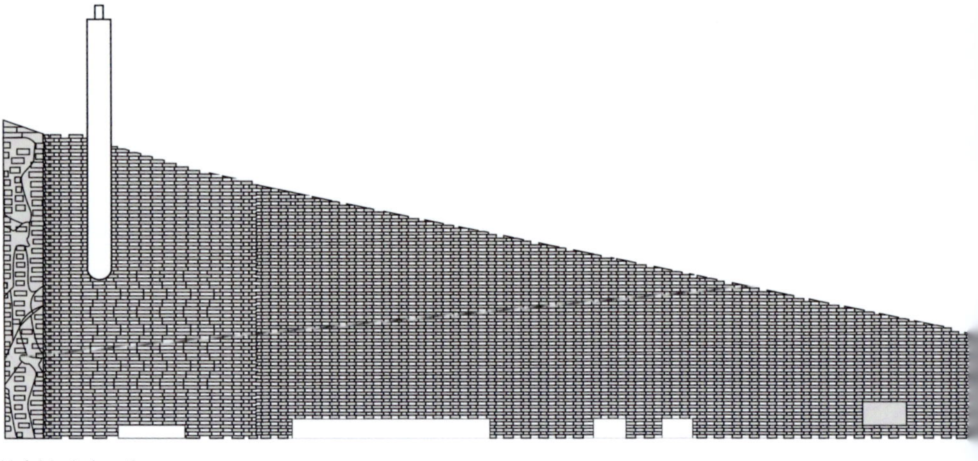

Unfolded elevation

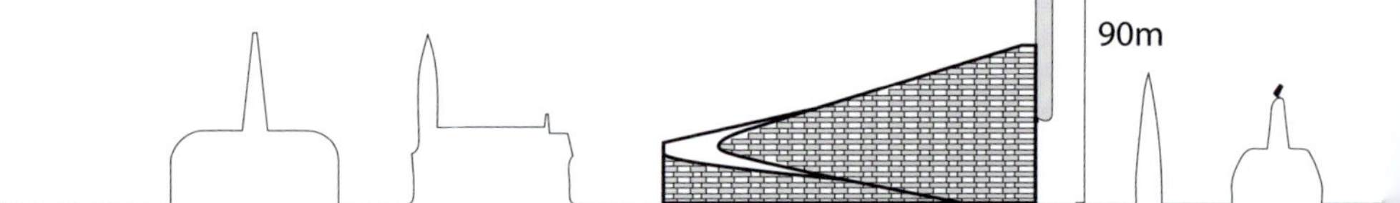

Elevation in context

of business because it's not about being wasteful about the plant. The plant could turn into a recycling plant, so you could suddenly go from burning waste as the best use of energy and an efficient transition to recycling 80% or 90% of our waste. Our waste currently is not 80 to 90% recyclable. We do not yet create products that one can just turn into something else. The first thing that has to happen is that we, through our design of the world, of the products, of the food, of the containers, of the packaging, we all need to work towards creating a circular economy. But to answer your question, now, within the four years since its completion, people have shown they love this plant. It actually has usage problems, because people are using it much more than it was intended. So, the wear and tear and the maintenance costs are higher, but that is actually a good thing. It is very exciting to see how Copenhageners have embraced it. It has literally made people travel to Copenhagen just to see it. Greta Thunberg toured it. Mayor Michael Bloomberg walked all over its roof. People are coming to Copenhagen to experience it, and I think it will have a positive change for other energy plants around the world. But we have a bigger question and responsibility, which is, how do we change our habits to become a no-waste society?

AS Thank you. In the Copenhill project, BIG's ambition to create world changing architecture applied the agency of a programmatic strategy to create strange, post-natural combinations, not wholly different from Bernard Tschumi's cross programming, or OMA's paranoid surrealistic method. So within this disciplinary context, can you elaborate on the programmatic strategy of mixing energy infrastructure and public recreational activities, which create a synthesis of unexpected combinations, and even surrealist effects?

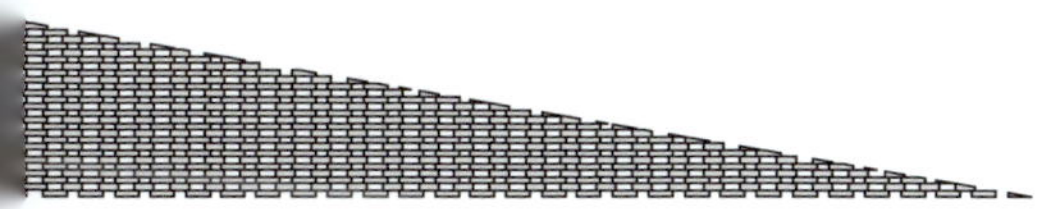

K-UB I will respond a little bit less academically, and more about people. We are working now in New York on the Brooklyn Queens Expressway, the BQE. It was conceived in the 1950s and was built in that period of time and into the sixties, and was just about getting people from Point A to Point B. The BQE was designed by traffic engineers, as one of Robert Moses's projects, who created a lot of infrastructure. The BQE also produced a lot of bad side effects. It split neighborhoods, it cut a lot of things off from each other and had profound economic byproducts, and, at the human level, we should not be designing infrastructure without thinking of people first – or I can even go so far as all species and organisms first. Here we have demonstrated that the birds and the bees have as much right to this area as humans; as much right to the area as the workers. We need to create for this complexity. We can make the world easier by mono single-use zoning of areas and declaring: this is where you work; this is where you live; and, this is where we create energy, but this compartmentalization does not work. We need to create more complexity. We need to design that complexity as a positive part of life, and then we need to co-exist within it, and I think we will then have much greater mutual respect. I would assume people will have much greater respect for this energy plant. School children take tours of the plant, and they'll have a much better understanding of their connectivity to this power plant than any other power plant. That is how I see it on a more social level. I think social infrastructure is what we have to talk about.

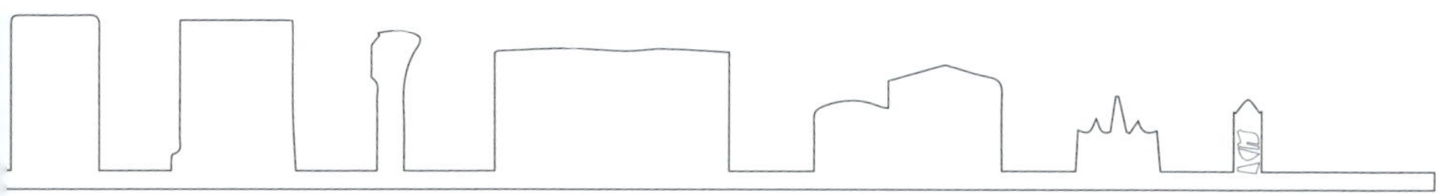

AS Thank you. One of the roles of the Copenhill Power Plant is to serve as an Environmental Educational Hub. Ultimately, does the architecture of a city's public institutions, infrastructure and technical apparatus have the obligation to educate the public? Can you comment on the expanded role of architecture to inform the public, and ultimately to educate its users? More broadly, what is the power of architecture to educate, and how specifically does the Copenhill Power Plant educate the public on green energy?

K-UB I think it's a continual process of education. So there is actually a room dedicated to teaching school aged kids about energy production, for dignitaries to meet up and learn about energy. They go to this plant, and there is a room dedicated for learning. They take tours. The spaces of the power plant are accessible. We have created a framework for much of this to happen, and it is now really up to the people who run this facility and for the programmers, but they now have a whole new way of interacting with the citizens. They can also have events that bring different types of citizens to the plant. While they are there, they can educate through screens, or through handouts, or through tours and personal experience. I do think that the education component was very high on our agenda and on our thinking of the function of this facility. That is also why the director stated she chose us: there were a lot of byproduct wins in choosing this scheme over another scheme. The architect is not engaged to create the curricula or the educational program. That is actually something that I think all of us contribute to, but it is driven by the people who run the plant.

AG The climate crisis has led to radical approaches to greening industry and infrastructure, and the relationship between architecture and its environmental impact. Processing residual household waste, this project simultaneously creates a biodiverse landscape with capacities to absorb heat, remove air particulates, and manage stormwater runoff, what is leftover after waste. BIG has published the Copenhill Power Plant project, arguing for what you call, "Hedonistic Sustainability", as the concept behind the design of this building, as well as many other BIG buildings. Can you please explain the concept of "hedonistic sustainability"? Does this notion imply the public enjoyment of clean infrastructure, and the environmental, social, and urban sustainability of this building to enable new experiences for the public to come closer to industry?

K-UB OK! Let's define what we see as hedonistic sustainability. Sustainability through the decades has been more of a Puritan approach to reducing resources. It means not taking hot showers, but cold showers. It means not flying, but maybe walking or boating, or taking the train. It means smaller windows, because you

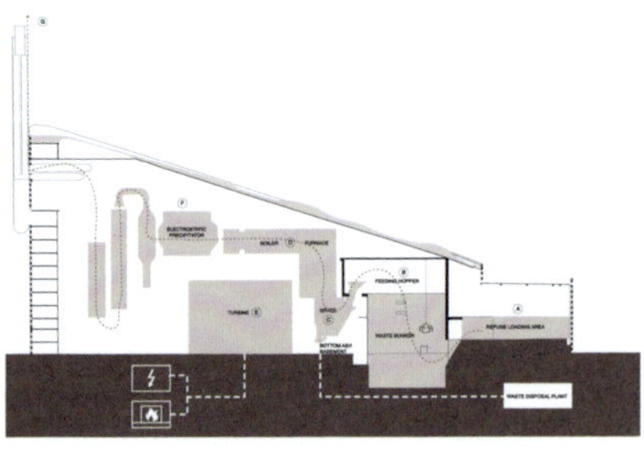

Building section of powerplant operation

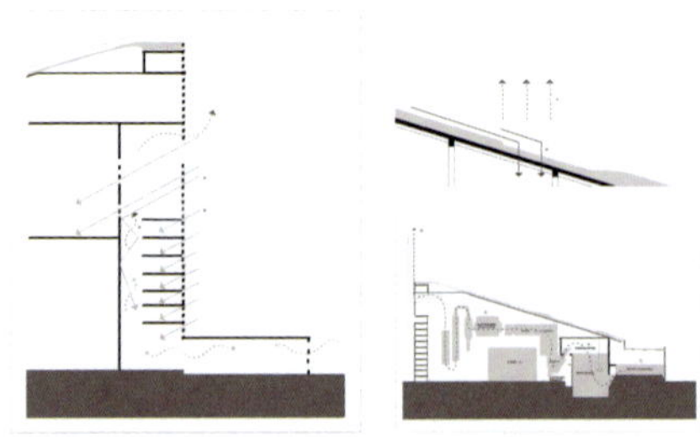

"The deciding factor in our winning of this project was that the director of Copenhilll looked at this project, and said the NIMBYs that she had always confronted in her decades of being in charge of the power plant, would turn into YIMBYs through our design of Copenhill. Yes, I want this power plant in my backyard. "
— Kai-Uwe Bergmann

need more insulation, and that's something where you are going to have a group of people that would reduce their enjoyment or lquality of life – you'll have a group of people, but it is not going to be all people. The way to get people to change their habits is to demonstrate that there is a higher quality of life with this approach and with this kind of idea about resource allocation. If people see that they can have bigger windows, if they can take hot showers, if they can take flights, they will very likely move towards that lifestyle than the other direction, and this is just in terms of thinking about mass adoption. Now, someone would ask "how could you take hot showers because you will need electricity?" Well, we have ample amounts of electricity, and it's called the sun. So if we have this sun, it is possible. We just need to now harness and build a world where we take the energy of the sun, and then are able to also pump it wherever we need it at a given time, even at night, when the sun is not there. Wind is the same way. Sometimes it's windy, and sometimes it's not. How can we actually balance out need and production? We feel that with a global energy grid, we could actually produce way more energy than the 10 billion people that are projected to be living on the planet by 2050 would ever need.

So, it's not a matter of designing for less energy. It is designing systems that produce more energy than we need in a renewable fashion that does not require more energy to be spent to harness it. Then we just need to be more intelligent about how we use it. It is really about thinking of the bigger picture and creating a more enjoyable and higher quality life. That way we can move very quickly to the adoption of hedonistic sustainability.

AS Awesome! As you mentioned earlier in your presentation, Copenhill is capable of

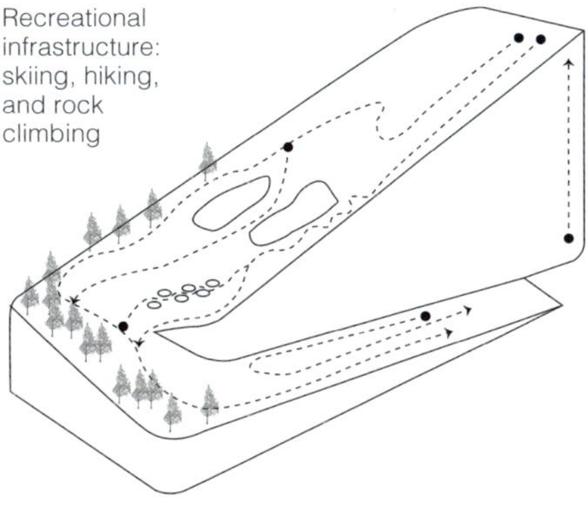

converting 440,000 tons of waste into clean energy annually, delivering electricity and district heating to 150,000 homes. Applying advanced technology in waste treatment and energy production, Copenhill is claimed to be the cleanest waste-to-energy power plant in the world. Can this building be understood as a prototype for other hybrid infrastructural buildings in Denmark, or elsewhere in the world? Is this kind of radical project possible to achieve in developing countries where budgets may be limited? And, were there any precedents you considered as examples of strange intersections of recreational infrastructure mixed with clean energy infrastructure?

K-UB So yes, it is a prototype in many ways, and we are currently in active conversations for a couple of energy projects elsewhere. I actually do feel that even in emerging economies this is a very viable concept, because oftentimes energy grids are the very source of global funding initiatives, like the World Bank or ESG funding. There are many different funding mechanisms to create transitional types of events like this. I honestly feel that on a smaller scale, medium scale, and large scale, this is very much implementable. The funny thing is that the waste-to-energy model was presented to America in the 1970s as a possible energy source, because energy prices rose very high. Tom (Verebes) might remember this. The fossil fuel companies were trying to run it out of business and they created marketing campaigns that claimed that waste-to-energy plants, which typically are in centers of cities as opposed to farmlands, are smelly, nasty energy plants within urban centers. They defeated the purpose, whereas Denmark truly adopted the waste-to-energy concept, because they had no place for the trash to go. Believe it or not, America puts all their waste into landfills and all of those landfills are actually an energy source. Maybe one day it will be cost effective to go to a landfill and turn it into an energy plant, because you have unlimited sources of waste. Just think of how ironic it is. We were called when press on this came out – I remember a call from the Pentagon. It was someone that was in Iraq, fighting in the desert to protect America's access to fossil fuels, and the General was basically saying, "Sir, you're telling me that the waste that we produce in this camp is actually fuel?" And I said, "Yes, sir". He explained how they actually put their waste onto semi-trucks, drive it through the desert and get shot at so that they could bury it under a bunch of sand. They literally had an energy source within the camp that they were actually taking out of the camp because they didn't want to smell it, all in order to defend fossil fuel energy. None of these things really make sense. If we have the knowledge, every municipality in the United States could be burning its household waste with incinerators and these clean technologies. This is a real thing. It's a proven technology. It's being used very effectively in Scandinavia and in other parts of Europe, and should also happen here in the US.

AS Thank you – this is so great to hear. Do you think that the concepts of Copenhill can be replicated to transform other existing power plants that also burn waste and convert to energy? In other words, do you believe other older power plants can be retrofitted as clean waste-burning energy plants, and then compounded with public, social, and recreational activities?

K-UB It is always going to be a big question of

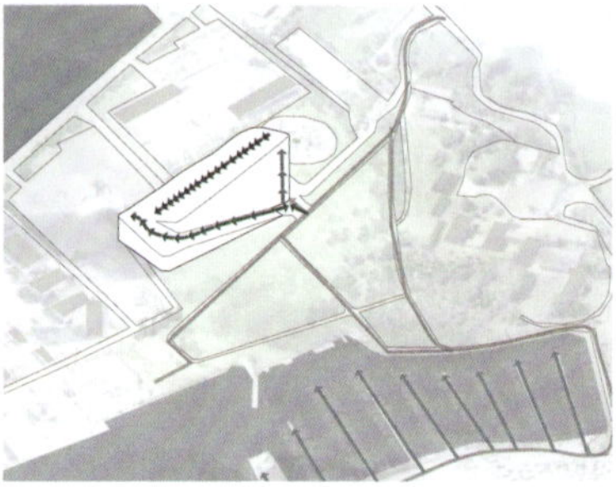

Urban context

retrofitting and the cost thereof versus building anew. They had that exact same question in Denmark with the old plant, and they decided to build the new plant adjacent to the old plant because it was more costly to retrofit. Because so much has changed – and you'll see that the square-footage of this plant is one fifth of that of the former plant – they produce the same amount of energy. So, even a retrofitting of an old plant with outdated technology does not mean a one-for-one transition. Other factors might come into play when deciding whether to retrofit or to build anew.

AS Thank you.

AG Shifting our discussion towards the façade technologies of Copenhill, a set of differentiated modules and patterns of ALU-Bricks wraps around the façade of the building, as a checkerboard of solid and glazed panels. How and why did BIG create a set of 3 distinct module patterns inset into the regular grid of modules, and what is the reasoning and possible performance of these design decisions?

K-UB A portion of the building is an office building which comes with certain code requirements in terms of the amount of daylight that reaches the office space. Some of the window openings also have to be operable for fresh air. And so, we looked at all of the different programmatic elements. There is an office building. There are the guts of the actual plants, and there is an elevator that takes you up to the top. There is a bar at the top of the roof, which also wants to be able to be used as an observatory. We quickly arrived at the design of a module that allowed for the right amount of daylight intake. It allowed for latrines to be placed, so that we could actually fill them with landscape and start growing vines or growing foliage on the façade. Then we needed to create openings for trucks to drive through, and for the skiers to come down and hit the ground. The façade pattern is a brick pattern that allows for a lot of flexibility. It addressed the corner by faceting it, and it was a very workable, flexible façade solution that allowed us to do everything that we needed to.

AS That's great. Our next question concerns the relationships of the Copenhill Power Plant project to BIG's larger portfolio of work. Further to your presentation, can you share with us the genealogy of the design of the Copenhill project within BIG's portfolio of preceding projects. Are there projects which led to Copenhill, as earlier prototypes that you developed further?

K-UB What a great question! If you know our books – *Yes Is More*, *Hot To Cold*, and *Formgiving* – in the back of *Yes Is More*, which came out in 2009, the year that we won Copenhill, there is a really interesting family tree that looks at all of our projects and how they are related. It is called "pragmatic evolution", and it looks at how our projects inform and build upon the ideas of multiple projects; that everything is a bit of an evolutionary kind of process. I would not specifically say that there is any one project that would be a precursor to Copenhill. The Mountain is a project that predates Copenhill, and, it too, has a fifth façade, which is a beautiful landscape on a roof structure. It is residential, and therefore all of the roof landscapes are individual gardens for the units. It implements the idea that the roof is actually something that should be enjoyed, and the roof is something that should be "birded", in that birds should be attracted to your buildings. That idea, I think, is definitely in a series of projects, and then became even more embedded in the Copenhill project.

AG Thank you. Please share with us how Copenhill has influenced your practice's recent and current work? In more broad terms, what has been the impact of the Copenhill project on your practice and more recent portfolio of projects?

K-UB As a piece of social infrastructure, I would say that any piece of infrastructure that we work on now, be it a power plant, or a bridge, or a highway, or flood management system, is only to realize that the world is a very big place. There are many pieces of infrastructure that are continuously and daily designed around us, and we, as architects, should be a part of their design and their thinking. Every time you come up against a really dumb gray wall that cuts you off from whatever other pieces of life there are on the other side, someone has made a decision to place a piece of infrastructure, a flood wall for example, that might not be the smartest use of concrete or of urbanism. So that is where we also have to be a part of that process. We believe that Copenhill has given us confidence. It has given us a little bit of proof that we can take something on the scale of the city and contribute, so that makes it a little bit easier each and every time we propose those kinds of large-scale ideas – but it's never easy. When you work at the scale of infrastructure, you are literally opening yourself up to, again, not just years, but perhaps decades of effort, and not just individual clients, but really a room full of hundreds, if not thousands, of people who have an opinion about what you're doing. So, it also requires very unique skills that I hope you are learning at NYIT.

AS This Beyond the Envelope series of presentations and interviews is set within a Master of Architecture course here at NYIT, and within our SoAD public series of lectures and events, and therefore your audience is predominantly students, as well as future architects. In this context, can you please share with us, from your point of view, any advice you may have for the next generation of architects?

K-UB Yes! Think BIG!

AS That's an amazing response. Thank you very much for your fantastic presentation. We are so honored to have this opportunity to interview you today.

TV Thank you very much, Kai-Uwe, for your enthusiasm to share your expertise today. Your generosity today is really greatly appreciated.

ASIAN GAMES 2023 HYBRID STADIUM / CONCERT HALL

Hangzhou, China, 2023 | Archi-Tectonics NYC LLC

Program Sports and/or concert events, foyer, bars, fitness center

Materials Planar solar glass, recycled aluminum & brass shingles, locally sourced bamboo, concrete base

Green Building Evaluation Label (GBEL) 3 Star

Awards Architizer A+ 2022 Innovation Award, CTBUH Excellence Award 2023, Luban Award 2021, BIM Award 2021

Solid	80%
Glazing	20%
Seats	6500
Glass Facade Modules	20%
Brass Shingles Facade Modules	6300
High	30 M
Floors Above Ground	2
Floors Below Ground	1
Site Area	47 HEC
Footprint	12,000M2
GFA	35,000 M2

INTERVIEW

Interviewee: Winka Dubbeldam, Founder and Partner, Archi-Tectonics NYC LLC, Professor of Architecture Weitzman School of Design, University of Pennsylvania, Director ARI Lab

Interviewers: Damini Srireddy, final year Master of Architecture student, School of Architecture and Design, New York Institute of Technology

March 29, 2023

Tom Verebes Thank you Winka for joining us! This is a very special opportunity for us to be toured through your pioneering project for the Asian Games in Hangzhou. I would like to introduce Damini Srireddy, a final year M.Arch student at New York Tech, who will launch into our interview with you.

Winka Dubbeldam Thank you for the invitation to join you here.

Damini Srireddy My name is Damini Srireddy, and I would like to thank you for your thorough, comprehensive, and enlightening presentation. The Hangzhou Asian Games Park for the 2022 Asian Games is the largest project ever undertaken and completed by Archi-Tectonics. This project comprises a vast 116 acre masterplan with the integration of seven buildings for the Asian Games, and the Village Valley Mall, a submerged valley as a shopping mall. The complexity of this project necessitated the use of Parametric Design & Building Information Modeling (BIM) for optimization, integration of information from all consultants to be consolidated into a central model for all consultants to work on, but also importantly, so the project could be managed remotely at a great distance. To recap, this project was designed in 2018 and for a large part built during the context of Covid-19, within a very tight schedule for completion for the Asian Games, and during a time in which there was a ban prohibiting travel to China during this time. Long before these tools were invented, architects were seeking clients and projects far away, due to economic necessities and the opportunities presented to internationally recognized architects. The use of BIM seems to facilitate a new expanded remoteness for a design team, yet with increased integration of consultants' information. Can you tell us about

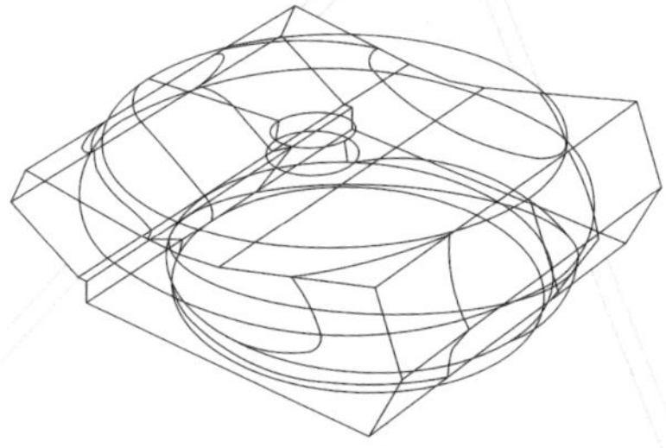

your experience of working remotely on this project with the use of BIM, especially given the travel ban, and also how your practice might be now in a position to work anywhere?

WD We had already built several projects in China, London, Paris, and elsewhere before, without Zoom, so we knew we could do this project. What was interesting about working on the Asian Games is that when we were halfway into the project, we had to switch to remote work. But it was surely not all negative. If you were inspecting this stadium in person on site, standing in the mud in front of it, you would never be able to see the top of the structure. During Covid, our local architect in Hangzhou would do drone visits in their daytime, which is our night time. The next day, we would watch the drone footage of each building being circled and we could stop the movie at any point, investigate a detail, and then, if we thought there was something super tricky going on, we would meet on Zoom with the contractor to discuss the issue.

Regarding BIM, we did not start with BIM. We started by designing everything in 3D using Maya and Rhino, then we gave the 3D model to the local architect & contractor to use for their BIM. This is becoming the norm and that is what they are building from. Also, by sheer coincidence, the LDI [local architect] person that was in charge of BIM, just loved our architecture, and was fascinated by the building. If there was a problem, he would call us, and we would work out details with him over Zoom. It was amazing to work with a local architect that loves your building, and would take the trouble of contacting us regularly. It is shocking how precisely the contractor built these buildings, and how precisely they followed all our drawings. In that sense, what we will definitely keep working with, is the idea that with a drone you can circle the building, and in your own time, go back to the movie and inspect the building at every height, which is extremely informative. If we had to drive by car from building to building, we would just not have had long enough time on site, and we would have had to move onto site for much longer to see everything. I am still super impressed with the contractor how they coordinated the whole project, because they had 300 workers on site every day. During the Covid pandemic, 300 workers would be on site for two weeks, and then this team would be off for two weeks. They would bring on another team in the meantime for 2 weeks, so there were two teams of 300 workers working two weeks on, two weeks off. They did that to be safe during Covid, and because we won the project only in May 2018, and the games were supposed to open in September 2022, so that meant the 7 buildings had to be done at the start of 2022, so they could still build out the interiors, the lighting, the air conditioning, and test all the facilities. The team managed to be ready for September 2022, but then they postponed the Asian Games for a year. The park, in the meantime, has been super popular and inundated by people camping, fishing, dancing and kayaking. It has been great to see. What we were hoping was for the project to operate first for the Asian Games, and then to be open for the city, but because of the delay, it was first open to the city. The hybrid stadium building has already been open several times for big events. At New Years, they had 2,500 students and faculty members celebrating, and the building's LED lighting was gorgeous. This hybridity is important, not only because of the reduction of carbon footprint, but also the building is to be for the neighborhood, and not just a "white elephant".

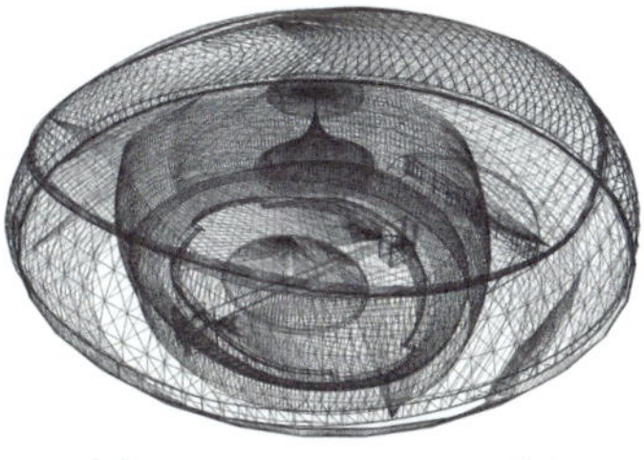

Formal concept based on the "cong"

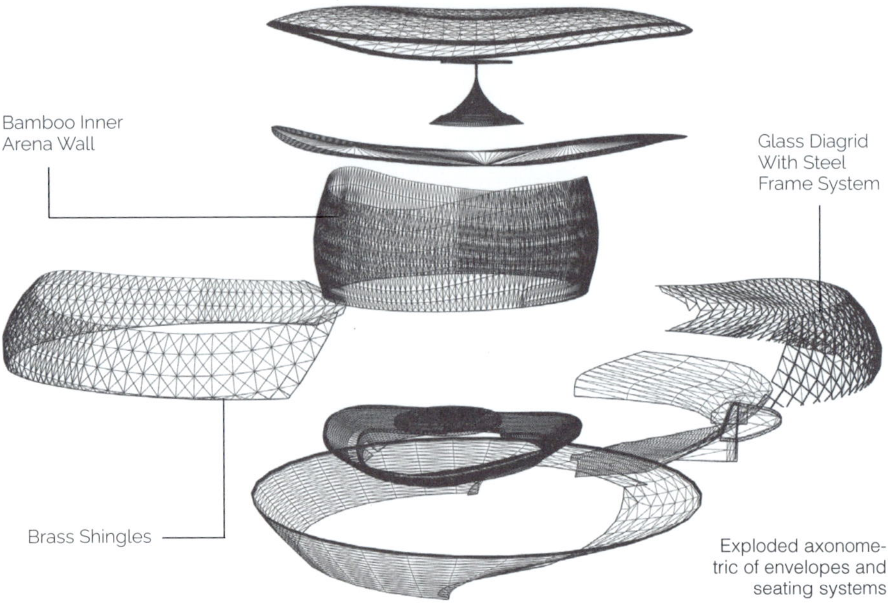

Exploded axonometric of envelopes and seating systems

DS In your presentation, and also in the few recent publications of the project in the architectural press, you highlighted the risk of these kinds of short term sporting events, also including the Olympics, becoming a "white elephant" – facilities which become unused, costly to maintain, and disruptive in the city's fabric. In our M.Arch course with Professor Verebes at NYIT, we have discussed, in relation to your project, the problem of obsolescence, dysfunctionality and decay of architecture over time, and strategies with which to futureproof an architectural or urban design project. We are keen to know more about how you developed the Asian Games project to be integrated into the city to remain an active urban landscape territory with thriving buildings and facilities which will accommodate a range of future uses, needs and desires. Your thesis focuses on the adaptability of HYBRID buildings – which are defined as multipurpose, and are transformable between sports and music and performing arts uses. Was the strategy of future proofing via the principle of hybrid buildings part of the competition brief, or was this proposition for the hybridity of uses in the two stadia in particular part of Archi-Tectonics' proposal?

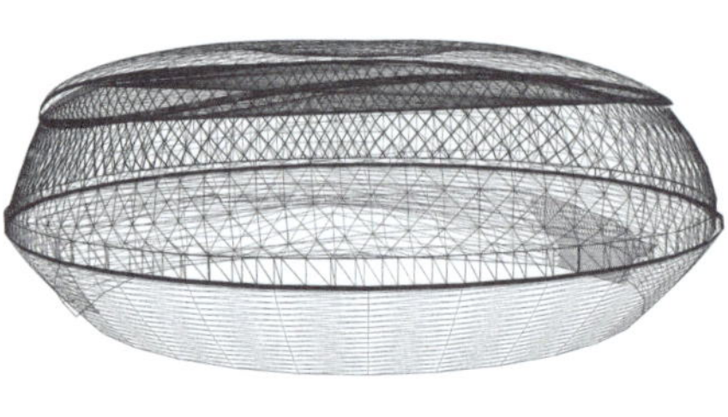

WD That is a very good question. Our client, the government, only stipulated what is called a "Sponge City", so they wanted the park to be sustainable. They had very strict rules of stormwater management & porous pavement, and we added the restoration of the wetlands. We also did a major study of local vegetation to bring back the local birds and insects to restore the local biome. We accelerated the idea of the Eco park to the 7 buildings, which was to have a LEED Platinum certification, and converted them into hybrid buildings that will be used after the Games. For example, an underground shopping mall is not very sustainable. You need artificial light, artificial air, which is the opposite of sustainable. That is when we developed a new shopping concept as a valley, as a connective device for the

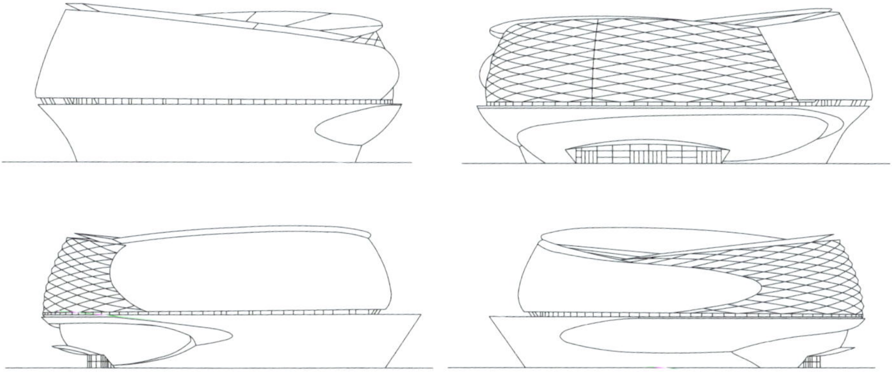

Elevations of sports theatre hybrid building

site, with natural shading, and natural light & air. The shopping pavilions have green roofs, and shops are placed along the edges of the valley, but the beauty of the valley is that it is also a continuation of the park.

The other benefit of the hybrid building concept is that it would allow us to make better buildings, to use more durable materials, create longevity and make them more beautiful. The Hybrid Stadium / concert hall's suspendome roof allows for the building to be column free, and facilitates its hybrid use. This lightweight roof is supported on the inner dome, and cantilevers over the lobby to carry the diagrid glass façade. It is an incredibly efficient and very lightweight structure. The diagrid has planar glass with custom designed fins, "eyelids" that negotiate the glass back to the double curved surface. The use of planar rather than bent glass saved significant costs just on the façade, and of course, it's much easier to maintain. The other surfaces are clad with brass shingles, that age naturally, do not need maintenance, and are parametrically optimized for the buildings curves in just 85 different shapes. By making the building's hybrids, they became permanent and instrumental for the neighborhood. Also, because we felt as the park is designed for the local people, we should also make the building's for the people, we were lucky that the client approved this, and I have to say it took very little convincing.

The most challenging point in the whole process was when they found a 3 meter diameter drain pipe for the city under the main road that bisects the park. We were told the Valley would have to pass under the pipe. Any tunnel had to be accessed by fire trucks with 5m clearance. We tested this deeper valley and the slope was just about doable. We did renderings with the pipe looking "pretty", but as you can imagine, it was not that easy. When we returned to Hangzhou however, we were told they moved the drain pipe, I don't know where it went. I didn't ask. That was definitely an amazing moment, because the Valley Village was the core idea for the connectivity of the 116 acre park

DS Architectural and urban design commissions commonly demand finality and completion of the project. The notion of a digital twin, at both the building and city scale carve out a scope of work for architects and urban designers to be commissioned to work in the post-occupancy stage of a project, on maintenance and future changes. In more general terms, can you elaborate on the problems of obsolescence and dysfunctionality over time,

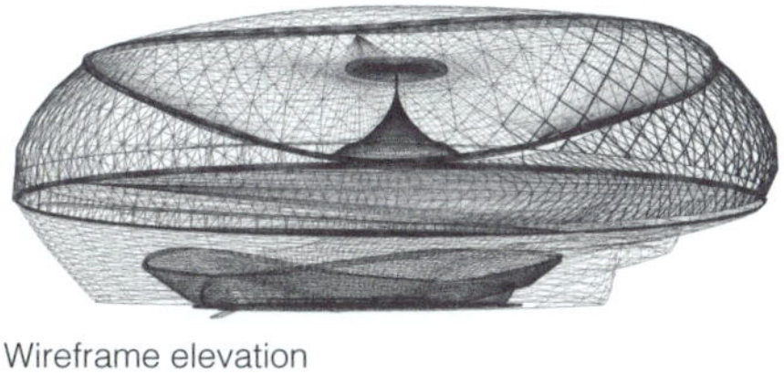

Wireframe elevation

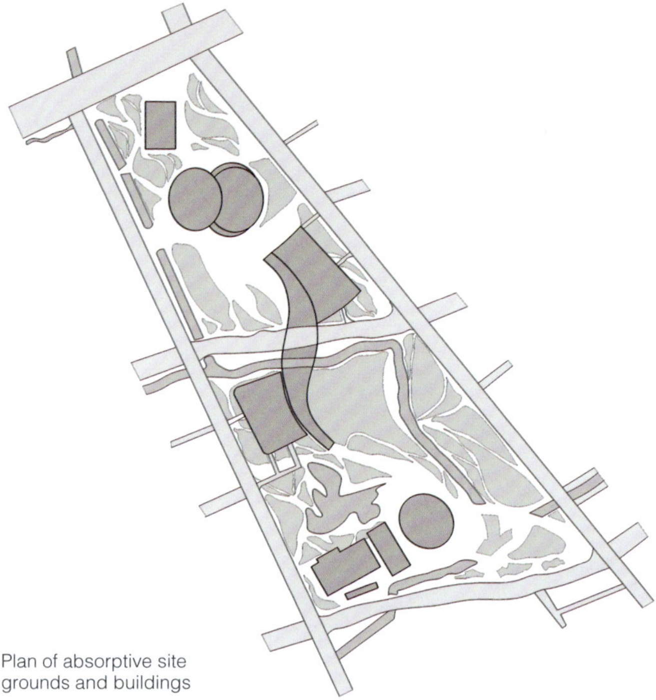

Plan of absorptive site grounds and buildings

and how this experience of proposing Hybrid Buildings helps to conceive the design of the future of an architectural and urban project?

WD Hybrids, as a typology, propose a more complex, embedded, and multiple being rather than a multi-functional or neutral space .

What I realized when I was working on this project was that a stadium typically is a one-liner, what you see is what you get. The Hybrid however needed to express its character and allow for multiplicity of use. I am interested in how architecture can change human behavior, and how we can be seduced to do other things.

By creating a hybrid, we also introduced an arena with hybrid seating, a redundancy of stairs and ramps through the six story high void, with upper & lower lobbies, and future areas for the concert hall. The building is conceived of intersecting ellipse discs, "wobbly disks", with intersecting surfaces allowing for fluidity of movement. Although the building seems symmetrical, it's completely asymmetrical, a hybrid with a complex geometry that is adaptable. We believe buildings should act as organisms, and breathe. To accommodate that, the building has a ring of automatically opening windows under the roof that let hot air out, and only the seats are cooled, drastically reducing energy use.

DS In our seminar, we have discussed the paradigm of temporal adaptivity and how to design for change within the larger scope of urban territories, as well as how buildings are adapted and reused along their lifespan. As a question: How can the hybridity of programming, or in other words, the transformability of a building for multiple uses at different times, potentially inform a more holistic approach to planning architectural methods to deal with variability, future flexibility, futureproofing, and the changing context, needs, and demands, of the built environment? Asked more simply and directly, how does The Asian Games project and its thesis on adaptability and futureproofing suggest a more general model of evolutionary change for architecture and urban design?

WD I think we are all going to face some serious challenges. It is just unreal what's happening now in nature – we have tennis balls of ice falling from the sky, wildfires, hurricanes and tornadoes that happen more and more frequently.

It would be odd today if we wouldn't think of new solutions that would introduce landscapes as eco parks that absorb the stormwater that we cannot absorb with our cities, re-introduce wetlands and re-naturalize the rivers with plants to filter the water.

We hope that this can also be an educational moment for the neighborhood – that you make the park and its buildings so beautiful that people will not pollute it with plastic, that they take care of it. It is a good sign that the neighbors go camping and fishing in the park, and apart from gardeners hired by the Government – local people are taking care of the landscape. The buildings as hybrids have created curiosity, as a strange attractor, and the visitors are talking about it, studying, photographing & filming it, the stadium does look a little bit like an alien coming from Mars. This curiosity will also allow visitors in the future to accept the building's changing persona, as it adapts for the future. It has been published quite a bit in news media in China, stating this is now a favorite spot to visit in China, which we are very proud of! I love the fact that people appropriate it, and that they feel they share a new identity or future with it. I am not sure this redefines the idea of evolutionary change for architecture and urban design, but it could well be a start.

DS Continuing our discussion towards the concept of the Asian Games Park as an Eco-Village, there are a number of architectural systems which are driven by agendas of resilience and sustainability. Perhaps the most substantial ecological move in this project is the "urban sponge" which you say acts as an absorptive lung which collects, filters and re-uses storm-water runoff. The Sponge City approach to landscapes and urban territories, as first championed by Yu Kongjian, has been adopted as Planning Policy in many of China's largest cities. In developing the design of the low-lying masterplan, comprising absorptive green spaces, wetlands and water catchments, and hardscapes, we can quote you in publications of the project how Archi-Tectonics, as the architect, worked on equal terms with the landscape architects, Melk. Can I ask you what you can highlight as the limitations of the discipline and professional scope of architecture? In another way of asking this, what is the position of the architect in a multidisciplinary design team on such a large site, with so many ecological and hydrological challenges?

WD Traditionally, the architect initiates the project, and hires engineers and consultants. It's a bit of a pyramid. As this invited competition was so large and the time so short, I realized it needed a new collaboration model. I sat down with my business partner at Archi-Tectonics, and asked him: "How many large competitions can we do and not win?" We can do the same thing all over again, and get the same results, or we can rethink everything. What about inviting the structural engineer and the landscape architect to be equal partners for this competition? We decided to try it out and invited Thornton Tomassetti and !Melk landscape architects. They accepted and we started.

From the beginning it felt very different, we had 3 offices being equally invested, and structures, building design and landscapes all evolved together. We all did an enormous amount of work. Our team ended up having the most complex daring project, but the clearest urban model, and we came with fully engineered structures. All that helped us win in the end.

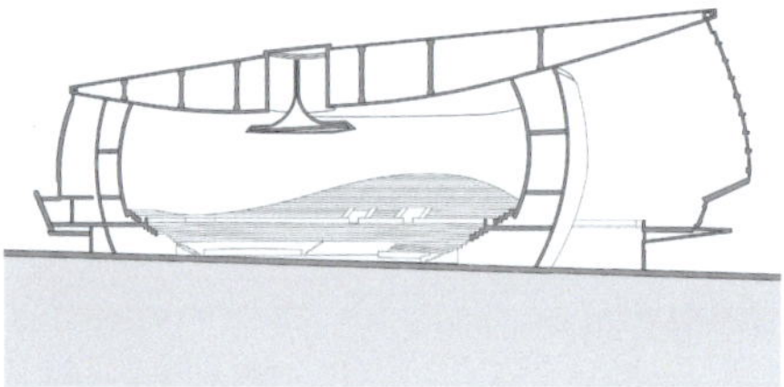

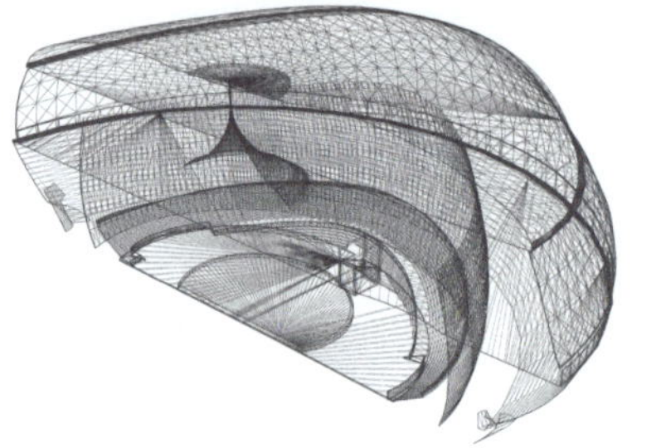

Sectional axonometric and section

We developed the master plan together with !Melk. As there is some Dutch heritage here, it was no coincidence that the idea of the Valley as connector came up in a Sunday phone call as we were brainstorming, inspired by a shopping connector in Rotterdam that is called the "koopgoot", Shopping Valley in Dutch. We translated that idea into a green valley, connecting the two halves of the park passing under a new viaduct and aqueduct. Ultimately we won because they loved the fact that we pulled the stadiums in the center of the park sections as hybrid attractors, and connected them with the valley. It was a bunch of really strange factors that the most complex scheme won, which doesn't often happen. We won because we collaborated on equal terms with the engineer and the landscape designer, to create an integrated holistic whole for the future of Hangzhou.

DS As a consequence of the Asian Games project in more broad terms, can you summarize the status of landscape architecture, landscape urbanism, or environmental planning to address the urgencies of climate change? Flipping this question, is architecture as a profession complicit in the acceleration of climate change? AND do you believe we can reshape our modes of practice in architecture to the extent to genuinely work towards the mitigation of the effects on our planet?

WD That is a really difficult question. Construction and households create up to 40% of the carbon footprint. So yes we are part of the problem. We have also had serious periods with political unrest, and social migration. I don't think architecture solves problems. But I do think architects' attitudes can help solve problems. Be more than a designer, be a thinker, be a team player, a pro-active collaborator who combines research with design.

Not to give up on complex shapes that enrich our lives, but to be smarter, faster and more engaged. Stand with your feet in the mud and take care of it. That is going to be an attitude we all have to adopt. The future lies in architects working in big multi-disciplinary teams, as we need all the experts we can find on nature, climate, and systems, not only architects.

DS Earlier, we had discussed hybrids as a programmatic concept. Can you elaborate on your thesis about the blurring of the distinctions of the categories of the natural and the synthetic, in how architecture and urbanism can manifest mutations, or other, more strange hybrids, between the presumed defunct polarities of the wild and the cultural?

As climate change challenges our environments we benefit from multi-disciplinary teams inventing new concepts. I believe that the architect's tool of expression is design that is inventive, sustainable and proactive. Beauty can be energy efficient and save money and resources, as we did for the Asian Games. That kind of innovation is the most important.

WD That is a super interesting question. We could say that any man-made park is already synthetic, because we have designed and planned it. We put green roofs on gigantic buildings. Nature is synthetic almost everywhere in the world. By now, 40% of our food is produced in irrigated fields in the desert that together cover 20% of the earth.

We are in the Anthropocene, human beings are the biggest impact on what is happening on earth. So, for better or for worse, we are part of a synthetic nature. Then the question is, how do you make the natural part of the synthetic better? And how do you make the synthetic more interesting? For example, our research right now is to work on buildings that absorb carbon, that produce oxygen, that mix biomatter with structural materials, so that our buildings become both structure and plant-like.

This also demands another kind of architecture and urban density. We feel that hybrids will only function and be used if they are expressing their "otherness" in a new taxonomy. We don't believe that a traditional building with some plants added are synthetic natures. So, to answer your earlier question, yes we can change 50% of the carbon footprint by just changing how much and what we build, and creating strange hybrids. Scientists and architects developed some really interesting possibilities in new building materials, 3D printed biomatter and optimized systems, but for the climate to improve it will take fast acceleration and rigorous action by us humans.

DS Focusing now on the largest and perhaps most complex building, the Table Tennis Stadium, we are interested in how the concept was developed from the Cong, a jade artifact with cultural relevance to the locality of Hangzhou. In which ways did the composite geometry of a hard line square figure and the curvilinear figures of this artifact become instrumentalized in the design of the stadium? To what extent is this object metaphorical, and/or how was it applied as a geometrical diagram in generating the form of the Tennis Stadium?

WD When we realized the singularity of a stadium's shape, and developed a hybrid concept, we knew something "other" was needed. On one of my trips to China I had admired a mysterious artifact called the Cong, a Jade stone intersection of a square and a disc found in royal graves. We were interested in the geometrical idea of intersection, to study newly found areas in the building that would not be otherwise there, to accelerate the idea of hybridity. The Cong is a gorgeous stone object that has mystery and an unknown use. I liked the idea that it had complexity and mystery, something we looked for in the hybrid. Initially I did look at the intersection of a square and a circle, and then realized the form had to be more self-similar, not binary – and create a level of complexity. That is when we designed the intersection and offset of two bulging discs, the brass shingled one and the glass diagrid one. On the interior the intersection creates slippages in and out of the arena, and onto the exterior terraces overlooking the wetlands.

DS The materiality of the Table Tennis Stadium is varied and pluralistic. Amongst other materials, the pallet includes a curved glass diagrid and solid brass shingles of the external envelope, as well as the curved shell of the inner arena in bamboo. Can you comment on the cultural significance or specificity of these materials? AND, Can you share with us how you decided upon this material pallet – was it perhaps related to some of the cultural and ecological criteria, material availability, and what may be buildable in Hangzhou/China?

WD This area of China is known for its huge bamboo forest. Bamboo is a very good, renewable material, it creates oxygen and in 7 years absorbs the same amount of carbon that would take a tree 40 and grows really fast. Both interiors for the two stadiums are clad with bamboo. It also makes for a beautiful contrast with the steel and glass diagrid. Bamboo brings warmth and a soft texture, so it was an easy choice – renewable and beautiful; a good combination. For the exterior skin, we used brass shingles because I looked for a material that ages beautifully, and has cultural relevance in China. The shingles are a hybrid of recycled metal with a very thin top layer of brass. But the beauty of shingles is in how you can parametrically optimize them to fit on a double curved surface, while being super textured like a fish scale skin. When studying fish scales it occurred to me, I should use planar glass for the diagrid, and together with our façade consultant Bill Logan created aluminum "eyelids".

To create a building that is maintenance free, you look at local references, natural renewable materials, and composites. The beauty of composite materials, like the brass shingles, is that they have multiple qualities. The bottom layer of the metal is strong, the brass doesn't rust and ages naturally. The durability is huge. For us, design is finding ways to make beautiful surfaces that are affordable, put together in new ways, and are more interesting.

DS Let's discuss the ecological building systems. Aside from the ecological infrastructure of the urban sponge, and the zero-earth strategy, the buildings in this project boast ecological cooling systems; natural ventilation; green roofs, and other systems. Did the competition brief call for these specific ecological systems, or did you make these proposals based on your values and obligation as an architect to work ethically with respect to the preeminence of environmental performance?

WD It was a combination of all of the above! The request for a 116 acre Eco Park came from the client, with storm water management and the use of porous pavement. Upon studying the site we found that there used to be more wetlands and proposed to restore them. We then proposed to make the buildings also for the future of Hangzhou to freeze the carbon footprint and add culture to an otherwise residential area. The client also stated that it had to be 85% green park, while asking for 7 buildings for a total of 2,000,000 sf. That was a huge challenge and required strategic thinking. The team devised a zero-earth method: where excavated earth of valley and wetlands was positioned on top of parking garages, fitness and exhibition centers, "earth buildings". It allowed for only the 2 stadiums to be visible, all other buildings are designed to be earth buildings, half recessed in the ground with walkable green roofs sloping over them.

In architecture, you have to be optimistic and

opportunistic at the same time. By digging out the wetlands, we optimized the Sponge City, but it also allowed us to use the cooled water to chill the stadium. Then, by only cooling the air under the seats of the visitors we were able to make it a sustainable building that received the Chinese equivalent of Leed platinum. The stormwater system of the park optimized the building systems. We added solar wing awnings to shade the Valley village, and to create lighting, otherwise it can be dangerous at night. How do you entice them to have the electricity on all the time? Produce the electricity. We all have to start thinking harder and be more engaged, and try and solve problems before they happen, and are asked from us. None of this was in the program.

DS In our analysis of the architectural projects in the Asian Games Park, we were taken aback by how the BIM processes used in this project enabled the design of the lightweight steel long span wing roof structure of the stadia, to save a huge quantity of material mass and money. You had mentioned working with the engineers, Thorton Tomasetti, on the suspendome, which is a composite ultra-lightweight structure. Can I ask you how will you take this experience of saving so much more material to further projects? Does the possibility of saving so much material point toward a more general theory and practice of minimizing the use and quantities of materials in architectural projects? Can we call this process and product "Computational Lightweight Structures"?

WD Computational Lightweight Structures are our favorite thing, especially when they cantilever out! Already in 2000 we created a folded glass façade for the 497GW building, you could say one of the early 3D parametric designs. I would send that curtainwall off to Standard curtain wall companies, I would clarify to them it is 90% standard, and only a 10% anomaly (I wanted the price to be "standard"), but of course, they all priced it 300% more. So finally, we moved away from standardization and custom-designed it with a great curtainwall engineer, Bill Logan. Even with that curtain wall we saved a lot of material and the costs were similar to a standard system. The double glass was folded in Barcelona, the custom aluminum mullions were extruded in Hong Kong, and the whole thing was put together in Brooklyn, and then moved to the site. This is when it occurred to me that innovation happens when you work straight with manufacturers, and you avoid resorting to standardization. I left the world of standardization in the nineties.

There are a lot of stigmas in construction and development about beauty and price, it is assumed that architecture is "expensive", which explains the state of buildings in the USA. I believe our challenge is to design things smarter than the standard, and to create beauty for any price. That requires prototyping, testing and collaborating to generate innovation. The only difference with industrial design is that in our case the prototype is often the full scale building.

The stadiums as hybrids required open column free plans, so very quickly the suspendome idea came up and was developed by the engineers, its lightweight structure is supported on the inner bowl, and cantilevers out to carry the diagrid façade, this saved a lot of steel.

DS What other options for materials and structural systems were considered in the design stages with Thorton Tomasetti? Please share with us how you arrived at this structural and material solution?

WD It was a brainstorm from the beginning. I kept saying to them we can't have columns when they first developed the structure. The roof was developed with the idea of the suspendome, sitting on the outer walls, and as we were interested in a steel & glass diagrid without columns, I eventually asked them if we could sit it on the inner dome. That was kind of a breakthrough, because at that point we could cantilever it out and carry the façades. It was a great and productive collaboration, and they are also a bunch of super fun people. We went so fast through those design phases, that honestly, if I think back, who did what exactly, is a blur.

DS Our next question concerns the relationships of the Asian Games project to the larger body of work of Archi-tectonics. Further to your presentation, can you share with us the genealogy of the design of the Asian Games project within the body of work by Archi-tectonics? Are there projects which led to this project, as earlier prototypes which you developed further?

WD That's a great question. Originally, I was doing the same as every other architect. Small projects first leading to larger projects. That changed in 2008 because of the financial crisis. What I realized and learned in that period is that it's actually super interesting to have smaller projects, as they are a great laboratory for the bigger projects. So, for example, I would probably never have thought of what I was doing with the Hybrid Stadium, if I hadn't just built the Inscape Meditation Domes in Manhattan. To test the domes, we had them prototyped 1:1 in California with a car design company. We used rotational grids and grid shells, and I was amazed how large a span you could make with the dome structure. These are relatively large domes for 45 meditating people.

Also the idea of integrating bamboo as both grid shell structure, the seating and the floor had amazing acoustic properties, the sound

deflects differently. This was a small project which was surprisingly intensely engineered. Ove Arup did the acoustics, the client hired incredible lighting people and sound engineers. It was the best of everything, and that was incredibly fun. It was a tiny project, but very inspirational and very inventive. Ultimately it became the inspiration for the 365,000 sf hybrid stadium.

DS This project is perhaps the most recently completed of all of the 21 projects in the Beyond the Envelope series covered from 2021 to 2023. Completed in 2022, it may be hard to map the Asian Games projects' influence on your practice's future work, but can you please share with us how you can forecast the influence of the Asian Games project, both as a masterplan as well as a series of buildings upon current and future work of Archi-Tectonics? Asked in another way, can you speculate on the future consequences of this project and its impact on your practice?

WD I am really interested in bottom up planning for cities, which means a set of acupunctures are developed that allow for economic, cultural, social, and urban growth. We developed this first for a client in Bogota, Colombia [2018], and when we were designing and planning the Asian Games park, we brought in a lot of those concepts into the masterplan. For example, the Ecp park as a social condenser, and the hybrid buildings as cultural generators, both are crucial for the future city.

It's always hard to predict how the future unfolds. We are interested in developing more bottom-up city models that combine sustainable systems with new natures, and architectures as synthetic natures, that reduce the carbon footprint by becoming plant-like.

DS This interview and the study of the set of projects in the Beyond the Envelope series of presentations and interviews are set within a Master of Architecture course here at NYIT. As such, your audience in this event, and this interview, are future architects. In this context, can you please share with us, from your point of view, any advice you may have for the next generation of architects?

WD I can share our educational plan at Upenn with you. We train our students for the next 25 years to be rigorous researchers and designers that are trained to lead multi-disciplinary teams. My advice: Do not be afraid. The future is complex, but that gives enormous opportunities for your generation. Be actively engaged in future challenges, think proactively, and organize yourselves. Understand that for architecture, design is your biggest tool. Never give up on design, but make it smarter, more intelligent, more rigorous, and more interactive.

DS Thank you very much for this special opportunity to interview you today, and for your enlightening presentation.

WD Thank you all for having me, and thank you for the great questions! Very intense!

TV Thank you so much, Winka, and apologies for the intensity of our unrelenting questions! Your presentation was absolutely amazing and thank you for your generosity with your time.

NATIONAL AQUATICS CENTRE / THE WATERCUBE

Beijing, 2008 | PTW Architects

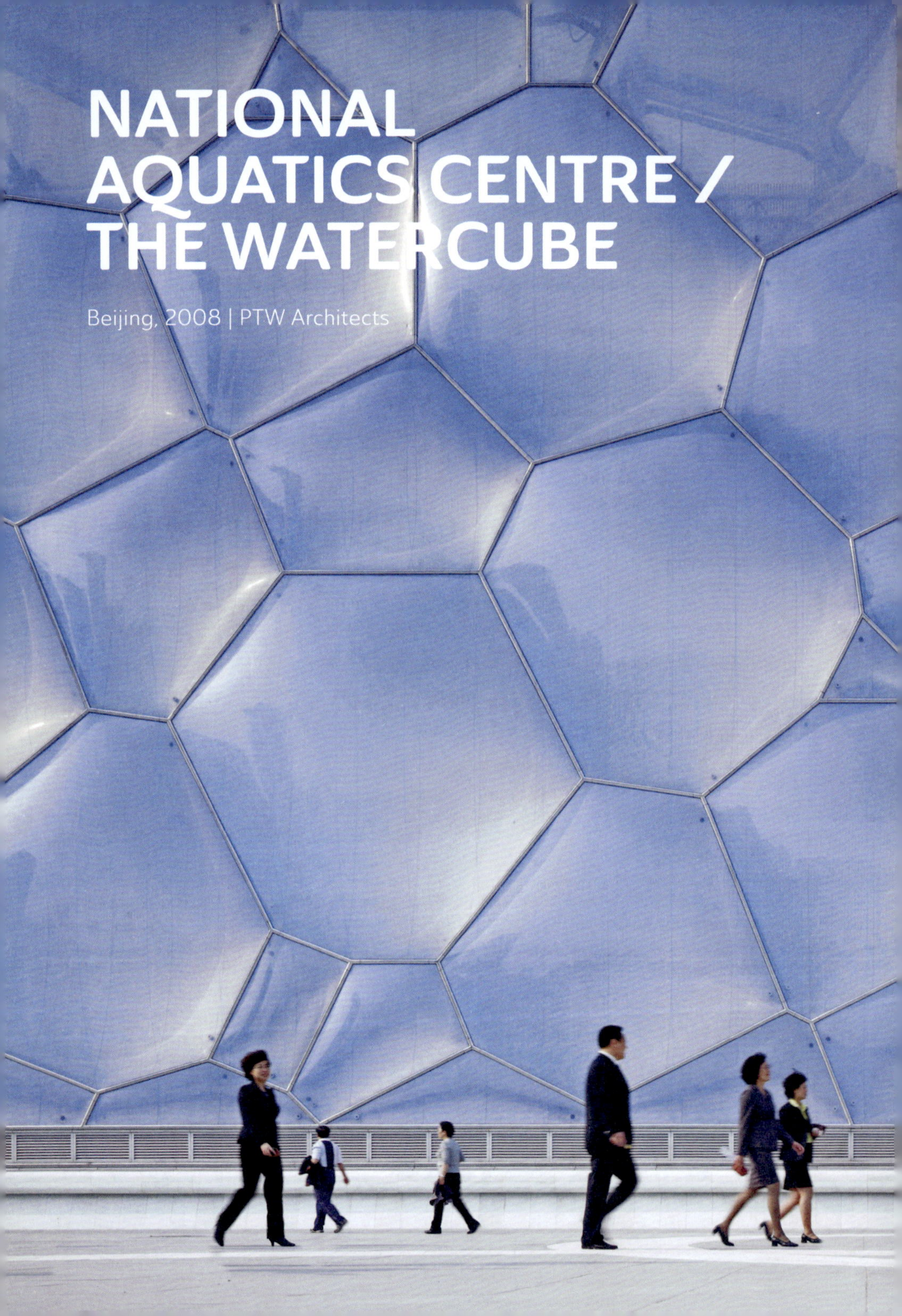

Program Main pool, Olympic demonstration pool, training pool, water park, tennis courts, gyms, shopping, cafés, performance stage

Materials Ethyl Tetrafluoroethylene (ETFE), steel framing

EXPERIENCE | 70,000 M2 GFA | 32,000 M2 Footprint | 1 70,000 Floors Below Ground | 5 Floors Above Ground | 31 M High | 4000 Etfe Bubbles on Façade | 100,000 M2 Area of Etfe Bubbles | 20% Solar Energy Collected on Façade | 30% Decrease in Energy Costs | 100% Glazing

INTERVIEW

Interviewee: Chris Bosse, Director, Lava

Interviewer: Riya Nerurkar, final year Master of Architecture student, School of Architecture and Design, New York Institute of Technology

April 24, 2023

Tom Verebes Welcome Chris! Thank you for joining us today, especially so early in the morning in Australia. We are grateful for your eloquent and in-depth presentation of the Watercube in Beijing – a building whose image is synonymous with the Beijing 2008 Olympics, and one which had pushed forward ETFE technologies.

Chris Bosse It really is great to be here to discuss the Watercube!

Riya Nerurkar My name is Riya and I would like to thank you for your exciting and immensely informative segmentation of the Watercube. My first question is focused on how facilities for the Olympic Games are often conceived as symbols of their host city and country, and how they serve to represent the host city and nation state. The Beijing Olympics was hosted at a time, fifteen years ago, when China had great ambitions to arrive on the world stage. The Watercube is a dramatic, and even an iconic building, in how it is instantly and easily recognized, and how it immediately became synonymous with the Beijing Olympics. As one of the key designers at PTW, can you tell us about who was your client for this project, and please describe your client's ambitions for the National Aquatics Center, and what was your remit to deliver those ambitions? In simple terms, what was the brief you received from your client?

CB It is very well observed how the purpose of the Olympics is always to mark a moment in history. It is also always an opportunity for a country or a city to make big changes and improvements. When you think, for example, about the Barcelona Olympics, their Olympic games were the first that I became aware of which had undergone this kind of transformation. Barcelona was a little bit of a derelict port city and an industrial city, and it was transformed into an amazing, vibrant tourist hub. The whole waterfront was cleaned up, the beaches were made accessible to the people, and the harbor all of a sudden became a destination. I first went to China in 2003. In Beijing, the five years leading up to 2008 were the absolute defining moments of the rise of

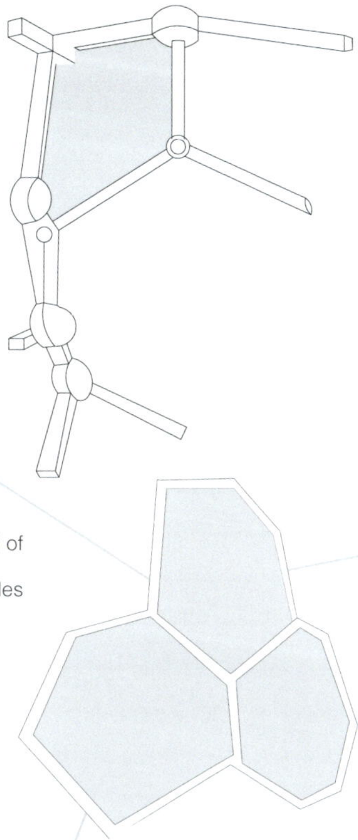

Detail of ETFE bubbles

China and its transition into a market economy. You saw the changes literally on a daily basis. The first day I arrived in 2003, you couldn't get a coffee. The last day working on the Watercube, you couldn't get away from Starbucks, for lack of a better example. There was really a huge transition. If you go to Beijing now, which I haven't been for three or four years, it is now full of Western technology, such as luxury cars, as status symbols. In a way, China is more capitalist than New York, and there are many superficial signs of this. It definitely was this big transition into a new economy. There are examples such as our local partner architecture firm that grew from 15 people to 4000 people, and at the same time, our Sydney Company was completely stagnant. Given this rise of China, the message to the world was that China is on the world stage. China uses international consultants, international technologies and actually exceeds international standards of sustainability, of construction methods of all kinds of associated disciplines. The ETFE bubbles are a good example of a façade wrapping material and a technology that was not available at the time in China. The Chinese approach was always to have these joint venture collaborations. An ETFE factory was agreed together with a German factory to start the production of ETFE in China. ETFE is now a product available in China with German technology and Chinese production.

There is a lot of this kind of technology transfer that happened during that period in design, architecture, construction materials and so on, which I saw as a really positive thing. Still, I think we really contributed to the development of China in the 21st century, and you can now see China as being one of the most advanced countries in the world, where now we are at a point where we can learn from their technologies, developing everything at a rapid pace.

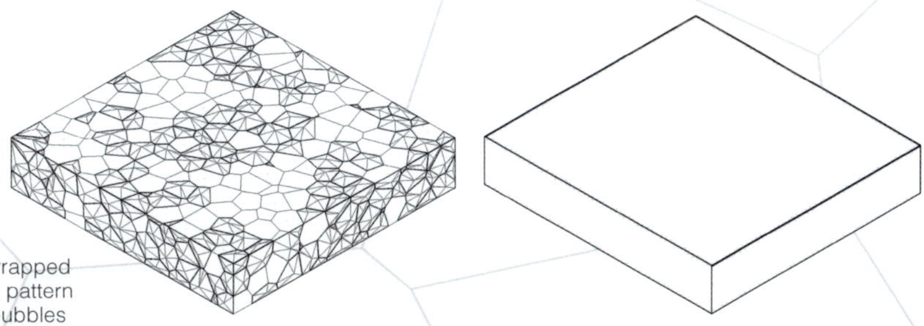

Volume wrapped in cellular pattern of ETFE bubbles

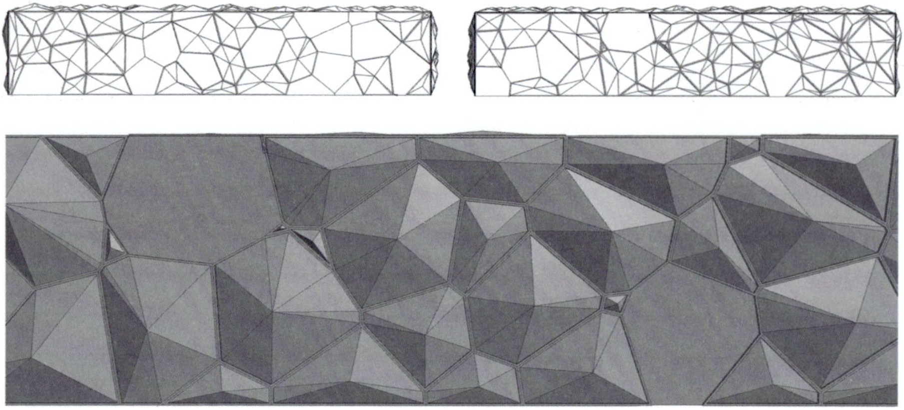

ETFE cellular pattern on façades

You also asked who was our client for the Watercube. The Olympics as a whole is not so much a circus, but it is a large global organization. Cities apply to host the Olympics and then they form an Olympic committee, so our client was the Beijing Olympic Organizing Committee. They held competitions with local and international architects and local-international juries. My understanding is that Rem Koolhaas was on the jury for our building, I also heard that Herzog de Meuron were also on the jury but this may have been an urban myth. Our proposal was selected by the jury, by the Olympic Committee and the chairman of the city. And the point I would like to make is there is nothing better for an architect than a competition that you win with the deadline for the building to be completed, because so many times you do projects and they end up somewhere and nobody really knows why it was not built. If you have a deadline like the Olympics, nobody can bail out of it. They had to build this. They had to deliver on the promise. The design was set. Every time someone asked, "Wouldn't it be cheaper to build a white box and just paint the public façade?", they would respond, "Yes, it would be cheaper, but this is the project that won and it has to be delivered and you better move on with it."

RN Thank you. My second question concerns the scheme for the Watercube, which had included public multifunction leisure and fitness facilities for use by the public both before and after the games. One of the risks of hosting the Olympic games is the possibility of the underuse or possible disuse of the facilities after the two-week sporting event. The term "white elephant" is often used to describe this condition. Can you share with us whether your project brief was to mitigate the Watercube becoming a white elephant? Was this risk communicated as a concern by your client? In other words, were you given the brief to make this project accessible as public recreational infrastructure before and after the Olympic Games, or was this a proposal for the building's use by the public PTW?

CB It is interesting that you mentioned this, and it is true for most Olympic precincts in the world, that there has always been the risk that they become abandoned or at least underutilized after the Olympics. It is madness to build an entire stadium just for one guy to run 100 meters in 9.2 seconds. If the stadium is in China, where the population is so vast, every time I have been back there, it is packed with people, there are markets, festivals, concerts, and ballets at the stadium, and there is always something happening at the Watercube. The people have really embraced the Watercube, and there is an urban myth that the Watercube is the second biggest tourist attraction in China after the Great Wall. So, every Chinese person in their life has to climb the Great Wall and see the Watercube. It is not a white elephant as such, and what we did in order to prevent that was with the multifunctional internal layout of tennis courts, gyms, and leisure pools. One third of the building houses a larger pool that you can go to with your family, buy a ticket, and spend the day in the leisure pool. There was always this public interface and it has since been refurbished multiple times. And after the Olympics, some of the seating was reduced from 17,000 seats to 6000 seats, and the additional space was transformed into commercial facilities, restaurants and shops. Then, for the Winter Olympics in 2022, the Watercube was transformed into a Winter Olympic venue for skating, hockey, and curling. I think this is ongoing legacy, and the best way to guarantee the survival of a building is to make it so special that people really look after it. I think people really love this building and they will refurbish it as many times as it is needed and they will always find a purpose for it.

RN Thank you. Were you surprised by the transformation or adaptation of the Watercube as the "Ice Cube", as the venue hosting ice-based spectator sports in the Beijing 2022 Winter Olympics? Did you ever anticipate that the building could be adapted in this way?

CB Yes, I think we did anticipate it. Even though we did not know that Beijing was going to get the Winter Olympics, the idea of multi functionality was always there. Because of China's Covid travel policies, I did not see the Beijing Winter Olympics, but from what I've seen, it worked out really well as a multipurpose sport venue. The difference between the winter and summer Olympics is that the water in the Summer Olympics is liquid, and in the Winter Olympics, it's frozen. It's not quite as simple as that, but essentially it has an ice surface on top of the pool. This is an important consideration. Many stadiums around the world have suffered the fate of being abandoned and neglected, and this has to do with budgets of course. If the Olympics are hosted by a country that cannot sustain the long-term activation of a stadium, it is a problem. So, a lot of stadia are recycled or upcycled, and sometimes they are dismantled and donated to other countries or other cities and so on, because it does not always make sense in every city to have twelve stadia. Another increasingly common strategy, by the way, is to have the Olympics hosted across multiple cities in one country, meaning the entire country can be upgraded rather than only one city. Sydney is an example where the Olympics were hosted in 2000, where for 15 years, Homebush Bay, the Olympic City, was pretty desolate, unless you have a Guns and Roses concert or a soccer match. Eventually, the whole precinct was densified with residential and commercial facilities, and now, after 20 years, it has finally become a bit of an active suburb. Even if there is a Guns and Roses concert with 80,000 people attending, they disappear 90 minutes later. That is always the risk.

RN The Watercube is activated for use as a venue for competitive water sports, as well as public recreation of a series of swimming pools. The building expresses the structure of water, and the aesthetics of foam and effervescence, as a basis for communicating its programming and content. Does the Watercube, and also the Ice Cube, deliver the expectation that a building should express the activities it houses, and what uses it is intended for, and who a building serves? Asked in simpler terms, can you please comment on the status of the western notion of the metaphor, as well as Chinese mythology, as tools with which to communicate the content and meaning of architecture?

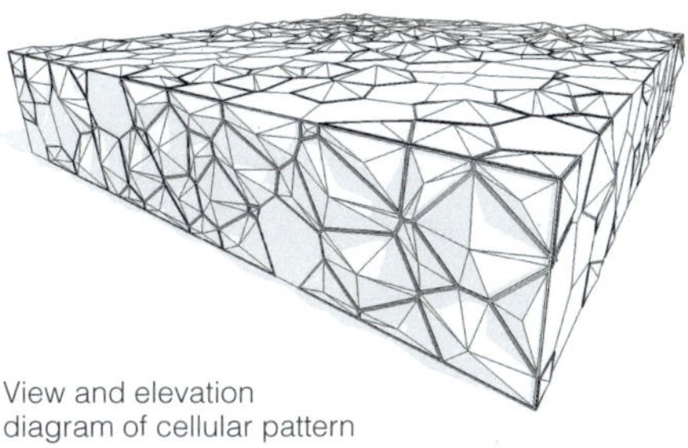

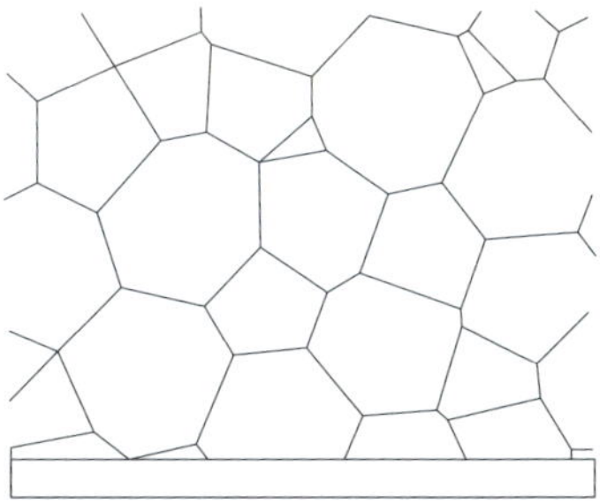

View and elevation diagram of cellular pattern

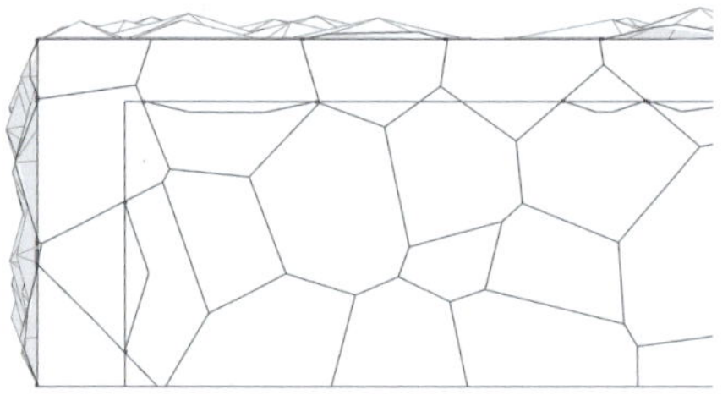

Elevation detail of ETFE bubbles

CB Riya, you've done your homework for sure! This is for other people to judge. We tried to communicate the content and I hope it does that well. I am still surprised how famous the building has become, to a point where at any dinner party in any country in the world, if someone mentions the Watercube in Beijing, people have an image of it. This speaks to the power of imagery and the power of architecture. Does it look like an aquatic center? I don't know. Did you know there were other ideas, such as an aquatic center needs to have a wave or something like that. We tried to not go for an obvious metaphor, but more abstractly of water. Zeit motif is a German word for a guiding motif. Once you have seen it, you have to come back at night because at night it is lit up and it becomes a completely different thing altogether.

As for Chinese storytelling, I am usually a little bit careful with this sort of cultural appropriation. It is also a metaphor, but it was very strongly embraced by our Chinese team members. Actually, they came up with an idea of circle and square with the square symbolizing the center of humankind and the universe. This metaphor is a very strong link which has to do with Yin–Yang and Feng Shui, which in the Western world, we are only now slowly starting to embrace.

RN Thank you for sharing this. The Watercube is an exemplary building in terms of its ecological performance, applying various advanced technologies in the early 2000s. The ETFE double skin is insulating, maximizes natural light and reduces the need for artificial lighting; it captures solar energy to heat the internal spaces; and harvests, recycles, and filters rainwater. With respect to reducing energy use, and minimizing the burden of the Watercube on the water infrastructure of Beijing, were these ecological building systems part of your brief, or did you, as the architect, push for an expanded responsibility of this building to endorse the mitigation of climate change, through better performing architecture?

CB This is a great question! Part of the 2008 Olympic agenda was to promote Beijing as a green city, and as a clean city. In China, the Watercube was one of the first buildings where this was even a consideration. You know, at the time, China was more about building bigger, better, faster, more, and not about saving energy or materials and so on. As soon as the Watercube was completed, it became a role model. Hu Jintau, the president of China at the time, stated publicly that the Watercube is a role model for China to become a greener, friendlier country with better air quality, better water quality and more open to the world. This is not an exact quote, but he said something along those lines. Architecture has traditionally been used in politics to demonstrate power with columns, architraves and strong Classical buildings. It is interesting how politics can embrace architecture as a message about sustainability, and about technology being smart, nimble, open, and transparent. In sum, the Watercube is a strong symbol of all these agendas.

RN When you were designing the project,

This is like a Pandora's Box – the more layers you peel, the more you discover, but it's not necessarily obvious. It was one of the first buildings to have this sort of layering. A good building should have this layering. It is not just something you look at. It draws you in. You want to discover more. You want to be between the façade and the structure. You want to climb onto the roof, you want to move through it and understand it.

Roof plan

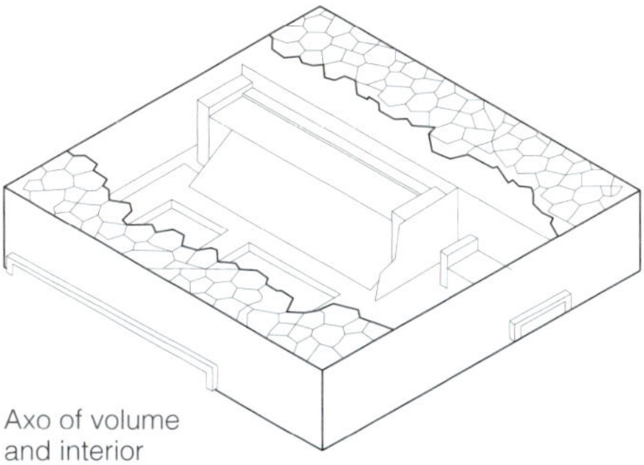

Axo of volume and interior

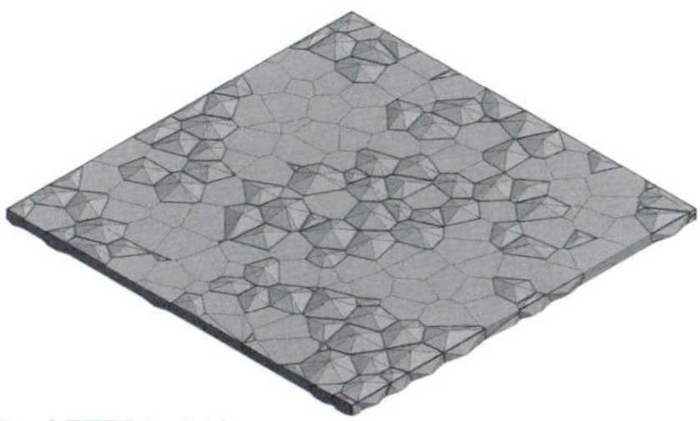

Roof ETFE bubbles

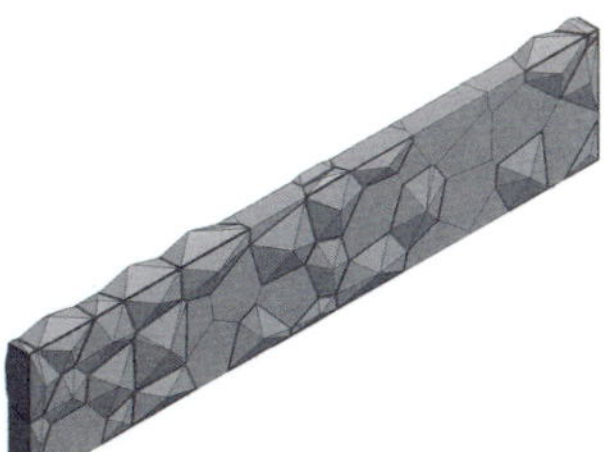

ETFE bubbles on façade

did you conceive it as a prototype for ecologically sound public recreation and social infrastructure?

CB Yes, all of that. A question we always had was "Can this be repeated?" The Watercube is not a model as such where you can say, this is exactly how every building has to look like, but every building could be approached in a similar way. We have never done an ETFE building again and we have never used a bubble structure again, but we have always tried to use these principles in our work at LAVA.

RN Our next question concerns the relationships of mathematics and forms found in nature to architectural culture. The natural formation of soap bubbles has been a fascination of architects for some time, perhaps most noteworthy is Frei Otto's research on minimal surfaces observed on soap-film bubbles. Although the envelope components of the Watercube are highly repetitive and buildable, they appear to be organic, non-uniform, and random. Although the Watercube was one of only a very few built projects applying the mathematical model of the 3D Voronoi diagram, perhaps shorthand for a more broadly defined three-dimensional polyhedral packing system. The spatial model of Voronoi packing, and other cellular or packing diagrammatic systems, was deeply embedded in the architectural culture of the 1990s and 2000s. Did you anticipate the impact of the design of the Watercube and its use of 3D polyhedral packing, upon a generation of architecture students?

CB No, I did not anticipate this impact. At the time, there were some important projects by Toyo Ito, Cecil Balmond, Herzog De Meuron's Bird's Nest Stadium among others. Herzog de Meuron spent decades talking about ornament and printing rucola leaves on façade, and then they moved into three dimensionality of ornament and structural expression. OMA, with the CCTV Tower, was also breaking up traditional typologies into a more expressive, three dimensional, loop structure. The Watercube was part of this family of thinking. All this came with the advancement of computation, because previously, to design the Watercube, you would have had to manually calculate

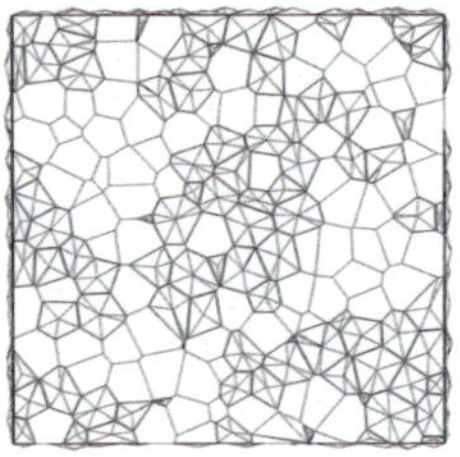

Roof plan

it. You have 22,000 steel pieces, but every change within the design would have required six months of redrawing and recalculating. Tristram Carfre was the lead engineer and one of the absolute superstar driving forces behind the project. He set it up as a parametric model where even if at a late stage of the project, you had to add a fire exit on one side, the whole structure could be recalibrated within minutes and every single steel member could be calculated for load, capacity, length, connection, etc. and printed out as a plot sheet for the steel manufacturing. Those advances in computation facilitated a new generation of projects which we now see all over the world. Sometimes, the appearance is appropriated or mistaken for pattern making. When designers designed a bubble building, or a building organized by Voronoi cells or an interesting emergent geometry, it is not necessarily about efficiency, about structure, about strength, or about the principles. It is good to go back to the origins and try to think about what you are actually trying to achieve. We still use these principles in our LAVA architecture projects, even in urban design. In terms of urban planning, consider a city like New York, which is based on a grid. The grid comes out of the necessity to bring some order to a new settlement. So, the easiest is a grid, and we name it A to Z and 1 to 10. And we have the possibilities of cities whereby the actual movement and flow and people within the city act much more organically and much more fluidly. We can now model movement and behavior of people in a much more dynamic way, and as a result, the cities that we can design today are not based on simple grids anymore. In the past, engineering structures, as well as urban planning, was based on this simplification. We have a column and a beam and that's your building. Now, we have this freedom all of a sudden where we can map the forces anywhere they flow, and we can come up with new emergent solutions.

RN Thank you. The space filling system of components is arrayed vertically on the deep, double-skinned 3.6m wide walls of the envelope, and horizontally on the roof, within a box that is partitioned and subdivided by polygons. In designing a thick, double skinned façade, during the design stages, were there other structural systems considered in the design stages of work? How did you determine the customization of the polyhedral structure, to reduce the components to only two different polyhedra, a twelve-sided, and fourteen-sided module?

CB Were there any other options considered? The propositions were benchmarked against other options, but the good thing about the design and maybe it is also a lesson, is that the structure and the space was all part of the same system. You could not all of a sudden put a square column in it, because it would have destroyed everything. You could not conceive of a more efficient façade cladding with square panels, because then we would not have much to structure. So, the lesson is, if you design all components of your building in a way that they become a necessity, then nobody can take anything away. In this building, you could not take anything away. You also could not add anything. It just was what it was, and that made it really strong. Otherwise, it would not have survived the economic ups and downs of the commercial reality of building.

RN I would like to pivot the next question to relate the relationships of the Watercube to your work afterwards both at PTW, and eventually as a founder and director at LAVA. Can you share with us the genealogy of the design of The Watercube? Are there projects which led to the Watercube, as earlier prototypes which you developed at PTW, or in research work, or teaching?

CB Before the Watercube there were many projects undertaken at the institute of lightweight structures by Frei Otto and his team. In my previous job in Germany between

2000 and 2002 we developed a number of projects based on these theories, including the bubble highrise Berlin with Charles Walker at the advanced geometry unit at ARUP. My late mentor, Seyed Mohammed Oreyzi, of SMO architecture in Cologne encouraged these experimental projects in the office and this is the legacy I took to Sydney when I moved in 2002.

Since leaving PTW there have been a series of projects that we at LAVA have developed from small to large, that came out of these research ideas of membranes, of coral structures, of minimal surfaces, and generally the relationship between nature and technology. We are looking into coral reefs, mangroves, and rainforests, as examples of ecosystems, and spider webs as examples for lightweight structures. We developed a series of projects, from very humble small pavilions and art installations into entire master plans. They all come out of a similar thinking, but they don't necessarily have the Watercube pattern or geometry. How can we develop for each typology the next step in this typology? What would an office look like in the future? What would a house look like in the future? How would a city look in the future? And how can the city, for example, become more natural as a human environment? The building that I am in at the moment in Ho Chi Minh City is an example of this. Residential towers all around the world are square boxes because it is simpler to organize them, and simpler to build them. The masterplan for this complex city garden was to have a series of towers that are like water drops within a landscape park, and this creates a completely different relationship of the buildings to nature and to the people. This is not necessarily more difficult to build or more expensive to build. It is just a little bit more effort, and you have an incredible new experience. This may be an example of how these organizational diagrams can be translated into other topologies. We also have a project in Vietnam which is an entire city block and we broke down the city block into hills and terraced landscapes, and this softens its street appearance, but also liquifies the internal experience moving through it. We also did a master plan for a peninsula in Sydney, Australia, on the harbor, and we created a new residential district based on mountain-like buildings that create a soft environmental ecosystem of relationships rather than square boxes. When I do LAVA lectures, I always end with a slide showing how I see the architect as an explorer between the natural world and our reality in the 21st century. We look at principles of nature, history, and everything that exists, but then find within that something new, immersive, and pointing towards the future. We now have the convergence of a video game aesthetic and architecture, and it is interesting how this aesthetic is full of nature, almost Avatar-like. In this cyber experience, where you combine nature and technology, we now have the emergence of AI (artificial intelligence), which I am sure you are dealing with at NYIT. You can type prompts, "city of the future" and you get an image like that, which otherwise would have taken you five years to design yourself. These images just come out of nowhere, and that always puts you into an interesting conversation of where do we stand as the architects within all that? Will we still exist as architects or will we be replaced by the cyborg, half sloth, half robot?

RN Thank you. This Beyond the Envelope series of presentations and interviews is set within a Master of Architecture course here at NYIT, and within our SoAD public series of lectures and events, and therefore your audience is predominantly students, and future architects. In this context, can you please share with us, from your point of view, any advice you may have for the next generation of architects?

CB The only advice I can give is along the lines of an image diving in the ocean. You are diving in the ocean of architecture, surrounded by history and designing the future, and you have to find within that what the future is that you want to live in and you want to be stimulated. You want to be surprised. You want to see familiar things. You want to see new things. One thing is for sure, though, the future is going to be different from the past. Twenty years ago, someone said to me that the acceleration of technology is coming and more inventions will be made in the next 20 years than in the entire history of humankind. And I asked, "Come on, how is that possible? Think about electric light or the steam train. How can you surpass this? This was before the iPhone; it was the beginning of the Internet; it was before 3D printing, and certainly before artificial intelligence. Within the last year, with Chat GPT and MidJourney, our life has been turned upside down.

You can only imagine what's yet to come. It is your job as architects, designers, and creatives, to understand the society that we live in, and to envision the equivalent of that for your built and virtual environment. That is why I think it is so, so important to say that if you want to be contemporary, you have to express the now in your architecture. Look at history for inspiration by all means, but design from today and for the future.

RN Thank you very much for your presentation and for the great opportunity to interview this evening.

TV Chris, this has been a tremendous opportunity for us to look back at the Watercube. Thank you for your generosity to share your reflections.

CB This was fun, and best of luck to all of you. Tom, let's hope to catch up soon in-person. Goodbye!

GALLERIA CENTERCITY

Cheonan, South Korea, 2010 | UNStudio

Program Department store, supermarket and food court, restaurants, kids' café, vip lounge, art center, cultural center, roof top terraces, parking garage

9.600	Luminair
12.400	Luminair
22.000	Led Light
13.500 M2	Media Façade
55 M	Atrium Height
2	
10	Floors Above Ground
6	Floors Below Ground
66,700 M2	Building Area
11,235 M2	Site Area
110,531 M2	GFA

INTERVIEW

Interviewee: Astrid Piber,
Partner, UNStudio

Interviewers: Aleksandra Zatorska, Jay Patel, M.Arch students, School of Architecture and Design, New York Institute of Technology

April 7, 2021

Tom Verebes Thank you, Astrid, for your presentation of the Galleria Centercity project, along with other UNStudio projects. You have presented so much information about the Galleria's design, its visual dynamics with the use of light and color. Your presentation elucidates the notion of the envelope as a site for illusory images and communication of information, in a unique assemblage of façade elements. Let's launch into the interview! I would like to introduce my M.Arch students, Jay Patel and Aleksandra Zatorska, who will lead this interview.

Astrid Piber Thank you – it is a pleasure to be here with you on Zoom!

Aleksandra Zatorska Sylvia Levin, in her book, *Kissing Architecture*, while describing the effect of the media façade, uses the term "mise-en-scene", a theatrical staging technique that transfers the audience to a different time and context. The analogy to cinematography is not random. The façade is made of vertical frames that change with time of the day and media content. "Mise-en-scene" also refers to the actors that are defined or emphasized by scenography. What kind of scene does the media façade of the Galleria Centercity stage for the viewers? How does the fusion of materiality and light media affect the subject, or the user or the public, with respect to their activity, programing, and didactic content?

AP The media façade is only activated by light at nighttime. For us, it was very important to also have the cinematographic effect during daytime, as a concept for the building skin that is static yet feels dynamic.

It is like a movie made in the early days of cinema, when every key frame was made as a drawing and the effect is of a moving image. What happens in the Galleria Centercity project is that the lines on the façade are static, but the viewer is in motion and that creates the dynamic experience.

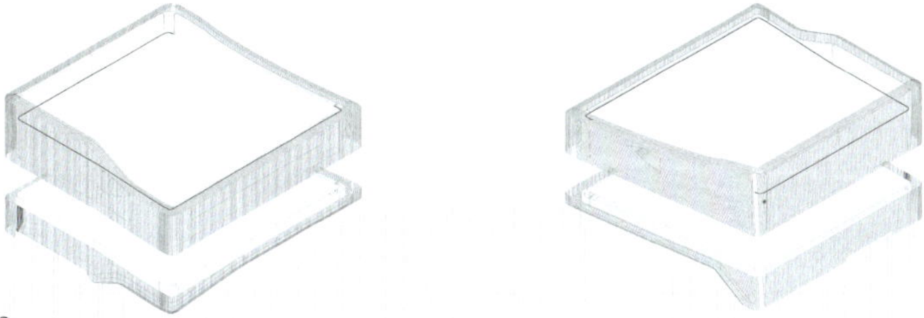

Axonometrics

During nighttime, the layer of color and light is added, which then emphasizes and breaks down the building mass. In the context of a media façade in Asia, this envelope is something special because normally all the lights are placed on one single façade as much as possible and with as much color as possible. Here, we were experimenting with dimming white light to have shades of gray or only a bit of color. That was quite exceptional and uncommon twelve years ago. It created a sort of different layer and an attraction, and also made it a canvas for people that have the skills to program different content on. On the four façades, basically every light is controlled individually, so any content, either through images or programming, can be displayed there. What we developed together with the lighting designers was also a program on site, a series of media content for special times of the year or special events that the client can choose from. It was the first set of scenes where you can develop an endless number of subjects. Think of it as a way to evolve the building and its content.

JP The Galleria Centercity is set in the context of East Asian behavioral tendencies in the large commercial spaces which enable community interactions hosted in privately owned public spaces, which serve to create social and cultural experiences. Was this path of research and the analysis of these social tendencies explored in the pre-design stages? Was there any involvement and collaboration with sociologists, original studies, and civic engagement, in the development of this social prototype?

AP This aspect of the project was not researched on paper or on a computer. It was researched through experience, because we had learned from our client which types of tenants they thought would have. Also, for example, we learned from a project we had done in Taiwan, where we realized that people went into a book shop to date other people. For us, as Europeans working on the project, the importance of such a place was really surprising. That is why I even tried to understand the importance of the food court in this context. Good food already establishes social cohesion. For example, the levels of the cooking classes attract different types of audiences at different times of day. It was not a process for which we needed to work with a sociologist. We looked at other department stores and observed what worked there and where people gathered and would meet. One thing that also worked out nicely was the study of the family that may go to such a store together, but they are not necessarily all interested in the same things. If you offer ways of enabling different experiences in a building, people will come back to have a coffee or to meet again and then go their

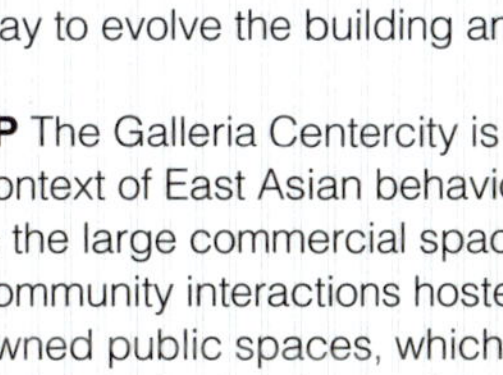

Elevation

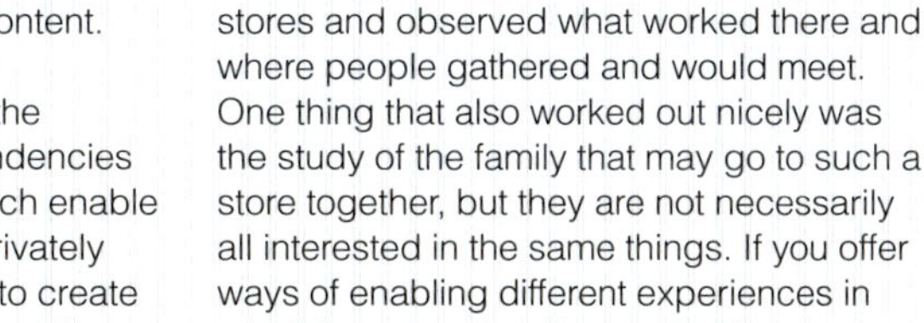

Axonometrics

own way as well. It's a bit more of a realistic experience than you would perhaps get at a standard department store. It's somewhere that you go to for one thing but unexpectedly do other things. So, we looked more at how groups of families come to such a place.

JP With its double skin façade and its materiality which helps to reduce reflectivity and harsh sunlight, what climate and sustainability factors were considered in the design stages? For example, how does rain protection work on the façade, and what other passive strategies were used?

AP The most important environmental consideration was to keep the heat out in order to reduce the requirements for cooling the building during summer. That is why a lot of areas are completely closed off, so as to not allow sunlight to enter the building. Even for the central atrium it was more beneficial to keep it closed, to avoid heat gain/heat loss. There was a long discussion about the void, whether the atrium should receive daylight or whether it should be lit with artificial lighting. There were several tests carried out to see how different lighting schemes impacted the different plateaus in different areas. In the end, it was decided it should be a closed roof with artificial lighting. Considering our intentions for the effects of the façade, one of the most important things for UNStudio was this idea of projecting the pixels but not in a cliché media façade way. Generally, when you look at LED screens, you need LED light sources at every five to ten centimeters to create a big image. But if you use one LED, you could make an image from illuminating an 80 centimeter by 80 centimeter dot source of light. Of course, it also uses less energy than any conventional media screen, especially in relation to the large media effect.

AZ In some of the publications, Ben van Berkel was quoted as saying, "No image is permanent in this building". This declaration refers to illusions of time, scale, light, and people. Both perception and physical qualities are blurred in the experience of media augmenting the building's presence. We see this as the effect of sensitive layering and rotation of those qualities. Could you elabo-

rate on the transitional, Illusive, and possibly immersive moments between interior and the exterior and their connectivity?

AP I started my presentation from the interior and the idea of the plateaus being organized around the atrium. The idea of the plateaus already breaks down the scale, because you do not perceive this 10-story building necessarily as ten stories high, but rather, as four main levels. This is the same design approach as we had done on the façade – that you don't know how big the building is. The connection is in these dynamic flows that enter from the plateau to the façade or the other way around. At the entrances, there is an inward transition, and even though it is a completely different concept, you do feel guided by it. One is more vertically oriented, and it moves us around. The one on the inside is something that moves you upwards. Once arriving at the plateau, you see the same façade from inside out and you also see the vertical lines, which re-establishes a link back to the context. You are immersed in a propeller effect, in a way. It spills you out onto the different areas and levels, where you can circulate and shop for different products. That way the perception of the space and its physical boundaries create these individual immersive moments.

JP The project's responsiveness to the building occupants' behavioral tendencies can be seen in the interior zones through the building's circulation and lighting strategies. On the other hand, the façade impacts the perception of passers-by. Is there a dialog between those two territories – the façade and the interior? If so, what kind of relationship is generated, is it a relationship between building and people, building user-passerby, or the contrast of interior-exterior material, and spatial and perceptual experiences?

AP During the design phase, we were discussing the effect of a drop of water falling onto the surface of a lake, and the resulting ripples. We saw the plateaus as something that spills out onto the façade. Every plateau starts the movement of these lines and these ripples. In daytime the optical illusion of the overlaying lines emphasizes these gentle waves, and at night we designed some lighting scenarios that exaggerate these waves even more. However, not all content scenarios at night follow the waves. Some also camouflage them, but there are many which play with the light that comes out of the plateaus. You see it from outside and then it spills over onto the media façades of the exterior. Through the lighting and the fluidity, the façade gets fully dematerialized and the building becomes "light" at night.

AZ The application of colored and polychromatic materials in the façades of some of UNStudio's built project has shaped the key identity in the office's projects. For example, the La Defense offices (1999 – 2004) use polychromatic reflective materials, or Star Place (2006 – 2008) with its media façade. We can see direct and indirect inspiration from these projects in the Galleria Centercity. Can you please share with us the extent of influence of the Galleria project (2008 – 2010) on the body of other works of UNStudio since the completion of the project?

AP The material experiments that were done for the La Defense offices had a big influence on the concept for the Galleria Centercity. In Almere, we experimented with three end points in the façade, tested several polychromatic materials and created a courtyard for people working there. We designed a kaleidoscopic effect. It very much influenced the Galleria projects because while we were working on the Galleria Centercity design in the studio, we were thinking about the dress for the first Galleria – Galleria Luxury Hall West in Seoul, which we designed in 2003 for the same client. There we worked with the different ways the glass was laminated and the contrasting day and night effect. We were also playing with this optical effect in the Talee Star Place project in Kaohsiung. There we had a concave façade with glass fins that had the colored LEDs fully embedded in the fixture holding the fins, absolutely hidden and bespoke and emitting colored light onto the glass surfaces. For that project we chose to not have colored foils laminated in the glass. The colored light appears to the

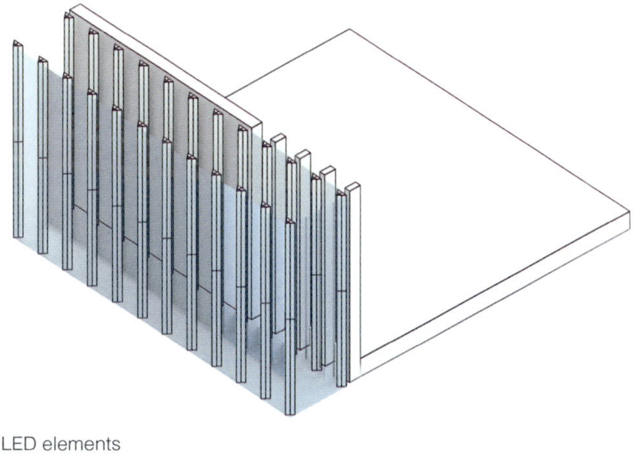

Detail of façade LED elements

Unfolded elevation

viewers eyes only because of a thoroughly tested frit of small dots on the glass fins. Also in Galleria Centercity in Cheonan, the color comes from the lighting fixture that projects light back onto a white façade surface. So compared to earlier projects, where the color effect is inherent in the materials, in Centercity the façade is a neutral canvas.

We started developing those animated façade ideas mostly around commercial projects, whether department store or shopping mall. It then took us from thinking about how we can integrate lighting, to how we can integrate sources for harvesting solar energy in the façade. For example, the Hanwha HQ office tower, which is a refurbishment we did in Seoul and completed in 2019. That was the first project where we integrated PV cells in the frames for the windows. We were triggered by this idea of how you can integrate PV in an interesting way that does not look like standard PV frames and still serves the purpose of harvesting energy, while also creating a new identity for the tower. In this sense, the Cheonan project, and all the previous ones I described, influenced us a great deal, literally taking us to the next solution; not of adding technologies to the façade in a standard add on fashion, but integrating them within the design. It is a common thread within UNStudio's work to integrate technical equipment in such way that performance is optimized while the design is simple and sophisticated.

AZ I also have a question about your current work regarding how human behavior is influenced. Is there something that you have learned about human behavior from your recent work, after completion of the Galleria project some years ago? Can you speak to how people experience a building? Have you created pavilions or smaller scale projects as prototypes to understand the relationships between the built environment and human experience? Is there some knowledge about this that was brought forward from the Galleria to UNStudio's next projects?

AP Yes, many things. We are continuously busy with evolving these types of experimental projects in our studio. One example is an installation that we made afterwards, the "Reset" stress reduction pods. The installation is a fully immersive experience that includes a colored wall where you can learn to de-stress because it measures your heartbeat and reacts to that using rhythm, sound, music to help you to calm you down.

The idea of this interaction is to positively impact our emotions and to create interaction between human & machine in order to produce intense atmospheric effects that engage with social health. Wellbeing and health have been of particular interest to UNStudio for some time now.

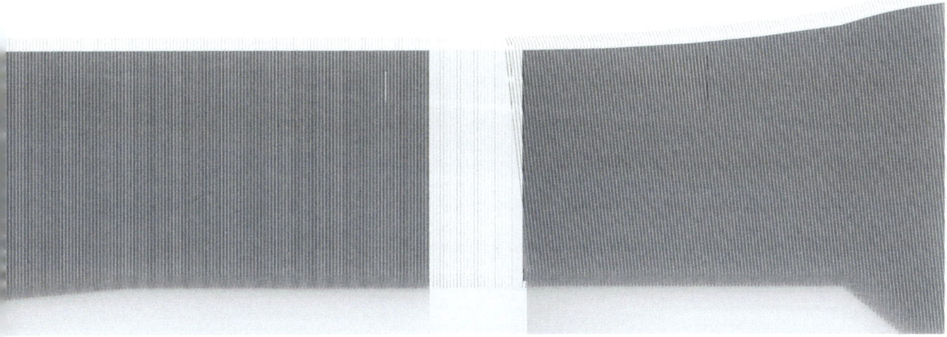

In every project we design, we strive to enable healthy environments through understanding behavior, making a conscious choice of materials and incorporating twenty-first century technologies that help human beings to improve the way they live their lives, work and travel.

AZ Thank you! We really appreciate your insights and being with us today.

AP Thank you – you asked some great questions!

AZ Wonderful responses! Thank you so much. Truly, we learned a lot.

TV Thank you so much! It is really such a pleasure to have you join us today. Thank you to Alexandra and Jay. I also learned a great deal about the Galleria Centercity project – some of the motivations and earlier work in this area; the design stages and decision-making, and for this opportunity to see some of the videos and photos of the prototyping you had shared, much of which is not published.

From interrogating and analyzing projects through discussion and spatial analysis, and setting this investigation into a discursive context from a distance, as we all currently are, which, even without our pandemic and all of our remoteness, we are very much at a distance, so I am grateful to you for sharing all of this information today. I think that UNStudio's expansion into "Sensing the Future" is also such a fascinating development in terms of what the service of an architect can become. I see this as an expansion of UNStudio's expertise, redefining what the professional product of the architectural studio is and represents an advancement of the professional scope of architectural practice. It is a very exciting development of UNStudio which is loaded with potential, and I look forward to seeing what the years will bring.

AP I am actually very thankful that this presentation and interview made me dig into our archives, because I realized firstly that there is not much published about the Galleria Centercity project. My team and I put a significant amount of time into this project and we are still working together, and it's very nice in retrospect to look back at those times. We are also still in good contact with the same client. This interview has triggered many ideas for me from the past, that at the time, we didn't see in the way we can now as we were maybe not so aware. Long afterwards, in reflecting on this project, like for every project, what we created can be assessed for how it took shape and how it worked. I think nowadays our approach would probably be very different, which is also good because different times impact our cities differently, and as architects, we can learn from our past work, long afterwards.

TV Well, I am grateful to you Astrid, for you looking into those archives! I think our discussion demonstrates how many architects think that our latest project is always going to be the best and it's the one we always want to show – a little bit like our most recent baby photos!

Our recent endeavor is often the most fresh in our minds, yet sometimes long past projects are influential, even though a particular project maybe did not get the attention it may have deserved in its time. The Galleria Centercity is a project which is not about a media screen, but actually more about a much deeper set of effects and affects. Looking back, I think this project, along with the Hanwha Headquarters, the Star Place project in Kaohsiung and Galleria Luxury Hall West, which you mentioned, are all emblematic projects of a certain kind of area of work about media to create immersive and illusory effects. So, when I selected this project for my seminar, I acknowledged it certainly was not the most well published of UNStudio's projects, but I think in a certain area of work, it is highly influential and super achieved. Thank you very much for your time today – we're grateful to you for your interest and support to join us.

AP Thank you!

TV All the best, take care, and I hope to see you live sometime soon!

AP Hopefully we will not be so remote soon. Good luck with your seminar! Thank you. Bye!

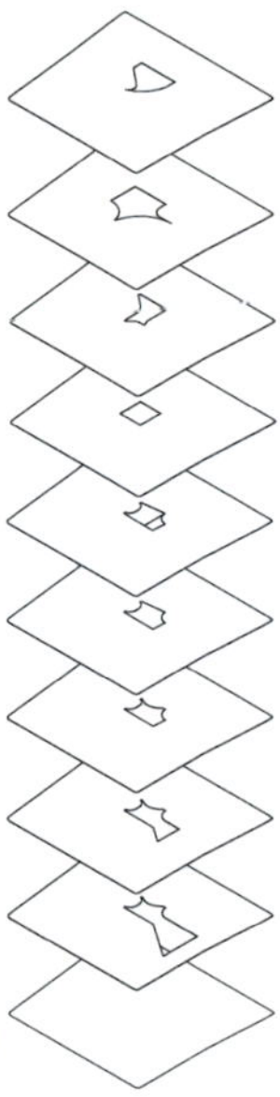

Axonometrics of floor surfaces and atrium void.

40
LANCÔME
sisley

100
사은 大축제
Dior

LEEZA SOHO

Beijing, 2019 | Zaha Hadid Architects

Program Office building, parking garage, retail

Solid	Glazing	Different Module Types	Façade Modules Total	Floor Atrium	Floors Above Ground	Floors Below Ground	Landscape	Building Coverage	GFA
42%	58%	734	4416	45	45	4	2,874 M2	40%	172,800 M2

INTERVIEW

Interviewee: Patrik Schumacher, Principal, Zaha Hadid Architects

Interviewers: Adam Giannios, Sohee Noh, and Aditi Pancholi, M.Arch students, School of Architecture and Design, New York Institute of Technology

March 3, 2021

Tom Verebes Thank you so much, Patrik, for the visual onslaught of your stunning presentation, which is as inspiring as it is overwhelming! Let's launch straight into the interview. Introducing Adam Giannios, Sohee Noh, and Aditi Pancholi, M.Arch students at New York Tech, who will ask you a few tough questions.

Aditi Pancholi My name is Aditi Pancholi. Our first question is focused on the ways in which you have developed the trope of the atrium. By the historical and etymological definitions, an atrium is an open-roofed entrance hall or central court in an ancient Roman house. Through a historical lens charting the trajectory of Interior Urbanism, the Atrium Effect is characterized by features as open terraces exemplified by the Bonaventure Hotel in Los Angeles, and several other John Portman Hotel projects, or the Ford Foundation in New York. The Leeza Soho project currently houses the largest atrium in the world. Can you please share with us how your client, Soho, supported the inclusion of this vast atrium in the design brief? Can you also discuss the legacies and further potentials of John Portman's atrium projects, through the Leeza Soho project? Was the atrium the outcome of the direct impact of any contextual or specific programmatic requirements in this project?

Patrik Schumacher An atrium was not originally required in Soho China's brief, but I was convinced it would make the project more attractive and I was at that time actively looking for a project to realise a mega atrium. I have always been a fan of John Portman, especially his fantastic atriums. I had seen his atrium projects in Manhattan, LA and Atlanta. I also had the privilege to meet him when I was appointed to become the first John Portman chair at Harvard's GSD.

I love the Portman concept of the atrium, but most of his atriums are lined with hotel rooms that have closed walls. I thought this concept can apply very well to office buildings. It's beneficial for offices to have intervisibility, and inter-awareness. Atriums also facilitate navigation in big buildings. You get some sense of what is going on in the building, avoiding the situation where everything is hidden on separate floors, where everybody disappears into closed rooms. Atriums allow visual communication across floors.

In the case of the Leeza tower we wanted to occupy and utilize the atrium more, projecting surfaces out into the atrium and making it more useful for circulation, but this collides with fire issues and other safety concerns like suicide. This is the reason why we haven't yet brought this vision of an atrium tower to full fruition. With respect to fire safety we are working on engineered solutions to overcome these restrictions. This is essential. This is a long term project to make the atrium more and more open and occupiable, full of activities.

Sohee Noh Hello – I am Sohee Noh. Firstly, thank you for your amazing presentation! Beijing is a climatically challenging context, with hot dry desert summer conditions and extremely cold winters. In general, how does the climatic context affect urban development in Beijing? Leeza Soho has a LEED Gold certification and China's Two-Star Green Building Rating. To what extent did Beijing's severe climate drive the design of the Leeza Soho tower?

PS One principle which I had learned decades ago is that these atriums are very useful as a climatic buffer. The atrium is not a heated space. But it is never as cold or as hot as the outside. With the atrium we can

catch daylight. We bring light to the interior façades and into the floors. We can also capture some sun energy in the winter. The glass enclosing the atrium is very transparent. In terms of the sun exposure management, the rest of the envelope operates with large full floor shingles with a dark glass. The next glass layer on the inside, receiving light from the atrium, could be fully transparent rather than darkened. The idea of layered glass makes sense everywhere in an urban condition where we believe that we should have interior urbanism, where we should open up buildings to the outside, as well as connect spaces across levels on the inside.

AP The next questions that we have relate to the thematic structure of our M.Arch seminar at NYIT, where we are looking at six different built projects that lie in relation to six different themes, one of which is "Form", focusing on geometry, articulation and expression. Leeza Soho makes a substantial contribution towards innovating the typology of high rise towers, challenging segmentation and serial repetition through the presence and formal expression of the interior atrium and resulting into different mass. How does the geometry of this project play a role in driving this? Also,

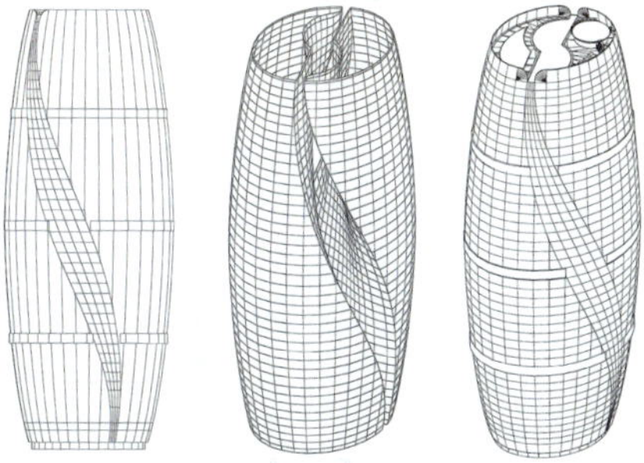

Mass and atrium

what stance does the Leeza Soho tower take in terms of its status as architecture icon especially within the recent political context of Chinese urbanization?

PS To some extent, we work with a relatively subtle geometry here. It is almost a kind of minimalism on the outside. However, there are subtle gradients in all directions. It's quite an elegant figure and there was the ambition for the Soho tower to become a sophisticated and upmarket product. During the design we were worried that the 'cut' of the atrium becomes too dramatic. We all know about the backlash against extreme or very unusual forms of architecture in China. We therefore made the outer envelope flush all around, rather than setting the atrium glass back as we had initially sketched. I also tested the idea to run the shingles across the whole envelope and let this form be even more neutral. We tried this but rejected it. I think this was the right decision, otherwise the view into and out of the atrium would have become too obstructed. The building is still quite subtle on the exterior. It is less dramatic than some of our other buildings. Of course, it is very dramatic on the inside. But that is private and a different matter. I understand where the Chinese are coming from. If we have a clash between multiple icons expressing different directions, you get urban chaos. In this sense, I am happy with the exterior expression of Leeza. We are exploiting the site condition to the fullest. We have retail on the ground and it is a sunken space around the tower. The tower is elliptical in plan. The elevational profile of the tower is also elliptical. So we are actually creating a relatively small footprint on the ground, leaving more public space. The volume – elliptical in both directions – is first swelling and then pulling back in, thereby offering the largest floor plate half way up the tower. The shingling actually helps to describe the curves with flat surfaces, especially as the radii get relatively tight. This is a more elegant solution than faceting a surface that wants to be curved. The shingling adds relief and dynamism rather than feeling like a compromise, as a mere faceting would certainly have been perceived.

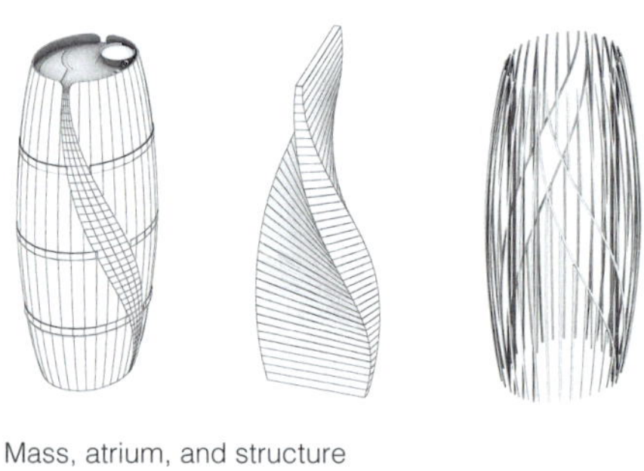

Mass, atrium, and structure

Only with very shallow curves does faceting become imperceptible, like in the case of our Vitra Firestation. So, I had noticed in some examples that the shingling helps a lot. The outcome is more elegant and deliberate. So that's why we went with shingles. I think this is very successful. There's also something interesting about the verticals. They shift rather than line up. This gives us more of a surface feeling, like a fish skin, instead a gridded articulation. The intent was to make it more seamless. It's indeed amazing how slick the tower looks. Also, I always like relief on surfaces. I went back to our Shanghai Soho project where we used large flat glass surfaces without mullions. I think it is a mistake. The inevitable deviations from perfect flatness become very visible and troubling and you realize why there was always a relief in traditional architecture. So the mistake we made in some past projects was to have a flat curtain wall on a large expanse of surface. Now, we are trying to find ways to create depth or relief in our façade surfaces.

Relief or depth also adds to the dynamic experience of the observers as they move. Deep façades vary much more visually relative to observer positions and view angles. Also, the play of light and shadow is more pronounced with deep façades.

Not only am I learning from our buildings, but also I was learning from many others. Sometimes, some of those details slip, and sometimes it is hard to notice those kinds of things in a drawing or mock-up. It is all a part of the life-long learning of the practicing architect.

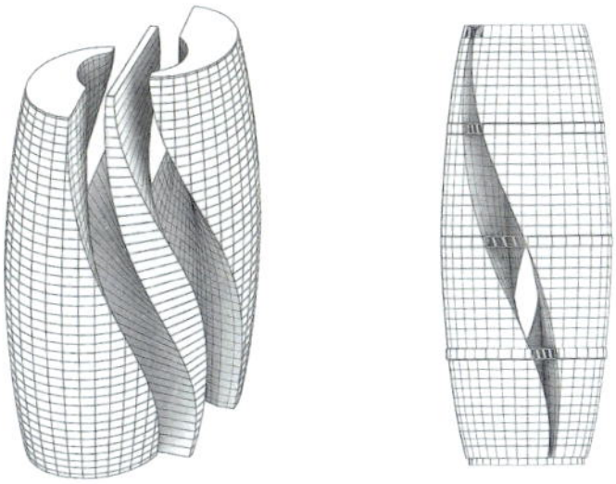

Atrium figure

Adam Giannios Thank you. It was great to see the inspiring approach in the short movie which you and Rosey Chan created about setting parametric architectural imagery to music. Regarding the impact of parametric design upon building design, you talked in *Wallpaper Magazine* about "…a paradigmatic sequence of animations…". Can you please explain this concept and methodological approach and how it can be understood through the design of Leeza Soho?

PS This video was from the beginning of parametricism featuring earlier office work, work from AADRL, as well as from our Vienna studio. It's all quite old by now. The main themes are variation and differentiation in the pursuit of adaptation. Urban elements differentiate according to an internal system logic or in adaptation to the landscape. The same idea plays out with respect to the differentiation of façade elements in adaptation to an overall envelope geometry and in adaptation to sun exposure. An early tool which allowed some of that was the software called Generative Components by Robert Aish from Bentley. For us, the concept became paradigmatic. I think the next step for me is also important, that this is not only a single system which modulates itself to varied underlying conditions, but that we can layer and correlate multiple systems in this way.

For instance, structure and envelope and internal spaces are three layers that each have their own logic but that can be correlated. Also, variation must not always be smooth. There can be triggering thresholds where quantity shifts into qualitative difference. In the case of the Leeza Soho façade, there is a sharp line that separates the atrium from the office spaces. However, there is also a blending operation: The depth of the shingling recedes as the envelope approaches the atrium, where the glass becomes wholly flat. The structural layer is not so evident in Leeza. That was a conscious choice.

The Macau Hotel project, in contrast, has a very strong expression of the structure. There is an atrium too. But here the atrium is not easily visible from the outside. Rather we introduced exterior voids that symbolize and index the atrium.

In another project I can mention, the One Museum tower in Miami, we have applied this idea of system correlation. Here the externally expressed structure that differentiates upwards correlates with the division of the floorplates into apartments. So, we were moving from three apartments per floor to two apartments per floor and finally only one apartment per floor in the top ten floors. This way we also get different balcony conditions. These balcony conditions transform gradually, not abruptly; the corner balconies shrink, while the central balconies increase. The skeleton thins out as we go up, and the corner splits open. This transformation of the exterior structure correlates with different interior products. For me, it's important that these variations, on one hand recognize the variation of loads and forces that accumulate at the bottom of the tower, imposing the need of more bracing and stronger elements but also that this differentiation can be picked up by the functional distribution of different types of products and spaces. That's the general theory. Now, these things come more to their fullest if you had more mixed use and more interoperating visible systems. The Leeza tower participates in this idea to a certain extent only. This makes sense for a single function building.

SN In which ways do you believe the Covid-19 pandemic will impact work environments in the long term? In your view, how does Leeza Soho forecast the intensely networked office as a safe environment in terms of public health? And also, what were the main considerations that were important while laying out the vertical array of floor plans and how does the design affect the corporate/work culture of the building, or conversely, how is the building shaped by its work culture?

PS This has been a theme for many years for me. It's about enhancing communication, intervisibility and inter-awareness, information exchange and collaboration. Why does a large company bring thousands of people into one central HQ building? To capture the work synergies that are generated by all the parallel work processes. It's to maximize the exchange of information and to catalyse a self-organising collaborative network. Work is project based. You have to find new partners within and across the office nearly every few weeks. In today's knowledge economy everybody becomes potentially creative. This technological civilization has an infinite ability to absorb innovations. This current condition is very different from fifty years ago, where massive fixed mechanical production systems could not absorb many innovations because it would mean you would have to rebuild the entire assembly line. R&D, marketing and financing have exploded compared to routine production work. The latter has largely been automated. Now we have 3-D printing, robotic fabrication, and the reprogramming of robotic production systems. You have software as service apps and can upload any innovation easily accessible to millions of people. That changes everything. This means also that we are working on many things, always with different and new partners. It is interesting that global telecommunications had not killed travel and face-to-face communication before Covid-19. The lock-down forced us all to continue without travel and face-to-face interactions. We discovered how well this can work. However, cities are not only about work. There is also social life in cities. As I am sitting here in Shoreditch in London, which Tom knows, where I live, as he had his office located here. While nobody was working in offices last summer (2020), everybody was still out and about. The clubs, bars and the nightlife here were humming all through the evenings and extended weekends. There is this desire to socialize. The pub opposite our office is where our people discuss continuously – so you need to live in an urban center, ideally walking distance from work, school, cultural venues. I believe in urban concentration, but I believe that some of us will remain more remote after the Covid experience. Perhaps the older generation will not be coming into offices so much and this will free up some space in the urban centers to have more residences. Some will move out of city centers, some offices will be vacated or reduced and some will now choose to move into the city centre. The much reduced commuting burden will allow us to create a walkable city with more urban vitality, for those of us who wish to live like this. I also believe it is more productive. Remote work does not offer the same networking and learning opportunities.

The other thing I am working on in terms of telecommunication, is the advent of cyberspace. There is an enormous amount of investment flowing into virtual event tools. There is a technology transfer from the gaming industry into the emerging metaverse industry. There are a lot of start-up companies for virtual conferencing, virtual exhibitions, virtual everything. We are also working on that, because all of our clients need that. We have full VR models anyway. Why not start using these technologies and allow staff and clients and anybody to roam around in these designed environments. That is what I am working on now. I believe some of that will happen rather soon. Telecommunication moves away from the paradigm of graphic design based on the magazine analogy, into the paradigm of architectural design based on the city/building analogy. I think it is feasible and viable. I believe that we should join these virtual worlds not only from home. Some of us will be gathering on site and then we will have virtual participants connecting in. I don't believe we will become physically isolated. We will be in our central office spaces with video walls and panoramic projections as windows into a larger virtual world where other remote groups or individuals join. There is a lot of technology coming in, e.g. AR glasses, holographic projections, or robots running around which project somebody's tele-presence. All the major companies are working on this. Whether it is Tencent, Facebook, Microsoft or Google. Architects should design these virtual spaces and cities. These should be designed together with and integrated with the physical spaces. Both virtual and physical design will share a single spatial visual language, iconography and semiology.

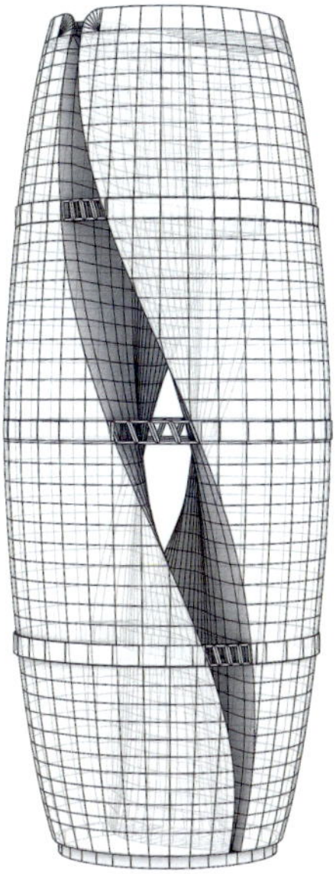

View of massing and atrium

AG In the past two decades, the portfolio of Zaha Hadid Architects includes a variety of Tower projects, including office towers, residential and hotel projects, in contexts around the world. In which way does the Leeza Soho project seem distinct and different when compared to previous Zaha Hadid Architects tower designs, and what interests have been carried from project to project? Also, how has the Leeza Soho project influenced other projects designed since Leeza, and finally how do you believe this project may influence current or future ZHA projects?

PS We worked on the idea of the big atrium in a series of projects for the Soho China client but also with other clients. What I'm trying to do is to make the atrium even more interesting. The atrium does not necessarily have to be conceived as one fantastic swoop but you could be more complex, more broken up, with only glimpses linking its parts, and there could be bridges crossing the atrium. In Tower C in Shenzhen, we do not have a mega atrium there, but several smaller atria. I would also like to foreground the structure more explicitly, and also vertical circulation systems. These notions lead me to nearly a hyper version of something which Richard Rogers tried to do in his fantastic Lloyds of London tower, but rather more seamless and more varied. I am working on all of these topics in recent studios at the AA, with clusters of high-rise buildings, conceived to be executed in different materials – concrete, steel, timber, and a mix of those materials. I am looking for opportunities where we can synthesize more subsystems in intricate ways. We also do urban projects, such as in Chongqing and Chengdu, where we have to design a whole cluster of buildings. These opportunities are what I am looking for, to realise my vision of a 3D, interconnected twenty-first century urban knowledge industry cluster with multiple public activations at higher levels. This is something I am initially developing with my students. Complex, optimized external structural skeletons, although materially efficient, are still economically taxing due to higher construction costs. The same goes for highly optimized/differentiated external shading systems. So that is why we cannot have everything in every project. Of course, every single project has lots of ambitions, as well as compromises. The compromises deserve criticism. What is nice about ZHA's overall accomplishment across all our projects, is that one can imagine how the best ingredients and innovations of the various projects could finally be brought together in a "super project". I think we will get there; we are moving towards it. I think that the construction industry also has to evolve further in terms of gearing up with respect to file-to-factory fabrication, on-site

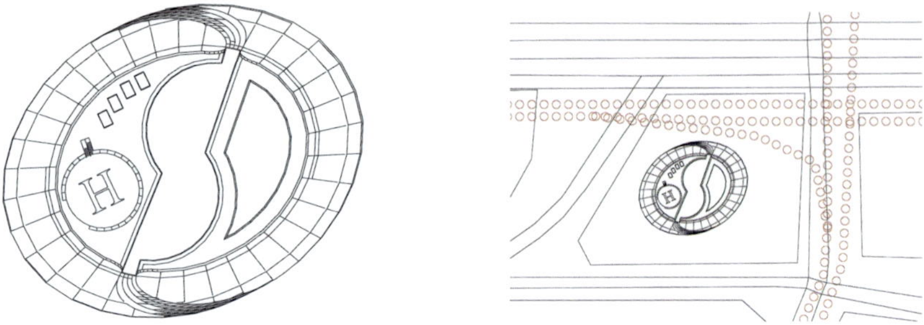

Plan and Site Plan

robotic construction etc. I think it's coming because in the end the material savings are projected. We must substitute information and computational intelligence delivering material efficiencies for labour intensive production. As that spreads, it becomes more economic to tailor-make solutions. Then these super refined and optimized structures and façades will, in the end, become economically compelling, as well as more eloquent, beautiful and light. Economic calculation has always two sides: benefits and costs. Parametricism will deliver on both sides of this equation. There is still a long way to go, and it is important that there are academic institutions like yourselves who are supporting this effort intellectually as well as creatively.

TV Thank you, Patrick, and thank you Aditi, Sohee and Adam, for leading our discussion. You have shared so many incredible insights on the Leeza Soho building, and as well as a series of projects which haven't been published yet. Just to wrap up, and although the interview questions were comprehensive, I have one more question for you. The Leeza Soho project contributes so many architectural advancements and innovations at the frontiers of contemporary architectural culture. It seems to me this project makes a break with some previous trajectories, tendencies and modes of expression in your office. Not only is this the largest atrium ever built, and much more vast than any other interior urban space designed by ZHA, and but I think there's also a break in some sense about a possible duplicity in the appearance of geometric simplicity from a distance, helped by the blackness of the building, departing from all-encompassing continuity of systems, as a sort of normative ZHA condition. I'm referring specifically to the structural expression of the atrium glass surfaces, in which instances of mathematical events mark shifts from concave to convex surfaces. These moments are quite extreme, discreet transitions in geometry, as an integration and of structure and surface.

I find it difficult to find this quality in ZHA's earlier trajectories, and it seems to be quite a new proposition in this project. In other recent or current projects, are you also working on this shift from continuity to discontinuous mathematical events found in the integration of structural and other tectonic systems?

PS Thanks for the observation with your keen eye on the details of the atrium's crease lines and the shifts between convex and concave. Yes, I think these are important elements in the aesthetic, as well as the overall elative muteness and subtleness in the exterior expression. Yes, we all love that and appreciate that and it inspires us also going forward. We have multiple cultures that are connected within ZHA, I am connected up with all of them. There are clusters of people who are following the path of refinement, subtlety and rationality, and others who are further pushing the "spectacular". Further, we have those who are very much in what I now call the tectonism paradigm, which I think is very important, but very tough to deliver in terms of the integration of sophisticated engineering knowledge and tools. Here morphologies are driven by structural engineering, environmental engineering and new fabrication logics.

This comes out of the research group venturing out into practice via smaller test projects and with some larger projects also. So, there are slightly different trajectories here at ZHA. They can be hybridized at certain points. We're a large firm, and we have a series of mature designers, as well as always young blood coming in.

It's true what you're saying Tom, but there is not a singular conscious trajectory at work. There is certainly not a single game of continuity across everything. Sometimes a threshold or break accentuates something and announces an event, and is integrated into a richer design. If there are not too many breaks, this is enhancing the experience. We are, on the one hand, in this game of seeking refined mastery over what we're doing within the intentionality, which we have developed. And then on the other hand, where we're also exploring new sensations and trajectories with these break-outs. We still see ourselves as connected to the academic realm and see ourselves operating within an avant-garde condition and research condition. Yet at the same time, we have to deliver on the large scale and also want that sense of mastery which we achieve when we have project lineages. I don't know yet where Leeza Soho stands in all this. It part of a lineage, but also sets a new accent. As I said, my own vision is to build up more complexity where such complexity is merited by site and program. Also I am working on a book on Tectonism. Leeza is not fully integrated with this vision which is more the next stage. However, this vision needs a project task which is more complex, mixed-use, with more systems at play than in this particular project. But again, what I do believe is that it is important that a design doesn't become overcrowded – trying to do too many things at the same time. I compare design sometimes to writing a political manifesto in the following sense: They have a primary headline, then a subtitle, then secondary and tertiary points etc. Its a hierarchy. A building should not be an onslaught of 100 simultaneous messages. It has a primary message which end-users should take in first, and then it should reveal other layers – it is the same when you do an exhibition design. So that's where this kind of toning down and suppressing of information, temporarily, makes sense. We must select and accentuate just a few things, initially. But the endgame must be an information-rich and interaction-rich environment. I believe that we have to reflect on our cognitive capacity to grasp an object, a space, and we need avoid creating an agitated onslaught. Let's say, that was the major failure of De-constructivism. This was not generalisable. Deconstructivist compositions often became so chaotic that you as designer can easily get lost in your own drawing. You go away for coffee, and you come back and don't know where you should continue to draw, where you had left off. If you get lost in the drawing, it probably implies a failure for end-user navigation also. That speaks for simplicity, which has been a value in architecture for thousands of years, and it's also a value in science and in writing. However, oversimplification is equally fatal. If social life becomes more complex , so must architecture. The whole point of parametricism can be summed up like this: enabling architecture to maintain legibility in the face of complexity.

TV Thank you. I think that Leeza Soho does delay the surprise of the atrium, from the exterior to the interior. It saves that sensation of the spectacular experiences of the building, which are in delay. And I think that this represents a quite mature sense of control and curation of an experience from a great distance to proximity, from exterior to interior. I would like to thank you genuinely for your graciousness and generosity for joining us today. We are, as you know, broadcasting this interview on Facebook Live, and will archive this interview with others on YouTubeLIVE, so our audience will be bigger and enduring. Thank you so much for joining us! I hope we get to see you sometime soon, once our world returns a little bit to some semblance of normalcy.

PS Hopefully later this year. Thank you. Great questions and discussion!

ALL Thank you!

丽泽SOHO

KUNSTHAUS GRAZ

Graz, 2003 | Spacelab: Peter Cook and Colin Fournier

Program Five exhibition spaces, offices, library, cafeteria, board rooms, meeting places, rest area

Materials Methacrylate, cast electronically

INTERACTION

100%	12	900 M2	930	1200	0	23 M	4	11,100 M2
Glazing	Roof Light Wells	Outer Skin	40w Led Light Rings on Façade	Façade Total Modules	Floors Above Ground	High	Floors Below Ground	GFA

INTERVIEW

Interviewee: Sir Peter Cook, Partner, Cook Belacevic Haffner Partnership Architects Ltd.

Interviewers: Ethan Ross, Vaibhav Vadadoriya, M.Arch students, School of Architecture and Design, New York Institute of Technology

April 27, 2022

Tom Verebes We are so thrilled to welcome you to New York Tech, Sir Peter Cook, to discuss your reflections on, "the friendly alien", the nickname for this incongruent architectural jewel set in the Baroque and medieval urban context of Graz. It is a floating, blue, shiny, smooth, three-dimensionally curvilinear bodily figure, with pointy nozzles on its roof to provide filtered daylight to its upper galleries. You have toured us through sixty years of drawings, and this event is indeed such a treat! My students will now ask some friendly questions, initially questioning why this alien blob is friendly, rather than adversarial, conflictive or unsettling in its host context. The Kunsthaus has rebranded Graz, not dissimilarly to the Guggenheim's famous "Bilbao Effect", for example. Welcoming you to this series, Peter is a career highlight for me, and it is a thrill for my M.Arch students. I would like to introduce our interviewers, Ethan Ross and Vaibhav Vadadoriya, M.Arch students here at New York Tech.

Peter Cook Thank you for inviting me. Tom, are we wearing the same shirt?

TV Nearly! I had this shirt tailored some years ago for a party in Hong Kong, and I have always called this shirt my "P. Cook Shirt"!

PC Wonderful! It seems then you have good taste!

Ethan Ross Hello, my name is Ethan Ross and my partner's name is Vaibhav Vadadoriya and we would like to thank you for your interesting and informative presentation. Our first question concerns the nickname of the Kunsthaus, "the friendly alien", which encapsulates the distinction of the Kunsthaus to the historic Baroque and medieval urban and architectural context of Graz. In retrospect, some 19 years after completion of this building, in which ways do you see the Kunsthaus as friendly to its context, to its visitors and citizens? More broadly, in your view, what are the responsibilities for architecture, and for the architect to adhere to?

PC Well, I think there are buildings that could be considered aggressive. I think there are

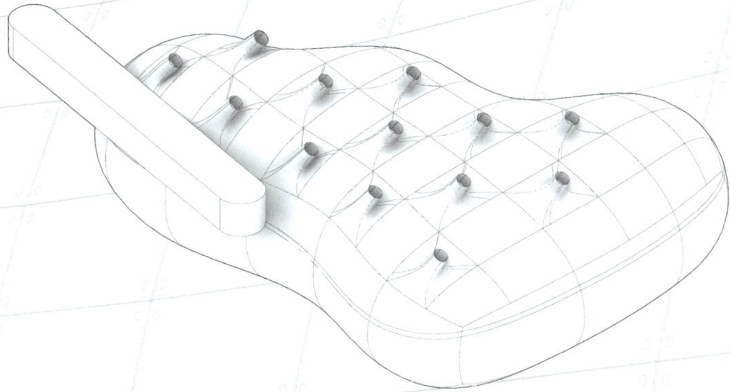

buildings where the tectonics are so pleased with themselves that they are actually uncomfortable to use. I'm always amused by buildings even those done by friends of mine, and I go to visit them and I had difficulty finding the men's room either because they dared to put it in a difficult position. I will refer to one late friend of mine, Zaha Hadid, and fortunately a living friend of mine, Ron Arad, both of them I think in their own way are design geniuses, but you try and find a toilet in their buildings. In a neo-classical academic building, you can always find the toilets and the stairs. Graz is a good city, and I liken it to a patchwork quilt. It has so many different types of architecture. But it never has any kind of architecture for more than three buildings in a row and then it becomes something else. Graz does have Baroque onion domes, so there were curvilinear buildings way back in history. The other thing is, which is strange, is that the Kunsthaus is very usable. I give an anecdotal reference that the day of opening I visited it for the opening ceremony, and no less than the Chancellor of Austria was there. We were chatting and we went together up the travelator, which is a gentle slope and we had an agreeable white wine in our hands, and despite his formal appearance, we chatted nonchalantly, and I believe the building created this informality and friendliness.

ER Throughout your career, you have been committed to the radicality of architecture. For Archigram, architecture was the site for experimentation with the intersection of culture and technology, empowering architecture with capacities to change society. Fast-forwarding some years, within the technological and disciplinary context or architecture at the millennium, building a double curved envelope, or blob, in the parlance of the 1990's and early 2000's was an ambitious goal. In which ways is architecture for you either, or both, a tool to serve society, or one to change it? In which ways does the Kunsthaus Graz install in built form these notions of how the radicality of technological experimentation in architecture can impact society?

I think your question is wrong. I think architecture is built to enliven your everyday experience. I think architecture's role is to take the things we do, that we have to do, we'd like to do and to take those that bit further.

ER Our next question concerns the art or curatorial context of the Kunsthaus as a "black box of hidden tricks," a multidisciplinary venue for new ways to present art of varied media, without a permanent collection. In the art world, the spatial options are most commonly either generic white cubes or black boxes, the Kunsthaus proposed a third space for the interaction of curatorial practices and artists with its architecture. How have the exhibitors in the galleries of the Kunsthaus responded to the specificity of the spaces of the galleries?

PC Your questions are academic and convoluted, but I think that what is interesting is that some artists cannot exhibit in there. They think the architecture is too present, but a lot of our artists have really enjoyed themselves in the Kunsthaus. The late Sol Lewitt, and Olafur Eliasson is another example, of people who have gone in there and said, “hey, right, now I'm going to play with this toy”. I know so many interesting museums have just white boxes inside them. Sometimes there is an abdication of the architecture that the architect likes to place as an emblem, and then you just go inside to a white box. Of course, there is another tradition, which is the concert hall, which is very often a box sitting inside a different box. There is a whole discussion which one could have about buildings where the inside is one building and the outside is another building, but I think straight functionality is one thing and extraordinary functionality is another. I did not think this building should be hurtful. I also do not think architecture should necessarily be very expensive. We built this building for 3% over the normal budget, but most art museums come out at about 15% or above their budget by the time they've been built.

VV Technology has the capacity to be applied by designers to enable the production of innovative architecture. The smooth skin of the Kunsthaus is made of 1,200 panels of 2cm thick transparent blue, pliable acrylic sheets, formed on molds, as you have shown in your presentation. The curved body of the building is punctuated by roof nozzles which point outwards, merging continuously with the surface of the envelope. Initially, the project was proposed with the nozzles responding dynamically and moving kinetically away from direct sunlight. What were the challenges of building a smooth, nearly seamless, architectural skin, and also, can we ask you what challenges led to the nozzles being designed as fixed in position rather than kinetic?

PC I think that in my own criticism of the nozzles, it would be wonderful if they could have been movable, but that would have cost a lot of money. They are too small. I will admit that they're not doing very much in terms of natural lighting. Their usefulness comes from particular artificial lighting, but to be really useful they should be about three times the size. In the library area of our Vienna University building, we do have nozzles again, but they are enlarged considerably, and from the inside they do light particular areas so they do have a particular effect. This is a criticism I have had. On the other hand, if you take away the nozzles, you just get a kind of “belly of the whale” kind of thing. I think the nozzle interests me – in our little blue Bournemouth project we had a single giant nozzle. If you had nozzles on top of Graz the size of those, we would only have space for three

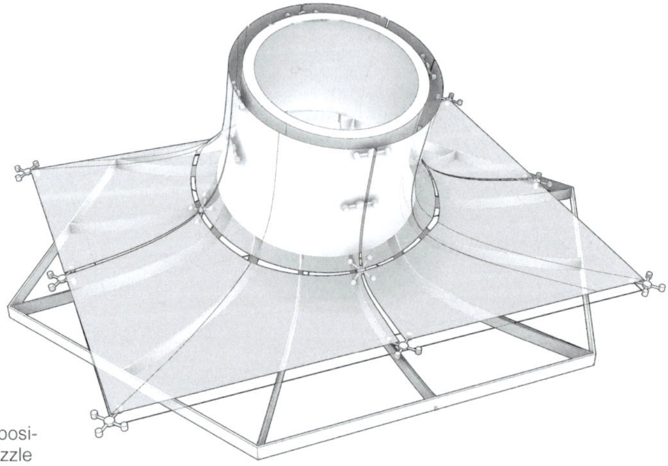

Detail composition of a nozzle

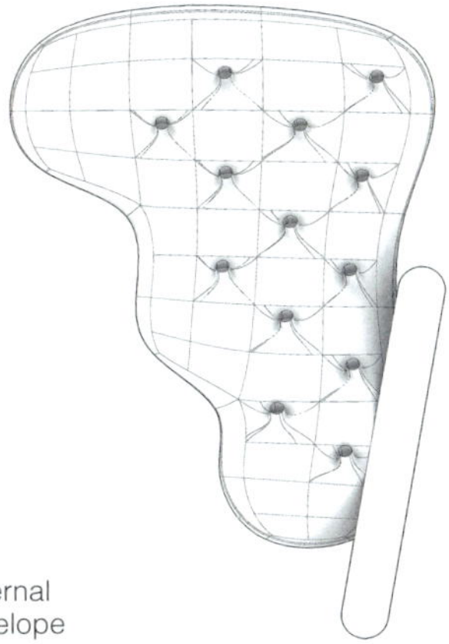

External envelope

or four nozzles and they would appear as outcrops. There is a lot to be done with the combination of natural light and artificial light, but making it come from the same zone therefore having a continuous character. The restrictions actually led us to a funny crew of local inventors we had rounded up for this project, who were good at inventing cars and planes. There is an old crafting tradition in that area. There are old ironworks in the city where crafting has been going on for 300-400 years. It is a good context for inventiveness. These people tend to hang out at the Technical University in Graz, so we found a lot of people to support the project with almost a craft nature. But the other thing is the budget. With the translucent parts in some of the public areas, we would have had much more ambiguity between the inside and the outside. We started doing that, but we got our fingers rapped. There are certain things you can do with budget and certainly stepping back, between us, in our other little blue building in Bournemouth, the budget was just sufficient for us to be able to have a very pure interior and a very total exterior, and to use a very non-local way of building things. The Arts University (of Bournemouth) was very generous to enable us to do a rather expensive building. To some extent, you get what you pay for.

VV In the sense of understanding a building as a public interface, do you see any parallels with ideas that recall the body of radical experimental architecture which was expressed in so many of Archigram's projects in the 1960s?

PC Yes, I suppose there are buildings which reveal themselves to be quite radical, but sometimes look quite ordinary. I am interested more and more in the vocabulary of architecture.

Most of what I have been talking about this evening has been about what things look like and the statement that they make initially, although sometimes I have been talking about the inherent kind of development of them, either through time or one thing laying upon the other.

Our little studio building is not as blue as Graz, but it does owe something to Graz, but it is a smaller building. It also has to do with art, it is to do with making art, with light. It is very direct in a funny way. Inside is on the outside even though there are so many layers in Graz. That might be a leftover of me being trained as a functionalist, before Archigram, that you do something, and that is what it is. My later architecture is fascinated by things not being seen. I am interested at the moment in hybrids as well. Something looks like stone and it actually turns out to be a derivative of plastic. It looks like you are not sure what it is until you get close to it. Also, I should mention the business of a building being an artwork. In Bournemouth we made the exterior of the building as a mural with

individuals inside making things. You see the interior, and it is largely an extended workshop – a making building rather than a sitting and talking building. I enjoy doing buildings where people make things, but I am not sure that I get off on office buildings, quite frankly.
VV In the 1960's, Archigram had championed, among other architectural paradigms, notions of indeterminacy, interactivity, transformation, change, and architecture as infrastructure. Archigram produced over 300 projects, mostly unbuilt in the conventional sense of an architectural project. From your perspective, can you share with the next generation of young, emerging architects, and current students, how you define an architectural project, and how has the notion of an architectural project changed since the days of Archigram?

PC What I would like young architects to do would be to actually look at things in my drawings, and in the buildings there is a subplot which I should raise here, is the role of the cartoon. I have done so many drawings which show people doing things in those buildings. In the case of the architecture school we designed in Australia, I have photographs taken of me unwittingly doing some of the things I was drawing. I am busy putting together anecdotes.

Architecture is about life. I feel myself wanting to contribute to the theater of life, helping things just to be more cheerful, just a bit more interesting, just a bit more quirky, and then seeing what people do with it. But I think looking is very important. A lot of what I do is a reflection upon something that someone has done or seen, or seen somebody doing.

If I am doing a building for something which I am very familiar with, for example, a building for post-graduate students, it is exactly what I have been dealing with for donkey's years. I have had thousands of conversations with students, and these run through my head. In my recent cartoons for university buildings, I depicted a shy girl in a corner, moving away from the noise, and another chap who is the loud guy in the middle of it. The first competition I won was actually was for elderly people's housing, but it was not built. It was all anecdotal. I thought how would I live in a restricted space. How would I operate? I designed it as a caravan. At the end of the day, I am not an abstract designer. When I write books, I do not have any

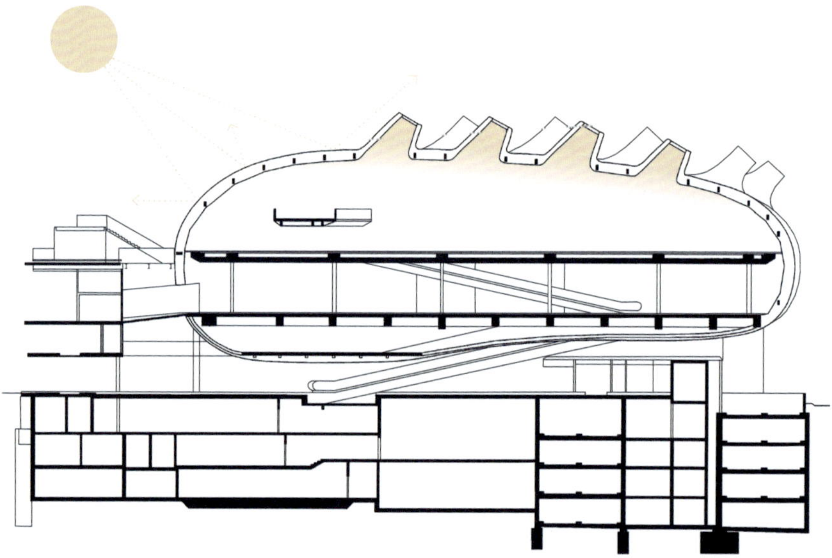

Section showing indirect sunlight throgh nozzles.

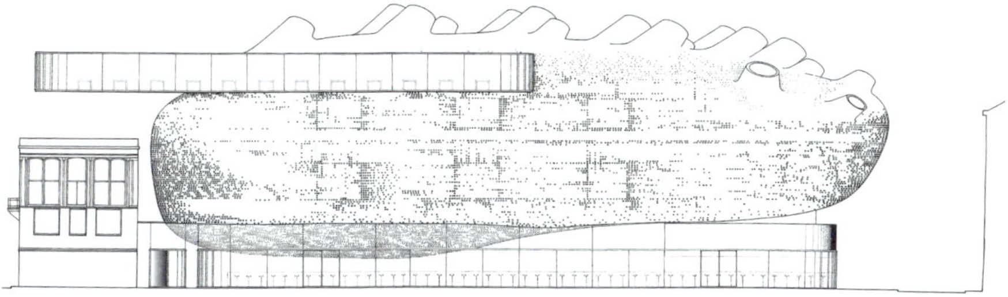

Elevation of mediated facade.

footnotes. It is all chit chat, not theory. I hate theory actually. I may have created some theory, but I find that the pursuit of theory has interfered with architectural education with disastrous effect, particularly in the United States. Oops!

VV Before designing and proposing the Kunsthaus together with Colin Fournier, you nurtured and developed experimental design practices as a professor and academic leader, at the AA, the Stadelschule, the Bartlett, and elsewhere. How did your background, working at the forefront of education in architecture, and your experience as an experimental educator, guide you to propose this radical and experimental building?

PC The drawings of the Kunsthaus were preceded by nine months of absolutely exhausting crying. One has lots of conversations in order to continue as a designer. If you're an academic, and I call myself a joke academic despite having three professorships, there are too many conversations. Sometimes you have to switch off. I have a lot of friends who are good teachers and have been very good designers. Then they get to a point where each time they try to design something, they are thinking all the problems, all the ways in which you could critique it, how they would

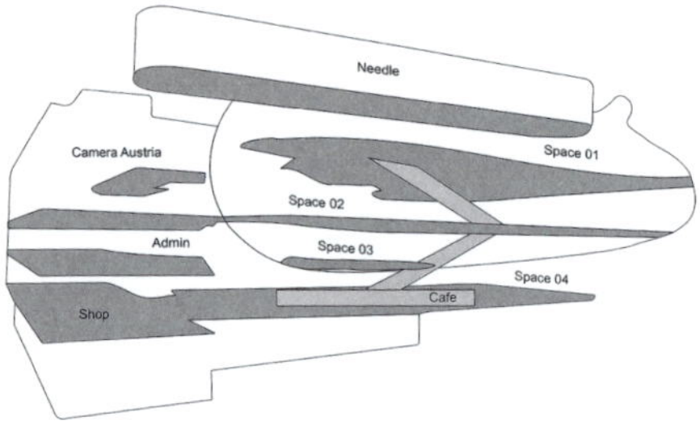

Program distribution.

critique it, and then how somebody else might critique it, and then they freeze. I have a sort of switch off, I say, "fuck it - we've gotten this far, and yeah sure, that might not work, but let's go with it". In designing, I have a cut-off point where I just say, "let's go with it".

ER For our final question, do you believe there is an avant-garde in today's architecture?

PC Not enough! I wish there was. I think most people are very scared at the moment. Everybody wants to be seen to be a good person. They want to do the right thing and want to be thought of as good. Everyone is a bit calm. It pisses me off, actually.

TV Peter, this is a great moment then to conclude and to thank you!

PC I should have presented more on the Kunsthaus, in retrospect.

TV Absolutely not! Your presentation was a fantastic visual tour of your drawings, of your thinking, and you narrated it so engagingly. It has been a great treat. On behalf of the dean, and our school, I thank you so much for the generosity of your time, for such a wonderful tour through 60 years of your work, and I wish you all the best, good health, and more productivity for years to come.

PC I hope to bump into you in the flesh soon.

TV I also hope we return to our previous normal soon as well.

PC All the best to you all!

MEDIA TIC

Barcelona, Spain, 2010 | Cloud 9

Program Public (Barcelona activa and oab – oficina de atención a las empresas, universities) and private (offices for information technology start-ups)

Materials Metallic main structure with bioluminescent paint, ETFE as sun protection, green roof

Metrics on energy "A" Energy Efficiency certificate, Net Zero

INTERACTION

60%	Solid
40%	Glazing
4	Different Façade Module Types
128	Façade Modules Total
4	Façade + Roof
8	Floors Above Ground
2	Floors Below Ground
3,640 M2	Landscape
22,940 M2	GFA

INTERVIEW

Interviewee: Enric Ruiz-Geli, Director, Cloud 9

Interviewers: Japheth Aleyakpo, Adam Giannios, Jay Patel, M.Arch students, School of Architecture and Design, New York Institute of Technology

April 21, 2020

Tom Verebes We are thrilled, Enric, that you have joined us today at New York Tech. Your Media TIC project exemplifies beautifully the issues encapsulated in our theme of "Interaction" – implying ways in which architecture can gain sentience, and better respond to the dynamics of the environment and user criteria. I would like to introduce our three interviewers today, Japheth Aleyakpo, Adam Giannios, and Jay Patel, M.Arch students here at NYIT.

Enric Ruiz-Geli Thank you. Tom, for hosting me. I am very supportive of New York Institute of Technology, so it is great to be here.

Japheth Aleyakpo Thank you for your amazing presentation, which has opened our eyes to features and functionalities of the MEDIA TIC project, and honestly, I have learnt so much from your presentation. The MEDIA TIC building was inaugurated in 2010. Located in the new science and technology district of 22@Barcelona, the building responded to a competition calling for an architecture about technology, information and communication. The building's active, adaptive and responsive systems create an interactive environment, as an incubator hosting technology thinkers, inventors, and entrepreneurs. This project has been rightly lauded for its advances in the discourses of architectural interactivity and smartness, mainly through the façade systems and their responsiveness to climatic and environmental conditions. Can you please share with us your approach to the competition brief, and your conceptualization of the Media TIC project, over a decade ago? Also, can you explain the affiliations of the Media TIC project to others researching interactive architecture in the early 2000s, perhaps also calling out any impactful projects, and their designers, in close relation to the Media TIC building?

ERG The first part of the competition was a big competition. I think about 80 projects and offices were competing. It was quite an international field of entries, and it was very tough. We focused our competition entry on just one goal. We promised light structure; we promised a membrane that will fight global warming; and, we promised a building which

will be Net Zero. So, we put our sticks on the fire. We declared there must be a Net Zero building in Barcelona. The competition program called for 18,000 square meters, which is a lot. Many of the proposals in the competition were 2 towers. The typology of the building that we proposed was a very compact building: forty by forty meters, with big openings and halls inside. The idea of urban density that is very much appreciated in Barcelona is what they saw in our panels. If you have a competition of eighty projects and everybody is proposing towers, towers, towers, that means shadows to the neighbors. It means impact to the street. But you don't produce public space with towers! Public space is crucial in Barcelona. In New York, public space can be created with a setback of a tower. If a tower is so high, there can be an overwhelming presence of the tower to the district. The district of the Media TIC is a residential district, so there is social housing around the block. We were one of the very few entries not proposing towers, so our proposal was very compact. I think the key for the city architect's support was "well, I'm getting a Net Zero and I'm not getting impact upon the social neighborhood".
That was very important. The difference in our scheme was a statement that we were not going to replicate Silicon Valley, silos, innovation here and social housing far away, instead we could have an innovative building and social housing on the same block. Is it impossible? Well Barcelona is saying to the world, No, it's not. So, our approach was to do a building showcasing innovation that is going to be an open house, towards social equity, for the competition jury.

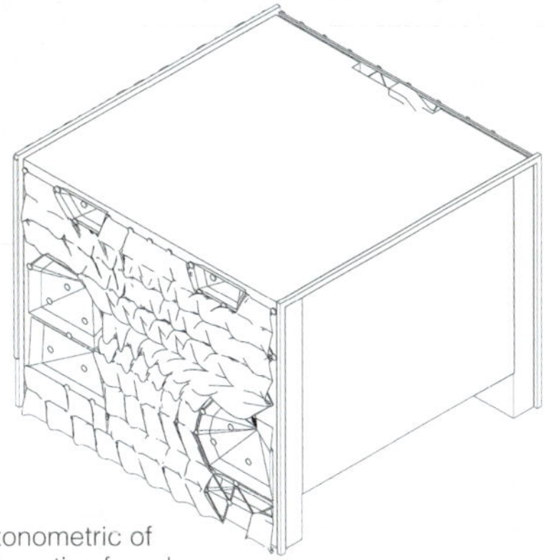

Axonometric of interactive façade

JA The ETFE air cushions of one of the façades are filled with nitrogen and mixed with tiny oil droplets. In the afternoon, the façade modules transform the façades from transparent to translucent, which blocks 90 percent of the sun's radiation, thus substantially reducing the building's heat gain. In maintaining this façades, can you please comment on the sustainability of this system, with respect to its longevity and maintenance?

ERG We are in a crucial moment. The glass industry is a large industry, led by big companies like Saint Gobin. Glass by itself is not enough. You have to have some plastic film inside to make the glass more efficient and smarter. Actually, the glass industry is using polymers, and the plastic industries, such as PPT, know that a year later this plastic can become yellow and fragile, and can break. They are interested in making plastic stronger, and more resistant to UV light. You have the glass industry entering plastics and the plastic industry interested in crystalizing plastics. What is very interesting is that ETFE, a crystalized polymer, sits exactly in the middle. It takes the best from crystal, the best from the glass industry, and the best from the plastic industry. As a middle ground material, ETFE has the lightness of the plastic industry and the resistance of the glass industry, and you get a forty-year warranty. But, do we want a forty-year warranty, given our ideas stand up for only fifteen years? Don't buy material that has a 100-year warranty because, believe me, you are going to kill some generations of builders, users, architects, and designers.

Polymers are interesting to me. The composite industry is extremely interesting. The composite industry is now turning plastic into recycled plastics, rather than using oil-based resin, they are using nature-based bio-resin. The future of ETFE is to start using bio-resins.

I was in Kuwait, talking to the industry who leads the oil interest in Kuwait, asking what was going on in their industry. In the oil industry, they are, interestingly enough, not interested in oil going into cars. Their profit for gas is $18.00 per barrel. If oil goes into the composite industry, their profit is $80 per barrel. They are very happy with electric cars. This is interesting, right? They are switching into other markets – for example, smart composites. Composites are used for 3-D printing materials. You start to see that oil is not only going to cars anymore, but is used in material for 3-D printing buildings. I am interested, because then we will not need to do mining for concrete or for steel. Aluminum was for some years the solution to framing. Now, as we understand that fabricating aluminum has such high energy consumption, and it is very hard to recycle. It is so energy driven, that suddenly, wood framing is attractive. We cut down trees, but we can plant more trees than we harvest. The Media TIC building is aluminum free. You have to know the materials of the future, but you also have to know which materials are the enemy; the blacklist of materials; the no-go materials.

AG Structurally, the Media TIC minimizes the need for large or numerous columns, increasing the visibility of the various transparent and translucent patterns of the envelope throughout the building. The primary structure is defined by a series of truss columns and beams. The truss beams, which are at a depth of two-stories, are inhabitable, and span the 35 meters between the two truss walls. Also, we note that the area with the greatest impact of the building's overall design strategy is in the lobby space where there are no vertical structures to disrupt the open plan setting. During the schematic design stage, how did you conceive the use of this vast space and the ways in which it stages the effects of the dynamic behaviors of the envelope?

ERG In 2002, I visited the Eden Project in Cornwall, England, (by Grimshaw & Partners). It was the first time I was introduced to ETFE. I was having a conversation with Grey Lynn and François Roche in the lobby of the Centre Pompidou during the Non-Standard Exhibition held there (in 2003). We were having a coffee, and I was thinking how the Pompidou lobby is in fact a warehouse. You can just as easily open a coffee shop in this lobby as you can install a running track. We asked ourselves, "What is the work that the incubators are going to be doing?" If you

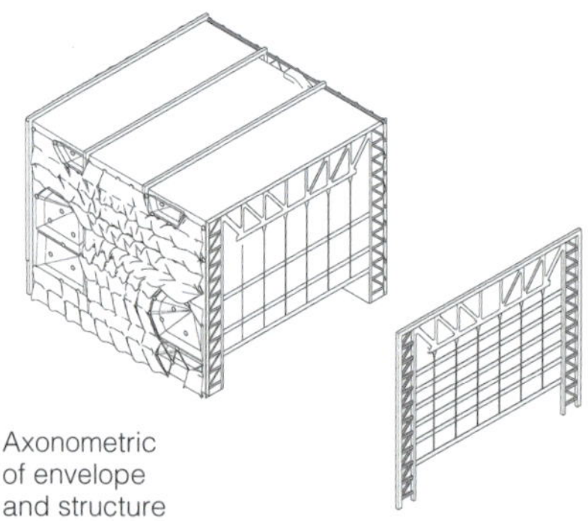

Axonometric of envelope and structure

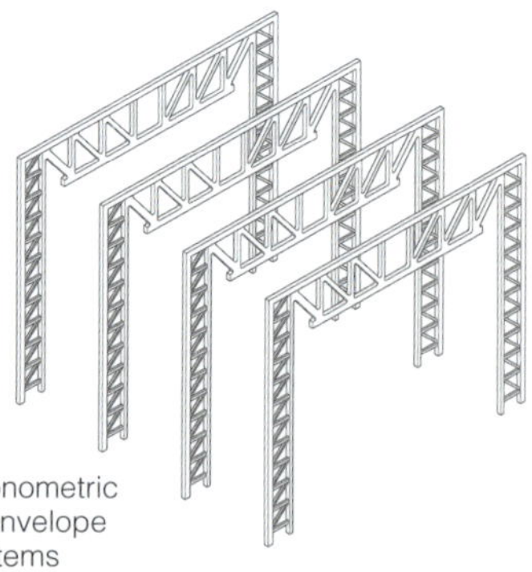

Axonometric of envelope systems

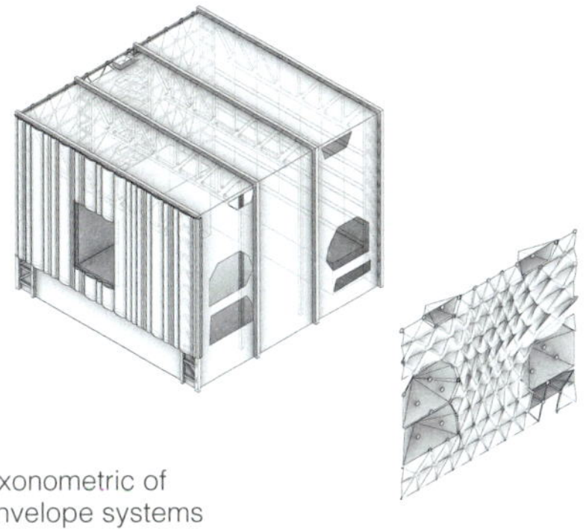

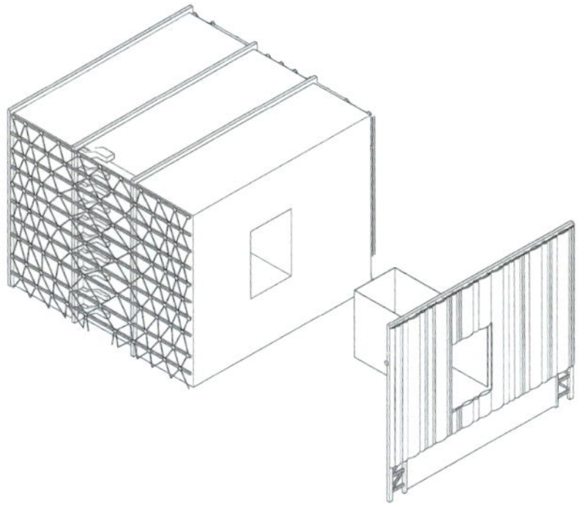

Axonometric of envelope systems

imagine as an architect, that your users are start-ups, we can address what a start-up needs. They need furniture, space, program, height... Are you allowing this start-up to be really a start-up? Have you told them what they need? I was under the impression that the lobby had to make everything possible. Maybe a museum is the only place where everything is possible for the artist to show. The best way to make sure to design the right space for start-ups was to design another type of museum space. Museum space enters the office space to enable anything. Now in the lobby of the Media TIC, for example, you can have people presenting an electric bike which they designed. There have been lectures in the lobby. They have used it as temporary offices. Or people are doing political interventions and demonstrations in the lobby. It's a place that the city is using in many ways, and we are very happy about that. These are the reasons we used the typology of a museum like Pompidou, or an office building. The owner of the building remarked, "This is not a museum. This is an office building." Lobbies are usually small, so you do not lose floor area. We lost some. In the lobby of the New York Times building, you find an artist installation, in a building which is locked to the public, so it is not a public building. The Media TIC is a public building, using public land with public funds, so it is public. No security, no entrance, no police at the door, no safety, no control, it's public. It's open.

JA In the Media TIC, a deep horizontal cut and a vertical punch through the slabs three levels above enable natural light to enter deep into the building. The resulting semi-sheltered transitional spaces are some of the key features of the building, The inflated ETFE cushions enable the building to react to solar impact in two distinctly different ways. In the design of Media TIC, are there any other considerations of passive techniques for light and ventilation?

ERG This is a great question. Let's talk about passive systems for a moment. Of course, in any team, you have structural engineers and MEP engineers, and we need to work together to form collective intelligence. You have to get the best from everybody to make the best design. Most buildings have their mechanical equipment on the roof. So, our first decision was to not have all the machinery on the roof, because then there would be no space for a green roof. We wanted a green roof. We wanted people to access the roof and for the terrace to be a public terrace. The first decision was to bring all the machinery down to the parking lot. The second decision was related to how Engineers very much like air to be controlled and managed as a sealed box. But this is a problem. It dries the air. The carpet makes that air very dry, and it has an electric field. The way to change this is to have openings to the terraces. By introducing this, there is airflow every time I go to the terrace for a meeting or a phone call. The terrace becomes a place for experimentation. At that moment, natural air is breathed into the office, so the humidity levels on the inside of the office are changed naturally by this airflow from the terrace. That is extremely important. The humidity levels of this air have to be,

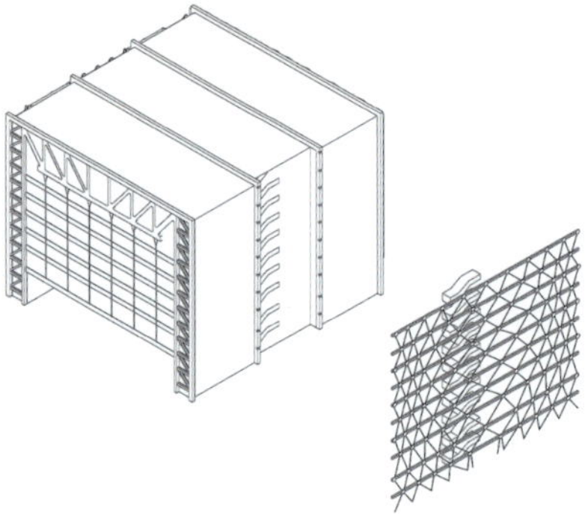

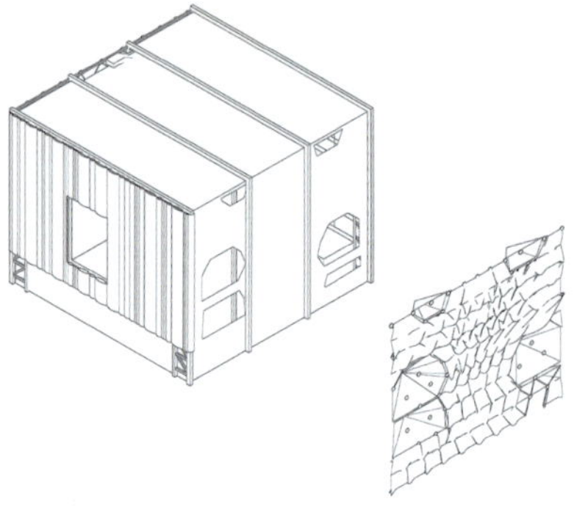

ideally in a sustainable world, at 60%. In my office right now, I'm sure the humidity level is at 48%. And in Europe, less than 52%, is not code compliant. What the building has to do is move the volume of air of the building out of the building three times per day. In a home, it's different. When the pandemic is over, and you go back to your university building, have a look at this. If a building has to move that volume three times out and three times in, the number of machines and the amount of energy consumption is huge. You can imagine the amount of volume to control the humidity inside. Instead, in a passive way, you only need to move the air one half of the volume per day because of window openings. You might produce 40%, 50%, or even 80% CO2 emissions using mechanical ventilation. We must have natural ventilation. It's healthy. Engineers don't like it, because their software indicates a loss of energy. If winter is only two weeks long in Barcelona, you are losing energy only during these two weeks. But in the overall year, it's peanuts. So how long is winter in New York? It's two months long. You may lose a little bit, but during the other ten months, you are extremely healthy. So, don't let the engineers take the lead on this issue. We are the green thinkers, and their software is not ready for this. But they have to understand, and you can get them the data from our building, and you can convince them with our Media TIC building.

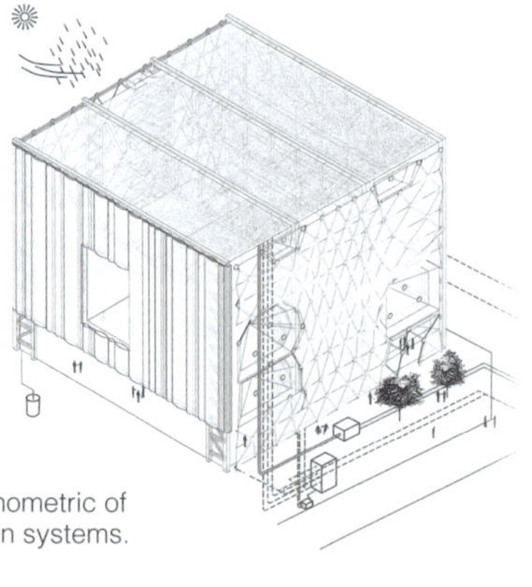

Axonometric of green systems.

JP Cloud 9's work boldly experiments with digital manufacturing, technologies related to energy efficiency, intelligent systems, and self-sufficiency. The Media TIC's enclosure is defined by two materials – a glass curtain wall and ETFE cushions. The cushions consist of several layers of ETFE and actuators that are linked with sensors on the envelope, while the distance between the layers in each cushion may be changed and the overlapping dot patterns create greater or lesser shading for the interior spaces. In response to the competition brief, what were the initial considerations for the smart and interactive design of Media TIC's façade? Can you please explain the process of how you conceived, tested, manufactured and installed these systems? Can you comment on the decisions about the material choices, and the electronic augmentation, and their effect on the cost of the project, perhaps when compared with normative and conventional office buildings?

ERG Let's first focus on the material performance aspect of your questions. For example, the three layers of ETFE have a thickness of 250 microns each layer. That is three times 2.5mm, all together 7.5mm of material. This building wants to be the best building in the world in 2011 with 7mm of material. It's not how much material and how much money, obviously, but rather what you do with those 7 millimeters. When I mean lightness, I don't mean our building is not 3% lighter than its neighbors. It's not 10%, or 20%. It's 70% lighter! The performance consequences amount to big numbers. When you are talking about ETFE, we can mention the curtain wall in the back. A curtain wall has to resist wind loads, and a big cost of a curtain wall goes into resisting wind loads. The wind loads towards the ground are lower than the loads several floors higher. If you have different thickness of the glass on different floors you can make a cost saving. A curtain wall normally has the same thickness as the glass all over, but that is silly. Also, if you have ETFE in front, actually this glass cannot receive the loads because you have the ETFE receiving the loads. And only 20% of the wind loads gets to the glass curtain wall, and the curtain wall only needs to resist 20% of the wind load. They do not perform independently – they work together. They help each other, and that helps in the economy of the building.

The good news about the economy of the building is twofold. If a building is a Net Zero building and is cheaper, the total cost of the building is cheaper than other buildings. That is why this building represents an ecological revolution, because every other building costs more.

In this competition, the jury said to me, "You are the winner, congratulations!" In our first meeting, they explained how this is a very important building for Barcelona, and they allocated a budget of $2,200 euros per square meter, which is a big budget. I thought that if I do this building with this amount of money, then it's not a revolution because it would be just another, fantastic, great, beautiful, and expensive building. But if I build a smart Net Zero building for market cost, then I am shaking up the industry. I'm shaking the industry to say at a market cost you can do a Net Zero. Sorry guys, no one has an excuse. Everybody needs to shut up. You see, this is why the Media TIC is a dangerous building. Because it disrupts the discussion about real estate, the cost of construction, and economic innovation. It's a troublemaker. For example, can social housing be built for market cost? This guy did a net zero building, so you can do it too. Nobody has an excuse. It took us a month to say to our client, "I don't think we need that much money." That was a strong commitment. I'm a socialist architect and live with a social agenda. That is why this building is a Net Zero building at market cost. Where is the money? There must be some trick here. The trick is that I am not spending money on decoration. I am not spending money on pouring concrete in the foundations. In fact, 80% of the building has been digitally fabricated using robotic fabrication. Structure is normally 30% of the overall cost, but if you say it's going to be 40% of the overall cost, investing in the structure to be built digitally, the 40% of the building is already built digitally. Digital Fabrication is very cheap, as you know. I am a pioneer, correct, but you are the first generation to have digital tools. You have the digital industry ready, and you have a pioneer example to demonstrate. Show us evidence. Well, you have the evidence. So, what are you going to do? (Frank) Gehry did not have the software but he had to produce the software in order to build the Guggenheim Museum in Bilbao. Your generation has the software, the industry set up, and the expertise. I am very interested in what your generation is going to do. Just to conclude about innovation, we spent the same money on construction as we did to produce patents. The fact that the construction of this project took 4–5 years, which is plenty of time for a start-up to produce patents. It's plenty of time for an architecture office to produce patents. So, we have been producing patents while we were doing this building. The patents are now owned by my office and they are shared with the

Plan.

builder and with the Mayor of Barcelona. He spent public money and got a building, but he also got five patents.

AG The portfolio of Cloud 9 includes a variety of scales and uses of buildings, located in various international contexts. How did the Media TIC project build upon your earlier design research into interactive and responsive architecture? In which ways did the Media TIC affect your projects, research, and teaching after 2010?

ERG I understand why you ask this question. It's really amazing. Tom, congratulations on your students for asking the best questions ever! Seriously, you are asking the right questions, Adam. Let me tell you a quick story. Our Villa Nurbs project in 2003 was a digitally fabricated house located two hours north of Barcelona. It was the very first of our projects which the *New York Times* published and it got everyone's attention. The owners, Emilio and Antolina, whom I am so blessed to know, have a family restaurant and this family was with me in the construction of the Media TIC building ten years later. Emilio was saying to me, "Enric, this is mine . . ." He was referring to the patent of the skylights of the Villa Nurbs project which was used in the membrane cushions. A house project produces a patent that later is applied in a public building. Imagine you have a first project soon after graduation for a neighbor or your Grandma's summer house, think about how innovation is going to follow your career and is going to get you to the design of the Media TIC. This is not a fake story. It is true. Emilio and Antolina are very proud that one of the most important buildings today in Barcelona is built with their innovations, their heart, and their private home. For example, our recent project in Taipei is real estate driven. Farglory came to see the Media TIC, as well as Virginia Tech students, among other Universities. We have had 28 universities from all over the world coming to visit the building. That was 8 years following the construction and then the CEO said: "Thank you. Welcome to Taipei". What did I just do? I gave him a tour of the building, and he then flew us to Taipei and he said, "I want a green building in Taipei," and we built it. We did not use ETFE because we don't replicate projects, but we did the first building with LEED certification in Taipei. It was the first building with green urban wind turbines. We fabricated the ceramics in Barcelona and sent it to Taipei. You start to see this also in Kuwait and in Virginia Tech, because we should be leading Net Zero buildings and this new agenda here at Virginia Tech and in US as well. I was appointed faculty at the AA because of this building. This building has propelled all our work internationally, and also in the field of education. I am often asked this question of the impact of the Media TIC, which I cannot answer easily. That is why I am pushing these ideas in teaching. If we have evidence of these green buildings, then how many Net Zero buildings there are in Europe? How many green architects are there in the world? Renzo Piano, William McDonough, Studio Gang, Mario Cucinella, for sure, Cloud 9, well, yeah. Ten? Fifteen Net Zero buildings in Europe, Europe, Germany? Come on, Europe is supposed to be great. We are no joke – we are green in Europe! There are a total of maybe six Net Zero buildings in Europe. So why is it not happening? Because there are no green architects, there are no green offices, or people don't have the skills. Tom (Verebes) is a pioneer. He is so ahead of the game. You are eight students here today, and maybe one will go back to their country and will push a green agenda. We can then multiply the numbers of green architects out there. So, this is why I am teaching alongside practice. In my Diploma Unit at the AA, I have had ten graduates per year, over nine years. That is a big group, and I hope they make it as activists of this green movement. Green can be passive, or high technology, or simply water collection. It is many things. It is not the Media TIC. It is your way. Every movement has three phases. The first phase was the pioneers. Well, we are the pioneers. Al Gore and Jeremy Rifkin are the pioneers. The second phase becomes a radical movement. I'm there, I'm the activist, pushing it. I'm sorry, if you are in the concrete business, we need less concrete and smarter concrete, that's it. Sorry. No more cheap concrete. That's the activist movement. The third phase is when green becomes mainstream. For example, as you know, everything is now digital. We don't talk about a digital movement anymore because everything is digital.

You are going to be the generation that doesn't talk about sustainability because you are making it sustainable. We are sustainable, not as branding, but as an option for the architecture you do to benefit your communities, your builders, and your clients.

Now everybody comes to us at Cloud 9 because of the work we do. You can build an ecology of clients because of the work you do. The project we are currently building is a retrofitting of a Calatrava building in Valencia. Your generation will be retrofitting buildings of Patrick (Schumacher) or you will be retrofitting buildings of our generation because they are not good enough. You will push that I am sure. That's my hope, but ultimately, you will do what you want. If you want to go into the concrete business, it's your call.

AG Thank you so much! This has been very inspirational for us graduating M.Arch students as we look towards our the launching of our future careers.

TV Thank you to Adam, Jay and Japheth, and thank you so much Enric! This has been such a pleasure to have you join us today for your presentation and this interview. I have learned so much and I am sure our students have also benefited greatly from this conversation with you. Although Adam had the last question, I have one more. I selected the Media TIC building because of a thematic topic in our seminar, called "Interaction" because of the ways in which the building and its responsive systems address the urgencies of climate change. Its responsibilities are embodied in the performance of the building. It builds a sense of intelligence into the architecture in its capacity to respond intelligently. Within our current era, we are shifting towards more artificial forms of intelligence, as strange concoctions of natural and artificial, human and machine – some label this era the Post-Anthropocene, or the Post natural. I have some questions regarding your position towards the concepts, methods, techniques and culture of artificial intelligence. If you were to propose and execute the Media TIC building now in 2021, what might be conceived and deployed differently from over a decade ago, with respect to greater access to big data and long data of users, climatic information, and our capacity to instrumentalize large datasets? Also, how can artificial intelligence facilitate a building's designers and managers to achieve Net Zero? Lastly, in which ways can you imagine artificial intelligence assisting the further advancement of what you call the Green Agenda?

ERG This is super crucial. This is really the next agenda. I'm very supportive of what you are saying, Tom. When I go back to visit the Media TIC building, I look at the performance of the building and I talk to the people working in the building and I try to understand several relationships. One relationship is the energy bill. The manager of the building keeps calling me to congratulate me on the energy bills. The energy costs are very low – we pay 8 and my neighbor is paying 100, but we pay 8. I thank him for calling, and I tell him I promised the building's energy use was going to be like this. But he keeps calling me. They are good calls. The other side of things is that sometimes I visit the building and suddenly the performance that day didn't work well and then I talk to the managers of the building to ask what happened? "Well, the technician didn't turn on the computer, and was not there, and went to have a coffee, and then came back..., and forgot the sensor and then..." Ok, so there is always a human condition there. I think it's great, when you drive a Tesla, it feels like I'm driving but the Model 3 makes some decisions to assist with driving. That is the collaboration I like: human and artificial forms of intelligence collaborating. I think that the Media TIC will benefit having at the same time both a digital manager and a human manager of the building. If there is data that runs the building, I could send this to you, but there isn't. Data is spread in folders. We are not able to look carefully at the data resource of the building. The collaboration between human and artificial intelligence will be very interesting.

TV I look forward to your future projects as technologies advance. I also welcome another chance soon to discuss the potential of artificial intelligence. Perhaps the benefits of AI for humanity will win over what may alarm many. Thank you Enric, for making so much time for us – this is one of the few great pleasures my students and I are having during the pandemic, sharing this event with our Facebook LIVE audience and eventual YouTube audiences in our SoAD-NYIT archive. We are grateful for your insights and ultimately, we admire the radicality of your activism to push a green agenda.

ERG Thank you all – I wish you all the best.

THE SHED

New York, 2019 | Diller Scofidio + Renfro

Program Galleries, theatre, rehearsal space, creative lab, event space

Façade materials ETFE panels, metal panels, curtain wall, exposed steel

Leed silver certification

Etfe	55%
Glass	45%
Weight of Deployable Shell	8,000,000 lbs
Outer Skin	45,000 M2
Etfe Façade Modules Total	148
High Moveable Shell	36.6 M
Floors Above Ground	8
Floors Below Ground	1
GFA	18,500 M2

INTERVIEW

Interviewee: Robert Katchur, Principal, Diller Scofidio + Renfro

Interviewers: Kyle Codispoti, Daniel Becher, M.Arch students, School of Architecture and Design, New York Institute of Technology

April 13, 2022

Tom Verebes Thank you, Robert, for joining us today at New York Tech to discuss The Shed, by Diller Scofidio + Renfro.

Robert Katchur Thank you for the invitation to be here!

Tom Verebes The Shed has been described in the architectural and art press as an anti-institutional institution. When selecting projects for this series, The Shed stood out as an exceptional contemporary example of an interactive environment. Emanating light through its transformable translucent ETFE envelope, the telescoping kinetic envelope of The Shed performs as a responsive creative environment, radically tailoring its organization to the particular cultural event it houses at any given time. The format for this event is a student-led interview. Allow me to introduce Daniel Becher and Kyle Codispoti, Master of Architecture students at New York Tech.

Kyle Codispoti Hello, I am Kyle Codispoti and together with my partner, Daniel Becher, we would like to thank you for your fantastic presentation. It is an honor to interview you about The Shed and more broadly about Diller Scoffidio + Renfro's work. Daniel will ask our first question.

Daniel Beecher Hello, and thank you for this great opportunity! Hudson Yards, also known as Billionaire's Playground, is the host urban context of this new cultural institution. It co-exists with commercial offices, high end residential, luxury shopping, and also serves as the northern terminus of The High Line which snakes through Chelsea. The Shed presents itself as a new anti-institutional institution, as a non-profit organization which was conceived in response to the 2008 Request for Proposals, issued by the City of New York. What was the architect's role in shaping the institution of The Shed, and its specific architectural manifestation, as the architects were on board much earlier than typically? Also, can you share with us the architect-client relationship?

RK I would say that while we did a lot of thinking and research about what it should be, we also had a consistent and deep relationship with the city the whole way along. Michael Bloomberg and Kate Levin, his cultural affairs commissioner, were with us every step of the way. We didn't know in the beginning who was ultimately going to run it from a day-to-day perspective, and how we should plan a building that would allow for any number of artistic visions to take hold. With Kate's help, we interviewed over 40 different New York City cultural institutions and asked them, "What do you regret most about your own facility?", and, "What would you ache to have?"

This is a sister institution that they could potentially take a show to. If you're in a theater of a smaller size and eventually you have a hit show and you want to move it up to a venue that has more capacity you could bring it to The Shed, things could be developed in concert. We met with any number of institutions, big and small, from the Guggenheim, the Whitney and the Met, as well as small theaters in Brooklyn, St Anne's and others, so that we could aggregate those different needs. A number of them shared their technical needs with us.

> Often, flexible architecture becomes generic in a way that is good for no one and is specialized for an abstract idea. We tried to take a lot of specific information and overlay it on all of the other specific information that we got and look for the common points, and for what would give us the biggest bang for our buck.

If we arrange power like this, if we arrange structural capacity in this way, what's the cadence and spacing that those things should all have – what are the right capacities in those systems? If you look at what Fashion Week puts on each year, there's a lot of show power that goes into those things.

We made sure that while we were trying to be responsible about how much power we put into the building, we made sure that the power we had there could get to each floor. There

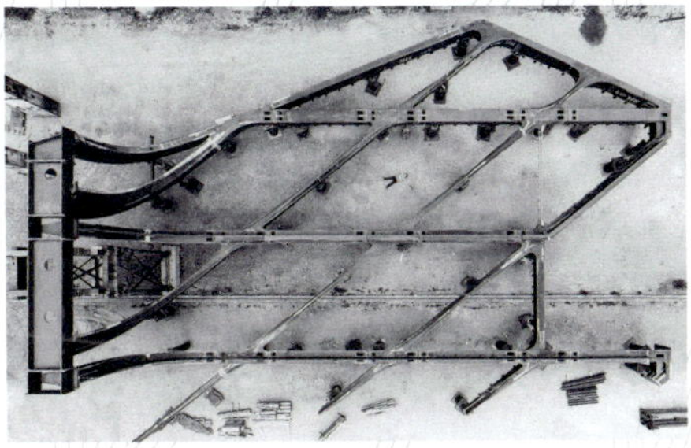

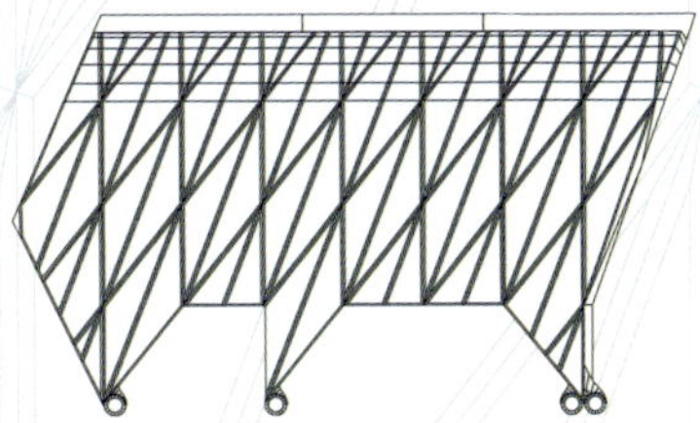

Elevation of The Shed on wheels

were centers distributed around the building that you can take down below through hatches and other things to make it all maneuverable. So, we took all of that, I'll call it raw data, and we tried to synthesize it into a formal technical program that took on more and more regular inputs from some of those other institutions. The Shed began, by that point, creating a Board, that could begin to respond to, and play off of, us. And as we designed, it was about maintaining flexibility and if it offered true flexibility, it became part of the program. Then in 2015, The Shed was moving along as an institution enough that they ultimately engaged Alex Poots, who gave it new heft and girth in its aspirations. He wanted to produce new work, which was something that was very much in sync with our hopes prior to his arrival, but he really breathed new life into it.

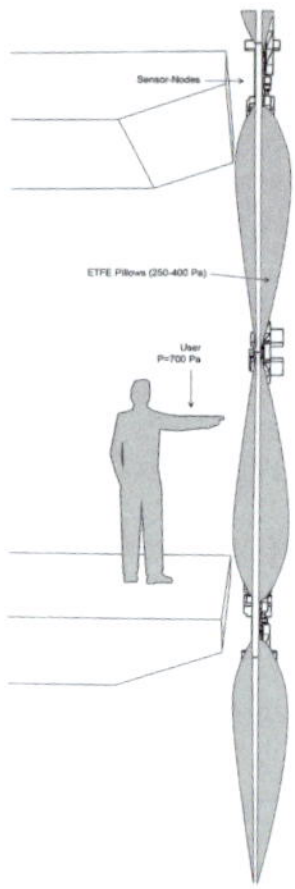

Schematic section of ETFE panels

DB Thank you. I would like to ask you some follow-on, more detailed questions about The Shed, and its physical infrastructure. Can you summarize the role of the architecture of The Shed in shaping the artistic activities which take place in its programming, including visual arts, performing arts, dance, theater and music? More specifically, how are artists challenged by the architecture of The Shed?

RK Firstly, if an artist is hosted in the McCourt movable shed component or in a location connected to some of the other spaces, then the show has to be visually powerful enough to take over the space and feel like it's present. If the scale of the event they're developing is something very intimate or something very small, the spaces within the fixed building can be reduced to create the level of intimacy they might want. We tried to take what we called the 80 - 20 rule. We wanted to make sure that we can accommodate 80% of what's out there very easily. Of course, there will always be a unique invention that does not fit the paradigm the way you envisioned. The part of this which is impossible is the unknown. We tried not to spend a lot of money or energy on things that would only happen 20% of the time. As far as our intentions, we tried to create a canvas that would easily support whatever the ambition was. Frankly, what the artists have done with it, I don't know if anybody has seen the Saraceno show that's on right now, it's probably the most exuberant use of that space. It's a 95 foot inflatable globe inside the room and you can walk off of the upper levels, climb up into the space 40 feet into the air and walk on a net. You see people in the middle of the space which is really tremendous. He has subdivided the galleries so that you can look very intimately at individual spiderwebs that have grown on small curios. That show touches all the different scales that we ever envisioned.

KC Thank you. Altogether, the kinetic systems of The Shed – its retractable roof and other interactive lighting, sound and seating systems – create a responsive and interactive environment. As you have presented, the intention is for the artist to interact with the space to alter it, on demand, through a set of kinetic systems, doubling in size. In this light, The Shed is a built manifestation of some of the ideas of interaction with intelligent spaces, charged with capacities to transform, present in Cedric Price's Fun Palace. Our research has focused on the flexible program elements that are achieved through The Shed's design and physical systems. As architects we are trained to work through a process to find our final product; making us intrigued about how the ultimate decision of the "expanding façade" came to fruition. Can you please further explain the process that led you to the design, and its tectonics. How can we now rethink the principle, form follows function?

RK The process that we undertook was a relentless version of what we called stress tests. We engaged a group of producers that took shows around the country and asked them to share with us. We overlaid many of the ranges of scales and shows onto our preliminary plans and examined what we could adjust. Could you bring this show from the Tate here? Could you bring that show from any number of institutions and how would it lay out here? If you said, I want to do an opera in a ring, how would it fit and what would the troubles be? Would there be a deal breaker in there? Could you accommodate its load? Could you accommodate its power needs? Could you accommodate its rigging needs? I mentioned communicating with over 40 institutions and then a smaller subset of them where we had really deep technical ex-

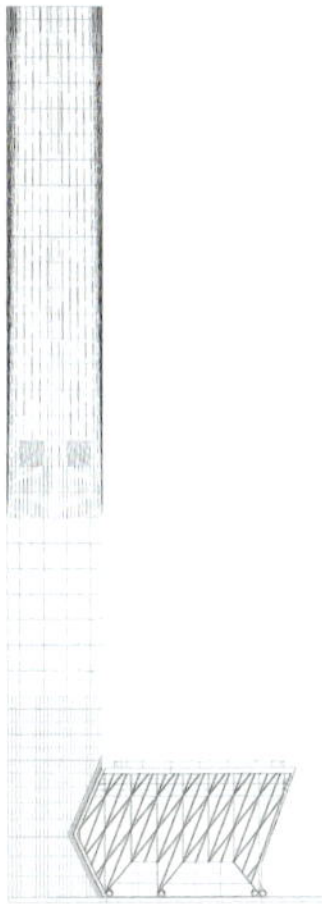

Elevation

changes. We were also doing that in parallel, while we were doing these stress tests. At the end of each phase, we tried to make sure that whatever happened for coordination, for cost control, for efficiency, we made sure we hadn't lost anything that we thought we shouldn't lose. It was a hard look internally to some degree. When you have a preexisting group of clients, they know what they need. They may not always be able to explain it well, but through the process that we typically go through, you kind of get to it. In this case, without the permanent people there yet we had to use surrogates which almost made us more rigorous about stress testing the plan.

KC Based on everything that you are sharing with us, we can determine that the architect's role within this project has a unique importance, because this approach to transformable architecture can lead to countless possibilities for the arts, community, and more. How impactful has this project been for Diller Scofidio + Renfro, in terms of the project's possible future role as a precedent for further research into architectural flexibility?

RK I would say The Shed is a very important project for us. We've begun to take all of what we learned here and apply it. Oftentimes, you have a client who says, "Well, I only have this much space, but I want that much stuff". How do you have this much budget and want that much stuff? I would say the lessons that we learned here have been invaluable in confronting those kinds of questions with new clients and new projects around the world. It's only going to continue to get more extreme as density increases in cities; as populations continue to grow, space will become more and more of a premium. So, the means by which you utilize that space will become more important. And it also, maybe more importantly, runs along the terms of environmental efficiency. Buildings should not become white elephants that aren't utilized in full force.

If I try to look far into the future, these issues are going to be more and more important as we try to be more and more efficient with everything we create and make in the world. Buildings are heavy, they're cumbersome, they're fixed, they're there for good, and they should be responsive for the longest period of time possible.

KC The Shed, through its kinetic behavior, can double in size allowing more possibilities that can be invited into the site. Due to this exchange, the scale of the project changes. In relation to scale, the assembly of the wheels feel as if they have a very specific design goal that expands the site's relationship to its visitors. We understand the project as a critique of a modernist notion of flexibility – most often expressed architecturally as a large fixed open space in which users have more limited control over the architecture's configuration. Why does The Shed need to double in size? How could the project for a cross disciplinary arts venue be achieved using a generic black box or white cube, as fixed volumes, rather than using kinetics to create flexibility?

RK Why does The Shed need to double in size? It was, to some degree, a dilemma presented by Hudson Yards itself, where 20,000 square feet of footprint was allocated to cultural need. At the same time, there was a mandate to find Fashion Week a permanent home. It had camped out in every major public

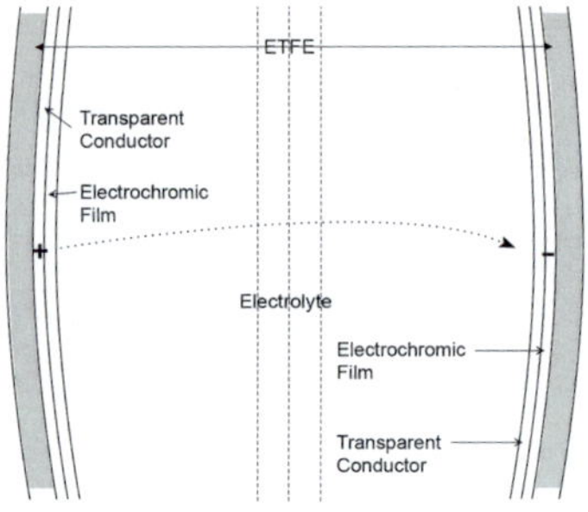

Schematic section of ETFE panel

space in the city, and every time it did there was conflict with the local neighborhood. The ability to host is extraordinarily expensive for this major industry in New York. When you look at a 21,000 square foot footprint for one event, which has three full length runways, and all that goes with it, somewhere between 600 and 1200 patrons, seated around that runway, the two do not align. Only at certain moments of the year does one need all of that dimension. Moreover, if you pair economic ups and downs, the trends that were in place in the artistic community at the beginning of the project were, for example, Richard Serra's large format mega projects, where one is installing massive steel pieces in very large spaces like the Guggenheim. There was a race going on to see who could have the biggest freight elevator in their institution. These elevators were becoming as big as New York apartments, maybe times two. That was the trend at that time. But of course, two years later when the economy fell out from under all of us, suddenly these institutions were struggling to put on medium sized shows. That's why we wanted the building to be responsive. If you just left it big and generic, you couldn't put a small intimate program within it, and have it feel right. It would feel like a white elephant with a very small jewel in it. That was the drive for the malleability of scale, but there's also a real need for outdoor public space, and every institution that has it. If you look at the Met's exterior gallery, it's a very popular space. The Whitney had put their large outside space at the south end of the High Line. These outdoor cultural spaces are in short supply. We felt we could offer a significant amount of space for chunks of the year by nesting it, and then expanding it when needed.

KC While we were doing our research, we were intrigued by the kinetics and engineering of the wheels driving the expansion and contraction of The Shed's spaces. Can you expand on the benefits that went behind the human-scale tracks, and why it was important to achieve this aesthetic to support its function?

RK We were interested in the wheels explaining to some degree even when the building was not moving, that it could move. The wheels do that just by being there. The scale of the wheel is directly connected to the weight of the building. We needed a certain amount of surface area to land that 8 million pounds and there are eight wheels total to bring down 8 million pounds to the ground. So, in really simple terms, not to talk about wind load and other forces, a million pounds is coming through that size of a footprint. The wheel touchdown point is just the bottom tangent point of the wheel against the rail. As you mentioned the rail is at a human scale, and we needed that surface to be a floor in a room, sometimes part of the Plaza, and other times placed so you can't catch your heel in it.

There are a lot of technical sides to it, like normal train station tracks are away from you, rail crossings at grade, are often humpty-bumpy things that cars don't tend to move over smoothly. Ultimately, there was the rail that was selected to cover that load. This is an eight-inch wide rail, which is several times bigger than a traditional commuter train line in the United States. It is the largest commercially available rail that is fabricated. It's used for gantry cranes in rail yards for shipping. We said we needed to stay within that limit. When you look at the weight of the building, and the decisions we made about the ETFE, the decisions we made about the acoustic liner system, every one of those fed all of those dimensions because of the rolling nature of the load.

DB Thank you for all this detail. In our seminar, we are looking at six pioneering built projects, analyzed in relation to a set of six themes. This week's theme is Interaction, with The Shed exemplifying this topic through its reconfigurable kinetics, but also through the experience of its visuality. Visually speaking, there are specific design decisions which create The Shed's presence, and bring attention to it in the context of the neighboring buildings of Hudson Yards, as a distinct glowing building at the northern destination of the Highline. Can you please talk more about the importance of materiality of The Shed, specifically the ETFE envelope, and how this material accentuates The Shed's presence in this context?

RK It was fundamental to the technical development of the project, how we shaped it and how we wanted this building to stand out against the commercial buildings that were around it. We wanted it to be unique. The tufting of the pillows, and the fact they have about a 22 inch standoff between their attachment points and the tip of the curve in the center of the pillow that gives it a soft appearance, is something that certainly sets it apart from its neighbors. The frit which we selected on the outer foil of the ETFE assembly, we selected specifically to give it a certain amount of mass from the outside. It also achieved the glare and the light control when you allow the room to be filled with light inside.

What is magical about The Shed's envelope is that it does control the light, but it doesn't entirely block your view, nor does it act like a sheet of glass. You are not just in a structural frame where you can see the buildings outside, it mutes the city and creates a more contemplative space within.

The ETFE was central to the exterior appearance, the interior appearance, and its appearance at night. We wanted it to be a glowing lantern. When we draw the blackout shades down, there's a lighting system within that cavity between the blackout shade and the ETFE that gives it a presence at night. We worked very hard to make sure that came off, and there are a lot of lights buried in those nodes where each piece of steel crosses making a pocket in there to house the lights.

DB Was this material choice and appearance, and their behaviors you have just described, something you wanted to achieve early on – or did the material specification and its possible visual effects come later in the design process?

RK It was very early because it was the obvious choice from a weight perspective. It had a dramatic impact on the shaping of the steel and the lightness that it could achieve. If we had selected something heavier we would have seen something that rather than 15% of the surface area in steel, would have been more like 30%. From our perspective, we did not want it to be like a lumbering, hulking piece of metal. We wanted it to look far more delicate. If you look at the individual members, they actually follow the structural diagram. The load is the smallest in the middle where we come together and it gets thicker as you come to the moment connections of the diagram grid.

KC Yes. I noticed that. Diller Scofidio + Renfro, as an architectural practice, have grown immensely and the office has taken on larger and more complex projects in recent years. Commonly, architects use precedents as a starting groundwork for their designs. Were there any past projects at Diller Scofidio +

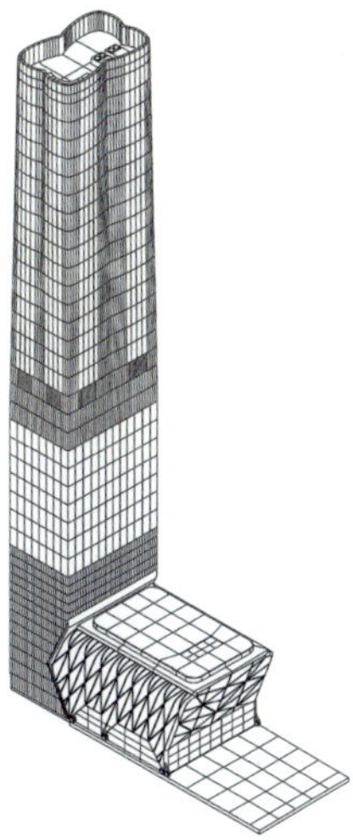

Axonometric

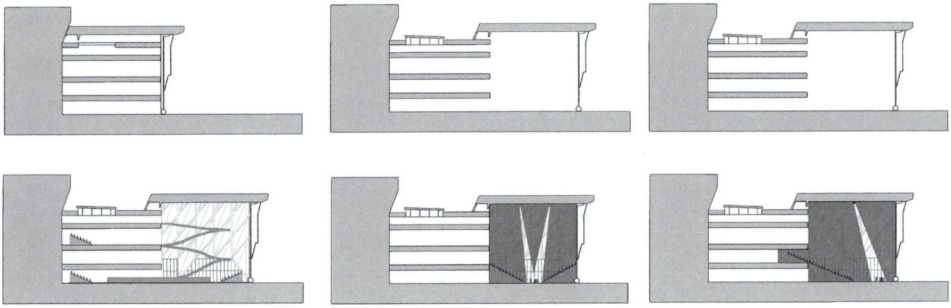

Sections demonstrating reconfigurations of the performance space and seating

Renfro that helped influence the design that led to The Shed?

RK I would say a couple of projects are imbued in the history of the studio. The first one I would say is the Blur project, which is an exposition. I'm not going to call it a building because it's really an installation on a lake in Geneva. It was a space frame that had several thousands of nozzles, and basically it expelled water pellets that instantly became a cloud, as it blew. You donned a raincoat and explored the exhibit with mist all around you. That took a naive aspiration, married up with a desire and need to tear apart the technical aspects of it to make it happen. This is foundational to the studio. The only way you're going to achieve those aspirations is by figuring out the technical side that would prevent you from otherwise achieving it.

That is the first thought I have on answering your question. The other one though, is a little less obvious. Lincoln Center was a big project that DS+R did with executive architects, as partners, and it took a lot of manpower, but what it took most, almost most importantly, was a tremendous amount of diplomacy. There were 22 separate city agencies that had to be negotiated with, from DOT to all the different utility providers, 13 separate cultural institutions within Lincoln center, and every one of them had a right of refusal. If you look at the history of Lincoln Center's redevelopment, there are many plans by many brilliant architects that never got off the ground. The cultural diplomacy required to hear everybody and to make sure that you take on board what they care about most, and to make sure that your proposal is responsive. So, there was a certain amount of drive and relentless listening that went into that process, and I don't think we would have been as well equipped to do The Shed project without that experience.

KC The Shed's many unique qualities have led to a successful design outcome. Were there any components that you learned through The Shed that have bled into new projects? Or in other words, what impact has The Shed had on projects in your office since its completion?

RK In the beginning days of The Shed, there were many people in the studio who thought, "well, this is a great idea", but who's going to build it. Who's going to pay for it? Why is this ever going to come about?" I think the principal lesson that we walked away with is to never say something is impossible. You might need certain things to fall your way, but whether it be a technical problem or a political problem, I think we carry the lessons out of it into each new project. Especially the ones that really want more than something that looks like it's feasible. I know that it has had an influence on a number of projects when a client says, "Well, I know I have to choose between these two". And we say, "Well, wait, maybe you don't have to choose. Let's see if we can find a way to overlap all the constituent needs of those two desires and make them harmonize." You might have to give up on having each of them a hundred percent of the time, but you might get each of them as much as you need them.

KC Thank you very much. This concludes our interview, and we really appreciate your time and the depth of your answers.

TV Thank you so much, Robert, for taking the time for your in-depth presentation, and also for this interview. We are grateful for your support for New York Tech, and for enabling this experience for our students. Thank you to Daniel and Kyle for leading this interview. Thank you, Robert, and also thank you to Liz Diller for facilitating this as well, and your admin team at Diller Scofidio + Renfro. Thank you.

RK It's my pleasure. Thank you all so much for having me. Bye!

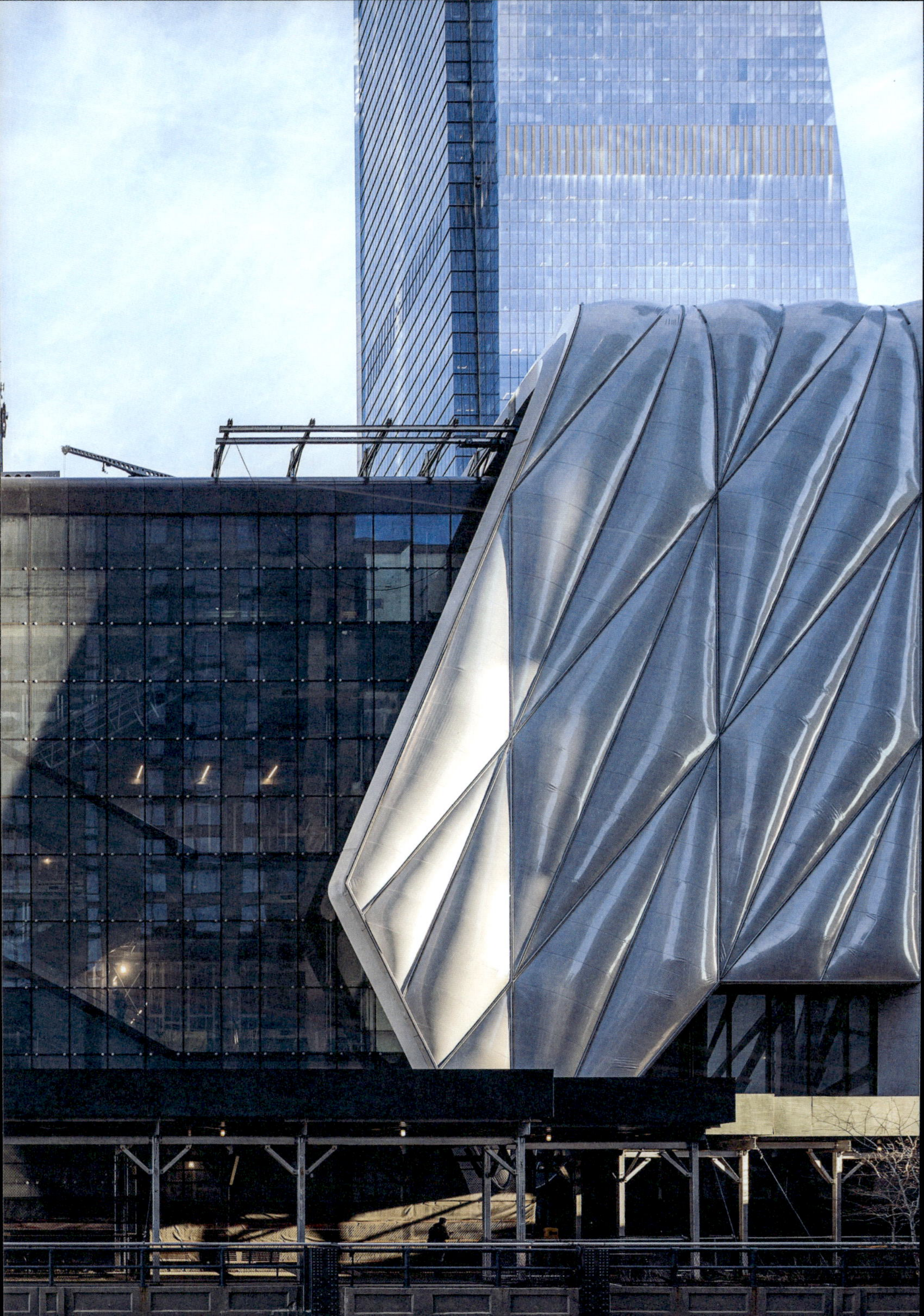

AUTHOR / EDITOR

Tom Verebes, PhD

Professor, School of Architecture and Design, New York Institute of Technology
Director, OCEAN CN, New York

STUDENTS

NEW YORK INSTITUTE OF TECHNOLOGY
School of Architecture & Design

Over three academic cycles in 2021, 2022, and 2023, Professor Tom Verebes, PhD, taught a graduate seminar course entitled Beyond the Envelope: Pioneering Architectural Technology, in the Master of Architecture (M.Arch) program at the School of Architecture and Design at New York Institute of Technology (SoAD-NYIT). These thirty-four students worked diligently and enthusiastically on their graphic analysis of the twenty-one projects included in this compilation. Born out of the context of the Covid-19 pandemic lockdown and remote teaching and learning in the SoAD-NYIT, the Beyond the Envelope seminar was first offered remotely on Zoom during the 2021 academic year. During this unprecedented time, Professor David Diamond, Director of the M.Arch program, and Tom Verebes discussed and enacted the idea of our SoAD-NYIT students interviewing the architect of each case study project, all of whom were working from home. These students are all now graduates of New York Tech, and this first-hand, direct connection to each architect created a unique academic experience for them during their final semester, helping to launch their careers upon graduation.

2021
Japheth Zino Aleyakpo
Adamandios Giannios
Yuti Kothari
Gyongok Tammy Noh
Sohui Noh
Aditi Sunilkumar Pancholi
Jay Patel
Aleksandra Zatorska

2022
Daniel Patrick Beecher
Kyle Steven Codispoti
Michelle Enkhbaatar
Adnan Quresh Jangbarwala
Francis Kwok
Dalton Lackey
Seth Patrick Mears
Ethan William Ross
Noah Seeback
Devanshi Sandeep Shah
Kaymar Thomas
Vaibhav Vadadoriya

2023
Anthony Acevedo
Anthony Dalto
Nidhi Manish Gohel
Amy Goldfisher
Alison Jean Iannucci
Steven Jean-Baptiste
Riya Girish Nerurkar
Vincenzo Luciano Orologio
Vishesh Jignesh Patel
Kashmi Sachin Shah
Adelina Sinanaj
Shivani Singh
Damini Sri Reddy
Meri Angely Sibal Syed

Tom Verebes is a Tenured Professor in the School of Architecture and Design at NYIT. He is also the Director of OCEAN CN, based in New York. Verebes co-founded the distributed network practice, OCEAN, in London 1995, and he has since directed OCEAN offices in London, Hong Kong, Beijing and New York. Among past academic roles, Verebes has served as Associate Dean for Academic Affairs at NYIT (2018-2020); Founding Provost of Turenscape Academy in Beijing and Xixinan, Anhui Province, China (2016-2018); Associate Dean for Teaching & Learning (2011-2014), and Associate Professor of Architecture at The University of Hong Kong (2009-2016). He was co-Director Design Research Lab at the Architectural Association (AA) in London, where he taught as Course Master from 1996 to 2009. He has held the position of Guest Professor at Akademie der Buildenden Künste ABK Stuttgart (2004-2006), and has held the positions of Visiting Professor at the University of Pennsylvania, Rensselaer Polytechnic Institute (RPI), Syracuse University, RMIT, Singapore University of Technology & Design (SUTD) and The University of Tokyo.

Among over 150 publications of authored books, chapters, articles and project features, including over 240 citations, Verebes' recent publications include *Shanghai Ten Folio* (ORO, AA Publications, 2017), his guest-editing of an issue of *AD*, titled *Mass Customised Cities*, (Wiley, 2015), and books, including *Masterplanning the Adaptive City: Computational Urbanism in the Twenty-first Century* (Routledge, 2013), *New Computational Paradigms in Architecture* (Tsinghua University Press, 2012), and *DRL X: A Design Research Compendium* (AA Publications, 2008). Verebes is currently guest-editing an issue of *Journal of Chinese Architecture and Urbanism*, titled, Chinese Cities of Tomorrow: Computing and Prototyping Intelligent Forms of Future Urbanism. Co-authored with Stefan Al, *The Urbanism Reader: Design, Culture, Technology, and the Future of Cities* will be published by Bloomsbury Publishers in 2024. In addition, Verebes has published numerous book chapters, and articles in issues of *Architectural Design AD, Architectural Review, RIBA Journal, 306090 Books, Urban China, Urban Flux, Archicreation,* and *World Architecture*. Verebes' work has been featured in over 50 exhibitions in venues worldwide, including the Venice Biennale, Beijing Biennale, Hong Kong-Shenzhen Bi-City Biennale, Seoul Biennale, Seville Biennale, Zoomorphic (Victoria & Albert Museum, London), Latent Utopias (Graz, Austria), Experimental Architecture (FRAC Collection, Centre Pompidou, Paris; Orléans), Archilab (Orléans), and Artists Space (New York). Verebes has lectured extensively in Asia, Europe, North America, Africa, and the Middle East.

PHOTOGRAPHY CREDITS

CCTV Headquarters
OMA/Philippe Ruault
PAGES 14, 32-33, 42
OMA/Jim Gourley
PAGE 42 bottom
OMA/Iwan Baan
PAGE 43

Absolute Towers
Tom Arban
PAGES 44-45, 54-55

MOCAPE
Duccio Malagamba
PAGES 56-57, 64-65, 66-67

One Vanderbilt
Raimund Koch
PAGES 68-69, 76-77

Ningbo Historic Museum
Lv Hengzhong
PAGES 16, 78-79, 87, 88-89

O-14 Tower
RUR
PAGES 90-91, 100-101

Chi She Pond Society
Schran Images
PAGES 27, 102-103, 110-111

Federation Square
John Goslings
PAGES 112-113, 122, 125
Trevor Mein
126-127

MAAT
Piet Niemann
PAGES 128-129
Hufton+Crow
PAGES 8-9, 137
Toni Cumella
PAGE 138
Fernando Guerra
PAGE 139

Tai Kwun Cultural Centre
Iwan Baan
PAGES 140-141, 148-149, 294-295

Mira
©Jason O'Rear, courtesy of Studio Gang
PAGES 150-151, 160-161

St. Mary's Axe
Chris Bosse
PAGES 162-163
Tim Griffith
PAGES 172-173

Emma and Georgina Bloomberg Center
Matt Carbone, courtesy of Morphosis
PAGES 174-175, 182, 184-185

Copenhill Powerplant
Rasmus Hjortshoj
PAGES 12, 186-187, 192, 198 bottom right, 197
Aurian Ghinitoiu
PAGE 19, 189
Hufton+Crow
PAGE 196 above and botom left

Asian Games 2023 Hybrid Stadium / Concept Hall
SFAP
PAGES 198-199,, 208, 210-211
Archi-Tectonics
292

National Aquatic Centre / The Watercube
Tim Griffith
PAGES 212-213
Chris Bosse
PAGES 222-223

Galleria Centercity
Kim Yong-kwan
PAGES 224-225, 234
Christian Richters
PAGE 233

Leeza Soho
Hufton & Crow
PAGES 28-29, 236-237, 246-247

Kunsthaus Graz
Colin Fournier
PAGES 248-249, 253, 255, 257, 258-259

Media-ICT
José Miguel Hernandez
PAGE 23, 260-261
Luis Ros
PAGES 270, 271

The Shed
Iwan Baan
PAGES 272-273, 281
Timothy Schenck
282-283

PROJECT CREDITS

CCTV Headquarters Client: China Central Television CCTV / Architect: OMA The CCTV project was led by OMA / Rem Koolhaas, former OMA partner Ole Scheeren (until 2010), partner David Gianotten and project manager Dongmei Yao in collaboration with partners Shohei Shigematsu, Ellen van Loon and Victor van der Chijs. / The design team consisted of project architects Anu Leinonen, Charles Berman and Adrianne Fisher together with Design team(A-Z): Alain Fouraux, Arianna Spaccasassi, Antonio Teles Branco, Beatrice Schiavina, Beatriz Ramo Lopez, Catarina Canas, Charles Gosrisirikul, Chris James, Christina Murphy, Chris van Duijn, Daan Ooievaar, Dan Cheong, Dirk Zschunke, Dorthee Dietz, Erez Ella, Fang Tieying, Faustina Tsai, Feng Pei, Fernando Donis; Florian Pucher, Gabriela Bojalil, Gaspard Estourgie, Georg Bucher, Gonzalo Laurentiu Coceanga, Hendrik Gruss, Guillaume Colboc, Hiromasa Shirai, Holly Chacon, James Harper, Jasmine Tsoi, Jeffrey Bolhuis, Joao Bravo Da Costa, Joao Gomes Branco Teodosio, Johannes Buchholz, Joris Fach, Joseph Monteleone, Keren Engelman, Kam Fai Tai, Laurent Troost, Lawrence Leung, Li Guilin, Liu Xiaodong, Lodewijk van Eeghen, Loy Tsao, Mamen Escorihueles, L. E. Tsao, Manuel Shvartzberg, Max Burianek, Max Rink, Max Schwitalla, Melissa Dowler, Menno van der Meer, Michel van der Kar, Paul Burgstaller , Paul Kroese, Pedro Costa Gama, Peter Lee ,Roberto Otero, Rodrigo Nunez Carrasco, Rodney Eggleston, Sarah Gibson, Shi Wenchian, Shiro Ogata, Steffen Ell, Steffie Wedde, Steven Smith, Stuard Maddox, Suse Koch, Tammo Prinz,Ted Lin, Tim Callaghan, Torsten Schroeder, Victoria Willocks, WangXinyuan, Wang Yunzhu, Wu You, Xu Tian Tian, Yimin Zhu, Yiannis Kanakakis, Yu Long, Zhaohui Wu; and Support team (A-Z): Lisa Aalders, May Yan Fan, Li Dan, Liu Aoshuang, Liu Yonghong, Sun Yongzhen, Ou Qiang, Wang Yimeng, Wang Yu, Wu Xinghua, Xu Yi, Zhang Yajuan, Zhao Xiaoyue / Architect of record: OMA/ECADI Interior designer: OMA/ECADI / Engineer: ARUP/FCADI—Cecil Balmond, Chris Carroll, Michael Kwok, Rory McGowan, Paul Cross, Xiaonian Duan, Craig Gibbons, Goman Ho, Richard Lawson, Alexis Lee, Andrew Luong, Chas Pope, design team / Local design institute: East China Architectural Design & Research Institute Co. Ltd. (ECADI).

Absolute Towers Client: Fernbrook / Cityzen Design architects / Design Architect: MAD Architects: Directors in Charge: Ma Yansong, Yosuke Hayano, Dang Qun / Design Team: Shen Jun, Robert Groessinger, Florian Pucher, Yi Wenzhen, Hao Yi, Yao Mengyao, Zhao Fan, Liu Yuan, Zhao Wei, Li Kunjuan, Yu Kui, Max Lonnqvist, Eric Spencer / Associate Architects: BURKA Architects INC. / Structural Engineer: SIGMUND, SOUDACK & ASSOCIATES INC. / Mechanical Engineer: ECE Group Electrical Group / Electrical Engineer: ECE Group Landscape Design / Landscape Architect: NAK Design / Interior Designer: ESQAPE Design.

Museum of Contemporary Art and Planning Exhibition MOCAPE Client: Shenzen Municipal Culture Buerau, Shenzhen Municipal Planning Bureau / Planning: COOP HIMMELB(L)AU – Wolf D. Prix & Partner Design Principal: Wolf dPrix / Project Partner: Markus Prossnigg / Design Architects: Quirin Krumbholz, Jörg Hugo, Mona Bayr / Project Architects: Angus Schoenberger, Veronika Janovska, Tyler Bornstein / Project Coordination: Xinyu Wan / Project Team: Javier Sancho Andrés, Jessie Castro, Jessie Chen, Jasmin Dieterle, Luis Ferreira, Peter Grell, Paul Hoszowsky, Dimitar Ivanov, Ivana Jug, Zhu Yuang Kang, Alexander Karaivanov, Nam La-Chi, Rodelle Lee, Feng Lei, Megan Lepp, Samuel Liew, Thomas Margaretha, Jens Mehlan, Ivo de Nooijer, Reinhard Platzl, Vincenzo Possenti, Pete Rose, Ana Santos, Jutta Schädler, Günther Weber, Chen Yue / Digital Project Team: Angus Schoenberger, Matt Kirkham, Jasmin Dieterle, Jonathan Asher, Jan Brosch / Local Architects: HSArchitects, Shenzhen, China / Local Interior Design: Jiang & Associates Creative Design, Shenzhen, China / Structural Engineering: Bollinger+Grohmann, Frankfurt, Germany / Mechanical Engineering: Reinhold Bacher, Vienna, Austria / Lighting Design: a·g Licht, Cologne, Germany / Cost Management: Davis Langdon & Seah, Hong Kong, China .

One Vanderbilt Client: SL Green Realty Corporation Architects: Kohn Pedersen Fox Team: Chairman A. Eugene Kohn, FAIA RIBA JIA Lead Design Principal James von Klemperer, FAIA RIBA Design Principals Jeffrey Kenoff, AIA / Trent Tesch, AIA NCARB Managing Principals Dominic Dunn, AIA / Charles Ippolito, AIA LEED AP BD+C Managing Director Andrew Cleary, AIA Senior Designer Darina Zlateva, AIA Job Captain Nicole McGlinn-Morrison, AIA Kohn Pedersen Fox Project Team and Contributors: Rachel Villalta, Katsunori Shigemi, Alessandro Boccacci, Steven Smolyn, Rebecca Kent Matthew Acer, Christopher Allen, Laura Austin, Theodore Carpinelli, Gera Feigon, Javier Galindo, Anton Gladden, Susan Green, Younhak Jeong, Algis Kalvaitis, Jerrod Kennard, Soroush Khajegi, Kiyong Lee, Mark Long, Meghan Malone, Stephen Martinez, Meg Mayell, Joseph Michael, Brandon Mut, Muchan Park, Jennifer Pehr, Burgess Rice, Stephanie Rogowski, Ian Siegel, Maxwell Strauss, Justin Whiteford, Lucien Wilson, Xin Zhang Engineers: Severud (Structural); Jaros, Baum & Bolles (MEP) Other consultants: AECOM (Eastside Access Consultant) AKRF (Environmental Engineer) Bramco Steel (Steel Consultant) Cerami & Associates (Acoustics/Telecom/Security Consultant) Code Consultants (Code Consultant) C.S. Caulkins Co. (Facade Maintenance Consultant) Delos (Well Building Consultant) Department of City Planning Domani Inspection Service (Special Inspection Demolition Consultant) Higgins & Quasebarth & Partners (Landmark Consultant) HMA Consulting (Security Engineer)

Howard I. Shapiro & Associates (Demolition Engineer) Israel Berger & Associates (Building Envelope Consultant) Kasirer (Community Outreach Consultant) Kenzo Digital (Observatory) Langan (Geotechnical/Civil Engineer) Lovett Silverman (Construction Consultant) Milrose Consultants (Expeditor) MTA Metro-North Railroad MTA Real Estate Pentagram (Signage Consultant) Rowan Williams Davies & Irwin (Wind/Snow/Ice Consultant) Silman (Preservation Engineer) Snøhetta (Observatory) Stantec (MTA/NYCTA Consultant) Stone Engineering (Security Consultant) AECOM Tishman Construction Corporation (Construction Manager) T&M Protection Resources LLC (Threat Assessment Consultant) The Friday Group LLC (Specifications Writer) Thornton-Tomasetti (Construction Engineering Consultant) Tillotson Design Associates (Lighting Consultant) VDA Associates (Vertical Transportation Consultant) Van Deusen & Associates (Vertical Transport Consultant) Vidaris/Viridian Energy & Environmental (LEED/Energy Consultant) Vibra-Tech Engineers (Vibration Monitoring Consultant) Waldorf Demolition (Demolition Contractor) Wiss Janney Elstner Associates (Stone Consultant) WCD Group/Emteque (Environmental Consultant) Contractor: AECOM Tishman Construction Corporation (construction manager) Any relevant suppliers: Boston Valley Terracotta (Cladding); A&S Tuned A&H Tuned Mass Dampers (Damper); Schindler (Elevator), Doka GmbH (Formwork); Banker Steel (Steel; ArcelorMittal (Steel).

Ningbo Historic Museum Architect: Amateur Architecture Studio, Beijing / Project team: Wang Shu, Lu Wenyu, Song Shuhua, Jiang Weihua, Chen Lichao / Structural engineers: Shentu Tuanbing, Chen Yongbing; Hu Jun, Construction supervisor.

O-14 Tower Owner: Creekside Development Company (subsidiary of District Investment & Development LLC) / Developer: Shahab Lufti, H&H Investment & Development LLC / Architect: Reiser + Umemoto Architecture / Partners: Jesse Reiser (Registered Architect) + Nanako Umemoto / Design Team: Mitsuhisa Matsunaga (Registered in Japan), Kutan Ayata , Jason Scroggin , Cooper Mack, Michael Overby, Roland Snooks, Michael Young, Neil Cook / Interns & Assistants: Tina Tung, Raha Talebi, Yan Wai Chu / Architect of record: Egra Progress; Project Manager: Joseph Sawaya / Structural Engineers: Ysrael A. Seinuk, PC; Ysrael Seinuk, Jaime Ocampo, & Wanlong He / Local Structural Engineer: EConstruct, Sameh El Ashri (director) / Consultants: Window Wall: R.A.Heintges & Associates / Lighting: L'Observatoire, Hervé Descottes / Local Lighting Consultant: Nouran Lighting / Concrete: Reginald D. Hough / General contractor: Dubai Contracting Company (DCC), Abdallah Yabroudi (president); Project Manager: Jihad Choueiri.

The Pond Society Chi She Client: Pond Society Chi She / Architects: Philip F. Yuan (Principal Architect) / Archi-Union Architects / Design Team: Alex Han, Xiangping Kong, Tianrui Zhu, Qinrong Liu / Structural Engineers: Rui Wang, Junchao Shen, Xiaofeng Zhang, Jin Wang / Interior Designer: Xuwei Wang, Xiaoming Chen / Construction Equipment: Yong Liu, Changying Jiang, Xi Li / Digital Fabrication: Shanghai Fab-Union Technology Co., Ltd.

Federation Square Client: State Government of Victoria + City of Melbourne / Architects: Lab Architecture Studio + Bates Smart: Directors: Donald L. Bates (design director - LAB), Peter Davidson (design director - LAB), Robert Bruce (BSA), Roger Poole (BSA), Jim Milledge (BSA); project director—Tony Allen; team/design leaders—Fulvio Facci, Peter Bickle, Attilio Terragni, Greg Bray, Roger Chapman, Stephen Davies, Doug Dickson, Gaynor Fox, Andrew Francis, Nicole Hardman, Derek Hawkes, Tim Hill, Dylan Ingleton, Steven Javens, Olda Kurdiovsky, John McNabb, James Murray, Edward (Ted) Sanderson, David Shultis, Peter Stevens, Bill Tucker, Paul von Chrismar; project team—Ben Albury, Helen Aldrich, Kate Allen, Lucy Allen, Sofia Anapliotis, Tony Antoniou, Jeff Arnold, Paul Bayley, Diego Bekinschtein, Leo Belci, Joanna Best, Estelle Bialek, Elly Bloom, Chantal Boisgontier, Philip Bowen, Rachel Breen, Richard Brenchley, David Bullpit, Annie Bunting, DeborahBurdett, Nina Burdett, David Burrows, Mike Buttery, Hamish Cant, Susie Calill,Raymond Cheung, Bo Christensen, Vincent Choi, Gianni Cito, Stuart Clark, Grant Cook, GeoffCosier, Veryan Curnow, Paul Davies, Rebecca Davis, Lance Decker, Alf Dennemoser, Mardi Doherty, Craig Douglas, Dierijk Drent, Andrew Drummond, Loredana Ducco, Jan Eastwood, Colin Edwards, Ron Elton-Baker, Nancy Everingham, Daniel Flood, Mat Foley, Warren Foster, Ronald Freiverts, Jack Fullerton, Lorenzo Galati, Eleni Gogos, Stuart Grandin, Olivia Griffith, Robert Gvildys, Kathie Hall, Arthur Hallinan, Stephen Hamilton, Prani Hodges, Sean Hogan, Brett Holmberg, Olivia Hrvojevic, Lewis Hunt, George Jockov, Peter Johns, Yiu Chuen Kan, Terry Kelly, Daniel Khong, Richard King, Lucy Knox-Knight, Barbara Kurdiovsky, Vicky Lam, Ashley Lane, Libby Langlands, Anne Lau, Elizabeth Laurie, Alex Lawlor, Rachael Lynch, Roxane Ludbrook-Ingleton, William McCorkell, Andrew Maher, Gus Mamar, Luca Mangione, Nicole Mandile, Esther Mavrokokki, Kylie Meacham, Amelia Minty, Rosalea Monacella, Cassandra Montgomery, James Mulvany, Dominique Ng, Johnny O'Hara, Luciano-Palma, Irene Papadimitriou, Adrian Parr, Andrew Partos, Peter Parry-Fielder, Stuart Paterson, Alex Peck, Sam Penfold, James Phelan, Toby Pond, Chris Price, Mathan Ratinam, Bhaven Raval, Stephanie Reiger, Jacqueline Ronalds, Robert Rudic, Chris Sawyer, Bianca Scaifek, James Service, Andrew Shaw, Jeremy Sheldon, Andrew Simpson, Daine Singer, Noel

Smith, Thomas Sloan, Robert-Stuart Smith, Valery Sverdlin, Waihan Tang, Simon Tiller, Blythe Toll, Mike Tollis, Quan Tran, Harold Trappe, Jim Tsoukatos, Ross Weeks, Jeromy Wells, Simon Whibley, Kristen White, Stephen Williamson, Andrew Wilson, Daniel Wolkenberg, Tom Yiantos, Jenny Yim, Casimir Zdanius. / Landscape architects: Karres en Brands—Bart Brands, Gianni Cito, Marie-Laure Hoedemakers, Rene van der Velde, Thierry Kandjee. / Civil/structural engineers: Hyder Consulting — Pat Strickland, Stu Jones, Ken McLeod. Structural / façade engineers: Atelier One — Neil Thomas, Dirk Zimmermann, Carolina Bartram, Scobie Alvis, Wayne Sanderson, Anil Hira, Andy Watts, Aran Chadwick. / Structural engineers (NGV): Bonacci Group—Stephen Payne, Roger Sykes. / Environmental Engineers: Atelier Ten — Patrick Bellew, Tim Elgood. / Services Engineers: AHW Consulting Engineers — David Worland, Roger Arnall, Hugh van Essen. / Fire Engineers: ARUP — David Barber. Signage and graphics: Tomato — John Warwicker + Sean Hogan. / Specialist Lighting: Lighting Design Partnership—Andre Tammes, Dhruvajyoti Ghose, Frederika Perey. / Acoustic Engineers: Marshall Day - Peter Fernside, Peter Holmes. / Project delivery: 1996 – 2000 (on behalf of the State of Victoria, and the City of Melbourne) Office of Major Projects—Dick Roennfeldt, Damien Bonnice – project director, Tjip Faber, Isabelle Johnstone. / Project delivery: 2000 – 2002: Federation Square Management—Peter Seamer, Stan Liacos, Emma Moore. / Building surveyors: Thomas Nicholas — Bruce Thomas, Con Nicholas. / Quantity surveyors and Cost PLanners: WT Partnership — Laurie Thomas, William Kennedy-Cooke, Phil Martin, Paul Huckin. / Programmer: Tracey Brunstrom + Hammond—Grant O'Donnell, David Goodman, Jiong Xhu. / Project managers: CCS—Colin Stuckey, David Fulton, David O'Connell, Peter Axup, Phil Flynn. / Public art curator: Vanessa Walker. / Artists: Paul Carter, Christopher Bell, Joyce Hinterding, David Haines, Scott Horscroft, Carl Priestly, Jon McCormack.

Museum of Art, Architecture and Technology MAAT Client: Fondação EDP / Architect: AL_A / Structural Engineer: Afaconsult / Other Consultants: Site supervision; project management: Tecnoplano LEED consultant: Edifícios Saudáveis / Energy certification: e3e / Landscape: Vladimir Djurovic Landscape Architecture / Restaurant and shop lighting: SEAM Design / Wayfinding: R2 Design / Main contractor: Alves Ribeiro / Selected sub-contractors: Ceràmica Cumella (ceramic façade fabrication) Disset (ceramic façade installation).

Tai Kwun Cultural Centre Client: The Hong Kong Jockey Club, Hong Kong / Architects: Design Consultant : Herzog & de Meuron, Basel, Switzerland / Partners: Jacques Herzog, Pierre de Meuron, Ascan Mergenthaler (Partner in Charge) / Project Team: Edman Choy (Associate, Project Director), Chi-Yan Chan (Project Manager), Vladimir Pajkic (Associate, Project Director, until 2011), Raymond Gaëtan (Associate, until 2012) / Abdelfattah Adan, Roman Aebi (Models), Maximilian Beckenbauer, Aurélie Blanchard, Emi Jean Bryan, Alexander Bürgi, Soohyun Chang, Julien Combes, Massimo Corradi (Digital Technologies), Duarte De Azevedo Coutinho Lobo Antunes, Dorothee Dietz, Peter Dougherty, Piotr Fortuna, Luis Gisler, Carl Kristoffer Hägerström, Kelvin Ho, Justin Hui, Kentaro Ishida, Anna Jach, Sara Jardim Manteigas, Hauke Jungjohann, Anssi Kankkunen, Rina Ko, Johannes Rudolf Kohnle, Dannes Kok, Pawel Krzeminski, Jin Tack Lim, Mark Loughnan (Associate), Jaroslav Mach, Donald Mak, James Albert Martin, José Ramón Mayoral Moratilla, Olivier Meystre, Lukas Nordström, Cristian Oprea, Leonardo Pérez-Alonso, Thomas Polster, Maki Portilla Kawamura, Tom Powell, Günter Schwob (Models), Oana Stanescu, Kai Strehlke (Digital Technologies), Fumiko Takahama, Zachary Vourlas, Kenneth Wong, Sung Goo Yang, Daniela Zimmer, Christian Zöllner (Visualizations) / Executive Architect: Rocco Design Architects Ltd., Hong Kong, China / Conservation Architect: Purcell, London, UK / Engineers / Structural Engineering: Arup, London, UK & Arup, Hong Kong, China / Facade Engineering: Arup, Hong Kong, China / Other consultants / Planning Consultant: Townland Consultants Ltd, Hong Kong, China / MEP Engineering: JRP Ltd, Hong Kong, China / Fire Engineering: Arup, Hong Kong, China / Lighting Consultant: Arup, London, UK & Arup, Hong Kong, China / Quantity Surveyor: Rider Levett Bucknall Ltd, Hong Kong, China / Contractors Management Contractor: Gammon Construction Ltd., Hong Kong, China / Façade Contractor: Josef Gartner & Co. (HK) Ltd, Hong Kong, China / Key Suppliers Aluminum Brick Production: Hycast Metals Pty Ltd., Sydney, Australia.

Mira Client: Tishman Speyer / Architect: Studio Gang / Associate architect: Perry Architects Inc. / Associate architect: Barcelon Jang Architecture / Structural engineer: Magnusson Klemencic Associates / Associate structural engineer: Bello & Associates / Civil engineer: Urban Design Consulting Engineers / Landscape Architect: INTERSTICE Architects / LEED / sustainability consultant: Thornton Tomasetti / Acoustic engineer: Papadimos Group / Lighting designer: PritchardPeck Lighting / Façade consultant: Heintges & Associates / Façade fabrication and installation: Permasteelisa / Geotechnical engineer: Rollo & Ridley, Inc. / Façade access consultant: C.S. Caulkins Co. Inc. / Accessibility consultant: Zachary Nathan Architect / Waterproofing engineer: Simpson Gumpertz & Heger / Fire consultant: The Fire Consultants / Parking consultant: Watry Design, Inc. / General contractor: Lendlease.

St. Mary's Axe Client: Swiss Re / Architects: Foster + Partners / Structural Engineers: Arup / Other Consultants: Project Management: RWG Associates / Construction Management: Kontor GTCM / Mechanical and Electrical Engineers: Hilson Moran Partnership Ltd / Cost Consultant: Gardiner & Theobald / Planning Consultant: Montagu Evans / Legal Advisors: Linklaters & Alliance / Urban Design and Conservation Consultants: The Richard Coleman Consultancy / Environmental Engineers: BDSP Partnership / Fire Engineers: Arup Fire / Lift Engineers: Van Deusen & Associates / Contractor: Skanska Construction UK Ltd.

Emma and Georgina Bloomberg Center Client: Cornell Tech / MORPHOSIS TEAM Design Director / Thom Mayne Project Principal / Ung-Joo Scott Lee / Project Architect Luke Yoo / Project Designer: Nicolas Fayad, Edmund Ming Yip Kwong, Jerry Figurski, Jean Oei / Project Team: Christopher Battaglia, Chloe Brunner, Debbie Chen, Chris Eskew, Stuart Franks, Farah Harake, Clayton Henry, Ted Kane, Hunter Knight, Jongwan Kwon, Ryan Leifield, Simon McGown, Brian Richter, Go-Woon Seo / Advanced Technology: Cory Brugger, Kerenza Harris, Stan Su / Project Assistants: Fiorella Barreto, Marco Beccuci, Paul Cambo, Vivian Chen, Tom Day, Justin Foo, Yong Fei Gu, Yoon Her, Sean Kim, Matt Lake, Sangyun Lee, Haidi Liu, Eric Meyer, Nicole Meyer, Jason Minor, Michelle Park, Vincent Parlatore, Conway Pedron, Danny Salamoun, Ben Salance, Suzanne Tanascaux, Matthew Tarpley, Ben Toam / Visualization: Stuart Franks, Jasmine Park, Nathan Skrepcinski, Sam Tannenbaum CONSULTANTS / Structural; MEP/Fire Protection; Sustainability; Façade; Lighting; Acoustics; Audiovisual/IT/Security/Smart Building Arup / Cost Estimator: Dharam Consulting / Geotechnical Mueser Rutledge Consulting Engineers / Code CCI, Code Consultants, Inc / Specifications: Construction Specifications / Water Proofing: Henshell & Buccellato / Food Services Consultant: Jacobs Doland Beer / Graphics and Signage: Pentagram / Visualization: Kilograph / Collaborating Artist: Matthew Day Jackson, Michael Riedel, Matthew Ritchie, Alison Elizabeth Taylor CONSTRUCTION TEAM / General Contractor Barr & Barr / Facade Construction: A. Zahner Company / Pre-Construction CM Tishman Construction Corporation / Owner's Representative Forest City Ratner Companies City Ratner Companies.

Copenhill Power Plant Client: Amager Ressourcecenter / Architects: BIG – Bjarke Ingels Group / Partners-in-Charge: Bjarke Ingels, David Zahle, Jakob Lange, Brian Yang / Project Leaders: Jesper Boye Andersen, Claus Hermansen, Nanna Gyldholm Møller / Team: Alberto Cumerlato, Aleksander Wadas, Alexander Codda, Alexander Ejsing, Alexandra Gustafsson, Alina Tamosiunaite, Armor Gutierrez, Anders Hjortnæs, Andreas Klok Pedersen, Annette Jensen, Ariel Wallner, Ask Andersen, Balaj Ilulian, Blake Smith, Borko Nikolic, Brygida Zawadzka, Buster Christensen, Chris Falla, Chris Zhongtian Yuan, Daniel Selensky, Dennis Rasmussen, Espen Vik, Finn Nørkjær, Franck Fdida, Gonzalo Castro, Gül Ertekin, George Abraham, Helen Chen, Henrick Poulsen, Henrik Rømer Kania, Horia Spirescu, Jakob Ohm Laursen, Jean Strandholt, Jelena Vucic, Jeppe Ecklon, Ji-young Yoon, Jing Xu, Joanna Jakubowska, Johanna Nenander, Kamilla Heskje, Katarzyna Siedlecka, Krzysztof Marciszewski, Laura Wätte, Liang Wang, Lise Jessen, Long Zuo, Maciej Zawadzki, Mads Enggaard Stidsen, Marcelina Kolasinska, Marcos Bano, Maren Allen, Mathias Bank, Matti Nørgaard, Michael Andersen, Narisara Ladawal Schröder, Niklas A. Rasch, Nynne Madsen, Øssur Nolsø, Pero Vukovic, Richard Howis, Ryohei Koike, Se Hyeon Kim, Simon Masson, Sunming Lee, Toni Mateu, Xing Xiong, Zoltan David Kalaszi, Tore Banke, Yehezkiel Wiliardy / Detailed Design: Jesper Kongshaug, BIG Ideas / Competition: AKT, Topotek 1, Man Made Land, Realities:United / Thanks to: A.P Møller Fonden, Lokale- og Anlægsfonden, Nordea Fonden, Fonden R98, Københavns Kommune, Frederiksberg Kommune, Tårnby Kommune, Dragør Kommune og Hvidovre Kommune / Engineers: Artelia, Rambøll / Consultants: SOH Wind Engineering / Landscape Architects: SLA.

Asian Games 2023 Hybrid Stadium / Concert Hall Client: Gongshu District City Village Reconstruction Department / Architect: Archi-Tectonics NYC LLC / Local Architect: LDI: Zhejiang Province Institute Of Architectural Design And Research (ZIAD) / Structural Engineer: Thornton Tomasetti NYC / Landscape Design: !melk NYC / Mobility Planning: MIC Italy / Contractor: China Power Construction Group East China Survey and Design Research Institute Co., Ltd.; Construction unit: Zhejiang Xinsheng Construction Group Co., Ltd.

National Aquatics Centre – The Watercube Client: Beijing Olympic Committee / Architect: PTW Architects + CCDI / Structural Engineers: Arup.

Galleria Centercity Client: Hanwha Galleria Co. LTD ARCHITECT: UNStudio, Amsterdam / Design team: Ben van Berkel, Astrid Piber with Ger Gijzen, Marc Herschel and Marianthi Tatari, Sander Versluis, Albert Gnodde, Jorg Lonkwitz, Tom Minderhoud, Lee Jae-young, Woo Jun-seung, Constantin Boincean, Yu-chen Lin / Interior: Ben van Berkel, Astrid Piber with Ger Gijzen, Cristina Bolis and Veronica Baraldi, Lee Jae-young, Felix Lohrmann, Kirsten Hollmann, Albert Gnodde, Martijn Prins, Joerg Lonkwitz, Malaica Cimenti, Florian Licht, William de Boer, Eelco Grootjes, Alexia Koch / Executive Architect / Site Supervision / Landscape Architect: Gansam Architects & Partners, Seoul, Korea / Design team: Kim Tai-jip, Han Kiyoung, Nam Myung-kwan, Yoon Chang-bae, Park Seong-beom, Kwon Na-young, Nam Young-ho / Interior: Lee Seung-youn, No Se-hyo, Ryu Heewon, Na Min-hee / CONSULTANTS: Façade Consultant: KBM Co. LTD; Light Designer: a.g. Licht, Bonn, Germany; Content Programmer: Lightlife, Berlin/Cologne, Germany; Way-finding Designer: Geerdes Ontwerpen, Delft, Netherlands; Visuals: UNStudio, Amsterdam and rendertaxi, Aachen; Structural Engineer: Kopeg Engineering; Electrical Engineer: Ilshin E&C; Mechanical Engineer: Sahmwon MEC; Civil Engineer: CG E&C / Contractors: Main Contractor: Hanwha E&C Co. Ltd; Façade Contractor Iljin Unisco, Korea; Interior Joong Il, Won Intertech, Artifort, Gawon, Creid, Hanmi, Sangwon S&D, and Daehye.

Leeza Soho Client: SOHO China / Architecture: Zaha Hadid Architects / Design Principal: Zaha Hadid, Patrik Schumacher / ZHA Project Director: Satoshi Ohashi / ZHA Project Associates: Kaloyan Erevinov, Ed Gaskin, Armando Solano / ZHA Project Architect: Philipp Ostermaier / ZHA Project Team: Yang Jingwen, Di Ding, Xuexin Duan, Samson Lee, Shu Hashimoto, Christoph Klemmt, Juan Liu, Dennis

Brezina, Rita Lee, Seungho Yeo, Yuan Feng, Zheng Xu, Felix Amiss, Lida Zhang, Qi Cao / ZHA Competition Project Directors: Satoshi Ohashi, Manuela Gatto / ZHA Competition Team Lead Designers: Philipp Ostermaier, Dennis Brezina, Claudia Glas Dorner / ZHA Competition Team: Yang Jingwen, Igor Pantic, Mu Ren, Konstantinos Mouratidis, Nicholette Chan, Yung-Chieh Huang / Local Design Institute: Beijing Institute of Architectural Design (China) / Structural Engineer: Bollinger + Grohmann (Stage 0,1), China Academy of Building Research (Stage 2), Beijing Institute of Architectural Design (Stage 3,4) / MEP Engineer: Parsons Brinkerhoff (Stage 2), Beijing Institute of Architectural Design (Stage 3,4) / Façade Engineer: Konstruct West Partners (Stage 2), Kighton Facade (Stage 3,4), Yuanda (Stage 3,4) / Lighting Design: J+B Studios Architectural Design (Stage 2), Light Design (Stage 2,3), Leuchte (Stage 4) / Landscape Consultant: Zaha Hadid Architects (Stage 2,3), Ecoland (Stage 4) / Project Management: SOHO China / Signage Consultant: Dongdao (Stage 4,5) / Fire Consultant: Parsons Brinkerhoff (Stage 2) / Traffic Consultant: Dazhengtong (Stage 3,4) / Contractor: General Contractor: China Construction Eight Engineering Division Corp., Ltd / MEP Contractor: China Construction First Engineering Division Corp., Ltd / Façade Contractor: Lingyun, Yuanda / INT Contractor: JTL, Qingshang / Landscape Contractor: Jingtai / Signage Contractor: Basalt.

Kunsthaus Graz Client: City of Graz, Austria / Architects: Spacelab, London: Peter Cook, Colin Fournier / Collaborators: Niels Jonkhans, Gernot Stangl, Peter Löcker/ Local Architect: Architektur Consult ZT GmbH – Domenig/Eisenköck/Peyker, Graz: Herfried Peyker, Dietmar Ott / Structural Engineers: Bollinger & Grohmann: Klaus Bollinger, Manfred Grohmann / Electronic Façade: Realities United: Jan Edler, Tim Edler / Lighting: Kress & Adams Museography: Bogner Cultural Consulting .

Media-ICT Client: El Consorci de la Zona Franca Ajuntament de Barcelona y 22@ / Architecture Cloud 9: Enric Ruiz-Geli (Principal architect) / Project architects: Javier Pérez Contonente, Francesco Ducato, Felix Fassbinder, Víctor Llanos Max Zinnecker / Project Team: Marta Arranz, Marta Banach, Luis Borunda Edouard Cabay, Daniel Corsi Nora Graw, Cristina Guadalupe, Konrad Hofmann, Patricio Levy, Albert Lopez, Mireia Luzarraga, Veronica Mansilla, Beatriz Mínguez, Alex Muiño, Federico Ortiz, Mireia Pallarès, Marisol Verges Hale YoungBlood / Models: Materialise Guillermo, Beluzzo LedsGo / Movies:Rubén Alonso, Javier Pérez Contonente / Bubbles:Pep Bou Structure Engineering: BOMA: Agustí Obiol, Alicia H / guet, Santos Valladolid / MEP Engineering: PGI Grup David Tusset Daniel Orduña / Technical specifications: Tècnics G3: Pilar Estrada, Felipe Rojas / Technical direction: Directors Josep María Forteza and Victor Forteza, Manoli Vila, Martí Santana, Aleix Samperiz / Project management: PAMIAS: Ángel Rotea, Héctor Yuste, Juan Carlos Caballero / Contractor and Industrial partners Dragados - Module A (under ground): Lluís Renom, Javier Charry / SACYR, SAU - Module B (metallic structure): Carlos Siscart González, Raúl Javier Fernández Cachón; Rodrigo González Álvarez, Vera Burriel Jarque / Francisco Ruiz Ortega, Antonio Montesinos Nietom / Monvaga: metallic structure Joan Buj Cotes Joan Masich Francesc Salas Victor Freixinet.

The Shed Client: The Shed, a non-profit cultural organization / Architect: Diller Scofidio + Renfro / Collaborating Architect: Rockwell Group / Landscape Architects: N/A / Engineers: Thornton Tomasetti (Structural, façade, Kinetic) Jaros, Baun & Bolles (MEP, Fire) / Other Consultants: Hardesty and Hanover (Kinetic Systems Consultant) / Vidaris (Energy Modeling Consultant) / Tillotson Design Associates (Lighting Consultant) / Akustiks (Acoustics / Audio / Visual Consultant) / Fisher Dachs (Theater Consultant) / Cimolai (Structural Steel Fabricator) / Vector Foiltec (ETFE Fabricator) / Code Consultants, Inc. (Code Consultants) / Van Deusen & Associates (Vertical Transport Consultants) Ducibella Venter & Santore (Security Consultants) / Other Means (Graphic Design and Wayfinding) / Entek Engineering (Façade Maintenance) / James R. Gainfort AIA Consulting Architects PC (Waterproofing) / Construction Specifications Inc. (Specifications) / Construction Manager: Sciame Construction, LLC.

BOOK CREDITS

Graphic design by Florencia Damilano
Art direction by Oscar Riera Ojeda
Copy editing by Kit Maude

OSCAR RIERA OJEDA
PUBLISHERS

NEW YORK INSTITUTE OF TECHNOLOGY
School of Architecture
& Design

ISBN 978-1-946226-91-4
Published by Oscar Riera Ojeda Publishers Limited
Printed in China

Oscar Riera Ojeda Publishers Limited
Unit 1331, Beverley Commercial Centre,
87-105 Chatham Road South, Tsim Sha Tsui, Kowloon, Hong Kong

Production Offices
Suit 19, Shenyun Road,
Nanshan District, Shenzhen 518055, China

International Customer Service & Editorial Questions: +1-484-502-5400

www.oropublishers.com | www.oscarrieraojeda.com
oscar@oscarrieraojeda.com